**Library Learning Information**

Idea Store®
Whitechapel
321 Whitechapel Road
London E1 1BU

**020 7364 4332**
www.ideastore.co.uk

Created and managed by
Tower Hamlets Council

# THE CHINA CODE

FRANK SIEREN

# The China Code

## What's Left for Us?

Translated by Thomas Rede

First published 2007 by
PALGRAVE MACMILLAN
Houndmills, Basingstoke, Hampshire RG21 6XS and
175 Fifth Avenue, New York, N.Y. 10010
Companies and representatives throughout the world.

PALGRAVE MACMILLAN is the global academic imprint of the Palgrave
Macmillan division of St. Martin's Press, LLC and of Palgrave Macmillan Ltd.
Macmillan® is a registered trademark in the United States, United Kingdom
and other countries. Palgrave is a registered trademark in the European
Union and other countries.

ISBN-13: 978–0–230–00135–0
ISBN-10: 0–230–00135–1

This book is printed on paper suitable for recycling and made from fully
managed and sustained forest sources.

A catalogue record for this book is available from the British Library.

A catalog record for this book is available from the Library of Congress.

10  9  8  7  6  5  4  3  2  1
16  15  14  13  12  11  10  09  08  07

Printed and bound in Great Britain by
Creative Print & Design (Wales), Ebbw Vale

# CONTENTS

# PREFACE

This book was written out of curiosity. It observes a phenomenon, which I am convinced, will have an important impact on our lives. This belief has developed steadily over the 13 years that I have been living in China.

I went to Beijing's first jazz bar with my Chinese friends. We also went to Ikea to buy the first Billy bookcase. I enjoyed parties in their first privately-owned apartments and toasted their first cars. Many had their first mobile phone before my friends in Europe. I also experienced the elastic nature of the Chinese legal system when my friends tried to get their rights upheld. Then there was also the corruption and the brutal competition amongst people trying to move to the top. It was only once I had lived in China that I realised the meaning of legal rights but also how important stability and growth are for a country. I had my run in with public officials who were so stubborn but then also more flexible than one would experience it in the west. I watched cities like Beijing and Shanghai grow. It fascinated me yet sometimes I was terrified and wondered whether it would all work out in the end. Deep in the west of the country I experienced breath-taking landscapes but then also mega-cities that were so massive, loud and unruly that everything which I had known before paled in comparison. I am also mightily impressed with what the Chinese have achieved in the last decade. An even greater challenge was to find out just how stable the new China is.

This book not only talks about a globalisation phenomenon, it is a global product itself and would not have been possible without the help of so many people across the world. At its completion people in seven countries were involved in its production: Germany, China, USA, Laos, South Africa, India and Britain.

First of all I would like to thank Stefan Baron, Düsseldorf, Germany, the chief editor of *WirtschaftsWoche* (The German Business Weekly), a brilliant journalist, who polished my articles, taught me not to give in, and to follow an idea clearly to its conclusion even if that means rowing against the tide. Thank you also to his wife Yin Guangyuan, Cologne, Germany, who has been an untiring mediator between the two cultures. I also have to thank Professor Dr Eberhard Sandschneider, the Director of Research at the Deutsche Gesellschaft für Auswärtige Politik (DGAP, German Council on Foreign Relations), Berlin, Germany. In a very impressive way he is in the process of modernising the DGAP so that it generates new ideas and theories instead of transforming other peopleís ideas into footnotes. Apart from his immediate support, it was a great incentive to follow his example with this book. I am also very grateful to the former German Ambassador to China, Dr Hans-Christian Ueberschaer, Bonn, Germany, for his immense assistance.

I am very thankful to my agent Barbara J. Zitwer, New York, USA, who took care of the book as if it had been written by herself. And Bob Breen, Düsseldorf, Germany, who translated the initial proposal. My deep thanks goes especially to Thomas Redl, Vientienne, Laos, for translating the book into English under enormous time pressure and keeping its spirit. Thanks to Yang Liu, Berlin/Beijing, for designing the cover.

Thanks as well to Catherine Moat and my brother Andreas Sieren, Johannesburg, South Africa, for polishing the work at short notice. Thanks to Vidhya from Chennai, India, for efficent project management and to Assistant Editor Alexandra Dawe in England for getting everything smoothly organized and checking the final proofs.

And I am grateful to Stephen Rutt, Global Publishing Director with Palgrave Macmillan, who had the confidence of placing this book in a prominent position on their publishing agenda.

When I first started this project I received incredible support from Kerstin "Anna" Wesendorf, the head librarian of Beijing's Goethe Institute. She managed to provide me with decisive books and articles at exactly the right moment, with the greatest efficiency. I would also like to thank her husband Dirk Brauns, an outstanding writer and journalist. His almost completed novel and this book are now so closely related that they have become inseparable.

My gratitude also goes out to Anna Vandenhertz and Professor Wolfgang Engler whose influence on me can never be underestimated, although they have nothing to do with China. This can also be said of Sabine Schneller and Dr Bernward Dörner whose suggestions helped to put me on the right course.

Kathrin Albrecht, Sonja Banze, Dr Leo Flamm, Dr Claus Knoth, Julia Kühn, Uwe Kräuter, Li Aihua, Petra and Otto Mann, Professor Dr Erling von Mende, Konstantin Menzel, Zhang Wei, Günter Schabowski, Dr Martin Posth, Erk Schaffarczyk, Justus Krüger and the Trier Gang of Sinologists provided additional support. (I am especially grateful to Dr Katharina Ahr who brought China closer to me and Sabine Lippelt who enticed me to China.)

Thanks also to Jürgen Kracht, founder of the Hong Kong-based consulting firm Fiducia, who generously shared his 30 years of experience of the Chinese market with me. Christian Sommer and Leif Goeritz, who are in charge of the German Centres in Shanghai and Beijing, were very helpful in spreading the word about the book. I would also like to thank a number of Chinese friends and acquaintances from Beijing's Ministry of Economics and various university departments who also assisted me, but who prefer not to be mentioned because they feel that their influence is more important than being named here.

This book is particularly dedicated to Peter Seidlitz, Geneva, Switzerland, who was at the beginning of the nineties the first German economic correspondent in China, and who enlightened this work with his clear and visionary analysis. He is a true pioneer, and there will be many generations of economic correspondents in China who will follow in his footsteps. Many of my colleagues, including me, are tremendously indebted to him.

I am also especially grateful to Bernhard Bartsch whose rigorous arguments refined the concepts and ideas in the book and through his practical support ensured that it was completed on schedule.

Lastly I would like to thank my parents who unrelentingly encouraged me to try a little bit harder, and now with the same wonderful patience urge me to work a little bit less. Finally and most importantly, thank you to Anke for enduring your human typewriter and for all you have done and continue to do for me.

FRANK SIEREN
Beijing, September 2006

# CHRONOLOGY

| | |
|---|---|
| 1368–1644 | Ming-Dynasty |
| 1405–33 | First Chinese journey to the West |
| 1433 | Capital punishment on international maritime trade and military naval expeditions |
| 1521 | Ferdinand Magellan reaches the China Sea |
| 1644–1911 | Qing-Dynasty |
| 1658 | German Jesuit Adam Schall is appointed Mandarin of the First Class, the highest distinction ever awarded to a foreigner |
| since mid-17th century | European traders on China's east coat |
| 1742 | Prohibition of the Christian religion is reintroduced in China |
| since 1760 | Operations of European merchants are restricted to the port of Canton and to certain months of the year |
| 1834 | The East India Company's monopoly on the opium trade collapses |
| 1838 | The Chinese court sends Lin Zexu as a special commissioner to Canton |
| 1839–42 | First Opium War |
| 1842 | 'Unequal Treaties' between England and China |
| 1851–64 | Taiping Rebellion |
| 1853 | Taiping forces take the former empirial capital Nanking |
| 1856–60 | Second Opium War |
| 1856 | British and French troups occupy Peking |

| | |
|---|---|
| 1894 | The Japanese enforce legal protection of foreign direct investments in China |
| 1894–95 | Sino-Japanese war |
| 1897 | German troups occupy the seaport-town Qingdao in Shandong province |
| June–Sept. 1898 | 'Hundred Days' Reform' of the Guangxu emperor |
| 21 September 1898 | Empress dowager Cixi comes into power; Guangxu is placed under house arrest |
| 1900–01 | Boxer Rebellion |
| 20 June 1900 | German envoy Klemens Freiherr von Ketteler is murdered in Peking |
| 27 July 1900 | Kaiser Wilhelm II in Bermerhaven exhorts German troops sent to quell the Boxer Rebellion to emulate the ancient Huns |
| 7 Sept. 1901 | 'Boxer Protocol' |
| 1904 | Siemens opens its first representative office in China |
| 1905 | Chinese merchants call for a boycott of foreign products |
| 1906 | Constitutional monarchy is established |
| 1908 | Emperor Guangxu and Empress Dowager Cixi die |
| December 1911 | Sun Yat-sen is appointed 'provisional president' |
| 1 January 1912 | Sun Yat-sen proclaims the republic |
| 12 February 1912 | Pu Yi, the last emperor of China, abdicates |
| February 1913 | The first Chinese parliament is elected (the nationalistic Guomindang wins) |
| 1914–18 | First World War: China allies with Great Britain, France and Japan against Germany |
| 1918 | Peace negotiations in Versailles: Japan is granted sovereignty over the German colony in Shandong |
| 4 May 1919 | 'Fourth-May Movement' |
| 1923–27 | First United Front |
| 1925 | Sun Yat-sen dies General Chiang Kai-shek proclaims his dictatorship in Nanking (Nanking-Decade) |
| 1927–37 | First civil war in China |
| 1934 | 'Long March' |
| 1937 | Japanese invasion in North China |
| 1937–45 | Second United Front of Nationalists and Communists |
| 1945–49 | Second civil war in China |
| 1946 | A coalition govenrment is formed under the leadership of the KMT |

| 1949 | The civil war breaks out again and ends with communist victory Mao in Moscow: Sino-Soviet treaty of friendship |
| 1 October 1949 | Founding of the People's Republic of China |
| 1950–53 | Military conflict between China and the USA in the course of the Korean War |
| 1953–57 | First five-year plan (focused on the development of heavy industry) |
| April 1954 | Abolishment of private business completed |
| 1954 | Deng Xiaoping is announced General Secretary of the Party and Vice-Premier |
| 1956 | China's first automotive factory goes into operation |
| February 1957 | 'Hundred-Flowers-Campaign' |
| July 1958 | Khrushchev arrives on a secret visit in Peking |
| 1959 | Mao is forced to resign as President |
| 1958–60 | 'Great Leap Forward' |
| July 1960 | Final and open split between China and the Soviet Union |
| 1964 | 'Mao-Bible' gets published |
| 1964–65 | Socialist Education Movement |
| May–Nov. 1964 | First negotiations between China and Germany over a trade agreement which does not materialize due to US pressure (four secret Sino-German talks in Bern) |
| 16 October 1964 | China tests its first nuclear weapon |
| 1965 | Germany for the first time delivers a rolling mill to China |
| 1967–76 | 'The Great Proletarian Cultural Revolution' |
| April 1971 | An American table tennis team arrives in China. Beginning of ping-pong diplomacy |
| July 1971 | The American national security advisor Henry Kissinger travells to China on a secret mission |
| October 1971 | China enters the United Nations |
| February 1972 | American President Richard Nixon visits China |
| October 1972 | Germany and China establish diplomatic relations |
| 11 May 1974 | Deng Xioaping becomes Prime Minister |
| 1975 | Germany organises the industrial fair Technogerma in Peking |
| 9 September 1976 | Mao Zedong dies |
| 1977 | Deng is appointed head of the central command of the People's Liberation Army |

| | |
|---|---|
| 1978 | Deng's 'Four Modernizations' of market economy |
| | China orders steel works and a coal-fired power plant in Germany; German banks give a 18 billion Deutschmark loan commitment |
| Fall 1978 | 'Wall of Democracy' |
| 1979 | The Special Economic Zone Shenzhen is established |
| | Thousands of students go West on scholarships awarded by the Chinese government |
| | Private craftsmen and small services are permitted for the first time since 1956 |
| | Price-regulation for 10,000 consumer products are lifted |
| | Founding of the China International Trust and Investment Corporation (Citic) |
| 1981 | Founding of the first Sino-German joint venture producing hair care products for the Japanese market |
| | In the course of its readjustment-policy, China cancles, among others, an order for a German rolling mill – then the biggest in German-Chinese history |
| May 1982 | First joint venture between a foreign (American Corporation) and a Chinese carmaker (Beijing First Automotive Works) |
| 1984 | The Volkswagen corporation signs a contract over a joint venture with Shanghai Automobile Industry Corporation (SAIC) |
| 1985 | Federal Chancellor Helmut Kohl visits China |
| | China orders a German steel plant |
| 1986 | First student rallies in Hebei province spread to Peking and Shanghai |
| 1987 | *Time* magazine declares Deng Xiaoping 'Man of the Year' |
| 1988 | The first German restaurant opens in the Lido Hotel in Peking |
| Spring 1989 | Independence movement in Tibet peaks in a rebellion in the Tibetan capital Lhasa |
| | State of emergency is declared in Lhasa |
| 15 May 1989 | Michail Gorbachev visits China as the first Soviet head of state in 30 years |
| 17 May 1989 | More than one million workers, employees and students protest against the the Chinese leadership in Peking |
| 20 May 1989 | State of emergency is declared in eight districts of Peking |
| 4 June 1989 | Bloody repression of the democracy movement on the Square of Heavenly Peace |

| | |
|---|---|
| June 1989 | The German parliament imposes sanctions on China |
| 9 July 1989 | Deng's 'Four point guideline': (1) Complete repression of the protest movement, (2) Improvement of economic parameters, (3) Continuation of the open door policy, (4) Coordinated economical development |
| September 1989 | Otto Wulf von Amerongen, chairman of the German Committee on Eastern European Economic Relations, is one of the first foreigners to visit Prime Minister Li Peng |
| 10 January 1990 | State of emergency is lifted in Peking |
| April 1990 | Carl H. Hahn, CEO of Volkswagen Inc., visits Shanghai and declares China the focal point of the companies Asia strategy |
| May 1990 | Former federal chancellor and editor of the German weekly *Die Zeit* visits Peking and meets Deng Xiaoping |
| July 1990 | The German government sends an under-secretary of state to China to meet Prime Minister Li Peng |
| October 1990 | The EU foreign ministers largely lift the sanctions imposed on China |
| November 1990 | German engineers help to build China's first nuclear plant |
| Late 1990 | The Shanghai Stock Exchange opens again after more than 40 years |
| 1993 | Chinese carmaker Brilliance China Automotive is the first Chinese company to be listed on the New York Stock Exchange |
| 1994 | German Chancellor Kohl visits China |
| | Installation of four state-owned major banks (Bank of China, Agricultural Bank of China, China Construction Bank, Industrial and Commercial Bank of China) |
| 1996 | First Chinese private bank (Minsheng) |
| | China's first investments into foreign oilfields |
| 1996 | The China-office of the liberal Friedrich-Naumann-Foundation is closed down and foreign minister Klaus Kinkel's visit is cancelled, after the Foundation invited the Dalai Lama as the leader of a government in exile |
| 1996 | German Chancellor Helmut Kohl is the first foreign head of state after 1989 to visit the People's Liberation Army |
| 19 February 1997 | Deng Xiaoping dies |
| 30 June 1997 | Handover of the British crown colony to China |

| | |
|---|---|
| 14 August 1997 | Onset of the Asian crisis |
| June 1998 | US President Bill Clinton visits China |
| October 1998 | IMF-meeting in Hongkong |
| since 1999 | German–Chinese 'Rule of Law Dialogue' |
| 7 May 1999 | American misslies destroy the Chinese embassy in Belgrade German Chancellor Gerhard Schröder is the first Western head of state to visit China to apologise to the Chinese government and the Chinese people |
| November 1999 | Signing of the first declaration of intent between the Chinese ministry of science and Transrapid International |
| 2000 | Paris-based writer Gao Xingjian is awarded the Nobel Prize for literature |
| 2001 | China enters the World Trade Organisation (WTO) |
| January 2001 | Contract concerning the construction of the magnetic levitation train Transrapid in Shanghai |
| Summer 2001 | International Campaign Against Terrorism and Separatism (Russia, Kazakhstan, Tajikistan, Kyrgistan, Uzbekistan and the 'Shanghai Six') |
| November 2001 | German–Chinese project over the production of a domestic jet goes bust in the last minute |
| March 2002 | The last German aircraftmaker Fairschild-Dornier declares bankruptcy after its China-plans fail |
| Fall 2002 | Hu Jintao inaugurated as new president |
| September 2002 | Chinese consumer electronics manufacturer TCL acquires its German competitor Schneider |
| 31 December 2002 | Prime Minister Zhu Rongji and German chancellor Gerhard Schröder inaugurate the Transrapid track in Shanghai |
| Spring 2003 | SARS-crisis Change of government: new policy of social adjustment under Prime Minister Wen Jiabao |
| October 2003 | China's first crewed spaceflight China secures natural ressources on a grand scale worldwide China foreign currency reserves increase to more than US$500 billion; the country increasingly buys Euros |
| August 2004 | British HSBC is the first Western bank to buy shares of the Chinese Bank of Communications China has 1.3 billion inhabitants, according to official estimates |

| | |
|---|---|
| November 2004 | China invests US$ 70 billion into Iranian natural resources |
| October 2004 | G7 finance ministers meet in Washington: the Chinese finance minister is invited for the first time |
| December 2004 | Chinese computer manufacturer Lenovo acquires IBM's computer section Chinese carmaker SAIC signs a contract concerning the acquisition of the British car manufacturer MG Rover |
| Since 2004 | China is the second largest consumer of German products |
| | The Chinese trade volume exceeds US$ 1 trillion BMW produces cars in China |
| 2005 | China begins to build up strategic oil reserves |
| 2006 | DaimlerChrysler produces cars in China |
| 2007 | One of BASF's largest and most sophisticated plants worldwide goes into operation in China |

# Chapter 1

# THE YELLOW PERIL?

## China is Getting Closer

Radical changes have at least one unfortunate characteristic: They are not immediately recognised as such. The Germans in particular have the tendency to bury their heads in the sand when they are faced with drastic change. They believe, with a certain air of authority that fundamental change can only come about through gradual transition. What is the point of making rash decisions when actually it is future generations who are at stake?

The effects of China's boom clearly demonstrate of how it can be a distinct disadvantage if one does not follow changes closely even when they are taking place on the other side of the world. Failure to quickly and appropriately adjust to these changes will result in missed opportunities. One is reminded of a family picnic being disturbed by the sound of rolling thunder. Everyone wants to polish off the last salmon canapé before making a beeline for the Range Rover … and then the heavens open.

China is certainly the good news that the weary world economy needs. This huge country has been booming for the last 25 years and in 2004 it had the largest share of growth in global production. It now has its internal problems under control so that they do not intrude on anyone else. Its leaders self-assuredly handled the Asian Economic Crisis, SARS[1] and the new challenges posed by the world economy, and have therefore also contributed to greater stability in Asia. At the beginning of 2004, just as China's economy was threatening to overheat due to the increase in senseless investments, the Chinese government immediately responded by applying practical measures. Instead of trying to shroud its own failures in a cloak of silence, China went about tackling its problems consciously and openly and thereby set the tone when it came to answering the criticism of the world's media. People began to ask themselves as to how this was even possible? According to western evaluations the combination of a population of more than a billion people, corruption, dictatorship and Manchester capitalism would be considered to be a highly explosive cocktail. Also the contradiction of growth and suppression seems unfathomable to the West. And yet none of this threatens to undermine China. On the contrary, as one has to unwillingly admit, it is getting stronger by the day.

In the background one can hear the creaks and strains of the world economy. Discreetly and unremittingly the Chinese are in the process of consciously modifying global statistics. As a result there has been an unbelievable release of energy, as 1.3 billion people want to concurrently scramble their way to the top. For decades they were either unable or forbidden to do so and at the same time the West insinuated that they were not up to facing the competition in the free market economy. In the meantime the Chinese have developed an astute understanding of these market mechanisms and are skilfully exploiting the dynamics of capitalism for their own purposes.

Up until recently the west were urging the Chinese to 'take courage', but the West would feel slightly queasy if they were to be offered this suggestion. If one has lived in China for more than ten years and has regularly travelled to the western hemisphere, one is more likely to save this encouragement for oneself and the established industrialised nations. It seems reasonable to assume that this distant country's rapid ascent and aspiration to regain its role as the Middle Kingdom will have a more lasting effect on the personal destinies of young people in the west than just about any other factor. Europe's future is being decided at a distance of eight thousand kilometres. Although there are only a few Europeans who have shaken hands with a Chinese, and there are even less who would be able to recall the name of a famous living Chinese person – apart from maybe the odd pop star or writer – China is already at their backdoor.

In a far more committed way than seemed to be the case initially, China has used globalisation to weave a fine web of dependencies around us. It is setting world standards that Germany, Europe's leading industrial nation ignores at its peril.

'Made in Germany' is no longer the norm in the country.[2] Nearly everything that Germans buy, ranging from dustbins and shirts to CD players, notebooks and container ships, is imported from China. China is not just the biggest producer of shoes and clothing, but also of mountain bikes, microwave ovens and mobile phones. It is even the world leader for high-tech products such as notebooks. China is also the world's largest producer of steel and in the first quarter of 2004 managed to double the output of the USA, triple the output of Russia and quadruple the output of Germany. Since 2004 China also manufactures more cars than Germany and only Japan and the USA have managed to stay ahead in this industrial sector.[3] At the beginning of 2004 anyone would have been accused of exaggeration if he had declared that the Chinese would buy the computer company IBM and the British car manufacturer MG Rover. *A year later, in summer 2005, anyone would have been called an enthusiastic China-aficionado if he had claimed that China would build state of the art Airbus planes.*

In 2004 China had already overtaken its wealthy neighbour Japan with an annual trade of more than a billion US dollars,[4] and has globally moved into third place just behind Germany and the USA, *a position the country held in 2005.*[5] Moreover, in the same year China also ascended into the top five of the world's largest economies as the country managed to double its trade volume just between 2001–04. People follow the movement of commodities. Lufthansa will have four daily flights to Beijing and Shanghai by the end of the decade. Jurgen Weber, the airline's CEO, has estimated that they will be transporting more passengers to these destinations than to New York.[6]

In the opinion of Jurgen Hambrecht, the Chief Executive Officer of the pharmaceutical giant BASF, 'There is no question that China will become the production base of the world', and their achievements also back up his claim.[7] The conglomerate invested three billion Euros in the establishment of a new chemical plant in the eastern city of Nanjing; and in 2003 BASF's largest chemical project in China already had a turnover of 1.6 billion Euros.[8] *And in summer 2006 BASF was already negotioating the enlargement of the plant.*

At the same time as being the 'factory of the world', China also dominates as a sales market since it promises the highest proportion of new market shares globally. It is for this reason that China has been able to attract more foreign investment than any other country in recent years – over 60 billion US dollars in 2005 alone, which accounted for 8 per cent of the global flow of investment.[9] One must add to this an export surplus of 100 billion US dollars – the highest since 1998, and this is in spite of their huge purchase of raw materials.

Additionally, China will be able to rely on a cheap source of labour in the coming decades. From a western perspective this may seem like a paradox: China's engineers and labourers are being exploited – but currently they appear to be quite content. They accept their working conditions, as hard as they may be, because never before in the history of China has their standard of living improved at such a rapid rate.[10]

These circumstances have enormous repercussions in the west. The value of western labour in is now being assessed according to Chinese salary levels, and this can be considered just as much a traumatic as an unavoidable reality. In the global economy people and their labour become a commodity whose value decreases with an increase in the supply. It is not only the German feeling of self-esteem but also the German economy that finds itself in a dilemma, for which there are only two equally unpleasant solutions. If salaries are cut, Germany will become more competitive, but then the workforce will have less spending power. The resulting decrease in consumption will in turn harm the German economy. On the other hand if German companies follow the path of their French, Japanese or American competitors and relocate a portion of their production in China, jobs will be lost in Europe and there will be a loss in tax revenue for the impacted countries. It may temporarily still be a 'win-win' situation – which is the hope of several heads of state of the industrialised nations – because we deliver goods to China.[11] However these conditions will change even faster than we anticipate, and China will be the first to sense it. Germany is currently leading the trend amongst the Europeans and has now become the largest European investor in China. *The years 2005 and 2006, however, mark a turning point. For the first time German exports to China are not growing anymore. This means that less and less of the products for China are produced in Germany; they are manufactured on site in China instead. It does not matter to the companies, but it is bad for Germany. Increasingly jobs and taxes are eroding.* The management consultants A. T. Kearney have estimated that just in the German chemical industry around 150,000 to 200,000 positions will be under threat in next ten years.[12] Also the middle class, the backbone of the German economy, face grim prospects. In 2003 alone the mechanical engineering industry had to compensate 24,000 employees due to the fact that ever-increasing numbers of machinery are being manufactured in China.[13] China's output is contributing to the erosion of the German industrial base. The business consults, Boston Consulting Group have predicted that by 2015, 1.4 million employees will no longer have their positions in the work force.[14] *The beneficiary is Asia.* 'You can feel it all over Europe', said Fred Kindle, ABB's executive chairman in summer 2006. 'A leaden state, which has been building up gradually and hence is not going to disappear over night. The Europeans are taking refuge to repressing the fact of the powerfull competition from Asia. They hesitate to confront the challenge. Instead they are trying to secure their past acchievments.'

Germany will be the first country to be hit by this wave, as it happens to be the 'export world champion'. The anxiety that the Germans feel today will soon be the problems that the English, the French and also the Americans have to face.

The financial elbowroom that is available in order to undertake fundamental reforms – so as to increase Europe's competitiveness – will depend on how quickly and forcefully China ascends to the position of the world's economic power. Many aspects of the standard of living, which the Europeans are currently trying to salvage, simply will no longer be affordable in a few years from now. Europe is not in a cyclical downturn; instead this is the start of the global transformation that is taking shape. Even if China's outstanding achievements are already dripping out the newspapers' business columns like sweet treacle, China is only at a new dawn in its evolution/development. In fact it has far from realised its full potential.[15]

## China Is Well Attuned to Globalisation

The global upheaval, the epicentre of which is in China, is being driven by an engine that is propelling the world in a new direction: globalisation. Migration, trade, wars, communication technology and travel have all played their part in putting people in touch with each other over the centuries. Nowadays global interdependencies have become so complex that they no longer are visible to the naked eye.[16] All of the countries in the world are being forced to co-operate ever more closely with each other. Of course economic globalisation is streaks ahead of both the political and social versions, and this has developed essentially because of three factors, which unfold with almost dependable certainty. Firstly, money flows to where the returns are highest and is withdrawn again when these fall. Secondly, companies, nations and regions pursue their share of the world market to assure future profits and improve their standing in the world. And thirdly, as new forms of media and fast transportation have evolved, companies have become less tied to particular places or countries.

China appears to be well attuned to these challenges. If one turns the clock back a quarter of a century, it was the time when the Chinese embarked upon some major economic market reforms, which however only made a relatively weak impact. Despite this predicament, they managed to turn their plight into strength by developing a knack for detecting the change in economic currents, which they had now begun to rely upon. Reluctantly they learned to accept that globalisation had been generated by people, but that it had not been invented by anyone in particular. Nobody had drawn up a master plan for globalisation but instead it had developed by coincidence due to the complex links which had built up as the result of people pursuing their various objectives in life. They also learnt that globalisation could not be forced into a certain direction – neither through mass demonstrations nor through the so-called capital.[17] Moreover they discovered with a certain sense of satisfaction and relief that even the most powerful country in the world, the USA is only able to influence globalisation, but is not able to direct and least of all control it. During the nineteen fifties and sixties the Chinese had already learned the painful lesson that it was pointless to try and block it. After the founding of the People's Republic Mao Zedong wanted to single-handedly modernise the country, but it was only at the end of his extensive rule that he realised that any country that tries to evade the rules of globalisation would be up against the rest of the world and would soon end up on the wrong track. As a last effort he invited President Richard Nixon for a visit and tried to lead China out of its isolation.

The economic boom that the Chinese ignited exceeded their wildest expectations and has had the west gaping with wonder/amazement.[18] In the opinion of George Soros one of the biggest names in the international financial world, they 'are the exploiters of globalisation'.[19] Optimists, such as himself, who have backed China's success, are increasingly being able to bring even stronger arguments to the table, namely: The global economy is dependent on the position of China's huge market and cheap production. The country has been able to break global economic records on a monthly basis. China's superiority is becoming obvious if one makes the comparison with India for example. India being the world's largest democracy, like China has to contend with a population of around one billion. During the eighties the two countries were on par, but since 1986 China's per capita income has tripled whereas in India it has not even doubled,[20] and China's gross national product is now almost twice the amount of India's.[21] A Chinese person is also four times more likely to be literate and India's child mortality rate is double that of China's. One is also able to find more than ten times the amount of mobile phones in China in comparison to IT-savvy India.[22]

Also from a historical perspective one would have to consider China's boom above average, having excelled even the USA, whose strong growth period during the twenties propelled them to the top position in the world.[23] Despite the numerous claims that have been made, it is surprising to discover that disparities in income, usually the main indicator of social instability, are not that alarmingly wide, as was disclosed in the United Nation's most recent Human Development Report. The distribution of income amongst its population is a little less favourable than that of the USA.[24] This is not to say that one should not be concerned with the ever-increasing divide between rich and poor purely on humanitarian grounds. However, these disparities have proved to be less of an issue for the stability of the country than was originally anticipated.

Considering that for last 25 years the Chinese economy has annually been expanding at an average rate of 9 per cent, the country will be able to squeeze Germany out of the third place at the 2008 Olympic Games placing it hot on the heels of the USA and Japan as the world's largest national economy.

'The come back of the middle kingdom is the most significant historical event of this century' Stephan Baron, the chief editor of the German magazine *Wirschaftswoche* wrote in the editorial of the world's only business magazine which presented its articles in German and Chinese.[25] One of the biggest German dailies even posed the question, 'Have we really reached the stage now, that Germans need to copy China's capitalism?'[26] Even hard headed business men like Heinrich van Pierer, the long-standing chairman of the board of directors of Siemens had strong words to describe China's economic growth by referring to it as, 'the latest Mongolian assault'.[27] Back in the days of the first 'assault' the whole future of Europe's royal families was in jeopardy.

A glance at the Chinese growth figures would confirm the following. Up until 1991 China's growth was still in line with the rest of the global economy, but then after a steady increase in the nineties it exploded in 1999. It was propelled even further in 2001, when other countries were experiencing the adverse effects of the global recession. Global demand was forcing western and flourishing Asian companies to relocate in, or at least buy from China because of the country's competitive advantage, so that they were at least able to supply their products at a lower price. These developments increased both China's economic and political leverage. The 'Taiwan issue' had already settled itself in China's favour, as now for example Taiwanese companies manufacture nearly 80 per cent of their IT products on the mainland. In the event of a dispute, China does not even have to threaten with an invasion. Beijing's leadership has the island's economy in the palm of its hand, as all it would have to do is confiscate the Taiwanese factories.[28] Now even the Dalai Lama urges his supporters not to 'challenge China directly on the delicate status of Tibet'.[29] Not even the most powerful politician in the world is able to stand in the way of such change. When President George W. Bush came to office in 2001 he still referred to a 'strategic opponent', but by the end of his term he had already taken the somewhat softer approach and spoke of China as being a 'diplomatic partner'. Indeed, it is now not possible to solve an increasing number of the world's political issues without China's input.

The sceptics claim that China's progress has been hugely overrated, and parallels are drawn with the fate of the internet boom – after the rapid ascent there will be an equally fast nosedive.[30] No one can rule out a crash, but there is a fundamental flaw in this comparison. China has a tried and tested business plan, unlike most of the internet companies: it sells market shares in return for the transfer of technology and know-how. That is the bottom line whenever western managers negotiate with Chinese entrepreneurs. As a rule it is the Chinese who benefit more from these alignments, because they can play off international companies against each other, while they have the trump card of being the market with the biggest growth potential. Incidentally, China does not build up massive debts like the internet entrepreneurs, which they then promise to pay back with their future profits. The China Inc. has already proved itself to be quite a profitable enterprise, considering that they have accumulated 853.6 billion US dollars in foreign exchange reserves (by March 2006) and only have minimal foreign debts. Let us not forget that Hong Kong has 120 billion US dollars at its disposal, which have not even been added to the equation.

Sceptics will once again bemoan the fact that even Japan, a much wealthier country, did not manage to fulfil earlier expectations. In the seventies and eighties it looked as if Japan would start to overtake the USA, but then in 1989 it ran out of breath and stumbled into stagnation. However even this comparison does not apply to China, because Japan had tried to take on the rest of the world on its own, and had already made sure that its own economy was not open to foreign investors. Japan had used every opportunity to single-handedly develop and produce its own goods and had managed to achieve amazing standards of quality and efficiency as a result.[31] The turn around came when the country could no longer support the system with adequate resources. China however has applied a strategy, which is more reminiscent of an oriental martial art, as it uses the energy of the global players for its own objectives by extracting their know-how. One has to add the fact that China will have a longer period of growth than Japan had, due to its considerably larger size and so will take at least five times as long to saturate its markets. This could mean a hundred years of growth as long as there are no unforeseen stumbling blocks.

While China's leaders do have a good negotiating position, they are far too shrewd to overplay this card. China has learned how to deal with the risks of globalisation from the numerous crises experienced by the USA, Japan and South America as well as by its Asian neighbours. Learning also from their own history, China's leaders have also developed a healthy mistrust of other countries. Just as the Emperors of the Han dynasty built the Great Wall over 2000 years ago to protect the country against the Mongols, the leaders of the 1990s erected a modern-day protective wall against global financial flows: the Chinese currency, the 'Renminbi', is not tradable in international financial markets, but instead is firmly pegged to the US dollar.

The country will therefore not be adversely affected by speculators on Wall Street or by Western creditors, as had happened to South Korea and Thailand during the Asian economic crisis.[32] China's only has minimal foreign debts and in the majority of cases agreements have been made for a long-term pay back.

Stock markets, the financial system and the real estate market are to a great extent protected from foreign investors. The wolves of globalisation have long picked up the scent, but China remains inaccessible for them. One could not just suddenly turn off the tap to stop the flow of China's exports, which are currently its main source of revenue. It is almost too late now to try and establish protective trade barriers as the western economy has already become dependent on Chinese products. One only has to look at Chinese exports to the USA, as nearly 65 per cent of them are manufactured by American enterprises in China.[33]

*When the EU in 2005 provoked a scuffle over textile quotas the Chinese could relax and watch the issue unfold. The European bulk buyers and manufacturers settled the matter among themselves. Buyers like Karstadt Quelle negotioated to China's advantage against the interests of South European manufacturers who wanted to protect their markets. The compromise they finally reached was a victory for China.*

A further advantage for the Chinese economy is the difficulty involved in transferring large amounts of money out of the country. Strict regulations governing the flow of capital ensure that money, which is generated in China, also remains in country, and does not disappear like Russia's capital to places such as Cape Town, St. Moritz and Monte Carlo, where it is then forever out the reach of the national economy. Money does end up in the wrong pockets, as China also has its share of mismanagement and corruption, but at least it is then spent locally. China's national economic statistics embody stability.

## China Is Fortunate to Have No Competition

China can afford to limit the extent to which it opens its markets to the world economy, because as a market of the future it has something akin to a monopoly. German and other international businesses do have numerous opportunities to invest in the established markets of their European neighbours or the USA, but the message has become loud and clear. With the increasing pace of globalisation, it has become obvious that China is unbeatable as a market of the future, given its heady combination of potential, stability, infrastructure, price levels and production capacity. There is no other large country that can match its stability. 'There are investment opportunities in many countries, but as far as China is concerned, you just have to be a part of it', is the opinion of Bernd Pieschetsrieder, chairman of the board of directors at Volkswagen, the largest European car manufacturer. It really does not seem as if any other developing country will be able to rival China in the medium term. Russia, which has been generously sponsored by the west, is not even able to keep up with its neighbours. China's gross national product was only half the size of Russia's back in 1978, and then not even a decade later it was the exact opposite, with the gap widening on an annual basis.[34]

China has also left India way behind, as India is now no longer in the position to be able to afford bold economic experiments due to the fact that it does not even have a quarter of China's foreign exchange reserves at its disposal.[35] South America is hardly in a healthy predicament as foreign creditors have put it on a drip, and its internal policies now require the approval from the World Bank and International Monetary Fund. Currency fluctuations, unpredictable demand and unstable governments have all contributed to the fact that there has only been limited foreign investment. One glimmer of hope for the South Americans is to be able to supply the Chinese market with perishable goods and raw materials.[36] The south-east Asian Tiger economies – Thailand, Singapore, Taiwan and South Korea – have all had to accept China's position as the region's leading economy. 'As a former entrepreneur I am aware that as a sizeable mid tier business, one is able to survive quite comfortably next to a global player', were the words of Thailand's Prime Minister Thaksin Shinawarta.[37] Even Japan is unable to avoid the pressure from its neighbour's competition, as it has become far too densely populated, expensive and inflexible. The country's economy has been stagnant for more than a decade and reforms have been far from effective, leaving Japanese businesses with little choice but to relocate in the more cost-effective China, so as to at least ensure their survival.[38] East Europe, which for Germans in particular, is so much closer than the Far East is also unable to compete with China's markets and low costs. A study conducted by business consultants Roland Berger concluded that the quality of Chinese products is not only better but also more reliable than those of Eastern Europe. This is particularly the case when one considers the large number of units that are produced and the pressures of competition. The consultants themselves were surprised with the results, which led them to comment that, 'our assumptions were the exact opposite of the reality'.[39] China shares the same problems with Eastern Europe as they both have bankrupt state enterprises and an inefficient financial system. However given these two alternatives China will remain the better choice for German enterprises for the foreseeable future. 'The risk of not being in China is higher than the risk of being in China' were the words of Von Pierer, which have by now become the mantra of the global economy.[40]

This unique position enables the Chinese government to stipulate the conditions under which foreign companies are allowed into the country. It enables China to access technology which it has not been able to develop by itself, and so now Germans, who work with the Chinese, have begun to realise that there are limitations to their perceived strengths.

Chinese economic planners have devised a system that could be described in terms of being a 'concubine economy'. Competing foreign companies are obliged to form joint venture companies with a Chinese parent company. They must then seek the favour of that parent company, much like the concubines of former times vis-à-vis the Emperor. In many globally important industries like the automobile, steel or chemical industries this is the prevalent system. The competitors Volkswagen and General Motors (GM) for example both share the same parent company, Shanghai Automotive Industry Corp (SAIC). This enables SAIC to play off Volkswagen and GM against one another as they are forced to compete for technology transfer, investments and a share of the market. This is also the situation in other industries, thereby ensuring that the foreigners are at a disadvantage/at the loosing end. The only way in which they can strengthen their position in the Chinese market is by dancing to the tune of their Chinese partners. This is reason why even the world's board of directors have not been able to collectively negotiate with the Chinese. It has not been possible for the Europeans to regroup themselves, so that even the large conglomerates are forced into the position of being China's employees. The Chinese capitalist state economy has taught their western capitalist competitors how to eat humble pie – even Karl Marx would have been surprised with this development.

Similarly Chinese politicians create conflicts of loyalty among the governments of powerful nations. The current head of state has to woo the Chinese during his official visit to ensure that contracts and licences are issued to his country's enterprises instead of those of the other competing nations. However, the upshot of this is that he manages to increase the rate at which western enterprises relocate overseas, resulting in a loss of both jobs and tax revenue. The only certain winners in this game are the Chinese.

China is therefore in a very comfortable position, as it not only controls an anti-globalisation shield but also a monopoly due to its potential market, and thereby manages to attract the benefits of globalisation without being exposed to its disadvantages. The country has also ensured the compliance of the world's conglomerates through it's 'concubine-economy'.

The Europeans on the other hand, are much more exposed to the forces of globalisation.

## China Is Stable and The USA Is Unstable

It is because of this stable economy that even the insolvent banking system, which despite efforts has only made marginal improvements, is less significant for China's stability than many correspondents have assumed. There is however a huge loss in growth potential because China's state banks continue to finance state enterprises, which do not even deserve the support; instead they could be backing the private sector, which would make a much more efficient use of these resources. One should not forget though that western governments managed to accumulate much higher amounts of 'bad credit', known otherwise as subsidies. These sustain bankrupt enterprises or whole industries mainly due to the social ramifications.[41] According to official figures the Chinese state is owed over 200 billion US dollars in 'bad credit' since it opened its market. However, this amount has not just been written off as subsidies, but instead it has gone through the books of the state banking system. If we assume that there has been a fair amount of creative accounting and that the figures are in fact twice as high, we would end up with a total of 400 billion US dollars in 25 years. It is not really such a huge amount if one considers that the Deutsche Bahn – the German railway – received almost half as much in subsidies from 1993 until 2003. In the meantime the railway has already managed to accumulate debts of more than 200 billion Euros.[42] (Apparently, as reported by railway minister Fu Zhihuan, the Chinese state railway covers its operational costs.)

The Kiel Institute of Global Economics has estimated that Germany annually distributes around 150 million Euros in subsidies.[43] This means then that it takes Germany only three years to amass the same amount of 'bad credit', which China accumulated in a quarter of a century. China's total burden of debt is equal to the amount that the EU spends in four years on farming subsidies. So, before we accuse the Chinese government of the futility of trying to sustain bankrupt state enterprises we should get a dose of reality and begin to sensibly evaluate China's power. The banks in China may be insolvent according to their balance sheets, but they are in fact very liquid because on average the Chinese deposit 40 per cent of their income in the bank.[44] In fact China's means of income generation are far from exhausted. The Chinese stock exchange is still being established and currently only a minority of Chinese state enterprises are listed on the international stock exchange. The airline Air China, *a member of Lufthansa's*

*Star Alliance since 2006*, managed to secure 1.07 billion US dollars for 30 per cent of its shares at the end of 2004.[45]

The Chinese national economy also does not have to worry about the bursting of the property bubble. The majority of private property owners actually live in their own property, and so they are not really affected by fluctuations in the market price as they mostly sell only in the long term. The sceptics believe that such stability is too good to be true and are worried that China is fooling the rest of the world with false figures/a numbers game. The Chinese government is of course not averse to whitewashing in just the same way that other countries do, but a simple rough estimate already clearly shows that China's success is not just a façade. In financial terms a national economy works much in the same way as a household economy: it can only survive if the available income lasts until the end of the month. If it does not then the only option is to borrow. Therefore in the same way that a family would not be able to conceal its debts from the bank, a country would not be able to hoodwink the rest of the international financial community. The figures of reported foreign debt are therefore as reliable as an enquiry of the credit investigation authority with a private German debtor. Countries also have another option when it comes to acquiring money: they can print it. However, this devalues the currency and essential goods quickly become more expensive. It would be difficult to cover this up. In 2005 the inflation rate was a moderate 3.5 per cent despite the overheating economy whilst national growth stood at 8.3 per cent.[46] If a currency is firmly pegged to the US dollar, as is the case in China, and one tried to allege that the currency is worth more than it actually is, it would lead to the development of black market – something which no government in the world be able to prevent. However in China there is no notable black market. At the end of 2004 the black market rate was not higher than 0.3 yuan per US dollar compared to the bank rate.[47] Given the current economic parameters China is therefore not in danger of experiencing an economic crisis as long as foreign debt, inflation and the black market do not spin out of control. However, if only one of these factors gets out of line one has to contend with social unrest as was demonstrated in recent Chinese history. But the Chinese economy has already managed to survive the pressures of the Asian economic crisis and the Millennium crash of 2001 and come out unscathed, whilst the American, Japanese and European markets crashed.

Particularly experienced German managers who have spent a considerable period of time in China intuitively regard the stability of the Chinese economy with a certain amount of scepticism. They are familiar with the daily chaos which they have experienced in their offices, factories and through their business negotiations. They also complain about the incompetence of the Chinese, their inability to think ahead and their unwillingness to take responsibility. On top of this they claim that they are oblivious of quality standards and alter the production schedule without rhyme or reason.[48] One therefore has to pose the question of how it is actually possible for China to be successful despite these conditions.

The reason it has been possible is because of the economy that they have set up. As long as they are still so favourable the Chinese are able to afford a certain amount of chaos in their daily lives. Incidentally, it is the same managers who are amazed that their parent companies – whether Volkswagen, Siemens or Allianz – are able to make a profit in many of their departments despite the incompetence, laziness and lack of planning. Once again they find an excuse, as surely the company must somehow be fiddling with the figures at the end of the financial year.

The fact that people's assumptions are worlds apart from the actual reality is not only unique to the Chinese economy. One can observe a similarly mismatched correlation in the USA – but there it is exactly the other way round.

The American way of life was established a while ago and as a result functions quite well. However the parameters of the national economy are quite alarming in comparison as the government annually spends almost 6 per cent more than it actually makes in revenue. This is twice the amount that the members of the European Union dare to disperse. At the same time the output of the American industrial sector is the lowest it has been for the past 20 years.[49] Now even Levis, the most famous jeans brand in the world, which are as American as Coca Cola, Marlboro and McDonalds (even though they were invented by a German in 1853), are being manufactured exclusively in China since 2004, instead of the USA.[50] American money has also been diverted to Asia, as the trade deficit reached a record high of 600 billion US dollars in 2004.[51] The deficit with China alone reached a record of almost 15 billion US dollars in November 2004.[52] The Americans have accumulated massive debts with the central Asian banks, particularly those of Japan and China, which have bought up US loans, amounting to 180 billion US dollars in 2004.[53]

'China is the most important force which helps to maintain the American standard of living', was the analysis of Andy Xie the chief economist of the investment bank Stanley Morgan in Hong Kong.[54] In 2004 the US national economy needed roughly two billion US dollars of foreign capital on a daily basis. Ten years ago most of the foreign capital actually stayed in the USA for a longer period as it was invested in enterprises and property. In the meantime foreigners have become much more cautious and mostly look for short-term investments, and now for example buy US dollars which they are able to sell at any time. They no longer have any faith in the stability of the USA. The German economy has also adjusted its US exports accordingly, resulting in a reduction of 5 per cent, whereas the volume to China has been growing annually by nearly 30 per cent.[55] The global economy grew by almost 5 per cent in 2004, which was mainly due to China's contribution.[56] However this was also the first time that China had a bigger share of global production than the USA, and so the USA's contribution to global production has stagnated. This means in fact that there has been a loss of economic power. China's share of global production has quadrupled to 13 per cent since the early eighties, if measured by purchase power parity. Instead of increasing during this time period the USA's share stagnated at 20 per cent, and so it has also lost its enormous lead over China. 'The viagra of the global economy', was the headline in one of the biggest European newspapers,[57] which actually hit the nail on the head, as without China everything would come to a grinding halt.

There are many signs that this will now be the beginning of a stage when the American share will also shrink. Congress therefore enacted new legislation in the autumn of 2004 that gives American companies the opportunity, within a certain timeframe, to transfer the profits of their foreign joint venture companies back to the USA at a favourable tax rate.[58] Incidentally this is on the condition that the money is re-invested in the USA and creates employment. Once this really starts to function it will particularly affect Europe because the profit margins are so minimal, and so it will be worth returning. This will also help to strengthen the current trend: Foreign investment in Germany has gone down by almost two-thirds whereas in China it has increased by roughly 25 per cent, involving some 53 billion US dollars.[59] Globalisation is the name of the game for this gang of thieves. The Chinese boom is forcing the USA to pull their enterprises out of Germany in particular, and to relocate them on home ground.

The rate of the US dollar is already being decided in Asia, as China alone has 20 per cent of the world's foreign exchange reserves at its disposal.[60] Asian banks also provide 80 per cent of all US dollar loans, which makes up the majority of their foreign exchange reserves.[61] However these they can change into another currency at the drop of a hat (such as the Euro), thereby putting further pressure on the US dollar. Foreign goods therefore become more expensive for the Americans, and so given these circumstances they should be thankful that the Chinese Yuan is pegged to the US dollar so that their purchases are not subject to an unfavourable exchange rate. Additionally, it is in China's interest that the value of the Euro goes up even further, and 1.70 Euro to the US dollar is hardly an illusory value. The strong Euro helps China in two ways, as firstly it forces European enterprises to flee the expensive European arena and to relocate their production in China, even if they are only manufacturing for the American market. Secondly, the low value of the US dollar forces the USA to buy their goods from China as other currencies such as the South Korean Won or the Thai Baht have a relatively higher value.

The USA is therefore currently much more susceptible than the Chinese to the vicissitudes of globalisation and they have far less room to manoeuvre. It would be possible to imagine the relationship between USA and China as being comparable to two neighbours living in the suburbs. One neighbour lives in a modest house, parts of which are still under construction. His younger children wear clothes that have been handed down by their older siblings and the family only occasionally goes on holiday. But nevertheless they do have adequate funds in their bank account to cover any unforeseen expenses such as the father needing to go to hospital, the heating breaking down or the children's education getting more expensive. The other neighbour on the other hand lives in a huge, lavishly renovated mansion, owns two cars and constantly takes his family on holiday. However, everything that they actually own belongs to the bank and their survival depends very much on fate treating them kindly.

The Americans have continued to live their lives with the notion that they are the leading world power – a role which nobody will be able to question for at least the next one or two decades. However, their relative perception of supremacy is rapidly changing. Whilst the USA is becoming increasingly unsure with its loss of supremacy and the way in which it confronts the challenges of the world, the Chinese are becoming more at ease/confident. The reality is that the Americans are on their way down and the Chinese are on their way up. People are aware of this, and realise that those moving up always have a better time than those moving down. Chinese students have recently begun to look elsewhere for their education, and so for the first time since 1971 there has been a reduction in the number of foreign students studying at American high schools. The Chinese are leading this retreat, resulting in a 45 per cent drop in the number of Chinese at American Universities since 2003.[62] This is not because they have been unable to get hold of a visa – they simply do not even want to apply for one in the first place.

## The Risks in China

Although China is much more stable than is generally assumed, it must confront problems at home which are more difficult to solve than the challenges currently faced by the countries of the European Union. China's greatest potential is also its greatest curse – its huge population. The creation of a social system that can provide 1.3 billion people with at least minimum standards of nutrition, medical care and education is currently way beyond the country's capacity.

The ongoing struggle to distribute inadequate resources is carried out with great severity and human rights are a frequent casualty. It is the rural population, which makes up some two thirds of the total population that suffers the most. The extent of the corruption and exploitation practised by Beijing's central government has been chronicled in Wu Chuntao and Chen Guidi's award-winning 'A Survey of Chinese Peasants'.

The literary couple spent two years in the province of Anhui and provided a detailed account of the tyranny inflicted by local cadres, the extortion of taxes as well as indiscriminate murders, which farmers in many regions are helplessly subjected to.[63]

People die of AIDS because they are treated with contaminated blood in state hospitals. Hardly a month goes by without miners being killed due to inadequately secured mineshafts.[64] Even in urban areas there is little chance of people being treated according to the rule of law if they are suspected of a transgression. Political dissidents, who question the power of the party, are pursued with unrelenting vigour. Although human rights watch dogs continually advocate that a healthy/solid state should not be afraid of granting its citizens their civil rights, this can hardly be said of the Chinese government. Non-political crimes are often dealt with in a very abrupt fashion. In April 2001, for instance, the government commenced a new round of its 'Strike Hard' campaigns against crime. According to Amnesty International, in the first three months more people were executed in China than in all other countries of the world combined for the previous three years. Between 1990 and 2000, the period of Jiang Zemin's leadership, Amnesty documented almost 20,000 executions, a figure government sources call 'exaggerated' and critics claim is far below the actual number.

'Every year there are roughly 4000 executions in China', was the claim of the dissident Harry Wu who, both during and after the Cultural Revolution, had spent 19 years languishing in Chinese prison camps. He made his statement in front of the human rights commission of the Bundestag, the German lower house, to elaborate on China's respect of human life, 'One would not even want to think of it in terms of a percentage, as that would amount to 80 per cent of all the executions in the world'.[65] He cited a further abuse of human rights, namely the trade in organs of those who have been executed and the so-called 'administrative detainment'. Many political prisoners end up in work camps without even having had a trial. Wu was unable to estimate the exact number of these work camps but there are probably more than a thousand. This means that the Chinese government has had a free labour force at their disposal, probably consisting of millions of 'workers'. The work camps therefore became a separate production branch of the Chinese economy, and their goods have been exported throughout the world. He also accused the Chinese regime of having used these prisoners as a means of applying pressure for their own benefits. Time and time again there would be the release of individual prisoners to ensure that the Chinese interests in other countries were pushed through.[66] These are circumstances that businesses and politics have increasingly decided to ignore as the Chinese market becomes more important to them. As China gains in strength on a daily basis it has at the same time become increasingly difficult to apply pressure on the country concerning human rights issues. The other argument is that as China becomes more prominent it is also at same time coerced into adhering to international standards as well as establishing the rule of law. If you want to play ball, then you also have to stick to the world's rules.

It would no doubt be possible to extend this list of Chinese problems. The country's environmental problems are appalling and according to a study conducted by the World Bank, China has 16 of the 20 worst polluted cities on the planet. Additionally, for example, Beijing manages to discharge the same amount of carbon monoxide as Tokyo and Los Angeles put together.[67] It would however be presumptuous to assume that China is not just as conscious of these problems as the western critics. The Chinese government makes the point – with some validity – that it took more than just a few decades to implement the so-called Western standards of civilisation much less than what the smaller countries took. There can be no doubt that the people of China have the power to fight for and secure more freedom, should they choose to do so. The country is too big and already too closely connected with the outside world for the government to be able to impose its will on a rebellious population. It is however unlikely that human rights abuses and social problems will lead to an economic collapse as we first thought. 'What is challenging about China', comments Nicholas Kristof of the New York Times, 'is that its government is simultaneously brutal to dissidents and is lifting more people out of poverty more quickly than any other country in history'.

We should therefore get used to a few paradoxical combinations (at least by Western standards) that will exist in China for the foreseeable future – macro-economic stability and social chaos, economic boom and corruption, dictatorship and freedom. It does look as though these extremes actually have far less influence on each other than we would have thought possible. The social chaos has so far not managed to undermine macro-economic stability and on the other hand it has not been possible to control corruption despite the economic boom. Nobody, including the Government knows how stable this 'stalemate' is going to be. It could possibly hold out for another 30 years after which we would be able to recognise a worsening of the situation according to the aforementioned variables. This does not in any way mean that it will be possible to ward off the danger.

Once China starts to spiral out of control there is not much that even the most powerful government could do. However, for the time being China's development project has social benefits greater than the costs.

## Germany Depends on China

One thing is certain: It is never wise to underestimate the strength of the competition. After all of these years of economic stagnation we simply can not afford to sit there and wait with the hope that China will trip up over its own feet. A few years ago the arguments were that China's share of the global economy was relatively small and that German companies had only a one-digit proportion of their global turnover[68] and foreign investment tied up with China.[69] Now however it has become almost impossible to reverse the current trend. China is able to call the shots when it comes to wage levels, working hours and production costs. If our engineers spared no efforts in designing a product then a margin would be slapped on top of it. Nowadays clients are asked how much they are willing to spend before an appropriately curtailed development plan is embarked upon. The Phaeton Volkswagen is the last great example of the wasteful use of German engineering talent.

Germany has had the largest growth in imports and exports with China, and has already become the biggest European investor in the country. German foreign investment declined in the USA and Eastern Europe in the last ten years, whereas in China it grew by 240 per cent.[70] China's influence on the German economy appears to be even greater if we take into consideration that China has a decisive influence in determining the rate of the Euro due to its foreign exchange reserves, and this of course hits Germany, being the export world champion, the hardest. Not to mention the influence on the demand for raw materials as this has already messed up the calculations of quite a number of German businesses and property owners. The price of crude oil increased by 40 per cent in 2004 alone. 'The Chinese demand is the driving force behind the global demand', was the conclusion of a report by the International Energy Agency (IEA) in Paris. The growth of China's oil-demand could double in 2006 to 5.8 per cent.[71] The massive increases in the price of oil are primarily due to China's huge demand, which now accounts for almost 80 per cent of this, and only secondly because of the war in Iraq.[72] China is not only in the process of securing its own supply, but is also managing to create fundamental changes in currently one of the world's hottest trouble spots. In the autumn of 2004 the state invested 100 billion US dollars in Iran's oil and gas reserves, an action that was almost unobserved by the global community, and so now it has become a kind of protective force for the Iranians.[73] If the Americans were to attack Iran, the Chinese would definitely have something to say. China will continue to drive up the price of oil and in 2005 it began to make arrangements for strategic oil reserves in addition to its normal consumption.[74] There have been similar developments with other raw materials. 'This is not just a passing phase, but it will continue or become even worse in the next ten to fifteen years', was Heinrich von Pierer's estimate.[75] This reduces businesses' profit margins and puts pressure on consumption. Nowadays, the state of the German Minister of Finance's household is already being heavily influenced by China.

China is in the meantime able to use a dilemma of capitalism, which economists have been debating for years: the limitations of growth. The populations of the industrialised nations are no longer in need of various material possessions, and they just about own everything already. The USA was successful in managing to prolong the period of consumption in the nineties through the promotion of the boom in the stock market but then when the bubble eventually burst there was an even bigger flood of tears.[76] In Germany there was a similar development: Private consumption was on a par with the European average until 2001 after which it collapsed. The corporations' investments in production facilities (fixed asset investment) suffered a similar fate.[77]

The western economy had already reached the limitations of its expansion by the turn of the century. However, the managers and entrepreneurs of the industrialised nations faced an enormous challenge because after all growth is the engine of the market economy. German entrepreneurs had never experienced such difficulties in trying to develop their businesses further. In the saturated western markets growth in most industries finds itself in a zero-sum situation. The success of one individual immediately means the loss of another. It is for this reason that China has become crucial as an arena of investment, as it provides the possibility to open up new as well as maintain old markets.

Germany only benefits out of this opportunity conditionally. Despite the fact that in 2004 the global economy grew at a rate which had not been witnessed for the last 20 years, Germany's international standing has seen its heyday,[78] as the Chinese have stealthily been hollowing Germany out from the inside. Let us not forget that England and France are next in line. The enormous German investments in China are of course good for the companies that have set up there, but on the other hand this amount is detrimental to the national economy. Germany became the export world champion in 2003, managed to secure jobs at home, but then it proved to be only in the short term. Since 2004 China has become the second biggest purchaser of German products (after the USA and followed by France), but it has particularly bought production facilities, which will then create jobs in China.[79] Incidentally the majority of the overseas business activities of German companies are also taxed overseas instead of in Germany. This has strengthened the downward trend of the economy that had previously managed to overcome other factors such as the reunification of Germany: The average German per capita income of US dollars 26,000 is now below the European average. If one compares the gross domestic product to the other industrialised nations, Germany comes out as the biggest loser in the last decade. It was overtaken by eight other countries and has now only been ranked globally in sixteenth place.[80]

German companies, however, are increasingly facing difficulties in the Chinese market. Many German firms have a hard time to stay a steady course. Giants such as Volkswagen, DaimlerChrysler and Siemens as well as the country's formerly famed Mittelstand or medium-sized businesses are lowering their expectations, postponing their time schedules, or are even busy working out exit-strategies. Even though the Chinese economy keeps growing fast the euphoric mood of German companies has gone sour. It was the often repeated credo of former chancellor Gerhard Schröder that in business, China and Germany find themselves in a win-win situation. His successor Angela Merkel was not heard uttering it during her first official visit as chancellor to China in May 2006. And she was right. Because the more the Chinese government is focusing the country's economy on domestic consumption, the fiercer the competition between the European and Chinese economies will become. We want to manufacture as many good, but expensive products in Europe as possible and export them to China. The Chinese government, on the other hand, is pushing for the maximum amount of goods for the Chinese market to be produced in China herself in order to create jobs and social stability in the country. Further the products should be as cheap as possible in order to integrate more domestic consumers and to reduce China's dependency on exports. And the Chinese are calling the shots in this conflict of interests. Eighty per cent of the car-parts for China-made Volkswagen Passat are already manufactured locally. Seventy per cent of VW's competitor General Motors Buick are produced in China. Eighty per cent of German carmaker Opel's Corsa model consists of parts made in the Middle Kingdom. Audi's degree of localisation is reaching similar proportions.

When one can hear the Europeans whimper it is not because they are oversensitive and looking for sympathy but because they have realistically realised that the situation will continue to worsen. The atmosphere changed in 2002 just at the stage when the Chinese economy was going at full steam. In 2000 only 8 per cent of the Germans thought that they were less well off than their west European neighbours, but by 2002 it had risen to 20 per cent and two years later it had already reached 23 per cent. In 1998 a quarter of the respondents had a pessimistic outlook of the future. The number had increased to 31 per cent by 2002 and even to 41 per cent by 2004, which was the highest reading in over fifty years.[81] Nobody gets pessimistic without a reason – not even the Germans. The respective moods in Germany and China form a stunning contrast indeed: A survey by the American opinion research centre Pew Research in May 2005 showed that nobody is more optimistic than the Chinese: 72 per cent said they were satisfied with their future prospects. Only 19 per cent opted for 'unsatisfied'. In Germany the results were the exact opposite: 73 per cent have a pessimistic outlook, only 25 per cent are optimistic. And the Germans are realistic. They realise that their hopes of deriving enough benefit from the Chinese boom to maintain their own standard of living will not be fulfilled. The Chinese boom is taking place in China and nowhere else. Eighty per cent of parts that are used to assemble a VW Passat in China are already being produced locally. The competitor General Motors uses 70 per cent local parts for its Buick.

The Chinese government is not forcing foreign enterprises to localise out of spite. It has the same problem as the German government, which is however about ten times greater: It must create employment at any cost. China's employment market annually receives a fresh supply of 8 million young workers.[82] The Chinese are still buying our machines but are beginning to produce their own, sometimes under licence, but more often as pirate copies. 'Our playing field is a lot smaller than I had expected', commented the manager of a European manufacturer of textile machines when he discovered copies of his machines in catalogues at the booths of his Chinese competitors during the annual Beijing textile fair in the autumn of 2004. Some had even gone so far as to use the logo of his German company. However the machines were not quite as efficient, but on average they did manage to achieve 80 per cent of the output, at half the price. The young manager was hit even harder when he realised that his customers from Malaysia and Turkey had also travelled to China to place orders for the cost-efficient copies of the German original. Additionally Chinese technicians were posing as customers at his booth in order to try and gain information about new technical innovations. 'It's completely pointless to complain about plagiarism', stated the manager of the medium-sized company, 'the lawyers are the only ones who profit and at the same time you shut yourself out of the market'. Competitors had also informed him that in some cases their turnover had decreased by 50 per cent.

Chinese market regulators support domestic companies to the best of their abilities – often in breach of WTO stipulations. They have passed legislation in some industries that prevents the use of machines, which have been manufactured overseas. Under these circumstances it is only a matter of time before Chinese engineers adopt our technologies and develop them further. The same could be said for the automobile industry.[83]

There is only one solution for the western and Japanese industry, as it has to try and maintain its technological advantage/lead. However this is also becoming increasingly difficult considering the Chinese competition, as China already spends more on research than Germany.[84] According to an EU Commission estimate, China's private investments into research and development will eclipse those in the EU by 2010, provided that the current trend continues.

Between 1998 and 2002 China advanced in the world ranking order of high-tech locations from 31 to 21 – level with France and in hot pursuit of Germany, which is ranked 15.[85] China's pool of talent is, of course, immense. Every year some 250,000 IT specialists complete their studies in China, compared to only 5000 in Germany. Even though the standard of education at all the Chinese secondary schools is not comparable to the German education system, the top universities are on a par with the world's best institutions. The probability that 5000 out of 250,000 Chinese graduates are more qualified than their German counterparts is considerably high if one takes into account its status as a developing country.[86] These specialists also proceed to work for a quarter of the annual income of their German equivalent and it should therefore come as no surprise that research and development is increasingly being farmed out to Asia. In 2004 roughly 80,000 IT specialists were registered as unemployed, which means that the share of unemployment in this industry has tripled to 7 per cent since autumn 2000.[87]

Additionally it does not seem very likely that the wage differential will be noticeably reduced within the next decade.[88] Not even German health care provision will remain in the country. The Dutch national health insurance scheme has been flying patients with long-term illnesses to Bangkok since the 1st July 2004 so that they receive treatment at a lower cost, as well as under better conditions and without the necessity of having to be on a waiting list. It would also not be far-fetched to imagine that European

patients will be flown to China in the near future, where they could be
treated by either Chinese or western medicine and be looked after by
English, German or French speaking nurses. Even China's age structure
works in its favour: the population under the age of 18 is greater than the
combined total populations of USA and UK.[89] A mere 10 per cent of the
population is over 60 years of age, whereas in Europe it has already reached
18.6 per cent.[90]

The atmosphere has also become correspondingly pleasant as young
people become more independent. In the daily routine of the middle class
there are hardly any reminders of life under a totalitarian dictatorship. The
new middleclass[91] in Beijing or Shanghai – much the same as the people in
Berlin, Frankfurt or Munich – are interested in their personal consumption,
employment prospects and their children's education.[92] Politics is much less
of a concern than the important issue of whether the first car should be
white, black or silver. Those who have enough money live in a modern
residential estate with international satellite television. Foreign newspapers
are expensive but available in all of the major hotels. Internet access is
cheap for everyone who needs it and it is possible to log on to international
mainstream sites in English. One only has to know a few tricks of the trade
to be able to get into those sites which have been blocked on the internet.
Almost everyone who can afford it is able to go abroad on holiday, which
after all amounted to 22 million people in 2003.[93]

One huge difference between the Europeans and the Chinese is the expectation that they have of the state. The Europeans, and the Germans in particular, demand a tight social security net but only have a slight inclination to
actually finance the state.[94] The Chinese are also not enamoured with the
idea of having to pay taxes, but then they also have low expectations of the
welfare state. This difference in the way people view their relationship with
the government often leads to misunderstandings when we make assumptions about China. A Westerner would never put up with the unreasonable
social demands of the Chinese state and therefore expects the Chinese to
react in the same way, and to raise objections. There are in fact civil movements within Chinese society but in general these are focused on concrete
social problems rather than the system. One therefore can witness demonstrations against corrupt managers of state enterprises who have failed to pay
the workers their salaries, or building contractors who have sold property
buyers defective units. However these are local conflicts that are also solved
at the local level. The desire to change the system or even the desire to democratically elect the government in Beijing in comparison is rarely an issue.

Official regulations governing elections, the division of authority and
the freedom to air political opinions have not been institutionalised either

politically or legally. But pressure is informally applied on China's leadership from two directions. Globalisation pressures the government to improve the welfare within society and to be more transparent, as people are aware of the situation in other countries. Additionally the pressure comes from foreign companies who want a better investment environment, which for example would require a functioning legal system. In reality China's population only has very few official rights but it does have a lot of power because no one and not even a government can force people to support it. If a government does not look after its citizens' welfare, people will look for an alternative. China's success shows just how well these informal controls work. The Chinese government needs to comply with them, as it is the only way in which it is able to stay in power. It seems that this form of conflict promises more progress than traditional forms of resistance headed by leaders.[95]

In China there are no civil rights advocates who can be compared to Mahatma Gandhi, Alexander Solschenizyn, Nelson Mandela, Lech Walesa or Vazlav Havel. A consumers' democracy is enough for people – at least for now. It would be a grave misunderstanding to assume that people from non-western cultures who do not have a democratic government based on the rule of law also do not have a concept of rights and independence. People do object to the west treating them like they have just come out of the forest.[96] Democracy is without doubt the best system that we could imagine. However just because we wish to see democracy everywhere it is pointless to underestimate the strength of dictatorship and the weakness of democracy. In the worst-case scenario politicians in a democracy can only react to short-term sentiment, because they have to win elections. In this case it is not possible for them to enforce their political agenda, and they overestimate the stability of democratic systems. In the best-case scenario dictators on the other hand, are able to make long-term plans, swiftly enforce their political agenda, and have a better sense of the social and political imponderabilities as they live with the fear that their illegitimate power could collapse. We will have to wait and see if China is such a case. The complacency of the parliamentary democracy becomes clearly visible when one sees it through eyes of China.

## Opportunities for the West

A shift of economic and political muscle to Asia makes it clear that the West and Japan are not in the kind of cyclical economic crisis that can be overcome just by perseverance and positive thinking. The global risk society poses new challenges for which there are no easy solutions.[97]

Under no circumstances should we sit back and watch these new developments without acting upon them. Once they have taken shape and become clearer, new opportunities will also arise. Germany will be the first country in the western hemisphere to be affected by these global changes. Due to the fact that a quarter of the German economy's jobs and a third of the gross national product are dependant on exports the country[98] is much more susceptible to international shifts in power, than for example France who only export half the amount.[99] It should be noted that the medium-sized businesses are particularly exposed.

The French find themselves in the following predicament. France lost their colonies at the end of the Second World War and then had to get used to playing a smaller part on the European stage. However this hardly affected their self-confidence, and so their 'group-feeling' is much less sensitive when subject to the forces of globalisation. From the French point of view, France and China are two 'grandes nations' who are able to approach each other on equal footing. At the same time the rules of the game are quite clear: If you are in the same social class, you stick together and respectfully address people using their family name. However it looks as if China will start to address France on a first name basis whilst still expecting France to use the family name. The English have also been very slow to realise that the size of their playing field is being determined by China. The fact that Great Britain controlled China for nearly two hundred years has still left its mark on British public opinion. Let us not forget that Chris Patten, the last governor of the Crown Colony of Hong Kong, which was handed back to China in 1997, was the EU's Foreign Commissioner until 2004. The English may be right in their conviction that if it were not because of their influence, Hong Kong would have never have developed into one of the most fascinating cities in Asia. However this is clouding their view of the growing influence that the emerging world power has on Europe. They might still believe that they have already got their reforms behind them, thanks to Margaret Thatcher. However they will also have to confront the global shifts in economic and political power.

The superpower, the USA, does have fine ears for global rearrangements in power. However their pride has affected their ability to be able to judge clearly and has resulted in their tendency to try to stand up against the inevitable. There is of course a huge danger that this gets them into trouble, because in the process of defending their individuality they have the tendency to overlook the fact as to who is actually challenging them – not just the Taliban, Al Quaida or Iraq but also to a great extent China. Whilst some operate destructively, there are others who do it constructively. There is no doubt as to who has got more chance of being able to assert themselves in the long run.

The Germans however do not have to concern themselves with historical baggage or political distractions when dealing with the Chinese. The country's history is brief and eventful and in this respect Germans only carry a small amount of historical baggage. They have already been able to use this to their advantage, as it was easier for them to position themselves at the head of the European Union than it was for the European states, which are stooped in tradition. Why then should this not be possible for the Germans to achieve when it comes to global integration? This is a great opportunity and the Germans should not miss it. Therefore the Germans need to be under no illusions and comprehensively concern themselves with the radical changes that are being driven by China.

As Sherlock Holmes said to Dr Watson before sending him on his first case, 'Don't develop theories before you know the facts'.[100] This certainly applies when making a sober evaluation of what is happening in China. If anyone thinks that China's boom is nothing more than belated modernisation or the logical way down a long-established road to development, they are limiting their options considerably. Even our current democratic standards are not necessarily the best and the only possible way to organise a society. The relationship between the individual and society for example is bound to be different in a country with a population of 1.3 billion people in comparison to a relatively smaller western society. The big question one has to ask when looking at recent Chinese history is whether freedom is more important than equality, or whether it is the other way round. It seems conceivable that in China the rights of the individual will permanently remain weaker than in the west. In any case the answer is anything but simple and even the Germans are far from unanimous when it comes to this question. As is the case with East Germans, the majority consider equality (56 per cent) to be more important than freedom (30 per cent). In the last ten years there was a reduction in the number of West Germans who placed a value on freedom, as it went down from 60 per cent to less than 50 per cent.[101] In China it would probably be even lower. In relation to this one needs to consider, to what extent one is allowed to limit the freedom of the individual in order to guarantee everyone's welfare.

China functions according to its own set of rules – a 'China code'. If we want to know how the world will change in the future, then we have to try and crack this code. This is just as important for our future as trying to unravel the genetic code. In order to do this we have to look at things from a Chinese perspective, which of course is not so easy. The sociologist Niklas Luhmann thoroughly examined the varying perspectives and did some pioneering research on this topic. His theory is that people operate in order to narrow the gap between their claims and a recalcitrant reality. The biggest possible mistake in this process is to believe that you are steering more than yourself. Exactly the same can be applied to countries and people. Luhmann argues that steering can only involve steering yourself. It sounds abstract, but it does describe a routine phenomena. Marriages end up in divorce because both partners steer past each other. Wars break out because both enemies are unable to find an alternative solution. Also many Germans believe that everything that is good about Germany is also the right thing for China. However China in fact steers itself completely differently.

The influence of the steering of strangers Luhmann describes as being the environment. This is something one is unable to influence. However because everyone is operating at the same time and following different goals they manage to disrupt each other. It is for this reason that one has to continually correct the way one goes about ones business. The Chinese are justified in judging the way they conduct their business differently to the Germans.[102] Our classic framework for passing judgement – capitalism and communism, the market and planning, dictatorship and democracy – does not really provide us with a great deal of information about China's actual position of power within the system of interwoven global connections. It has already become noticeable just how unwieldy these ideas are when one applies them to China.[103] If one manages to mistake one for the other then it is possible to make some seriously false judgements. Everyone orientates themselves by their own construction of reality, in other words by their own code.[104] Because of this Luhmann concludes, 'Whoever pursues an end will then have to play with this end against the world'.[105] Nobody is able to go about his or her business without competition. The West is also not able to do it without it. We would be wise to learn just how solid our values and standards are whilst we concern ourselves with China.

## China Is Going Its Own Way

China's self-image differs from our image of her in two fundamental ways. While some are waiting for the big crisis to happen in China, the Chinese are convinced that their big crises have already been overcome. And while we perceive China as emerging from its status as an underdeveloped country, the Chinese are convinced they are in the process of reclaiming their former mantel of glory.

China's decline is indeed a thing of the past. It is some 150 years since a collapse that seemed at the time like the end of a civilisation, but was in retrospect no more than a blip in the long history of China. It lasted a good 120 years and ended with the death of Mao Tse-tung in 1976. The Chinese have not forgotten how far they plummeted from their former pinnacle of success and how brutally hard the landing was. The disaster, which struck the late Chinese empire, should give Germans who were born into affluence an idea of what is at stake.

That China was once the Middle Kingdom gives its people self-confidence. And the more closely China becomes integrated in the world, the more people remember that China has always gone its own way. The historian Ray Bin Wong who is the Head of the Asian Institute at the University of California demonstrated in his highly acclaimed study 'China Transformed'[106] that the development model of the European nations cannot be universally applied and that in fact China operates according to another set of rules. At the same time the historian Kenneth Pomeranz brushed aside old notions of China's backwardness by providing evidence that at least until the beginning of the nineteenth century people living along the delta of the Yang-tse river – the most developed region of China – had the same standard of living as people in the most developed regions of Europe, and England in particular. The income per capita was also just about the same amount. The standard of hygiene, which used to be a determining factor in the level of development, was in no way below Europe's. In fact the use of soap and hot water was 'a more integral part of Chinese life',[107] and they also had access to clean water. It was not only the Chinese cities, but also Asian cities in general which were 'streaks ahead in relation to public health'.[108] The death rate, an important indicator of the welfare of the people, was actually lower in China in comparison to Europe and the Chinese also reached the same age. The Chinese were doing so well that on average they were even having fewer children between 1550 and 1850.[109] The population growth was higher (1550–1750) and then for the next one hundred years about at the same level as Europe's. The cities were traditionally bigger and more cosmopolitan. In the fifteenth century Europe's biggest city had 150,000 inhabitants whereas in Canton alone there were 200,000 foreigners consisting mainly of Arabs, Persians, Indians, Africans and Turks. In 1840 the turnover of goods in Shanghai's harbour was already higher than London's.[110] Right up into the eighteenth century Europe was globally regarded as 'not a very exceptional economy'.[111] It was only at the time of the industrial revolution, from the middle of nineteenth century onwards, that the Chinese economy was overlapped by Europe's.

Historians have celebrated Pomeranz's research 'The Great Divergence'[112] as being, 'the greatest and most important contribution to a new understanding of the reasons and the mechanics', for the differences between China and the West.[113] In order to gain a clearer understanding of the tradition in which the Chinese see themselves today, the arguments of the Californian historian will be more closely examined in the following chapter. Pomeranz supports the Chinese perspective that China after about one hundred years of major problems – that almost led to its breakdown – is now in the process of returning to the position of being the world's leader in social progress. The business skills that the Chinese exercise nowadays did not just land in their laps. Their boom is a Chinese boom, which has been, and also will be, cleverly directed by the elite. If one considers the time scale involved as a society develops, then the 150 years that China was treading water can hardly be considered to be a long period of time. As soon as the parameters of economic policy were in place, there was a reawakening of century-old business acumen, for which China could count on the help of the numerous Chinese entrepreneurs who have successfully survived in Hong Kong, Taiwan and Singapore.

## The Demands of Globalisation

In simple terms, the different regions of the world pursue three different strategies in order to promote their global influence. The Americans try to do it with the force of arms, the Europeans with values and the Asians – especially the Chinese – with merchandise. Until well into the eighteenth century the force of arms, or in other words the law of the jungle, was the most efficient way of making oneself more powerful. The wars in Korea and Vietnam, the Cold War and more recently, the third Iraq war, have demonstrated to the USA the increasing difficulty of achieving and maintaining dominance through the force of arms. The Chinese, on the other hand, seem to have developed their own method that is more effective in increasing their influence in the world – as swift and penetrating as it is inconspicuous. The invasion of Chinese products is barely noticeable, but represents an influence far more subtle, long-lasting and powerful in effect than any military incursion.

If we want to come up with a survival strategy, we need to do more than examine the individual features of China's path of development. We also need to decipher the common elements of civilisations that hold the world together.[114] It is important to recognise the demands which both Germany and China are equally subjected to. The Polish-English author Norbert Elias spent a considerable part of his life examining this 'process of civilisations'[115] and demonstrated that there are certain similar ways in which societies develop the world over.

The Chinese leaders in the early nineteenth century found it difficult to acknowledge the fact that there are demands which no one, and not even a massive empire like China, can avoid. As leaders of the Middle Kingdom they had got used to being able to give directives according to their own terms. The idea that nations have to compete against one another was completely alien to them.[116] However globalisation had already cast a net over the world which was, 'more complex, far reaching and tightly knit', as Elias discovered.[117] History has often repeated itself, in that nations have already become dependent on each other long before their leaders actually realise the fact. It is important to adjust oneself to the continually evolving weaves and twists. 'No one is able to stand outside of this/remains unaffected. No one is able to steer the motion of the whole', was the way in which Elias described the course of events.[118] Progress is the result of competing desires, experiences and plans eventually guiding themselves into a new direction – something which no one individual had previously planned. Certainly the goal must be to at least be able to see through the mechanics of the process.

Globalisation therefore appears to be a paradox. On the one hand it makes the world more homogenous because every nation needs to deal with certain demands in a similar way. On the other hand it makes the world more complex, because every country has its own goals and values and its own path that it follows.[119]

China's leaders had underestimated both factors for a long time and had therefore missed the opportunity to find their niche within this weave of the global community – one which brings out its strengths and softens its weaknesses. Nations or even unified groups of nations have no chance of success if they try to swim against the main global current. China had already come to this painful realisation. Firstly the emperors and aristocrats resisted integration but then their successors hesitatingly began to accept the overwhelming demands. Nowadays they are the masters of integration.

At the turn of the twentieth century China, the Middle Kingdom, had to unwillingly admit that it was unable to compete economically without the west. However today the west needs to realise that its economic system is unable to function without China. Germany's current position within Europe could be referred to as being a kind of economic middle kingdom. These radical changes in two acts are far from over. Both acts have a common motive. Established countries find it difficult to recognise the concept that there is unavoidable change. They are incredibly stubborn when it comes to adapting to new rules of the game. The adaptation to change in both cases involves accepting your weaknesses and in the worst case coming to the decision to step down, with the hope of being able to rise out of the long-term changes with new vigour.

## The Crisis Barometer: Monopoly on Power and Self-Esteem

When does one begin to take a national crisis seriously? What are the signs that go beyond all national economic figures, which every country accepts as an unmistakable indicator, that one is not really attuned to new global conditions? In any case wealth and democracy will not offer any protection. In fact the opposite is true because wealth enables us to put up with critical problems for so long that we reach the point when it is no longer possible to solve them. Additionally, democracy in its present stage of development has the distinct disadvantage that one is seldom able to reach a majority consensus when dealing with unpleasant realities.

As if reading a barometer, one is able to use a nation's self-esteem and the stability of its monopoly on power in order to register just how great the actual burden is on the country, independent of its wealth and political system. Both factors have an effect on each other and the bigger the country is the more difficult it is to balance them out.

Due to the understandable fact that nationalism has aggressive overtones, and that one's bond to a country does not only consist of negative elements, it would be more sensible to use the neutral concept of self-esteem. Nobert Elias who devised this concept defines it as being, 'a feeling of having a personal bond, identity and sense of belonging with your own country'.[120] This concept also appears in contemporary literature. The author Jana Hensel nostalgically titled the first chapter of her book *After the Wall*, 'The Wonderful and Warm Feeling of Self-esteem'.[121] Globalisation and a sound local feeling of self-esteem go hand in hand no matter whether it envelops Meckelnburg-Vorpommern, Germany or the whole of Europe.[122] Self-esteem helps people to make more effective use of their strengths in globalisation's competitive arena. As the Chinese strategist Sunzi put it over two thousand years ago, 'know yourself and your enemy and you will win one hundred battles'.[123] However is national self-esteem not a sectarian counterforce to globalisation? Is one still allowed to think in terms of national categories in the twenty-first century? Of course one is. In fact one should combine all of one's strengths so that they both motivate and make one's own country look good. The Chinese are particularly good at this. Seldom has a nation been so uninhibited when it comes to talking about themselves. They have an unquestionable sense of unity/belonging, which is somewhat surprising if one considers the historical baggage. As they are on the way up they obviously are not so bothered by it. About sixty million overseas Chinese who are living in South East Asia, America and Europe also share this feeling of self-confidence.

A sense of unity is one of the strongest influences on progress, economic welfare and political stability. As in the case of Germany, it starts to become obvious just how important its function is, once a country's self-esteem begins to falter. The second scale that allows us to compare the competitive edge of nations is the monopoly on power. A state is only able to function if it can uphold the rule of law and order. Laws are only worth more than the paper they are written on if they can actually be enforced and delinquents are actually punished. When people have the impression that the state is no longer able to represent their interests they will begin to take their fate into their own hands, and demonstrate like never before. At that stage the monopoly on power is in jeopardy. Countries, which are unable to ensure stable legal conditions, are given a wide berth by the world's capital.

## China Is Creating a More Just World – At Our Expense

Globalisation, instead of having the effect of releasing new energy, has many people worried – as they are convinced that they are on the losing team. They react by either getting angry or as if they had been mummified. In autumn 2004 Heiner Geisler the CDU politician, best-selling author[124] and well-known Christian gave the anger that has resulted because of these global changes a new voice. Geisler has said what is on many people's minds, but that does not mean that one has to agree with him.

One look at China should make any left-leaning politician worth his salt rejoice at such a gigantic redistribution of wealth. Never before has so much money been channelled from the First to the Third world as with the investments in China. The industrial nations have so far transferred 530 billion US dollars into the country.[125] Furthermore it profits from every exported product labelled 'Made in China'. In 2003 exports amounted to some 440 billion US dollars – a growth of almost 40 per cent over the previous year. The boom is not evenly distributed but according to Francois Bourguignon the Chief economist at the World Bank, 'even the income of the poorest of China's citizens has increased fourfold in the last twenty years'. In the meantime the country's average per capita income has risen to over one thousand US dollars. It was only 25 years ago that famine was not uncommon in China; today it is almost out of the question. Bourguignon is under the impression that it will continue to be an uphill climb: 'China has got a rosy future'.[126]

For the first time ever one country has succeeded in reversing the long-term trend of global income development: in 1820 the per capita income of the poorest compared with the richest country in the world was 1 to 3. In 1992 the ratio was 1 to 72.[127] One of the few prognoses that the Nobel Prize winners for Economics agree on, is that China's meteoric rise will lead to a more equitable distribution of the world's wealth over the next 50 years. 'The per capita income in countries like China will grow more quickly than in the more advanced countries' is George A. Akerlof's prediction.[128] His colleague, Milton Friedman, agrees with him, 'The main reason for today's imbalance is the difference between developed and underdeveloped countries. This difference will decrease in size in the course of globalisation.'[129] Lawrence Klein concurs: 'Growth is so promising in China and India that poverty has already been reduced to a considerable extent.'[130] William F. Sharpe, the biggest sceptic in the team, is still using a probability of 60 per cent that there will be a more even distribution of wealth.

Even Joseph Stiglitz, the leading critic of global institutions, is sure that 'the Chinese will have higher incomes. Even when it is no longer growing at the same rate as in the last 25 years, the imbalance between China, the EU and the USA will decrease substantially.'[131]

Paradoxically, what the critics of globalisation demand at their demonstrations is in the process of happening throughout China. It must be a sobering realisation for them that the redistribution of global wealth would come about without their campaigning. It is not the political pressure of critics that has changed the world, but, of all things, the very global economic system they denounce. It might even be said that to some extent globalisation is devouring its critics. Large parts of the developing world, and particularly those in Asia, will soon be able to grow because of their own stamina and will no longer be dependant on our aid. China is playing a leading role in reducing global poverty. One of the UN's development goals is to halve the numbers of people in the world who have to survive on less than a US dollar a day by 2015. According to Kofi Annan the UN General Secretary this goal is attainable, 'only on the grounds that China is able to bring almost all of its citizens out of this category, even if the proportion of those in poverty will remain unchanged in most of the countries in Africa'.[132] This is the greatest challenge that China should be measured against – and it is a challenge that is within reach even with a slow-down in the economic boom. If one does gauge China's performance according to this goal, then one puts pressure on its government to ensure a more equitable distribution of economic gains within the country. In this process however one should not lose sight of the fact that even then China is still denying its citizens basic rights.

The good news is that there is a chance of a better world. The bad news is that the way the world is going, every day as the Chinese become richer we grow poorer. Years ago we would have used the racist expression 'yellow peril'. But it is not the huge mass of Chinese who threaten us. They are just acting shrewdly according to the capitalist rules of the game that we established in the first place.

The big question is if our humanitarian values will be able to stand up to the strain. We will have to find out if we are tough enough to be able to adapt to the new global circumstances in which we have less and others have more, without resorting to a raging fit. It will be an enormous challenge for us to live in a world in which the Chinese no longer want to sit and listen to us telling them what is right and wrong or good and bad, but instead in a world in which they will increasingly be able to determine this by themselves. And we can already be sure of the fact that they will do many things differently and that there will be precious little that we can do about it. One of many questions that would need to be answered is whether we would agree to only being able to have one car per family on the grounds of the scarcity of the world's resources and environmental concerns, so that at least each fifth family in China is able to own one. That is both the big surprise and the huge dilemma of the early twenty-first century: capitalism is putting China's leadership in a position to distribute the world's wealth more equitably – at our expense.

# Chapter 2

## THE CRISIS OF SELF-ESTEEM

Globalisation made a relatively late appearance in China. This had more to do with China than with globalisation. In the second half of the seventeenth century – after the invasion of the Manchus who established the Qing Dynasty after toppling the Ming Dynasty in 1644 – the Middle Kingdom increasingly isolated itself from the rest of the world. From that point until the beginning of the nineteenth century the country enjoyed a brisk economic boom and solid stability, which caused the pride of the ruling classes to turn more and more into arrogance and also to reject any of the innovative drives that came from the outside. The country's boom was to a certain extent an internal affair. 'We already have everything',[1] Emperor Qianlong informed a baffled Lord McCartney in 1792, who had been sent from England by King George III to negotiate trading concessions with the Chinese court.

The absolute rulers of the former Qing Dynasty were more open to foreign influence and nurtured their contacts with foreigners, even though it was already considered to be a sign of weakness[2] and could be used against them politically. The young Emperor Shunzhi (the second emperor of the Qing Dynasty who ruled from 1638–61)[3] came under enormous pressure when he granted the German Jesuit Adam Schall, who was his teacher and friendly father figure, a certain amount of influence at the Chinese court.[4] His successor Kangxi,[5] whom the Jesuits had cured from malaria, still commissioned foreign architects, artists and mathematicians and even issued an edict at the end of the seventeenth century that allowed the Jesuits to preach Christianity. However from the start his orders were also treated with suspicion. It was in 1742 when the representative of the

Pope fell out with the Chinese court over the issue of whether Chinese Catholics should consider Rome or Beijing the highest authority that it was once again forbidden to practise Christianity in China. There was to be no other belief which would question of the power of the divine emperor.

In the opinion of the Chinese leaders even the exposure to foreign customs and habits was dangerous. It was for this reason that the few European traders who arrived at China's East coast from the middle of the seventeenth century were only able to do business with selected Chinese, – mostly representatives of the British trading company, the East India Company. To have even stricter control over foreign trade, which involved mainly the exchange of wool and metal products for tea, it was decreed that from 1760 onwards all transactions were only be conducted in certain months in the port of Canton. During this period the European traders, consisting of Englishman, Portuguese and Dutchman, who had come up the Pearl River in their small boats from the Portuguese colony of Macau were only allowed to stay on Shamen, a small river island in front of Canton. Female company was forbidden and they had to obey strict rules governing their exit permission. They were allowed to visit the flower gardens of Canton on the eighth, eighteenth and twenty-eighth of a particular month under Chinese surveillance and in groups of no more than ten people. Just as before, all trade had to go through Chinese middlemen – the 'Co-Hongs'. No matter what happened, the foreigners were forced to comply with the so-called 'Hoppo', the official from the central government responsible for trade issues.

In many ways these rules remind one of the restrictions that one still has to put up with if one wants to do business in China. Just like the old days there are considerable barriers for foreigners to enter, even though China has been a member of the WTO since 2001 and should have opened its markets.

Whereas the Chinese were not particularly interested in overseas countries in the seventeenth and eighteenth century and even the Europeans only considered the Middle Kingdom an additional market, China and the West have now become competitors, yet at the same time they are dependant on each other. The Chinese need overseas technology and investment and the industrialised nations on the other hand need to open up new markets. As China currently finds itself in the position of having a global monopoly because of its growth market the Chinese are increasingly able to demand higher 'entrance fees'. These days it is not so much hostility towards foreigners but rather the mercantile ambition to close a good deal that motivates these barriers.

China's domestic boom ensured nearly two hundred years of peace and maintained the power of the divine emperor for longer than in any major European nation. One reason for this was because of the Confucian discipline, which the Chinese people had internalised and another was because of the administrative power of well-educated officials. Moreover, an extensively prosperous economy also ensured that there was a good atmosphere. Unlike today, the high standard of welfare resulted in the Chinese having more children and in the eighteenth century alone the population doubled to 300 million.[6] This huge population was unified by a feeling, a strong sense of national pride that had matured over the centuries which really helped the emperors to rule their people. The conviction of their superiority over the rest of the world seemed unshakable.

A nation's pronounced feeling of self-esteem is a key factor for the population's unity and motivation. Whether it is in a dictatorship or a democracy, the person who heads the state cannot afford to ignore this feeling. A dictator who does not manage to establish a strong feeling of self-esteem will be reliant upon different means of oppression and therefore one way or other is doomed to failure. The feeling of self-esteem is more than national pride. It grows out of the feeling that people are willing to stand in for one another. It is something active which incorporates the acceptance of others as well as a mutual feeling of dependency.[7] It is the 'sense of belonging', to which Sir Ralf Dahrendorf is referring.[8] 'An enterprise in cooperation for mutual benefit', was how the British philosopher John Rawls phrased it.[9]

Even in places where the citizens elect their government democratically, a strong feeling of unity and an ability to reach a consensus within society are fundamental requirements for implementing drastic reforms or daring to embark on brave new ventures. In the one and a half decades of a unified Germany, no politician has succeeded in generating a sense of community. Although they have tried countless times, the divide between East and West or rich and poor has still not been overcome. In comparison China, at the beginning of the twenty-first century represents a stable entity, which has managed to endure and unify its people during times of crisis. Even during the enormous strains of the Cultural Revolution the Chinese people managed to stick together.

The fate of a nation depends not least of all on the resilience and flexibility of its collective self-esteem. That is one of the secrets of China's success today. Despite the Chinese emperors having intermittent difficulties in keeping their giant kingdom together – as during the Ming and earlier Qing Dynasty (around 1650–1830) – China was predominantly calm and stable. The Qing emperors in particular, not being Han Chinese and as

Manchurians – belonging to a minority group knew – how to integrate ethnic minorities into this huge united kingdom. Anyone who wanted to pull out had a big price to pay; they lost their status as a Chinese and so with that their collective superiority over other groups of people. What then was the real value of the Koreans' or the Laotians' independence? Even the Mongolians – who had ruled half of Eurasia a few centuries before – found it difficult to nurture their national identity once their reputation had faded. There was no other country that the Chinese considered more desirable than China. It had grown and now belonged together.

As the superior Middle Kingdom China also lacked competition. The Chinese minorities were unable to shift sides to further their autonomy – as the Alsations and Saarlander had done in Europe. In the Europe of the new era it was difficult to get a collective frame of reference until the end of the Second World War as it was characterised by internal competition. The small, young European nations rubbed against one another like tectonic plates. One war followed the next as the rulers tried to redefine and lay down the new borders of their territory, and so the inhabitants of the border areas had to get used to belonging to a different country at different times. A feeling of unity that established itself under the rationale of the inhabitants' common purpose was therefore hardly going to develop under these circumstances. Even among the upper classes there was only a weak sense of national self-esteem. The European aristocrats felt a much greater common bond amongst themselves – one that transcended national boundaries.[10] One was more a noble than a German, and so European history consisted of a competition between similarly matched noble families. It was exactly this battle for supremacy that eventually brought the nobility to their knees and was to result in the establishment of new country borders between the seventeenth and twentieth century. Because every royal kingdom needed ever-increasing amounts of money to finance their wars of expansion, they became dependant on their middle classes who both paid and collected taxes. The nobilities' assistants, the bourgeois elite, soon began to ask for more than money for their services. They also wanted to be members of the more refined social circles. The previously accepted value system therefore started to rock from side to side, and so the system, which had humbly subjugated its citizens under God and the divinely legitimised, crowned heads of Europe was replaced with a type of order of subjects where both the rulers and subjects had to be equally subjugated – the 'belief of the permanent value of national characteristics and traditions'.[11] A nation does not just consist of a social class, but instead it encompasses everyone who lives within its national borders, in essence therefore every citizen. Those who had made a special effort to secure the welfare of the nation also had the right for a better status. Herewith the patriot was born and the appetite for expansion gained a new momentum. Instead of noble families going to war it had now become nations.

At a distance of 10,000 kilometres the members of the Chinese court could only shake their heads in disbelief when they heard about the hullabaloo in Europe. The Middle Kingdom had surpassed the phase of squabbling mini states almost 2000 years earlier. Qin Shihuang, the first emperor of China had unified the country in 220 BC,[12] and since then the central power of the emperor had remained largely uncontested. In any case the personnel who had been given their heavenly right to rule changed with the dynasty that was in power at a particular time. The Chinese believed that as long as Europe was still catching up in their efforts to modernise and the European elites were busy wearing each other down, there was nothing to worry about. The news of war, insurrection and social unrest only confirmed their conviction that the place was inhabited by 'barbarians'.

The welfare of the Chinese had resulted because they had a similar capitalist economy as the English. This meant that there was a similar degree of the division of labour, intricacy of trade and freedom of movement within the regulations of the state. The American historian Kenneth Pomeranz confirmed what his dear colleague John K. Fairbank had indicated 20 years previously, 'On closer examination we see how little the Anglo-Saxon merchants of the 19th century appreciated the finer structures of Chinese business-life'.[13]

The land, commodity and labour markets had a similar degree of freedom as they had in England – certainly freer than they are today. Fairbank described China as being a 'huge free trade zone'.[14] Production was also comparably high in both countries. The English were more advanced in simple manufacturing and the Chinese were better in agriculture. The state supported the economy. The national trade in China had advanced similarly to the international trade in Europe. The capital costs were just about the same in both regions and so was the surplus in cash. The European economic boom was characterised by capital whereas the Chinese boom by labour.[15]

However there were limitations for both of these regions of the world, which were to become very useful for China 150 years later; the consumers and the land started to become scarce. The hinterlands of East Europe together with Russia were economically just as fruitless as the Chinese provinces of Anhui, Hunan and Hebei. Something had to happen if both regions wanted to secure their standard of living. The Chinese were right in their estimations that the English were not more technologically advanced. In fact the opposite was the case; the Chinese were leagues ahead in hydro technology. European specialists in the eighteenth century were well aware of this; a Welsh Association for the Improvement of Agriculture set themselves the goal to attain the level of technology, 'so as to make things bloom like in China'.[16] The Europeans imitated the Chinese in both textile production and the manufacture of porcelain. In the 1840s numerous engineers in the steel industry still reported back to their headquarters in England that Chinese as well as Indian steel was better and also less than half the price.[17] Even the steam engine, which had been conceived in Europe, was developed in different societies before the eighteenth century. A Jesuit who had already demonstrated a working miniature model to the Chinese court in 1671 had taken both the Chinese and western development impetus into account. As the American historian John Fairbank summarised it,

> The fact that Eurpoeans were more mobile, that the Portugese and Dutch opened India, later China and Japan for European trade, only highlights how in many things the Europeans were lacking.[18]

Pomeranz came to the conclusion that the differences, which the Europeans played to their advantage, eventually leaving China economically way behind, were much more negligible than has been assumed until now. 'Europe's advantage was just as much based on geographical coincidences as on technical skills, rather than on non-existent advantages in the efficiency of the economy's market as a whole'.[19]

Nevertheless the Chinese missed something crucial. There was an important aspect of the European development that the Chinese telescope had failed to focus on – and this would eventually oust the self-confident Chinese emperor from the throne. The stronger the feeling of self-esteem grew on the European continent along nationalist lines, the more secular it became. Everything ended up being put to the test, cardinal virtue, bravery, honour or faith in God, as well as the numerous courtly rules of conduct. National integrity became more important then personal honour; aspirations of national power replaced the force of God's will. Life became, to use a concept of Max Weber's 'internally secular'. The age of secularisation had begun.

The new self-esteem turned life in Europe upside down. The ruling classes were torn in both directions: On the one hand the nationalist sentiment strengthened the unity of their own associations of power, but there was a high price to pay for it. With the elimination of the line of command from God, through rulers to citizens, the subjects were no longer willing to be disciplined and they demanded a share of power. 'Vive la roi' came to be 'Vive la France'. Parliaments, in which nationalist self-esteem found a new home, substituted the absolute sons of God. Inherited thrones and government administration offices shared a common value. And every step of renovation was the result of fierce power struggles. The French underwent the hardest break with the French revolution and then suffered the most serious setback with 'divine' coronation of the emperor Napoleon. In Great Britain the conflict between its citizens and the aristocracy gave rise to the constitutional monarchy. The royal family was able to retain its pomp and pageantry and which remains to this day a great symbol of national identity. However its power was steadily withdrawn and transferred to the parliament. The Germans were the least convincing in their transition. After a late and brief parliamentary experiment in the form of the Weimar Republic, they plummeted into an appalling combination of dictatorship and racist nationalism under Adolf Hitler, and it was only later that the victorious Allied forces of the Second World War forced them onto the right path.[20]

For about 250 years, from the early eighteenth to the middle of the twentieth century, shifts in the European feeling of self-esteem led to a new dynamic in politics, new institutions and a new society. Only China remained set in its old ways. The emperors basked in their supremacy and ensured that just enough sunshine radiated on their citizens. The economy was still blossoming and self-confidence glowed. However around the beginning of the nineteenth century the Chinese system started to become too sluggish and complacent. In the opinion of the leading elite China's society had reached the end of its historical development, and that all that needed to be done was to repeat previous achievements in order to retain their fine standing. The term 'barbarians' for foreigners gained increasing popularity and replaced the periods commonly used term 'people of the western ocean'.[21] The 'locked-up self-esteem'[22] consolidated itself into a structured supremacy. John Fairbank in this connection refers to a 'contrast between the foundations and the superstructure'.[23] The government, 'was hardly capable of innovation, but the population and therefore also the economy were in the process of enormous growth'.[24] China not only shut itself off from the global economy, but also disconnected itself from political progress, something that can only develop whilst competing with other nations.

These are basic patterns that are also not unheard of in the West. Countries who are convinced of their own economic strength are seldom willing to modify. But this belief is often only the result of an unrealistic overestimation of their abilities, which is particularly astounding when the economic statistics clearly paint a different picture.

The competition between the individual Chinese provinces was not fierce enough to actually trigger a contest at the beginning of the nineteenth century.

And so individual provinces were still quite comfortable economically during the reign of the Manchu emperors. In any case the Chinese were used to a central government, which was still powerful enough to enforce their rules of conduct from the top down. Even at the end of the nineteenth century it was possible to swiftly extinguish the few large, yet isolated revolts that occurred during this time. It is true that there were also problems such as overpopulation, natural disasters and poverty, but the undercurrent of discontent that swept through the kingdom never grew to be vehement enough to force political change.

It was exactly this stability that caused China to fall behind. The Europeans had to develop alternatives in their hour of need. Thousands emigrated to America, the 'new world' because of a scarcity of basic provisions. China in comparison was so large that the poor were to a certain extent able to migrate within their own country during hard times, whereas well into the eighteenth century the English, French, Spanish and Portuguese sailed around the world in order to establish new territories and markets. In the process they brought the inhabitants of distant and less-developed countries in Africa, South America, and South East Asia to their knees. These people then had to manufacture products and mine natural minerals according to the conditions that had been stipulated by the Europeans, so that these could be profitably sold in Europe.[25]

However China was too big and mighty and also far too developed, so that such methods of conquering were a not possible. Moreover the British had already had the experience in India that waging a war against a huge kingdom can become a very expensive affair and that will take a long time for the investments to amortise. In spite of this the Europeans did not want forgo the opportunity of the Chinese market, and they felt that the small trading posts positioned on the island in the South Chinese Pearl River delta were far from adequate.

As gentle persuasion had been ineffective the West eventually decided to barge ruthlessly into the Chinese market, as it was under tremendous economic pressure. The Chinese sold tea and silk for silver and the British wanted to desperately trade products for Chinese goods so that they would not lose massive amounts of silver. And so from about 1800 onwards China was integrated into the global economy without having given its official consent.[26] As it turned out there was a product that the Chinese did not have, which was widely popular, constantly in demand, paid for in silver and was to a certain extent produced around the corner in India, Britain's most important colony – the narcotic opium. In Europe opium had caught the attention of socially conscious politicians relatively early on, who were able to ban it due to the considerable costs to the health care system. In comparison, the

Chinese government did nothing about it at this time. It was not only the foreign smugglers who were making a lot of money in the business, but also Chinese dealers who were able to distribute the drug into the country's interior, where the foreign traders had almost no foothold or distribution network. In the 1840s there were already one million coastal inhabitants addicted to opium, which was in fact 1 per cent of the entire population. By the end of the nineteenth century there were already twelve million addicts[27] which took an enormous toll on the country's economic power and social stability.

At the beginning of the nineteenth century China was still a successful country. The emperor was aware that foreign businessmen were increasingly infiltrating his country, ignoring his regulations, and this was having an immensely negative impact on both the state and society, yet he failed to respond appropriately. Economic laissez faire, which up that point had been one of the empire's strengths, had now become the exact opposite. The Chinese leadership acted as if paralysed, they neither fought against, nor legalised the opium trade. As a result they mostly harmed themselves, as the state was unable to raise revenue either through fines or taxes. The West has at least been able to minimise the social costs of alcohol and tobacco with such an income. It can be considered representative of the increasing paralysis of the Chinese state, that the opium trade was eventually stifled by the British Parliament and not by China. At the beginning of the twentieth century the liberal party in England won votes with the promise, among others, of curtailing the 'unrefined trade'.

China was hit by a cold blast of air; 1834 saw the collapse of the state-run East India Company's monopoly in the opium trade, which resulted in private traders taking over a large part of the business. One of the entrepreneurs, William Jardine played a leading role in uniting his competitors to exercise pressure on the British government. They were fed up with having to grovel at the feet of the emperor's trading representatives and having to depend on the Chinese trading houses such as the Co-hongs to gain access to the domestic market. After all the opium trade was important for Great Britain because it increased its purchasing power in India and thereby also strengthened the foundations and ensured the stability of this gigantic distant colony. At the same time Jardine also petitioned the Chinese government to relax the strict import restrictions on opium.

Whilst the Chinese court continued to ignore the global transformations, their subjects had long since recognised the sign of the times. They knew how to take advantage of the state's dwindling authority, had become wealthy through the sale of opium and were also faster at distributing the drug throughout the country. The consequences were devastating. What had started as a social problem now became an economic problem. Opium not only turned people into addicts but it also affected the economy. China was to a certain extent exchanging silver for ailing drug users. After one hundred and fifty years of stability inflation now began to take off. Silver became scarcer and so farmers and property owners had to spend more of their earnings in copper to be able to pay their taxes in silver. Their buying power plummeted. A wave of unemployment spread through the country. Business people were unable to finance their trade in the interim. The empire's balance of trade became negative. Only one thick heavy noose tied the country to import from the outside world – the opium trade. This sole import was enough to make the country weak and susceptible. The global economy had China hooked.

The situation had become so bad that it was bearable only in a haze of opium, which accelerated the negative trend even more. 'The Chinese are smoking opium because they are lazy', was the opinion of the intellectual Chang Chih-Tung at the end of the nineteenth century.

'Laziness arises when there is nothing new left to do. There is nothing left to do if you have no new ideas, and the reason for this is that you don't learn anything new.[28]

The opium dens destabilised urban society and the military. It also rocked the state's monopoly of power and the Chinese people's self-confidence and the century old feeling of self-esteem began to fade.

There was no other alternative, the Chinese court had to take action. Lin Zexu, the provincial governor of China's central province Hunan was assigned especially to Canton at the end of 1838. His initial attempts to go up against the Chinese traders were somewhat half-hearted. However three months after having taken office he began to apply harsh measures; he had the foreigners' opium confiscated and stopped the trade; numerous foreign traders were placed under house arrest. The British, who for the first time in their colonial history, encountered a country that refused to show them respect, at first decided to give in. However their envoy did demand financial compensation for the loss of the business.

The Chinese told themselves that this kind of crisis was not going to send their country off the rails. Even though they would always have to face difficulties. It would not be too long before they would start to go uphill again. They were not going to abide by the biased rules of the 'barbarians'; they would trip over their own feet soon enough, as it is well known that arrogance precedes the fall. It was unimaginable that China could be defeated or that the currents of the global economy could undermine one's power in the country. Even into the 1860s it had not occurred to them that there could be weaknesses or faults with the system. In fact the state philosopher Confucius could have given them one or two bits of advice:

> If you are able to rule your own kingdom, who will dare to slander you? If we are united, strict and sober, and if we follow the rules, they (the foreigners) will not attack or slander us.[29]

In 1839 the emperor's emissary wrote a letter to the British Queen Victoria,[30] which her Ministers decided not to present to her. The message was in accordance with the aristocratic code of honour that had been common in Europe two hundred years previously:

> If it is not permissible to harm your own country, how much less should you harm others, and least of all a country like China? The riches of China have to serve the profits of the barbarians. The Laws of Heaven will not tolerate this. (…) [From now on] you will surely see to it that your subjects will cease to violate the law.[31]

Instead of concerning themselves with international power play and sharpening their competitive edge, the Chinese believed that they were able impose their values and rules on the rest of the world. China thought that England was nothing more than, 'a hand full of rocks in the western ocean', and on top of that it was 'far too populated with inadequate supplies of food'.[32] The Europeans on the other hand profited from the fact that they were experienced in competing amongst themselves. The nations had become better and better at this reciprocal competition.

Wars were a common means of asserting interests of political power in this competition of nations. However the Qing Dynasty had forgotten what it was like to engage in a power struggle with another nation. China had not attacked another country for ages, let alone been attacked by one. Added to this the ruling body had over the years become so power-blind that they were not even able to apply their famous battle tactics, which the strategist Sunzi had developed in the fourth century. It did not foresee any problems and therefore was also not able to, 'use the power of the opponent for one's own purposes', or turn a 'disadvantage into an advantage'. Instead they complained bitterly that the foreigners had upset the 'heavenly harmony' – a harmony that should have encompassed more than it actually did.

For the thousands of Chinese traders who made their money from opium and other goods, personal gain was more important than the damage that resulted from their actions. Indeed it had become more important than the affiliation with their own country or the humility they should have felt for their god-like rulers. However there were other Chinese, and particularly those who were in direct contact with foreigners whose self-esteem was strengthened excessively. They felt their own powerlessness and therefore started to adopt an extreme attitude:

> We will definitely kill you, chop off your heads and burn you. We will skin you and eat your flesh, and only then will you see our strength. Because like beasts you cannot read written characters; our speech has to be loud and vulgar for your instruction.[33]

The British were slowly beginning to lose patience. A rational dialogue along diplomatic channels was now no longer an option. As research by the Harvard historian James M. Pollack has demonstrated,[34] when they eventually did resort to bearing arms in 1839, a war broke out that nobody wanted. It was not a 'clash of cultures', but rather a dispute between a backward country and a progressive one. The British fought for global free trade and the Chinese court for heavenly harmony and to be left in peace.

Admiral George Elliot who was dispatched by England to open China for the British traders was determined right from the start not to become engaged in any massive military manoeuvres. Even though he was sure of the support of the West and many Chinese traders and had the use of better weapons, he had to reckon with the fact that the Chinese would put up bitter resistance in defending their motherland. For this reason his troops occupied the entrance of Canton and then he renewed negotiations. The treaty, which followed in January 1841, was hardly worth the paper that it was written on. Both sides soon had the feeling that they had been disadvantaged. The hesitant envoys were replaced and only four months later the next round of negotiations had started. After Chinese soldiers had attacked a British patrol the British began to systematically conquer one port after another. They encountered considerable resistance as the Chinese felt that they had lost face as they had been attacked by a foreign power. In the city of Zhapo numerous families committed suicide rather than to fall into the hands of 'barbarians' – so deeply engrained was the Chinese self-esteem.

This however was not enough for the Chinese to match the British firepower. A year later, in August 1842, the emperor surrendered as the British secured Shanghai and the old imperial city of Nanjing, as well as blocked the big canal, which was China's most important transportation route. The southern ports had to be opened to the British, the Chinese state was almost unable to collect any customs duties and foreigners could no longer be prosecuted by the Chinese judicial system. Since the door was opened it was first the French in 1843, followed by the Americans a year later, who managed to have similar rights sanctioned on the grounds of a most favourable clause.

These 'unequal treaties' were a reflection of the new balance of power. They also clearly indicated that the British seemed to have a guilty conscience because of the opium trade. Although they did force the emperor to replace the value of the confiscated opium, there was no mention of the word 'opium' in the treaty. Maybe opium was just a political pretext to use colonial measures to bring China to its knees? Or did England's economic interests outweigh efforts to press for liberalism within the market economy? The assessments of various historians are quite diverse in this matter. John Fairbank is of the opinion that opium was a reason rather than the cause of the war. However, the British historian David K. Fieldhouse believes that the opium trade was an integral part of the British economy.[35] The Australian historian John S. Gregory on the other hand came to the conclusion that England's main goal was to reliably and permanently open China up for traders, investors and diplomats rather than for colonial administrators: 'The foreigners had imperialistic but not colonialist purposes'.[36]

The pride of the Chinese court had been hurt and it was unwilling to comply with the agreement. It tried to undermine the arrangements and boycotted the trade wherever possible. When Emperor Daoguang, who had been responsible for the signing of the treaties, died in 1850 he was succeeded by Emperor Xianfeng, and with him came a more hard line approach. He wanted to prove himself as a mighty ruler and once again strengthen the self-esteem of the Chinese through political achievements. His aspirations were not totally without prospects as China was no longer on Britain's list of priorities. Lord Palmerston had in the meantime become Prime Minister, even suffered from a vote of no confidence in relation to the China question, and it was only after a re-election that he managed to safeguard his China policy. Nevertheless India was far more important for the English and its army had its plate full on the sub-continent. The Chinese and the colonialists engaged in skirmishes for a period of 15 years, until the British embarked on a major offensive in 1856 with the aid of the French. This time the emperor experienced first-hand that he was only conditionally the master in his own empire. The English and the French occupied Peking, the government had to flee and the emperor's summer palace was burnt to the ground as it apparently harboured forces that were hostile towards foreigners. The colonial masters now had control of all the important Chinese ports from the southern city of Canton to the northern city of Tianjin. The Americans, Russians and Japanese went on to secure free access to China for themselves. The treaties that were signed after the war determined England and Portugal's relationship with China in particular right upto the 1990s. Only then were Hong Kong and Macau were handed back to China.

The Chinese should have at least been able to judge the global balance of power realistically after this massive defeat. However the court's strategists were caught up in a fatal combination of superiority and helplessness. Added to this was sluggishness, which is characteristic of large empires when they are required to realign themselves or to rectify their course. China strayed further off course. It was only over several decades that the realisation that China was only one country among many, and that despite its size it was required to reach a consensus with others, slowly began to filter through to the corridors of power. It also slowly dawned on them that in the age of global industrialisation it was no longer conceivable to function without the West. In the words of the German historian Jurgen Osterhammel, the opium war therefore was, 'not the invasion of a rigid and stubborn Asian society through the dynamic herald of Western modernisation, and it was also not according the contrary assessment – simply the attack of sinister imperialists on virtuous contented Orientals'.[37] He accentuated one of the turning points in Chinese history. If one considers the USA's political actions in the world today, then one could infer that great empires generally have the inclination to develop an obstinate self-esteem, which becomes an obstacle for the way the rest of the world operates. Could this be a characteristic of a declining world empire?

China had not always led such a solitary existence. Quite on the contrary, two hundred years before explorers like Christopher Columbus set out to circumnavigate the world, Admiral Zheng had sailed to the Persian Gulf and South East African coast in ships which were almost five times the size of Columbus's Santa Maria.[38] He had porcelain, silk and lacquer ware on board which he bartered for luxury goods such as exotic spices, ivory, rhino horn, fine wood, pearls and diamonds. The Chinese went on seven extensive journeys between 1405 and 1433, which totalled a hundred ships and 28,000 sailors and soldiers. They probably sailed all the way to Australia – 300 years before Captain Cook. Europe, as the Arab traders had informed them, was not really of much interest as a trading partner, as they could only offer wine and wool.[39] Zheng He and Vasco da Gamma missed each other by a mere 80 years. Louise Levathes wondered what would have happened if da Gamma had run across the Chinese fleet in his nutshells. 'Would he have still dared to sail across the Indian Ocean?'[40] In any case, the natives of the African city of Malindi appeared to be quite disappointed when the Europeans landed on their coast, after their grandfathers had told them about the arrival of colossal ships.[41]

The decision of China's leaders to rein in their curiosity of the world had more to do with a series of unfortunate circumstances rather than strategy. The progress on the high seas became a bone of contention for two factions of the palace, namely the Confucian advisors and the eunuchs.[42] The emperor Zhu Zhanji had managed to cleverly balance the influence of the two factions. However after his death in 1435 a child emperor followed him, and the eunuchs took the opportunity to seize power. In addition to the sea-going vessels they also controlled the secret police and the tax collection agencies. When China went through a period of economic difficulty the Confucian faction felt that the opportunity had arrived to weaken the position of the eunuchs. Although only 50 years previously the Confucians had been huge advocates of navigation they now totally reversed their stance out of sheer opportunism in this power struggle. Fan Jin took on the task of securing the interests of the Confucians with the emperor, and tried to convince him that China was so superior as a civilisation that there was no need to engage in international trade.

> Let the people of the Middle Kingdom have a breather. Then, they will be able to focus on agriculture and learning. The distant peoples will give in on their own accord, distant countries will come under our dominion, and our dynasty will last for ten thousand years.[43]

Even so the emperor did not take any action, so that two years later Fan's colleague, Yang Shiqi broadcast an even clearer message, 'China should not degrade itself by fighting with wolves and pigs'.[44] In 1433 Zhu Zhangji banned international navigation, whether for trade or war, on the penalty of death. In 1477, a whole generation later, it was not even possible for the eunuch Wang Zhen, the powerful chief of the secret police to revitalise shipping. When he demanded records of previous expeditions and ship design plans he was informed that they had 'been lost'. A Vice Minister added that in case they had not been lost, 'they should be destroyed'.[45] Such a huge amount of money and countless people's lives had been invested without ever having got back anything meaningful in return.

The Confucian faction was therefore responsible for depriving China of a distinct advantage in the competition of nations. Levathes concluded from her research that,

> Ironically [China] withdrew from the sea precisely in that historical moment in which the European powers dared to leave the safe Mediterranean coasts further and further behind and attempted to find an ocean route to the Far East.

However it was not until 1521 that Ferdinand Magellan reached the Chinese sea, and then it took another quarter of a century before the Portuguese permanently settled in front of the gates of China in the province of Macau. Political squabbles had thrown a spanner in the works of China's revolutionary navigational technology. Navigation did however serve the purpose of strengthening the Chinese self-esteem, as is impressively documented in a play from the Ming era (1615) about one of Zheng's expeditions to Indonesia. When the Indonesian kings demand porcelain as tax, Zheng replies, 'You want porcelain – that's not too difficult…'

'What is porcelain made from?' asks the King of the Sulus.

'Do you not know your majesty? Zheng He answers, 'In our country porcelain grows on trees. I can show you some porcelain trees if you don't believe me'.

'Of course we would like to see them', said the kings.

The curious kings went below deck to have a look at the trees at which point Zheng's soldiers took them captive.

It was not only the Confucian faction in the fifteenth century, but also Confucianism as a philosophy, which stood in the way of modernisation, rather than helping it. This became very obvious in the nineteenth century. The Confucian values of loyalty, which were untiringly spread throughout the country, served the primary purpose of educating the population in obedience to the state. People did not only have to follow one straight line of command from the emperor, there were also rival leaders who competed for their loyalty. Above this there was also the development of relationships based on loyalty and dependency among the family clans, which were tightly knit through friendship, marriage or business. These relationships were much more complex than traditional Confucianism had predicted. People do not only have the tendency to obey their elders but also to build up networks. The Chinese self-esteem, which was meant to be based on Confucianism, only partially fitted into the complexity of the daily life of the Chinese. Norbert Elias goes so far as to say that these interconnected webs are continually expanded and become more tightly knit as mankind advances further,[46] because they make life easier and safer. With the wealth of knowledge that originated from Confucianism, it was this sociological trend in Chinese history that always went against the expectations of the scholars. It is far more difficult to plan a society and to directly steer it from the top to the bottom, than the Confucians thought. Elias commented,

> Nobody takes the lead. Nobody stays outside. Nobody can control the movement of the whole, unless a vast number were able to understand

the large figuration which they constitute together, and survey it from the outside.[47]

After the collapse of the Ming Dynasty, the Chinese academics who tried to figure out what had gone wrong came to the conclusion that Chinese society was impregnated with an 'extreme individualism'.[48] This was a concept that was in direct contrast to Confucianism. However the idea that a nation, a powerful group or even one person was able to determine the development of a society is an illusion according to Elias. This recognition on the other hand is the foundation of a modern understanding of self-esteem. Even a single powerful ruler is a part of the interwoven web and is also dependent upon it, as he needs to find out what it takes to cement his nation together, as he is only able to participate in deciding how their pride is going to take shape and how impassioned it becomes. Elias's pretext is that in all configurations of leadership there are many individual experiences, aspirations and plans that are in competition with one another, which balance themselves out into a new direction in a long-term development process. The self-esteem of the Chinese had to come down from its high pedestal. The concept that China is only one part of the interwoven web of nations, which cannot be evaded, made its way to the emperor's throne only in the last quarter of the nineteenth century.

A pioneer in this tiresome course of events was the political essayist Hsueh Fu-Cheng, who in 1879 made the following sober declaration on China's standing in the world:

> You can't find a place in the whole wide world with which they [the Europeans] have not already established relations. When [the legendary rulers] Yao and Shun had to react to this development, there was one thing they could not do. They could not close the doors and live in isolation. That is why the Empire has to change. The world is no longer divided, Chinese and barbarians are no longer clearly separated. Instead, China finds herself in an integrated world in which she and the distant lands are closely related.[49]

These are the first famous comments in reference to globalisation in recent Chinese history. The long-cultivated concept of dualism between the Chinese and the barbarians began to crumble and was slowly replaced with the competitive mechanism of social change:

> When there is little social change [in an integrated world] the laws ruling a society accordingly change very little. But when there are great changes

going on, these laws must change as well. The reason for reforms is not that [the rulers] want them; no, they are forced by the times and circumstances. The progress of the European nations is based upon their energy and cleverness in competition with one another. If we want to reach their level, we have to change our economic policy (…) accordingly. (…) If we do not enforce reforms they will get rich and we will remain poor. (…) Without reforms, they will be connected, but we will remain isolated. United they are strong, whereas we may easily collapse. (…) In order to eclipse others we have to study their methods before we can conduct reforms. After the reforms we will perhaps be in a position to overtake them.[50]

It was now a question of being able to push this realisation past the hard-liners. In the 1870s a trusted aide of the famous widow Empress Cixi was able to push several reforms through, which were to narrow the gap with the West's lead in development. Components of the reform programme included the establishment of a Chinese shipping company for trade, the dispatch of students to the USA and the extension of the existing telephone cable that had been laid on the seabed from London to Shanghai up to Tianjin and Peking. However the reforms got stuck, due to the fact that the conservative Qing officials had only limited interest in China's integration into the power network of nations they rather they wanted to heave the country back into its old position. The reform programme was not about 'strengthening through international competition' but rather 'self-strengthening'.[51] Nevertheless, Feng Kuei-Fen a Chinese intellectual who was probably the first philosopher who used the term 'self-strengthening' in the course of the Chinese reforms, asked a vital question whilst looking at the European colonial powers in 1898: 'Why are they small and yet so strong, and why are we so big and yet so weak'?[52]

One of the possible answers was given by Liang Qichao,[53] one of the most famous writers of modern China,

In the last thousand years there has not been one epoch without change. But this means that it takes new laws even to govern an old country. Those who insist that we need no reforms should understand that it is precisely our tradition that calls on us to adapt. It is written in the Book of Changes: 'When there is exhaustion let there be change. After the change there will be new unity'.[54]

These considerations were given a more current dimension because of a short and violent war. During an attempt to save their influence in Korea, the Chinese army met Japanese troops with similar intentions in July 1894.

The fighting dragged on until January 1895, resulting in the annihilating defeat of the Chinese, who thereby also lost their vassal Korea. On top of this they had to pay war debts amounting to 10,000 tons in silver, and open four additional ports, which included Chongqing located deep in the hinterland on the banks of the Yang-tse, as well as release the island of Taiwan and the peninsula Liaodong in Southern Manchuria.

This additional defeat continued to gnaw at the Chinese self-esteem. Recalcitrant contemporaries like Tan Ssu-Tung[55] now demanded a bid for freedom. China was to break away from the entrenched forms of governance of the old Manchus and to cancel the 'unequal contracts' with the foreigners. Tan wrote in 1898 that if one pays attention to networks between China and other foreign countries, between the upper and the lower classes, between men and women and also between oneself and others then reforms would be the most effective.[56] The understanding that networks are more useful than orders and Confucian obedience started to gain more weight. Furthermore Tan was convinced that trade with the West could also be beneficial for China. The emperor and especially above all the conservative forces went on the defensive even more strongly. Tan Wrote,

> If a nation is pushed into the whirlpool of world historical change, the traditionalists will only hurry its downfall. But those capable of change will seize the opportunities of competition and move on.[57]

Eventually the young emperor Guangxu's struggle to issue an edict was successful in 1898; which historians were later to describe as 'the most revolutionary in Chinese history'.[58] With the support of a small group of advisors he tried to encourage the country to embark on a more open approach:

> We should choose those aspects of Western business that keep us connected with modern times and use them to elevate our country to the level of other nations. We should get rid of useless, hollow and self-deceiving practices – they will only slow us down. (...) We should crack the shell of slackness that enlaces our system.[59]

As impressive as this 'counter-speech' was, which had come out of the late emperor's era – it was to take another one hundred years for China's team of leaders to actually open the country to the world. At first narrow-mindedness prevailed at the turn of the twentieth century. After only one hundred days of reform the widow empress and the military ended the renovation programme. A few of the reformers were able to flee into exile and six of them were executed. The imperial edict was annulled. The court once again withdrew itself onto a high plateau with its pride, which was hardly in keeping with reality. The echelons of power had registered that the West no longer wanted to get along without China, but reforms can only be effective if the political establishment has a clear and sober understanding of its own position and spreads these perceptions to the lowest level of administration. The nineteenth-century debacle did manage to imprint a fundamental question onto the collective memory of China and its leaders, which to this day determines all political and economic decisions: What is the balance between the dependency on foreign countries and self-sufficiency so as to optimally guarantee unity, order and prosperity in China? This question has overshadowed all the ideological arguments that were to lead to turbulence in the ensuing hundred years.

It was not its technical and economic abilities that prevented China from keeping up with the other nations. The military backwardness could have been avoided, as Japan had successfully demonstrated. There were also enough progressive Chinese politicians in the nineteenth century who wanted to help the rigid political system make some headway. However the rigid Chinese self-esteem stood in their way and even was exaggerated in times of crisis. Chinese history has shown that soporific self-certainty can also become a trap. On the other hand confession of one's own weaknesses provides an opportunity for judging oneself realistically and through this process powerfully invigorate the feeling of self-esteem. It is even more important to know one's strengths as one can then build on top of these.

China's pride was the secret of its success but it also head to its downfall. In the twenty-first century Germany is in the process of making the same mistake. China's leaders encouraged their people by telling them that, 'We are strong!', but had forgotten that in this situation a dynamic feeling of self-esteem that drives people to engage in competition with other countries is what cements a country together.

# Chapter 3

# THE DECLINE OF POWER

> If we ignore the people and lose their hearts, who will support our rulership?
>
> Widow Empress Cixi, 1900

Peace is threatened when one fails to recognise its presence. Particularly in times of long-lasting peace people tend to overlook that peace is not just a matter of course but rather that the state clasps it with all its power. It has the monopoly over the internal application of power, and to ensure that peace prevails is one of the most important achievements of modern nation states. Without the state's monopoly of power a society is unable to function. However, just how quickly it can be undermined by those who no longer feel that they are being represented by the state is easily underestimated.

The monopoly of power is especially crucial for a functioning state as it is so closely connected to the monopoly of taxation; by offering security, the state receives money from its citizens. With this it can improve security, which in turn provides its citizens with more liberties. A fall in the revenue from taxation is always an important signal for the beginning of a crisis for a state. If it has less money at its disposal it will be forced to decrease its expenses and therefore will reduce its spending on social interests, which will only intensify its citizens discontent. A downward spiral is set in motion; self-esteem and the monopoly of power, the two forces that sustain a state, begin to diminish on an increasing scale. Finally this results in a perception, which Norbert Elias has described as follows, 'one feels as if one is a detached outsider in a deteriorating society; one is convinced that this society is on its way down, and one hopes that it will cave in'.[1] This is the predicament that the people of China found themselves in in the middle of the nineteenth century, at the start of the national decline of the Middle Kingdom.

The feeling of self-esteem and the monopoly of power have a direct relationship with one another: A society with a strong sense of community will only have to use limited resources to implement general rules of behaviour. However the deeper the social divides, the more intensely the state is required to safeguard the observance of law and order. A state that has a stable monopoly of power but no feeling of self-esteem is a terror state, which enslaves its citizens. Its leaders, as for instance in Sudan, only manage to control people through fear and terror. A feeling of self-esteem can only develop against them, but not with them. People only conform to the state's monopoly of power because they are forced to, and not because of conviction. Germany however is a country where its citizens still obey the state's monopoly of power as they are assured by it, but at the same time are estranged from those who govern. On the other hand a state with pronounced self-esteem and a weak monopoly of power ends up reeling in a rush of feelings, as in, for example Russia. Then, as in India, there are also countries with a weak self-esteem and a weak monopoly of power.

Whilst the monopoly of power presides over the adherence of rules and directives, a strong feeling of self-esteem is founded on understanding and self-control. When both of these counter balance each other, the determinants for peace and prosperity are established, irrespective of whether this is a democratic state or a state that is headed by a dictatorial regime. The political system is only the means with peace and prosperity being the purpose. A dictatorship such as the Chinese one does therefore not necessarily have to be insecure and unstable, and a democracy such as that of Germany is automatically secure and stable.

If the feeling of self-esteem and the monopoly of power weaken simultaneously, the society concerned will be disconcerted that it will no longer accept essential reforms and will be unwilling to pay taxes. Then the situation may develop where the aggressive element of those dissatisfied no longer allow themselves be controlled by the police, as there is a lack of funds for the maintenance of order. Chaos develops. Thus a that a state must try to defend its monopoly of power with all its strength, and its citizens should only take the risk of challenging it in the most extreme of emergencies. One should not forget that even in good times social order is imperfect and may become unstable. It is only possible to maintain standards of living as long as they are embedded in a functioning society. In the mid-1800s the Chinese leadership in the middle failed to recognise this link; the Germans at the beginning of the twenty-first century also seem to have difficulties in coming to terms with this. The situation is much more uncertain than the state generally believes, and this means that it may – although not necessarily become a lot worse.

Despite the fact that the monopoly of power denotes the foundations of peace, it is still regarded with distrust. This because again and again leaders have succumbed to the temptation to arbitrarily use power against the people on whose behalf they are exercising this power. Progressive states have therefore created checks and balances to ensure that it does not abuse its power. However one cannot rule out this risk completely. The debate about the police state addresses this issue.[2] However this is the price to be paid for the monopoly of power. Today, at a time when the weaknesses of Western nations are an open book, it is no coincidence that the American economic and cultural theorist Francis Fukuyama has once again supported the enhancement of state institutions. In his book *Building States* he wrote,

> The idea that nation building is at the top of our agenda, and not reducing the role of the state, may seem absurd to some. For the previous generation, afterall, the dominant trend was to criticize too much state, and to relocate activities from the state sector to the free market or civil society.[3]

Here, Fukuyama addresses a key point: In a state where people do not comply with laws because they are not afraid of being punished it is not possible to build a strong community in the long run, where there is a stable feeling of self-esteem. This is just as unlikely in a country where everyday life is shaped by the salvos of rivalling rebels. 'The weakness of states is a national as well as international problem of the first order' he wrote. 'For individual societies as well as the global community, the decline of the state does not lead to Utopia, but to catastrophe'.[4]

The critics of the police state and the advocates of the strong state are certainly in agreement: A functioning monopoly of power is a requirement for a civil society enveloped in a lively self-esteem and vice versa.[5] If people can live in security, if conflicts are only resolved by force in exceptional circumstances, if things people own actually belong to them and if they believe that the state is powerful enough to secure their standard of living, then it is possible for national pride, which is based on what has been mutual accomplishments, to flourish. On the other hand this feeling of self-esteem relieves the monopoly of power.

The Western colonial powers' military actions in the nineteenth century demonstrated that the monopoly of power and self-esteem were out of balance in the Middle Kingdom. The Opium Wars were not the cause of the Chinese crisis, as Karl Marx had written in an article for the New York *Daily Tribune* during that time, 'the authority of the Manchu empire fell apart in front of the British weapons'.[6] It was much more the case that the weapons accelerated the already advanced process of internal disintegration. Even with their modern weapons the English would not have succeeded if they had been faced with the unimpaired self-confidence of the Chinese. It was only possible for the colonial powers to acquire colonies, concessions and exclusive trading rights from the Chinese because there were sufficient numbers of powerful Chinese collaborators, who were more interested in trading with the foreigners than they were in the welfare of their own motherland. Emperor Dao Guang who had obviously recognised the connection between state authority and self-esteem wrote in 1878, 'What matters now is appeasing the people. As long as the people remain loyal we can deal with those foreign bandits'.[7]

Dao Guang had inherited some major problems: China's population had doubled itself to 300 million in the peaceful eighteenth century. At the turn of the century the economy began to falter under these pressures and so the advent of opium trade was considered a saving grace. What the Chinese traders interpreted as a financial blessing was to totally dismantle the state authority in the following decades. Globalisation taxed its first tribute. Because the Chinese had to pay the foreigners for the opium in silver, silver became scarcer and therefore more expensive. The unfavourable exchange rate primarily burdened the farmers in the interior of the country, while their income was in copper and they however had to pay their taxes in silver. Taxes therefore increased for the farmers without an actual increase in the tax rate. Moonlighting and tax evasion blossomed (as in Germany today). Ever-increasing numbers of people were convinced that success was more likely by pursuing their interests either without or against the state. Corruption escalated and became an even bigger problem.

From 1810 onwards Emperor Jia Qing tried vigorously to fight corruption in the country as well as the propensity for wasteful behaviour at his court. However he no longer had the power to actually enforce these measures. It was already too late to reform the administration of the grain-taxation system. The agency that was responsible for transporting the rice from the Yang-tse delta to Beijing, which had been collected as tax, had long stopped following the directives of the government and was acting independently. Smugglers had also infiltrated the state salt monopoly at the beginning of the nineteenth century. A substantial part of the tax revenue that had been paid at the provincial level never even reached Beijing. In fact the entire administrative machinery had already started to skid dangerously out of control. Until then it had always been the pride of the Chinese state as a mechanism that was considered to be especially effective. This was already so at the turn of the first century when the Romans at the other end of the Eurasian continent were still dependent on the unreliable assistance of powerful private individuals. The rigid selection process of the elite for state service had however ensured that young thinkers, which the country so desperately needed at the time, were not even instituted in the first place. Many of those who had been selected as career officials now began to turn against the state as they sensed the decline of power of the emperor's court: 'Many ranking officials began to weave networks of dependants and assistants. Funds for payments were raised by tapping public resources', is how the China historian Jonathan Spence described this gradual decline.[8] The more that economic circumstances deteriorated the harder it became for people to secure their standard of living. In the power vacuum that the crumbling monopoly of power had left, a romping ground developed for gangs, local princes and secret societies.

Lin Qing was one of the many ringleaders, sect members and charlatans who ensured that there was unrest in the empire. In 1808 he founded a sect and called himself, 'the eternal ancestor in our original homeland in the world of true emptiness'.[9] Like the dubious investment fund managers of the new economic phase, he relieved the farmers of their money and promised to return ten times the amount once his sect had seized power in China. He never got that far. In 1813, as he was preparing an assassination of the emperor, he was imprisoned and executed by order of the Chinese leadership.

The 'eternal peace', which China's emperor was supposed to proverbially guarantee, was now in danger. With that the unspoken social agreement between rulers and subjects had become invalid. The emperor tried to conceal this decay of power with reform rhetoric. What is unpleasantly familiar for many Germans nowadays happened: there were many political proclamations, but in fact very little was actually implemented.

At first the threads of disrespect towards the emperor's court began to loosen the formerly tightly woven self-esteem. It did not take long however for the relationship to be ruined. One reform document noted, 'In former times the people loved their leaders, compared them with their parents and respected them like the heavens (...) Now the people in the empire hate their leader, regard him as an enemy and refer to him as a dictator (Tufu).'[10] 'Who knows', wrote the political observer Karl Marx in 1850, 'perhaps one will be able to read the following on the great wall: Republique Chinoise – Liberte, Egalite, Fraternite'.[11]

However as similar as the French and Chinese were in the rejection of their leaders, they were quite different in their notion of how things should continue in the future. That one would have to revolutionise the political system was still completely unimaginable to the Chinese. They regarded the French revolution as being 'luan', which means chaos in Chinese.[12] They were on the lookout for a strong leadership personality, whereas the French fought for civil liberties, democracy and the abolition of the feudal system. Sect leaders were suddenly in business in China and they soon built up their own empires within the empire. The most famous of these was Hong Xiuquan (1814–64),[13] the leader of the Taiping movement. One night in 1843 he had the following dream: he saw himself as the Chinese son of God, who with sword in hand fought at the side of his Godly father and his "European" son Jesus Christ, in order to bring the Middle Kingdom back on track. His real life until then had been a somewhat unsuccessful existence: he had managed to fail the examination for provincial officials in Canton a total of four times. However now his dream was to prove itself to be more useful for his career than a recognised qualification. The two people who first believed in his vision and became his disciples were his cousin and Issachar Roberts a fundamentalist Baptist teacher from the USA who had established a church community in Canton. He went about teaching Hong the art of sect leader rhetoric. Once this was complete Hong and his disciples set off in search of followers. The teacher proved himself to be the most skilful at winning farmers over to the cause. When they had managed to amass 2000 people in the province of Gaungxi the teacher was arrested for planning a rebellion. Hong immediately replaced himself with two farmers who were confident orators, and so were ideal for integration into his house of faith as messengers of God and Jesus Christ. Soon after Hong was to become the leader of nineteenth century's biggest global mass movement. In 1850 Hong's movement already had 20,000 members which subsequently increased to over one million; added to this were uncountable numbers of silent sympathisers. British missionaries who had been received by Hong described him as being, 'of unsound mind and incapable of leadership'.[14] He managed to put people under his spell with a particular mixture of superstition, anti-Western morals and a pop version of Christianity. His lofty goal was, 'the heavenly kingdom of the soaring peace'[15] where the Manchu demons at the Beijing court, who opposed the real God, would have nothing to say.

Hong's rapid ascent reflected the ailing Chinese self-esteem as much as the immobilised state, which was incapable of stopping the preacher.

Especially the poor, whose high tax burden left them with little more than they needed to survive, were particularly enamoured with Hong. Added to this was a lack of food, because of brisk population growth, which also had the effect of driving up the cost of living. Especially those people who were unable to afford vices demonstrated with Hong against tobacco, alcohol and opium consumption as well as gambling and prostitution. The liberal undercurrents that characterised the French revolution were almost non-existent.

When the Taiping and their supporters realised how defenceless the state was against their movement, they decided to take up arms. Their warriors were also made up of the brave female regiments of the Hakka minority. The government troops tried desperately to keep the rebels under control and to defend the imperial court's monopoly of power. The Taiping rebels, to their own amazement, managed to fight their way from the Thistle Mountains in the interior of the country all the way to the old imperial city of Nanking by March 1853. Commando troops, who were disguised as buddhist monks, blasted through the mighty city walls. A little later Hong set up his quarters in the palace of the former emperor of the Ming Dynasty.

It was only thanks to the mistakes that the megalomaniac Hong was about to make that the Qing Dynasty did not collapse by the middle of the nineteenth century.[16] Hong enjoyed incredible popularity as a moral apostle, but when he tried to abolish private capital in Nanking and establish a type of 'communal fund' as well as regulate the markets of the occupied cities he turned huge sections of the population against him in the blink of an eye. They were quite content to have a strong leader, but they had no interest in socialist economic structures. Even his promise to redistribute wealth more equally was far from popular since this meant that one had to part with one's savings. The resistance gathered and Hong had to use force increasingly to retain his power. His rocket-propelled ascent had made him blind to a realistic estimation of his own power base. Therefore he also rejected the opportunity to unite with the rebel leaders of other regions to collectively topple the Manchus. He wanted everything but in fact was logistically overburdened with the leadership of his own sect. After only seven years in which he had taken control of the middle Yang-tse region and had nearly seized Shanghai the power of his sect was expended. He attempted reformist drives that he had copied from the leaders in Beijing. However he had meanwhile lost the power to actually implement his innovations. His disciples lost interest in him and so the Chinese son of God eventually committed suicide. In July 1864 government troops were able to take back Nanking.[17]

Once again the leaders behind the walls of the Forbidden City had made a narrow escape. They had considered the Taiping rebellion much less of a threat than the Western allies' plundering of the summer palace a few years earlier. This may have been due to the fact that the internal Chinese rebellion had taken place at a considerable distance from Beijing. In fact the colonial encroachments were much less of a danger: The foreigners only wanted to make China compliant as a trading partner but the rebels in comparison wanted to topple the emperor, drive his followers from the court and seize power. They already got quite far and had failed because of their own mistakes, not because of the imperial troops. It was even more fatal that the Beijing advisors lulled the emperor into a false sense of security. 'If people nowadays hear of the rebels, their hearts will be full of pain and sorrow; men and women will flee and the cooking fires will be extinguished'.[18] It is now no longer possible to determine whether they only wanted to calm the Emperor down or they had underestimated the seriousness of the situation.

The development of states and how the resulting monopoly of power becomes more and more pronounced are embedded in the larger configuration of the civilising process. Norbert Elias proved in his extensive research that all nations follow a 'process of civilisation', which heads in a similar direction (although at different speeds). Thus, during the history of their development people increasingly strive towards controlling their environment. Elias speaks a little emotionally of the 'triad of fundamental controls'.[19] Subsequently people did manage to exert more control over nature. When centuries ago thunder and lightning would have had people slaughtering a sheep to appease the Gods, nowadays we don't even bother to pull the television plug out of the socket. Instruments, machines and buildings protect us from the forces of nature. In the following stage of development people organised their communal living arrangements. They established institutions and administrative systems to coordinate a large society. For this they needed rules of conduct, and so compliance with these rules was surveyed and non-compliance was punished. People came to the rational conclusion that the sole right to punish members of society should be handed over to the state, and thereby the state received its monopoly of power. As wrongful behaviour could now be determined objectively and punished by independent authorities, pressure built up on the individual. The control of nature and of society was thereby followed by the control of the individual over him or herself. Those who were the quickest at being able to comprehend the risks and opportunities in their interconnected surroundings and use them to their own advantage could go a long way in the increasingly complex societies. Even those who were comfortably positioned were seized by these pressures against their will. Elias wrote,

> The fear of loss or even decrease of social prestige is among the most powerful driving forces behind transformation, which is evolving undesigned.[20]

*In Szechuan in summer 2008?*

Societies or even nations that are characterised by people who react to state-directed external control develop themselves in this interconnected mix of unplanned pressures – over the generations – into societies in which those people who are guided by their own self-control dominate. The conscience to a certain extent substitutes orders. It is however always possible for a set-back or a collapse to occur. Sometimes separate sections of a society take certain steps before others do, but no matter what gets in the way, everyone will eventually again follow the original direction.

During the course of this process people become more independent, and at the same time they take on more responsibility. They must learn to think in terms of ever-bigger connections. A division of labour occurs in the economy. Because life now becomes increasingly complex, more and more people are forced to come to an agreement with larger groups. This leads to the development of networks. The individual on the other hand who is able to adapt his behaviour the fastest becomes, 'more differentiated and always more regulated on an even and stable basis',[21] and has huge advantages and is more successful than the person who finds it impossible to adapt or compromise.

History has demonstrated that nations who functioned in this way were also economically more successful. The state used its monopoly of power to support and secure the advancement of the society, by ensuring that inconsiderate infringements of the regulations were penalised. The state-enforced and socially desired self-discipline eventually became habit through this process. The super-ego was established, to use the famous expression that was not accidentally coined by Sigmund Freud at the beginning of the twentieth century. Because at that time firmly grounded self-control had for the first time became a fixed component of people's lives in some of the European countries. The individual was given the burden of having a greater amount of responsibility towards the general public. Although this transformation came about without planning, it did not take shape without a distinctive order: 'an order which is more forceful and stronger than the will and reason that individual people have formed themselves'.[22] People were increasingly able to get along with one another peacefully because of their own volition (and without the state). It was a mixture of guilty conscience and realisation that forced them to do so. The further that people develop themselves, the more the monopoly of power is regarded as a matter of course.

In crisis situations where the monopoly of power is at stake, the rulers therefore have to offer their population solutions that are appropriate for their stage of development. If a majority wants more political freedom and independence, the rule of thumb is that this points to a more stable self-control.

A state that now demands obedience is more backward than its citizens. If the overriding desire is to have a strong leadership personality, it would be a sign that the people are still more characterised by externally-regulated control. A state that would offer free elections under these circumstances would trigger off a new uncertainty. Democracy, self-determination and independence are therefore not the cure-all for stabilising the state's monopoly of power and securing a functioning state during times of crisis.

The standards according to which people live and societies function have developed over centuries. Even if none of the Chinese leaders were pronounced social theorists, the successful ones amongst them were able to effectively rule the country precisely because their style of leadership was appropriate for the stage of development at that time. They knew that leadership had to be built on a stable monopoly of power, which only remains secure as long as the right degree is applied to ensure the welfare of the citizens. To find out how social unrest breaks out it would be logical to examine the somewhat cumbersome differentiation between self-control and external control in societies. Those that are dominated by external control rebel because they are looking for a leader who is able to obligingly and convincingly tell which direction to follow; those that are dominated by self-control demand more independence, autonomy and a share in the decision-making process. Both of these motions are freedom movements: one group wants to free itself from an unsatisfactory leader and the other group from overwhelming pressures. If those leaders who are fighting for their political survival muddle these two movements up, it could mean an end of their power. The one who gives people more civil rights when they are yearning for a new strong hand to guide them will ruin the existing order and plunge the country into chaos. On the other hand, the leader who tries to control people who are looking for more freedom strictly will need to reckon with continual resistance. Keeping in mind that a stage of development that a society has reached can once again be lost. In the past demagogues who have been able to mobilise majorities in society for their own means have continually been able to attain power. The huge popularity that sect leaders like Hong Xiuquan had in China shows that people's self-control had not developed to the extent that it had in France by the middle of the nineteenth century. The leaders who promised order, firm decisive actions and moral cleanliness were so in favour that the people were prepared to fight at their side and give up their loyalty to the weak emperor. In comparison to the Western colonial powers – who suddenly forced China into the whirlwind of globalisation and thereby international competition – the Middle Kingdom was backward.

The competition among nations put China under pressure to develop faster than was appropriate for its internal dynamics. What was then needed was someone who could modernise along with a strong leadership personality so as to breathe life into the battered self-esteem. It almost took one hundred years until Mao succeeded in giving the people what they were looking for.

Chinese intellectuals in particular who had studied abroad did not want to admit to the low level of development of Chinese society. This is how the dissident Zou Rong, who was just twenty-year-old, living in Shanghai's foreign quarter, called upon his countrymen to topple the tyranny of the Manchus and to take matters into their own hands:

> The government is yours, control it! The industry is yours, run it yourself! The army is yours, lead it! The land is yours, guard it yourself! The inexhaustible treasures of the soil are yours, exploit them! In short, you are entirely capable of revolutionary independence.[23]

Zou's theories received an enthusiastic reception, and particularly from expatriate Chinese.

The later founder of the Republic, Sun Yat-Sen distributed thousands of copies of Zou's proclamations to his followers in Singapore and San Francisco. Sun and his followers, just like Zou were inspired by the assumption that all that needed to be done was to apply the proper leverage, and soon China would be as advanced as the West. However they underestimated the speed at which even economically advanced systems develop into liberal societies. Zou's attempted revolution came to a tragic end he was sentenced by a court comprising both Western and Chinese judges to two years in custody, which he never survived. Both the Qing government and the foreigners living in Shanghai were angry at his attack on their monopoly of power.

Although the Chinese people were not ready for a revolution there were rebellions all over the country. Often not even a religious leader was in need of being able to recruit a force of 30,000 to 50,000 men. They were the victims of the economic crisis who gangedup together: farmers whose plots did not produce enough yields to feed large families, and also single men who were unable to start up families due to the shortage of women in China. They were the victims of the widespread custom of killing female infants, because sons were traditionally worth more. They plundered their way through the country and for years whole sections of the land were in the grip of fear and horror. For instance one rebellion in Jian, in central China, went on for 17 years before the government troops were able to restore peace to the area.

The foreigners watched the country with grave concern. It was quite clear in their minds that the only way that they would be able to expand their trading transactions in China was if it was peaceful and orderly. They therefore acted comparatively moderately. Already in the second Opium War their intention had been to scare the imperial court and ensure its compliance but under no circumstances to topple it.[24] As far they were concerned there was no one who was able to stabilise the country like the emperor – even if he managed to do this only poorly.

It was for exactly this reason that the colonialists were unnerved by Hong Xiuquan's attack, even though this did distract the court and Hong did spread Christianity – if a somewhat radical version of it. At first though the colonial powers held back completely.[25] As the Taiping rebels grew more powerful the more they feared for the stability of the economy, as the rebels were bitter opponents of opium consumption. In 1862 they eventually helped the government troops in the defence of Shanghai. One troop of soldiers which was known as, 'The Ever Victorious Army' was founded and initially led by an American adventurer, until a British artillery officer took over.[26]

The monopoly of power was so important for the economic stability that it forced two bitter enemies to fight side by side. Added to this foreign businessmen were supporting the religiously motivated fight against the Muslims in the north-west of the country with donations and credit. Here a leader by the name of Ma Hualong who let himself be revered as the self-proclaimed head of a sect had managed to build up over five hundred fortresses. The movement, which began around the same time as the Taiping rebellion proved itself to be more persistent, not least of all because the conflict between the dominant ethnic group. The Han Chinese and the Muslim minority had already existed long before – and incidentally still exists until today. It was only in 1873 that Ma was defeated decisively. This was a very important step for the Qing. 'The ambiguous state of the treaty ports aside, China in 1850 could once more be regarded as a united empire under the rulership of the Qing', is how Spence summarised the events.[27]

All the same it was only a temporary calm; in fact it was more a case of catching one's breath rather than a stable leadership. The state once again had the monopoly of power, but under the surface discontent rumbled worse than ever. As much as the colonial powers – with the British taking the leading role – lent the emperor support so that he could uphold his monopoly of power, they simultaneously forced him to abide by the 'unequal contracts', which served the interests of the Western economy exclusively.

National humiliation ran deep and the court tried frantically to come up with a strategy which would re-establish power on Chinese terms. If the court was unable to do this by itself, then it was surely better to share power with local leaders in the interim, rather than to lose it to the foreigners.

Consequently leaders in the countryside were raised to the status of nobility. They received the privilege of taxation and were able to obtain a share of the income. In return they had the task of keeping the rebels under control. The Australian historian J. A. G Roberts asserted that,

> Without there being a formal redistribution of power the power-balance between the bureaucratic system and the gentry shifted in the direction of the local forces.[28]

The emperor tried to strengthen his monopoly of power, but in reality had lost further power. Political and economic reforms would have been necessary so that the team of leaders could be on an equal footing with social developments. However, according to Roberts the central leadership lacked suitable economic constructs. 'The economic measures taken only show that the restorative leadership had no clue about any economy aside from self sustaining farming economy'.[29] The emperor's advisors were convinced that the cause of China's misery was its inferior weapons. They demanded a better-equipped army and the development of a navy. If the 'historical inertia', as John Fairbank describes the condition, had prolonged the power of the Chinese leaders, it now had begun to work against them.

The acknowledgement that even the Middle Kingdom was able to learn from the West reluctantly spread through the imperial court's tiers of leadership. Prime Minister Li Hongzhang came up with the motto (rang sich zu der devise durch) 'Chinese teachings as foundation, Western studies for application'.[30]

This was not even a political formula of compromise, but the level of argument that the emperor's think-tank had advocated for ages. One advisor demanded that one should 'learn from the superior technology of the barbarians', whereas another felt that the basis of Confucianism needed to be supplemented, 'through the methods which are used by different countries in order to increase strength and prosperity'.[31] However they were still in the dark about the actual connections: They were not open to the acknowledgement that the power of nations now needed to be valued according to new criteria. It made no sense to them that in the competition of nations that the size and the wealth of the population could be weighed up against the global economic networks of a country. The progressiveness of the Chinese leaders was akin to the bound feet of their women: they only managed to move forward by taking small and considerably painful steps.

The economic reforms, which the court finally struggled to push through, were correspondingly half-hearted. All one needed to do was amass Western know-how and high-tech goods and the crisis was solved. The first joint ventures between the Chinese state and private foreign enterprises were established – an economic practice whose advantages China knew how to use perfectly well for its own benefit from the 1880s. The French assisted in building expensive and dated ships. A shipping company was formed in collaboration with Jardine Matheson & Company, a British trading house based in Hong Kong. A few of the coalmines were modernised by British engineers. And in Shanghai the first modern Chinese cotton factory was built, so as to end the ten-year monopoly of the colonial powers.

However such selective measures were far from adequate. Additionally the provincial princes had much more important things to do than to discuss economic reforms with the central authorities. Their primary objective was to secure their own power base. The taxation system, as far as it still was actually in operation, was geared towards creaming off the highest possible amount from the traders' sales revenue. Long-term investments were therefore not an option. In any case the realisations of the Beijing elite had failed to filter down to the middle level of China's administration. It therefore resulted that in 1866, a leading administration official forbad a Beijing school from opening a department for Western astronomy and mathematics.

The court was not exactly unaware of the fact that its orders were going unheeded. It was for this reason that radical reformers, who were present in the court, gained the attention of the emperor at the end of the century. A group of six advisors were able to convince him to give up his traditional role as the mediator between opposing currents and to put his full weight behind Western reforms. It was a leap over one's own shadow. For the first time in centuries China orientated itself according to the achievements of a neighbouring country: the Japanese Meiji government, that had managed a transition 30 years previously. In a sensational edict on the 11th of June 1898 the young emperor announced nothing less than a new modern China.

In numerous additional edicts he described how the areas – which are normally in need of reform in every crisis of the state – such as education, economics, bureaucracy and the armed forces were to be modernised. The old crusty examination system was to be disposed and new Western subjects such as mathematics and physics were to be introduced. Industrial policy was to be more actively planned and coordinated. The Ministry of Finance was to create a modern budget plan. The army was to be beefed up with a fleet of more than thirty modern battle ships and the troops were to be trained according to Western standards. Additionally Guangxu wanted to fight corruption and simplify bureaucratic procedures. The surplus officials were to be transferred to the offices for central economic planning.

This initiative was however stopped in its tracks even before it had the opportunity to get started. The young, enthusiastic reformist emperor lacked the necessary experience in power politics to the overhaul of the system. He should have ensured more support for his approach from his inner circle. Now the opposition had become so fierce that he had managed to catapult himself offside. After only one hundred days he was impeached. The widow Empress Cixi, who had conducted official functions before Guangxu and whose support he had never managed to win over, proclaimed in an edict on the 19th of September that the emperor had requested that she should once again take control of power.[32] Guangxu was placed under palace arrest and from then on he no longer had the company of young intellectuals rather his concubines. His six advisors were arrested and executed.

The empress was not the only blatant opponent of reform. The officials and landed nobility were also not prepared surrender to their privileges for greater reforms. They preferred to fight independently, sometimes with and sometimes against the foreigners, but always against the lethargic court. The widow empress was not unjustified in fearing that Guangxu had primarily created chaos. But she was also able to secure the monopoly of power for only a few months. The more the international economy integrated China into the interwoven web of globalisation the more its backwardness came to light.

New sects, secret societies and political protest movements were born. The last major rebellion that the imperial kingdom just managed to survive was led by a group, who came to be well known as the 'Boxers'. This obscure association whose members were kick boxers and avidly followed strict simple Confucian beliefs such as 'respect your parents' and 'live in harmony with your neighbours'[33] first surfaced in the province of Shandong in 1896. At the time this was a hopelessly overpopulated region, that was particularly afflicted by famine, floods and bandits and was also continually plundered by colonial rulers. The Boxers' intention was much less to bring the downfall of the emperor but rather to drive out the foreigners who for them were the scapegoats representing the miserable Chinese state of affairs. There were regular attacks in which two German missionaries became victims in 1897. This provided a welcome reason for the Germans to penetrate into China and to annex the port of Qingdao in Shandong as a colony. Through this there was a clash of two nations neither of whom were in the mood to reach a compromise:[34] the Chinese wanted to re-establish their damaged self-esteem at any cost, and the Germans wanted to become colonisers in the blind rush for group-ideal of a late developing nation.

As the Germans had settled themselves in the home province of the proud Boxers they became a particular focus of hatred. On the 20th of June 1900 a fighter murdered the German envoy Klemens Freiherr von Kettler on a street in Beijing's diplomatic quarter. When the envoys' quarter came under fire shortly after that started of the so-called Boxer War. As the imperial court was neither willing nor capable of keeping the rebels in check, the colonial powers had to send in their own armies to save the besieged diplomats. No country did this with more delight than Germany. The emperor William II slung the notorious Hun speech at the Chinese from the port of Bremerhaven. In the high-pitched tone of the national upstart he threatened the weakened giant, as he fired up his soldiers: 'When you meet the enemy, then the same one will be beaten! No pardon will be given! No prisoners will be taken! Whoever falls into your hands shall be crushed! Just like a thousand years ago when the Huns under their king, Etzel made a name for themselves so that they now still make a mighty appearance in folk and fairy tales – so may for a thousand years the name of Germans in China be validated through your actions in a way, that a Chinese will never again dare to look down on a German'.[35]

The Chinese were fully aware that it was the weakest of the European nations that bellowed the loudest. The pompous tone of the German emperor matched the loudmouthed diplomats that he had sent to China. Only their wives were able to outdo them in excessiveness, as the former Austrian emissary, Arthur von Rosthorn cabled to Vienna: 'The ladies belonged to a certain group of "excessive patriots" who swore that they would like to have ten sons so that they could sacrifice them for the fatherland. Paula said justifiably that this was either hypocrisy or bore witness of an unparalleled inhumanity.'[36]

In this way the imperial court and the foreign powers were unable to find a common Modus Vivendi. The widow empress tried to use the popular Boxers as a catalyst for a new Chinese self-esteem and specifically protected the rebels with an edict that was issued in 1900. 'Today China is extraordinarily weak. We can only depend on the hearts and feelings of the people. If we push aside the people and lose their hearts, then what else is left for our country to support itself on?'[37]

As they had surrendered themselves to the economic problems, the opposition against foreigners came just at the right moment. 'The foreigners have behaved aggressively towards us, they have hurt out territorial integrity', went an imperial decree, 'kicked our people with their feet. (...) They suppress our people and our Gods. The common people have to endure great hardship under them and thirst for revenge. This is why the brave followers of the Boxers have burnt churches to the ground and killed Christians.'[38] The authorities looked the other way as the rebels pounded foreigners during street battles. In the words of the envoy von Rosthorn, 'There could be no doubt in the mind of anyone who has seen a horde of Boxers that the strapping country lads did not bear a personal grudge against the Europeans, and had probably never even seen a European. They regarded these foreign people with naïve amazement. And the other thing that we noticed about them was that they were all both similarly and well dressed. Hereby one could conclude above all that the uprising against the foreigners was not a spontaneous movement, but instead that it was being directed and subsidised from a higher position.'[39]

There was now the development of a 'feeling of unity', which according to Spence, 'now had to be mobilised if the Chinese people were to survive'. The 'national outlook', which Cixi valued from the Boxers, was nothing other than an extremely sick version of the Chinese self-esteem. It aligned itself with an over-valued group-ideal instead of reality. Not only the elite, but the man on the street was conscious of this ailment. 'Hawkers and rickshaw drivers, sedan carriers, canal boatmen, leather workers, knife sharpeners and barbers'[40] were all after the same thing.

Every attack on the foreigners weakened the court even further. It was a state of anarchy: foreigners and sects could do exactly as they pleased whilst the court withdrew to the safety of Xian. The empress attempted to demonstrate her resolution by beheading five dignitaries as traitors. Eight colonial powers, which in Europe were hardly innocent about what was going on, assembled a joint army in China and marched to Beijing. Court advisors such as the viceroy Liu Kunyi and Chang Chih-Tung implored the widow empress to comply. When it became obvious that the Boxers with their fighting techniques had no chance against the artillery of the allied forces, Cixi had to look for the support of the foreigners once again.

The besieged diplomats became aware of this shift and hoped for an immanent rescue: 'At the beginning of August we received a cart full of watermelons in her name', von Rosthorn reported, 'even those of us with the French envoys received a couple'. However through this action the court gained little respect for itself. The foreigners allowed themselves a prank, 'by carving a face into the rind the after the consumption of the interior and placing it with a candle on top of the German barricades at nightfall. The Chinese, who either felt that they were being mocked or as result of their superstition believed it to be a ghost, got terribly excited and the usual screaming and wild shooting started up again'.[41]

In August the French, Japanese English, Germans, Russians as well as Indian Sikhs and Rajputs liberated 'long, dark figures with mighty turbans'.[42] The commando of the German General Field Marshall Alfred Graf von Waldersee arrived after the Bereihung had already been carried out.

Cixi was lucky that the European troops were still convinced that the monopoly of power was in no better hands than those of the imperial court.

Despite this they were happy to receive a royal reimbursement for the reinstatement of national order.[43] In the 'Boxer protocol' they dictated reparations, which amounted to four times that of the Chinese state household's annual expenditure.[44] Additionally they permanently stationed their military in the Beijing headquarters, whilst the Chinese had to reduce their military installations.

The West was obviously not aware of how weak the Qing state had become in the meantime. The Germans who were still inexperienced as colonisers also underestimated how dangerous a wounded feeling of self-esteem could be. As the ultimate humiliation they demanded the dispatch of a delegation of atonement. In 1901 this delegation led by the brother of the Chinese emperor had to apologise in Berlin for the murder of the envoy von Kettler. In addition a wreath of atonement was to be positioned at the spot in Beijing were the diplomat had been murdered.

The Boxer rebellion had been crushed, but the court was in bigger difficulty than ever before: it had lost its regional influence as well as its influence in relation to the foreigners. This was to become deeply entrenched in historical memory. When China once again opened up for the international economy at the end of the twentieth century, the politicians always adhered to the golden rule that the prize of economic opportunities always had to be tied together with the attainment of power. When the imperial kingdom was going under there were different conditions: the foreign-induced drives for modernisation were of little benefit for China. In 1894 for example the Japanese had already succeeded in ensuring that foreign direct investment was legally and thereby legitimately protected. Due to this foreign direct investment increased by tenfold to 962 million US dollars in the following ten years.[45]

The West managed shipbuilding as well as the manufacture of tobacco in China. Even electricity and gas were in Western hands. One single American electricity concern generated more electricity than all the Chinese producers put together; one American soap manufacturer was solely responsible for producing more soap than half of all the local competition. The West controlled 47 per cent of the cotton industry and even 93 per cent of the machine-assisted coal production. Nothing, absolutely nothing indicated that China would posses a similarly high world market share of important products a good hundred years later.

The number of free trading ports rose from 15 in 1870 to 40 in 1900.[46] That the increase in trade in the concession ports was 'for the most part a continuation of the brisk trade which had already previously existed in China', as Fairbank noted, was a poor consolation for the Chinese.[47] The Russians and the Japanese who had already encroached in Manchuria after a brief and severe war in 1894 expanded further into Northern China.

A particularly grotesque testimony of the times that demonstrated the loss of power of the court was a report of a ladies coffee circle which the empress hosted for the wives of the Western diplomats shortly after the end of the Boxer rebellion. If until the end of the eighteenth century the imperial family was treated with the highest respect and humility, the grade of respect had now almost reversed: the empress sat down 'next to me and presented the dishes', reported the wife of an Austrian diplomat. 'Whilst doing this she drew her own chopsticks between her lips in order to show me that they were sanitary, and then used them to personally place a few morsels in my mouth. She spoke to me with regret about the Boxer disturbances and assured me that everything had happened against her will.'[48] Even the tables had been laid in a European way. 'Also the serviettes were of very colourfully printed cotton fabric and mine still had a label "Made in Germany" stuck to it.'[49]

In addition the emperor now only played the role of an extra in his own palace. 'One time when I was not quite sure of what to do with my cup', reported a tense Austrian lady, 'I placed it into the hand of a young man who was standing next to me, whom I assumed was a servant. He took it and looked around him with a shocked expression searching for help. Then several eunuchs rushed towards him, took the cup and threw themselves onto the ground in front of him and began to kowtow. It was at this point that I realised to my shock and horror that so as to have my cup cleared away, I had given it to the emperor of China.'[50]

The two-thousand-year-old Middle Kingdom had reached the end of the road. The widow empress was comparable to the straw-man representative of a large company. The court had to negotiate with the allies for loans so as to actually be able to continue ruling the country.[51] In 1906 the advisors allowed the establishment of a type of constitutional monarchy.

Their realisation came too late. Competing governments had already established themselves at the central, provincial and local level, whose budgets were partly financed by foreigners who were capable of turning off the tap at any moment. Administrative reforms that promised more independence was undermined by the local elites. High-ranking Qing officials who were on the board of state enterprises and trading companies, became self-employed and took the best of the state's assets with them. 'The problems unveiled by the attempted reforms can give one an idea of the fragility of proto-democratic institutions and the difficulties they met when introduced into an unprepared environment',[52] is how Spence sums up the situation. External control was the dominating force. The people had to help themselves, as the court was no longer in a position to do so. In 1905 the Chinese merchants called for a boycott of all foreign goods, which actually only lasted for four months. It was the first time that the Chinese strengthened their unity through a collective punitive action (Strafaktion) against the foreigners. Entrepreneurs and the managers of certain groups tried to get foreign infrastructure back into the Chinese hands between 1904 and 1907. However they lacked the necessary capital.

The old empress Cixi died in 1908, one day after emperor Guangxu. The father of the new child emperor Puyi, Prince Ching tried to give the reforms new momentum. However even though the personnel had been replaced there had been no change in the powerlessness. The few successful endeavours of modernisation, as for example the repurchase of the railway lines by Chinese and foreign investors, was eventually paid for by the West. This dependency was appalling: without money it was not possible to reform and without the foreigners there was no money. Added to this the approval of loans had been linked with concessions, which were not in the interest of the Chinese state. The court was no longer capable of re-establishing the monopoly of taxation and power.[53]

The finale is the same the world over. At some point even the army is no longer willing to prop up a weak government. Even the progressive, worldly Minister of Defence Yinchang was unable to rally the soldiers around him in the long term. He had a German wife, spoke fluent German, was fascinated by German bravery and weapons and was thoroughly determined to bring the Chinese army up to the German level of operation. But there was no money for new weapons. Despite this the old army was wound down, and the new one never got to its feet. The promises, which were to keep the soldiers loyal to the flag, were never realised.[54] The consequence was that many of the soldiers were won over by the foreign students to take part in the revolutionary struggle. For example, in the autumn of 1911 the insurgents already had a third of the army that was stationed in Wuhan on their side, which totalled 6000 men. When three revolutionaries were executed after a raid against bombers on the 9th of October of the same year, the eighth pioneer battalion began to mutineer. By the evening three other units as well provincial government of Hubei had joined the protest, which had just like the other provincial representatives been installed a few years previously by the imperial court. All over the country the units of the Manchu regime started to fall off like autumn leaves from the trees.

The final nail in the coffin for the two-thousand-year-old imperial kingdom did not however come from the military but from the economy. Sun Yat-sen, the doctor and revolutionary, who had been gathering young followers for a military coup in Southern China since the beginning of the century, managed to convince the British to stop granting any substantial loans to the court. As a result the money ran out and the emperor was ruined. At the end of December 1911 Sun was appointed as the 'provisional president'. On the 1st of January 1912 he announced the establishment of the Republic. The mighty imperial kingdom had crumbled into itself, without having been defeated by anyone; it had lost against itself. One hundred years earlier, it had been a matter for the emperor to be at the centre of the world; in the second half of the nineteenth century he had to struggle to remain at least at the centre of China; at the turn of the century the widow empress was only concerned with being able to rule in Peking, and right at the end the court was no longer financially independent and was hardly able to guarantee its own protection.

On the 12th of February 1912 the last emperor abdicated and a left behind a society which Spence described in the following apt way,

> In the midst of an alertly lurking and dangerous world, the Chinese people, unexperienced in the art of self-government and dealing with its institutions, had the chance to take their future into their own hands.[55]

This was a unique moment in Chinese history: the mechanisms of external control were no longer taking hold, and the mechanisms of self-control had not yet been developed.

This phase is typical in the development of states. 'The lower order underneath the powerful autocratic elites, whether they be monarchical or dictatorial turns into an inveterate habit,' wrote Norbert Elias.

> Populations which have acquired this habit typically find it difficult to be ruled in any other way, no matter how unsatisfied they had been with their leaders. The transition to a non-authoritarian regime makes it necessary to learn new social techniques that make more difficult demands on one's own judgement and on the people's self-control. Normally peoples only gradually work their ways out of long eras of autocracy, during which they have acquired the habit of having external discipline and supervision imposed on them. In situations of serious crisis they are prone to relapse into an autocratic phase.[56]

There is hardly another country in which the courtly elite disintegrated so suddenly as in China. There was great insecurity. The desire for a regime that was founded on a broader participatory decision-making process was not widely spread throughout the country. If one follows Elias's theories then China had to adjust itself to unsettled times. The reaction to the abdication of the emperor indicates that he is correct in his analysis. This is because the citizens in no way regarded it as being a liberation from the yolk of the monarchy. Massive celebrations were not the order of the day.

Whichever political system would now be installed, it had to be built on the ruined foundations of court. The Chinese feeling of self-esteem, which had united the kingdom for hundreds of years, was deeply wounded. The people no longer identified themselves with the state and so instead they conducted business with foreigners at the cost of the Chinese economy or pledged allegiance to local leaders with whom they could identify. China was also bankrupt. This was not really the best time for encompassing political reform, and least of all the time for economic reform. China had become globalisation's football. The central links between China and the rest of the world were under foreign control and thus the West was able to determine China's future.[57]

In a way similar to which whole branches of key industries in the industrialised nations are closed down these days without provoking any massive strikes, the allies had conducted a very modern war campaign. With minimal military expenditure they had managed to gain considerable control over the country. For the first time in China's history it had been vanquished by powers that were socially, technologically and politically equal to them. Instead of wasting their time in the interior of the country, the new intruders acted as doormen of the kingdom and controlled the entrance fees in the form of trading tariffs and all sorts of taxes. So too the drives of innovation that washed over China came primarily from the foreigners. The West could be thanked for the fact that Shanghai was a glittering world city at the turn of the nineteenth and twentieth centuries was due decisively to Western influence and involvement. (The fact that Shanghai at the turn of the twenty-first century is a metropolis, which is hot on the heels of New York, Tokyo and London, is the result of Chinese strategy and construction capacity.) The imperial court had let someone else take control of the rudder. 'Foreign capital in fact had control over all the strategic areas of the Chinese economy'.[58]

The shame went to the bone and characterised China: even at the turn of the twenty-first century Chinese politicians paid very careful attention during negotiations for the entry into the WTO, not to lose their control over imports and exports. Just like other countries China ensures that at any time it can control the influence of overseas enterprises with hidden regulations. Foreigners should bring progress, assist with investment and be guests in a proud country, but never again be able to determine the direction of development. In the nineteenth century it was less to do with the Western imperialists, rather it was the hesitancy of the court itself that stood in the way of

China's modernisation, as they allowed the foundations of the state to be undermined. China had fallen into one of the biggest traps that stable and successful countries can fall into: peace is threatened once one fails to recognise its presence.

The downfall of the monarchy left a society which had been torn from its tradition but had not arrived in the new world. In a haze of foreign-financed reforms and the inspiration of alien concepts, only a few of the government advisors had recognised that in fact it was too early for a republic.

One of them was Liang Qichao. 'The sacrifices of 1793', he clearly analysed the French revolution,

> paid off for France only in 1870, and the reward did not meet the expectations. If today we attempt to gain liberty at the cost of immeasurable suffering we may be rewarded only 70 years later, and god alone knows what will have become of our ancestral land by then.[59]

For many decades China was a society caught between two roads. Life was characterised by an upheaval. Nobody knew which direction the journey was going to take. After several hundred years of stable dress codes, there was for example the development of new fashion trends. 'On the road one wore chequered Jagerpatschen (ankle high house shoes made of felt), green or lilac socks, together with sock supports which were fitted on the outside over the trousers so that one would be able to see them better, and a stiff, black, European hat that was completely embroidered with lilac lotus flowers'. The Chinese Foreign Minister wore a tailcoat lined with sable at a ball. 'The leggings looked like drain pipes and the expensive pelt hem at the bottom of the trousers did nothing to enhance their beauty. Another high-ranking official had had a magnificent frock coat tailored for him – made out of blue brocade with pink lapels and a pink collar. The usual company had made an appearance in a strange mixture of half Chinese and half European dress. One could see gentlemen who considered the combination of a tailcoat with sports trousers or long trousers with a sailor shirts to be refined.' The Chinese were colourful on the outside but on the inside they yearned for order.

# Chapter 4

# THE KINGDOM WITHOUT A MIDDLE

> Eight hundred men! Two hundred were of some use, two hundred were inactive and four hundred were not utilized. What did they manage to achieve? They were not even able to reach an agreement over the rules of procedure.
>
> President Yuan Shikai, 1914, in reference to the first Chinese parliament.

At the beginning of the twentieth century the Middle Kingdom was comparable to an African backwater republic. China still existed but the Chinese state had ceased to function. The central power had collapsed. The army consisted of unreliable legions that attached themselves to this gang, or that governor, depending on who promised the best protection and the highest pay. The state's monopoly of power could not be upheld with these opportunists. The influential local rulers on the other hand no longer saw a reason to follow the new weak leaders in Peking. Because as great as the desire was for a strong leadership – if nobody offered, then one would rather rely on oneself in an hour of need.

Uncontrollable and unpredictable violent outbreaks were the order of the day. Taxes disappeared into the pockets of those locally in command and the citizens were stirred up through the governance conflicts of the powerful. People felt extremely insecure and longed for the good old days when a strong leadership had ensured stability in the entire kingdom. However, such a situation was not on the horizon. Even at its weakest days the imperial court had at least still been able to unify China, which was no longer a surety, yet it was still a standard for orderly conduct. Now the kingdom had broken down into an assortment of power blocks.

The nationalists led by the intellectual Sun Yat-sen and the power-hungry Yuan Shikai were nominally the new rulers, but their power was only regional. They were not even able to unify the president and the parliament or the civil and military forces.

So what was the next step to be? 'The most pressing task in drafting a practicable constitution according to which legal elections could be conducted throughout China', was the opinion of the American historian Jonathan Spencer.[1] In fact Sun had, during the long years in which he had sought support in the West for his Chinese movement of renovation, conceptualised an encompassing state system upon which the republic was to be built. However this meant taking the second step before the first. Because what China needed more than a constitution and elections was leadership, which as always ensured that important functions of the state were under one directive, and that the feeling of self-esteem and the monopoly power were once again strengthened, so that a stable balance would result. The new nationalist president Yuan Shikai, who within a few days had snatched the state leadership from Sun, was a successful officer, but not the strong personality that the country had needed. The small, ball shaped man with the black moustache not only lacked the necessary charisma to bridge the disrupted chains of command. He also did not have any political ideals that overrode his personal gratification of being in power. A decade earlier Yuan had assisted the widow empress in removing the progressive reformist emperor Guangxu from the playing field and in crushing the Boxer rebellion. Almost as soon as he had been nominated as the General Governor of Beiyang[2] out of gratitude, and consequently was at a far distance from the imperial court, he built up a strong army in his province so as to be able to reign independently in any way that he desired, free of any control from the central authorities.

The lack of transparency about the situation was not improved by the fact that in February 1913 – for the first time in Chinese history – about 10 per cent of the Chinese, accounting for 40 million people, were allowed to vote for a parliament. The clear winner was the nationalist Guomindang (KMT) party, as they were the only ones who were even half-way organised. However within a few days the election result was rectified with an iron fist. The KMT leader Song Jiaoren was murdered on the way to Peking, which had obviously been carried out under the order of President Yuan.[3] After this, in 1914, he forced the frightened KMT parliamentarians to elect him as President for life, and used this term of office to ban the KMT as being a party that was a threat to the state. The manipulative monarchist had after a brief transition as a republican become a dictator whose instructions were followed out of fear rather than conviction. In the long term, this was simply not enough. Yuan completely disbanded the uncohesive parliament one year after the elections: 'Eight hundred men! Two hundred were of some use, two hundred were inactive and four hundred were not utilised. What did they manage to achieve? They were not even able to reach an agreement over the rules of procedure', he complained bitterly.[4] The citizens, as much as they had even been aware of the proceedings, were not particularly touched by this end of the parliamentary system. Indignation and mass protests, which had earlier been generated by the wounded nationalist sentiment through the actions of foreigners, never took shape. However even through this measure Yuan, who had moved into the Forbidden City as the new emperor, never became a great leader. Just around the next street corner, and out of earshot, he was referred to as the small man with the big mouth. Why should the provinces forward their tax revenue to him? Why should the foreigners hand over the customs duties they had accumulated to the central authorities if tomorrow one could not even be certain if they could still act forcefully?

Yuan had exactly the same problem as the imperial court from his first day in office: without money there is no power. The government ran up a monthly deficit of 13 million yuan that could only be financed through new overseas credit, the so-called 'redevelopment loans'.[5] Yuan momentarily had the impetuous hope that his credit standing could be transferred into power. He negotiated a loan with the allied consortium that was worth over 25 million US dollars.[6] Whereas the Americans were still cooperative, the Japanese gave the President a lecture in credit economics: they declared that they were only willing to make funds available if the monopoly of power was handed over to the Japanese police in the regions that they had occupied; after all the President lacked the authority to ensure law and order anyway. Yuan had to accept that creditors have more leverage, and had to give in. It was a high price to pay: there were mass protests because the proud Chinese did not want foreigners to tell them what they could and could not do in their own country.

The rule of this man without principals or charisma trundled along. Yuan stepped up press censorship, tried to reintroduce Confucianism as the state religion and finally announced that he would be crowned emperor, after his advisors, amongst whom there was a far-sighted American,[7] who recognised that the country lacked a symbol of central power. However Yuan was not a suitable candidate. Even his own clan abandoned him. Yuan eventually called off the emperor's coronation. Who knows, perhaps he would have tried it another time if he had not unexpectedly died in 1916. The last central authority in China – if it still deserved this name – disintegrated with Yuan's death. His successor reinstalled the parliament and brought the child emperor Henry Puyi out of exile. Yet after one year he had made such a bad impression that the provincial military turned their back on him and ended his brief rule.

Duan Qirui, the new prime minister was more skilful in the way he went about doing things. He knew from the mistakes of his predecessors that China's wounded self-esteem needed to be resurrected. Because of the limitations of his playing field, it seemed to him that the most practical option was to heal the internal political wounds with a successful foreign policy. His bold plan was for China to engage in the First World War and, of all things join forces with its most severe colonial suppressors namely Great Britain, France and Japan to fight against Germany. He was fascinated by the idea that China would be able to achieve a military success in the distant Europe. As the Japanese gave a helping hand by providing new loans, he was able to send a mere 1600 Chinese to support the troops in Europe.[8] Their main task however was only to clear the battlefields in France, however it was for the first time that China had taken part in a global conflict, and at long last were on the winning side when Germany signed the armistice on the 11th of November 1918. The victory struck a deep nerve in the nation's soul and for one historical moment the nationalist feeling of the Chinese was re-ignited. Totally beside themselves the masses destroyed the wreath of atonement, which the Qing court had had to put up for Klemens Freiherr von Ketteler, the German envoy murdered by the Boxers. China proudly sent a six-man delegation to the peace talks in Versailles, who were supposed to reclaim Germany's colonial territories in Shandong. Premier Duan, probably due to a lack of experience, had totally underestimated the global political climate. His envoys had to ascertain that their creditors and occupiers had other interests and were in no way prepared to count China as one of the victors. Even before the Chinese ship had landed in Europe, they had already agreed that the German colony was to fall into Japanese hands.

Almost as soon as the message had reached Peking, the masses were back on the streets, but this time it was the anger at their own weak government that drove them.[9] It was the first time that the people's displeasure voiced itself not only in the capital of Peking, but in numerous other cities. The revolts which were to be recorded in history as the '4th of May Movement' (the 4th of May 1919) reached their climax in a mass demonstration in Peking on the 30th of May, after British and Indian soldiers had shot a dozen young demonstrators. Massive strikes ensued in Shanghai. The people did not really protest so much for democracy, the division of power, freedom of the press or against corruption but instead it was much more about the strength and independence of their nation.

China was caught in a dilemma: the pressures of globalisation on the one hand demanded that the country had to modernise itself politically, as the countries that China had to compete against were already far more developed and possessed a strong government with advanced political structures in which a parliament played a central role. On the other hand the Chinese neither had practice in debating nor in striving to reach compromises. The majority of the population was used to following orders and instructions. The concept that they now had to suddenly make decisions by themselves in their own regions caused anxiety for most of them. Added to this the huge power struggles between the different factions were an unsuitable breeding ground for a new political initiative that was groping its way forward.

The extent of the instability becomes clear when one looks at the number of victims. Between 1900 and 1949 there were up to 18 million Chinese civilians who lost their lives through political unrest, 9 million in wars and revolutions and more than 14 million as a result of famine – all in all more than 40 million people.[10]

As bungled up as the situation was, China did not find itself in a historically unique or unusual predicament. The biographies of nearly all states are characterised by such phases, in which they have manoeuvre themselves into a position where there is a disconnection between development targets and the level of development and in which they are put under considerable stress by opposing currents. This is for example how the German Reich found itself, in a very similar dilemma at almost the same point in time.

Germany's flaw however was due to the fact that it had not been in existence for very long. There had only been German provinces. Even after the disintegration of the 'Holy Roman Empire's German Nation' in August 1806 the Reich had remained splintered. While China to some extent had existed for too long, Germany had not been in existence long enough. The rulers of successful nations such as France, England or Russia were not really able to take the muddle that the small German states had caused through their squabbling until the end of the nineteenth century, seriously. The Germans' perception of self-value suffered under their own weakness in the same way as that of the Chinese had. 'The national pride and the collective self-esteem of the Germans was also more brittle than that of the English or French who had undergone a more gradual and smoother development', wrote Norbert Elias.[11] It was only in 1871, and so therefore centuries after their neighbouring nations, that Germany almost managed to ascend to the rank of great European power. Unity had not been the reward of the people's struggle but instead it had been organised by those in command, nevertheless it was followed by a phase of euphoria. The hope was that one would soon be able to draw level with other nations and evolve into an equally radiant Empire. However, naturally one wanted to become a little bit stronger. Its residents image of Germany though was primarily that of a huge, mighty Empire, their neighbours considered the Germans to be boastful. So they tried even harder to prove that they were able to achieve what they had intended to they wanted to narrow the divide a little between claims and reality, and so they started to invade their neighbours. It turned out though that their neighbours had evaluated them correctly: Germany lost the First World War and received written confirmation in the Versailles Treaty that it was a second-class nation in Europe. Just in same way that Chinese were controlled by their colonial masters the Germans were now dependent on foreign powers when it came to addressing central national issues. So they were only able to maintain a quarter of their armed forces[12] and for decades had to hand over a large portion of their tax revenue to the victors as reparations. The parallels that have been drawn between the Chinese and the German history may seem to be surprising and a little bit contrived. Norbert Elias however saw that within the mechanics of the process of civilisation, which runs as similar course even though this may be in different parts of the world and at different times. The emperor had to abdicate in both countries, and in each case the decisive impulse came from external forces. In China, as in Germany, the emperor's rule was followed by a weak parliament. In the eyes of many Germans it was regarded as only as a 'gossiping den'[13] while the Chinese were hardly aware of their parliament. In both cases they introduced institutions that were on a par with the leaders in development of competing nations, yet these did not correspond to the level of development of the population at the time. What we already know about the Chinese, also characterised the Germans for a long period of time is that:

> The yearning for external discipline and supervision by a strong ruler, which frequently increased in critical situations, was tightly knit with the insecure standards of self-control, which has been mediated to the Germans by their tradition. In the 1920s and thirties one still saw sentences such as: 'Parliamentary democracy may be just fine for the Americans and the British, but it is not suitable for us Germans. It is un-German. What we need is a strong man who enforces law and order among us.' What the Germans still had in mind was the kind of unity that they had dreamed of for centuries, a total unity without a trace of discord.[14]

The German self-esteem was just as wounded as that of the Chinese. Both were tossed backwards and forwards between the demands of the modern world, their own overblown notions and their actual levels of development. The new political institutions were not firmly rooted in the minds of the people. A characteristic of China's predicament after the collapse of the imperial kingdom, as well as Germany's after the end of the First World War was that the new government was subsequently hardly in a position to uphold their monopoly of power. The military and police forces that were essential in ensuring peace within the state were only partially able to fulfil this task.[15] Actually the Germans did not have to contend with rivalling armies rather with political cliques, however the destabilising effect in the comparatively small country was similarly great: 'The communists had a private army, the social democrats had a private army, the national socialists in the same way with their 'Socialist' Army and the conservative middle class with the "steel helmet" '.[16] The insecurity of large sections of the population was the reason they accepted a dictator who promised to strengthen the dispirited self-confidence, make them forget the shame of the lost World War and help Germany achieve the peace, welfare, greatness and abundance of power, which had never existed up before.

One and a half decades after the Germans, the Chinese similarly pinned their hopes on a central leading figure, Mao Zedong. Both the Germans and the Chinese had the advantage that their populations were sapped of energy because of war but most so because of the economic crisis. Both were able to ease their ascent because they were not from an established, recognised social class and so in a quite undisturbed way were able to play up their folksy origin. To a great extent they relied on their charisma. Eventually the deciding factor was that both leaders built up armies and paramilitary organisations that conducted their fight for the monopoly of power in such a skilful, hard and systematic manner that they were finally able to gain authority.[17]

Most of all though, their formula for success was that they were able to revitalise the feeling of self-esteem. Mao could recapture the pride of the Middle Kingdom and promised the return to an unrivalled national greatness, which the Chinese believed they were due rather than their current standing in the world. Hitler who was unable to evoke a former radiance called upon an alleged superiority of the German 'race'.

Belonging to the Germanic race provided an access for far more people than belonging in good aristocratic or bourgeois society, and, among the young, a place among ranking officers or the universty fraternity.[18]

One should not exaggerate the parallels, but already a superficial comparison clearly indicates certain historical patterns: Spun into a process of long-term globalisation the biographies of nations in comparable circumstances proceed according to similar patterns, and these are independent of cultural differences, national characteristics and local differences. Among the pivotal points in this process are the feeling of self-esteem and the monopoly of power.

From this point of view one can more understandably portray the course of events over three decades from the 4th of May Movement in 1919 to Mao's founding of the People's Republic on the 1st of October 1949. The main reason why the new leaders were unable to establish themselves was their catastrophic economic situation. Firstly they had lost their control over foreign trade and then they had let the foreigners take what were weak industries, out of their hands. Foreign investment was beneficial for factory owners but hardly for the national economy as a whole. The Japanese had taken over further sectors of industry in the north of China, and the few sectors that the Chinese still controlled themselves were largely unprofitable and could not stand up to foreign competition. In this way the Chinese gradually lost access to their own markets. At the same time the state had to invest a large portion of its slim budget in the army so as to provisionally buttress its monopoly of power. This led to an erosion on both sides: the state revenue dwindled whereas the indebtedness and dependence increased. In the 1880s the government had to borrow 1.25 billion US dollars.[19] Numerous Chinese companies had to take short-term credit from the Western banks, which drastically increased their interest rates. The exchequer did not even profit from the property boom in the harbour city of Shanghai. Apart from a small lease the profit was divided up amongst the foreigners.[20] Between 1919 and 1928 industrial production grew by around 300 per cent,[21] but the lion's share went to the foreigners. In 1913 there were 166 enterprises that were financed by overseas capital, in 1936 there over 800 and in 1937 foreigners were responsible for 60 per cent of national production. They already had such a high proportion of foreign trade since 1870. During the First World War the amount of overseas investment was around 80 per cent of the entire volume of capital in China. However the influence of the West was still restricted. In spite of the high investment, 'the foreign economic expansion did not lead to a revolutionary transformation of the Chinese economy', wrote the Peking historian Lu Aiguo.[22] In large parts of the country China's economy was characterised by agricultural and pre-industrial handicraft production.

The unrest and regional splintering made it impossible to build up an integrated economy at that time.[23] In the interior of the country – and out of the reach of the foreign economy and central authorities – there were so-called warlords who managed to turn off the revenue tap to the state. All in all there was a good dozen of these mighty warlords whose territories consisted of one or in some case several provinces; and which were infiltrated and surrounded by several hundred smaller military despots. Independent of which role they played – whether military strategist, entrepreneur, political reformer or bandit – their strength depended on how successful they were in appropriating the money that was actually meant for the central state for their own private gains. And so they set up monopolies for consumer goods, sold opium or controlled railway lines and roads. It could never really go anywhere because the warlords were only able to improve their power base by forming a coalition with other warlords, which as a rule broke up relatively quickly because of the stubbornness of the current leader.

There was a stalemate that gave the state a weak grip on the situation, because the warlords never declared their separation from the central government, even though this existed more in people's minds than it did in reality. 'It was difficult to see the dividing line between forces of order and forces of disorder', wrote the German China historian Jurgen Osterhammel. However there was still the dream of a strong united China during times of civil war, even if every warlord hoped that he would be the one who would be able to fill the central state's power vacuum.

In the mid-twenties there was, as has already been mentioned, the formation of two power blocks each with strong leadership personalities: the nationalist Kuomintang led by General Chiang Kai-shek after the death of Sun Yat-sen[24] in 1928, and the communists with whom Mao Zedong had asserted himself as the leader. Both camps were aware that their power would only last if it was underpinned by with social and economic reforms. It was also clear to them that China's future did not lie in the political patterns that had been pre-moulded according to Western value concepts, such as dictatorship and democracy, a market economy and a planned economy or communism and capitalism. They formulated their own goals and expectations according to the level of development and culture of Chinese society, in a tone which from today's perspective would appear to be authoritarian, but was in fact well suited to the expectations of the people. A solid feeling of self-esteem was the key to success for both leaders. Sun emphasised more strongly that the individual would have to give back to the community whereas Mao was one of the first to bring up the subject of global pressures. In 1912 Sun Yat-sen had already had the experience as the transitional president of the first republic of how the first liberal democratic beginnings can be turned into a military leadership. He concluded from this experience that it was not the most progressive of all political systems that was best for China. 'The individual should not have too much freedom but the nation needs to acquire absolute freedom. It is only when the nation has realised its freedom, that China will become a blossoming state. In order to achieve this everyone will need to sacrifice their freedom.'[25] Mao merely classified China as being a part of a much bigger movement of competing states:

> the tide of change is raging over the world. No power can stop it. No one can weaken it. What is the biggest problem in the world? The biggest problem is nourishment. What is the strongest power? The strongest power is the unity of the population. Once the population is really able to achieve this unity then we will no longer need to be scared. Not of the heavens, not of ghosts, not of the dead, not of the bureaucrats, militarists or capitalists (...) But only those who go with the change will survive; those who oppose it will be defeated.[26]

In order to give their convictions mass appeal they shrouded these with the paper mache of catchy, well established, international ideologies.[27] It is true that they had to adapt their theories to the conditions in China so that they could become a part of Chinese national pride and no longer have the trace of Western imports. Neither communism, which Mao adhered to, fitted to China exactly in its original form, nor did an earlier version of the social market economy which was favoured by Sun. Due to the fact that China did not have an industrial proletariat the communists were forced to declare the whole of China a factory in which the Chinese workers were exploited by their Western colonial overlords.[28] Sun, in contrast wanted to modernise China economically, so that there would not even be the establishment of a bothersome proletariat in the first place who could give the entrepreneurs grief. His notion of a beautiful world therefore consisted of 'capitalism without capitalists'. Importantly both theoretical concepts bloomed in a competitive environment.

Normal political life is dictated by totally different measures of success: weapons, luck, strength of leadership, coalitions and the fight for the favour of the bureaucratic middle class who were close enough to the masses that needed to be convinced in the long term.

Until the mid-thirties the nationalists were clearly in the lead and felt to a certain extent that they were the sunny boys of Chinese progress. They had toppled the emperor and professed to have instigated 'the most civilised revolution that the world has ever experienced'.[29] (A claim that the East German civil rights campaigners predicated with more correctly about sixty years later.) The KMT power base was in the progressive cities like Shanghai, they were favoured with the support of the foreigners and the great ideal became the Western republics. Although they had democratic legitimisation, they quickly came to realise that the issue of power would not solely be decided through ballot papers. As they were unable to advance militarily into the north of China, Chiang Kai-shek proclaimed a dictatorship in Nanjing after Sun's death in 1925.

The greatest success of the so-called Nan king decade[30] was the creation of a new sovereign Chinese state with modern national institutions.[31] For the first time in Chinese history there was a division of power. A central Chinese bank was established; foreign debt was categorised in a new way and for the first time a standard Chinese currency was introduced with the Chinese silver dollar.[32] Taxes were collected on domestic trade and a loan distribution system was instituted, from which the farmers also were able to benefit. Added to this the nationalists improved the electric power supply and the transportation infrastructure.[33]

However it was not actually possible to implement the reforms everywhere as the Nan king regime was unable to ensure stability across the country, which was a necessary condition for reforms. The officials who were supposed to give up on old privileges refused to comply. The state was not in the position to collect income tax until 1936. In any case there would have hardly been anything to take from the poor farmers as the loans had disappeared into the pockets of the landlords.[34] A law, which was to have improved the relationship between the actual yield and the rent of the fields in favour of the farmers, was never modified. So too the farmers were not allowed to use the new roads as they were exclusively for the use of the military. The budget deficit grew annually by 20 per cent.[35] A large proportion of income was used for military expenditure so as to fend off enemies both on the inside and the outside. The crucial investments in industry never materialised and the global economic crisis of the late twenties did its bit to strangle exports and overseas investment. There was run away inflation (between 1942 and 1945 at an annual rate of 230 per cent).[36] The Nan king dictatorship was forced to confess this to the landlords and the urban capitalists and was unable to carry out its great intentions.

The communist movement until the end of the twenties was comparable to a fire in a haystack – at times it flamed up with more smoke than fire and at other times it only slowly smouldered. They did receive sporadic support from the protest movements of the urban intellectuals. But it was hardly possible to explain to farmers and workers how the globally encompassing ideologies of Karl Marx and Friedrich Engels were to improve their lives. Additionally the KMT pursued all rival groups. In June 1928 the

Communist Party of China (CPCh) even had to stage their sixth party day in Moscow, because there was not a safe place for them in the whole of China. The communists were only able to operate underground in the cities, and it almost looked as if Chiang would succeed in disbanding them. The reason that events turned out differently was because of one heretic, who had always resisted following the directives of the Moscow Comintern agents to seek the support of the urban proletariat. Mao, whose heart always went out to the farmers, had fortified himself in a safe upper valley where through carefully well-thought out land reforms he had managed to gain considerable backing from rural communities. The rich farmers were treated generously, and were not immediately dispossessed, as pure Marxist doctrine insisted. His soldiers protected the farmers instead of plundering them. However by doing this Mao risked expulsion/exclusion from the party. But his 'Jiangxi Soviet', a type of allotment as the first outdoor experimentation of Chinese communism, became the only region in which the CPCh was successful. Around 1930 Mao governed an area not quite the size of Holland, with a population of about five to six million.[37]

Instead of using money and weapons to win people over onto his side – just as most of the gangs and warlords had tried to do – Mao offered political alternatives, which appealed particularly to the farmers. Chiang Kai-shek, who had unsuccessfully attempted this, therefore felt threatened and so, on the 12th of April 1927, he mobilised an armed force against the communists. This was the start of a civil war which was to last almost an eternity. Eventually Chiang managed to encircle his adversary with a force of one and a half million soldiers. Mao now had to choose between idly watching the massacre of his surrounded followers – as after several months the food supplies had begun to run out – or daring to escape through the front lines. On the 16th of October 1934 the communists, totalling about 86,000 men and five women, managed to break through the ring of KMT troops. It resulted in a witch-hunt, where the communists were pursued all over the country by nationalist Chinese forces, which were ten times as powerful and technically far superior. The communists managed to cover 12,500 kilometres on foot, horseback and mules and eventually two years later with only 8000 survivors they reached the northern Chinese province of Shaanxi, that lay 150 kilometres south of the Great Wall.

The 'long march' became the founding myth of the communist party. Mao was its undisputed leader. The sensitive and affable intellectual Zhou Enlai became his closest and most trusted companion. He came from a well-to-do civil servant family and it was not long before Deng Xiaoping, the son of a socially conscious land owner who himself was a roguish pragmatist, came to be his lifelong opponent. They discovered their particular strengths and weaknesses during the long march and managed to become an entity that ultimately succeeded at the end of the forties to once again give the Chinese empire a common direction.[38] Yet their varying social origins and the enormous strain of the march, should not be underestimated.

Certainly the long march could just as well have become the last march of Chinese communism, if it had not been for fortunate circumstances that came to the rescue of the communists. The KMT had to fight another enemy that was much more powerful and gnawed away far more intensely at the national pride of all the Chinese: the Japanese. These aggressive neighbours had already attacked Manchuria and Shanghai at the beginning of the thirties and were working their way deeper into the heart of the country. In the summer of 1937 580,000 Japanese soldiers were deployed in north China and occupied the former imperial seat of Peking. Within a short time important cities like Taiyuan, the capital of the province of Shanxi, as well as Jinan, the capital of the coastal province of Shandong, were in Japanese hands (the former German colony Qingdao already belonged to the Japanese after the end of the First World War).

As long as the Chinese were still fighting amongst themselves the Japanese had an easy game to play ahead of them. There was no adequately established institutions, and no general powerful enough, to force the rivalling factions of the civil war to the negotiating table, eventhough they were all concerned about China's future as a nation. However the one who would have been first to exclaim, 'Collectively we are strong!' would thereby only have admitted their own weakness. Eventually a young campaigner by the name of Zhang Xueling dared to move forward. In a raid that took place in Xian under the cover of darkness and mist, the young warlord kidnapped the mighty Chiang Kai-shek in December 1936. He wanted to force him to unite with the communists and together fight against the Japanese. Chiang had no other choice than to comply. The national armed forces was amalgamated with the Red Army national armed forces. As had not happened for a long time, China once again spoke with one voice.

The tasks of war were divided regionally. The communists looked after the north and the KMT focused south of the Yang-tze River. However it was not possible to push back the Japanese who were better armed and tactically more skilful. In 1942 they had integrated all of the economic centres including Shanghai and Hong Kong into their ambitious 'Asian welfare zone'. Never before had China been so at the mercy of a foreign power as now; and never before had the central state been so barely visible. 'China for the Chinese', the battle cry of the 4th of May movement in 1919 was a distant dream. The

Japanese troops carried out devastation and massacres on a scale that made the suffering of the civil war pale in comparison.

Just like a bad Hollywood movie, an unforeseen hero came to China's rescue. No matter how successful the Japanese had been with their Asian invasions, they were no match for the USA. The Japanese emperor surrendered on the 2nd of September 1945 after the atom bomb was dropped on Nagasaki. The USA had only hastened what had finally become the clear defeat of the Japanese. Immediately there was fresh activity on the Chinese front lines. The united front between the communists and the nationalists fell apart. On both sides there was the spark of hope that one would be better at bringing about national unity, on one's own rather than collectively.

The deciding factor at this stage was logistical speed. Who was going to be the first to fill the vacuum in the areas that had been occupied by the Japanese, and requisition the weapons which they had left behind? The Russians mainly assisted the communists and the USA supported the nationalists. The communists were not only closer in achieving this goal but had also used the turmoil of war in their favour. Whereas the nationalists had brutally bent the population to their will, Mao had succeeded in creating a social alliance with the farmers. They protected the villages from the Japanese without committing any offences when it came to the processions of the village inhabitants. In return they were supported logistically. Guerrilla warfare, land reform and 'mass line', the unified alignment of his followers, were the three pillars upon which Mao, who had flourished in the turmoil of war as a first rate strategist, built his system. The guerrilla war was to wear down the opponents and the land reform was to improve the prospects of the farmers. Nevertheless he took great care in building up the self-esteem of the people. He had to succeed in being able to grasp their desires and feelings and to give these a political mould. As strange as it might sound, with the communists the customer was king. It was the humility of defensiveness, which characterised them, as they had realised through their numerous defeats how quickly one could loose the support that one had gained.

The nationalists arrived too late and for this reason the majority of Japanese weapons and territories fell into the communists' hands. Within ten years they had managed to become an equally matched opponent. In the autumn of 1945 the CPCh had 2.7 million members and governed over one hundred million people.

And so the balance of power between the two main rivals tilted in favour of the communists, especially as the KMT troops only managed to harm themselves. The soldiers let their anger out on the civilians and had the reputation of being corrupt, unorganised and inefficient. Even the Americans who wanted to help the KMT regain power began to doubt the reliability of their partner. The communists knew how to take advantage of this fact. In order to bring the Americans to their side, they had already during the war spread rumours that they were actually inveterate democrats. Briefly after the arrival of an American delegation to Yan'an in 1944 Mao came up with the idea of eliminating the term 'communist' from the name of the Party. One year later Zhou Enlai continued the charm-offensive when he met General George Catlett Marshall, who was later to be awarded the Nobel Peace Prize. Zhou fawned Marshall by assuring him that it was the sincere wish of the CCP to install a US-style democracy. On top of that he talked the American envoy into believing that nobody in the CCP was interested in a close alliance with the Soviet Union. Rumours that Mao would plan a trip to Moscow were not true, Zhou assured his guest. If the chairman would go on holidays abroad, Zhou quipped, he would much rather go to the USA. And Mao himself instructed General Lin Biao: 'Tell them that we are fighting for political, economical and military democracy. Avoid the term "class-struggle" '. The razzle-dazzle was a success. Unfaltering support for the KMT ceased to top the American agenda.

In order to avoid a division of the country and so as to be able to fully concentrate on the geopolitical challenges in Europe and East Asia, the USA instead hit the emergency brake. In January 1946 General Marshall, who was later to develop the Marshall Plan for Germany, managed to persuade Mao and Chiang to form a coalition government under the leadership of the KMT. However the agreement only existed on paper. China also would have needed a Marshall Plan so as to once again build up the country economically. Instead inflation rose so quickly between 1946 and the middle of 1948 that prices increased by four zeros. The national government introduced a new currency without having deposited any reserves. Business men were forced to exchange gold and foreign currency reserves for Government Certificates, and when the Government eventually increased the tax even on daily necessities, it resulted in stockpiling of goods. The once blossoming economy finally collapsed after nearly one hundred years of reform experiments. And so both sides used the short spell of peace to prepare themselves for a new war.

Morale among the KMT troops by then was so low that the communists succeeded in planting their spies at crucial positions among the enemy military. War began in January 1949, was short and severe and ended with the victory of the communists. The army, which had become well-equipped, along with the support of the population were the deciding factors in this outcome. On the 1st of October 1949 Mao proclaimed the People's

Republic of China in front of the Gate of Heavenly Peace. Chiang and his following had to flee to the pirate island of Taiwan.

The communists had won the war and profited from the desperate economic policy of the nationalists. It is noteworthy that it was not the size of the army or progressiveness of the political system that tipped the balance in this post-imperial power struggle, but instead it was the movement, which had the greatest appeal to the population that succeeded in gaining supremacy.

And in this regard the communists were far ahead of the KMT. Nepotism and corruption of Chiang's government were legendary. The Generalissimo's brother in law, for instance, Prime Minister T. V. Soong, in 1949 caused the largest trade deficit ever in Chinese history – with illegal currency trading that benefited nobody except himself, and drove entire industries into bankrupcy. Exasperation among the population was growing, and many called the regime simply a gang of thieves. Instead of enforcing the law, Chiang allowed himself to be guided by his family loyalties and personal feelings.

Mao knew no such sentimentalities. Compared to the KMT-government he seemed to wear a clean shirt. Rumours about the brutality of the land reform were trickling into the cities, but the troubling news typically met with incredulity. More often than not people either thought they were merely temporary excesses of a cruel war or took them for nationalistic propaganda. Support for the KMT government was rapidly dwindling, and in case of doubt people were prone to exonerate Mao. Still, enthusiastic supporters of the communists were the minority in China. In 1950 Lin Biao told a Russian envoy that the population had not been particularly elated about the change of government. What finally made them lean to the side of the CCP was their disgust of the discredited and corrupt KMT-regime. The new communist leadership on the other hand complied, in the early years, with the popular need for law and order after a long period or war and chaos. The communists scored points with determined campaigns against widespread crime, and by the end of 1952 drug-traficking and brothels were a thing of the past even in the notoriously nefarious Shanghai.

The future success of the communists was however not only going to be dependent on their ability to react to their people, but also to global shifts of power. It was important to find the balance between the population's level of development and the pressures of globalisation. A leader can from time to time play against the world and against his people, but he cannot win. It is tempting at this stage to make the comparison with Germany's current predicament.

Hardly a single Chinese citizen in the middle of the nineteenth century would have imagined how drastically it was going to go downhill. This situation demonstrates that good political theories are often worth less than a good sense of the concerns and desires of the people. The young Mao had this sense.

# Chapter 5

## THE 'HEAVE-HO' ECONOMY

*A dead pig does not fear the boiling water.*

Mao Zedong

Mao had saved China. It was more than having won a war and having helped communism in gaining a victory. With Mao China once again had strong leadership. The Chinese were once again governed by the Chinese, in a functioning state that directed and protected. Although China was no longer a Middle Kingdom, it was just like before one of the biggest nations in the world.

Whatever one's position is regarding Mao – when he died in 1976, China was in many respects in a better position than it was in 1893, the year of his birth or in 1949, the year that the People's Republic was founded. China was once again unified, had strengthened its position of power and had managed to free itself much faster from the entanglements of the Cold War than the Soviet Union. After the American President Richard Nixon had paid Mao a visit in Peking in 1972, the European nations and the USA lobbied equally to open the door for China so that it could find its way back into the global community, and they could also profit in the process. This changed nothing about the trail of suffering that Mao left behind, the arbitrariness with which he ruled and the chaos that he had caused. But it was exactly because Mao had, according to the criterion of Western values, all the characteristics of a cruel tyrant that it is difficult to look at his leadership from a sober perspective. If he had exhausted the Chinese people by driving them to the threshold of pain and had millions of dead on his conscience, he had for three decades at least managed to hold the country together. In addition, China's position in the power struggle of nations was considerably more favourable than it had been centuries before. It is difficult to weigh up which share of the successes of his leadership were on account of external coincidences, convenient circumstances and unpredictable social currents and whether China would have developed much better under a different social system. In order to understand where China's power comes from, which we nowadays feel in Germany and which is starting to change our lives, such deliberations are initially secondary to other understandings.

When Mao moved into Peking in September 1949 and had driven the Kuomintang troops onto an island at the edge of the empire, the population was euphoric. After decades of nervous vigilance and the oppressive atmosphere of civil war the 'masses' gained fresh hope, and the intellectual elites also betted on the charismatic leader, even if this farmer's son despite all of his eagerness to learn could never be one of them. 'I was so proud of China and so full of hope and happy that exploitation, misery and foreign aggression would come to an end', stated an enthusiastic doctor, who had returned to China after having lived overseas for 17 years, even though he would not have classified himself as a communist. 'There was no doubt in my mind that Mao was the great leader of the revolution, the creator of a new great (chapter in) history'.[1] Even the few Western foreigners, mostly entrepreneurs who were still living in Shanghai in 1949 who had traditionally backed the republican troops of Chiang Kai-shek, now hoped that the communist leader would re-establish order. This was in spite of the fact that their home countries were clearly positioning themselves on the other side of the iron curtain. 'It cannot get any worse under the communists, but it could get better, no it will get better', is how the Hong Kong business magazine, the *Far Eastern Economic Revue* described the atmosphere in 1949.[2]

Mao's charisma had invigorated the people. 'The Chinese people have arisen', was the declaration with which he proclaimed the Peoples Republic in his sing-song Hunan dialect on the 1st of October 1949 whilst standing at the Gate of Heavenly Peace – the first gate of the Forbidden City, in which the emperors had governed for centuries. At his feet hundreds of thousands broke into wild applause. However as intoxicated as the people were from the victory, Mao was not. In the old film clips, probably the most important record in the history of Chinese filmmaking, Mao comes across as an unemotional observer as he receives the congratulations of the people and his comrades. It was probably in this moment at the latest that it became clear to him: people who applaud, want to forget, are not on their guard and are defenceless. Mao was to use this optimistic defencelessness to brutally consolidate his power. *Perhaps he was able to take the population to the threshold of pain unflinchingly precisely because in every step of the Long March he had gone well beyond it.*

Two huge hurdles now stood before him. One was that Mao was now, as the new leader, part of a shattered political system whose directive only reached the power elite and their vassals in the provinces, not the broad masses of the population. For generations the state administration had been incapable of steering the social and economic changes of the whole country. The other was that for one hundred years China had missed connecting with global economic development. And after decades of civil war the economic reserves and powers of resistance were almost sapped. Corrupt bureaucrats and local elites took advantage of that which was still left. The flow of goods had been interrupted and cities and villages were cut off from each other. The few commodities that were still available became more expensive by the day.

To stabilise his own power, Mao had to secure the Party's monopoly of power over the huge national territory and to permanently get the people behind him. Only in this way would he able to face the rest of the world with a strong China. To achieve this he had to change the people's longing for law and order into an obedience of his system. In this process he justified any means that were necessary. People were allowed to be tortured and killed, as long as this served the purpose of stability and preventing the masses to rise up against him. Communist ideology, in the name of a huge China, could be moulded and polished, where it stood in the way of Mao's goals.[3] Contradictions were allowed to erupt, campaigns were allowed to fail and people had to starve and die as long as it happened in the name of progress. Whoever stood in the way was pushed aside. 'A dead pig does not fear the boiling water', Mao was in the habit of saying.[4] China was to become a Middle Kingdom again at any cost, and a modern one at that, with Mao at the top. Surprisingly the huge fascination with the 'Great Chairman Mao' was sustained over decades despite all this suffering. This fascination of him still holds true: as before Mao pictures can be seen hanging in taxis and student bars, even though nowadays nobody is forced to hang these effigies up.

In many respects Mao was still a Confucian emperor. He continually had to prove his heavenly mandate by the means of his charisma. 'As the Son of Heaven, the ruler had to constantly prove that he still held the heavenly mandate – by the welfare of the people', as the German sociologist Max Weber described his role.[5] That was not an easy task. The ritual and Communist leadership cult were only able to briefly gloss over the fact that the empire was in a disastrous state – as the superstitious Chinese population had for thousands of years been conditioned into rating floods, droughts and other natural disasters as a sign of displeasure of the heavens with the particular ruler at that time. Even in July 1976 when an earthquake in the vicinity of Peking took the lives of 250,000 people, it was seen by many Chinese as being a definite sign that the Gods were calling Mao on his deathbed to join Marx and Engels.

Already in 1949 Mao moulded his political visualisations into a programme, whose title – like so many things, including the Mao suit – he had copied from Sun Yat-sen: 'On democratic dictatorship'. The question 'dictatorship or democracy' that dominated the discussion along the border between the two Germanys in the fifties, certainly only played a minor role in China. Mao who was a marketing genius had chosen the two terms for a completely different reason: he wanted to avoid the development of a negative connotation as the word 'democracy' had a flat aftertaste for the Chinese, since Sun Yat-sen's Republic had disintegrated into chaos, and yet still give his politics the tone of participatory decision making. In his programme report depicting the path to the 'Empire of Great Harmony' he demanded amongst others that wealth must be distributed equally and fairly and that the people should have power over the 'lackeys of imperialism (…), the land owning classes and the bureaucratic bourgeoisie'. He was convinced that, 'we (…) have to awaken the masses and ally ourselves with those nations who are willing to meet us on an equal footing'.[6]

This meant – in a more modern and succinct way – nothing other than that he wanted to re-establish the Chinese feeling of self-esteem and integrate the country into the modern world. Already in the past it was imperative that 'The only way to save the country was modernization, and the only means to modernization was learning from other nations'.[7] And this was particularly valid for the future. In this respect Mao differed considerably from his predecessors, the emperors. However Mao suspected that for many Chinese one or two things would not mix well together. They hoped, after having been shaken by their experiences with their colonial overlords, that China would now finally be able to make it on its own. 'This is a ridiculous notion', Mao countered. 'Even when the victory has been won, it is impossible to consolidate it without such support.' He certainly had to admit that his previous attempts to learn from the West had not been particularly successful.

> The imperialistic aggression has shattered the illusions of the Chinese. It was odd – why did the teachers time and again resort to violence against their pupils? Throughout his whole life, Sun Yat-sen appealed countless times to the capitalist nations to help China. But it was all in vain; on the contrary, he received nothing but rude rebuffs.[8]

So the only alliance partner that remained was the socialist brother state of Russia. China and Russia, 'were similar in their economic and cultural backwardness. Both countries had fallen behind, China even more'.[9]

Mao was brought to a head:

> World War I shook the whole globe. The Russians achieved the October Revolution and founded the first socialist state in the world. The revolutionary energy of the Russian Great Proletariat and working class, until then only latent and invisible for the foreigner, suddenly erupted like a volcano under the leadership of Lenin and Stalin. The Chinese people and the entire human race began to see the Russians with new eyes.[10]

It must have been difficult for Mao to not only extol Russia as an ally but also as a shining example of the creation of a socialist state, as he had already managed to get himself into a dispute with Moscow's Comintern agents in the twenties and thirties, as they had wanted to give China's young communist party its directives. Mao however needed a precedent to which he could appeal in order to consolidate his power. The cheerful message was that just like in Russia the socially weak and the huge majority of the Chinese were to have a voice. Mao made it very clear that this was not going to be a walk in the park. In response to the accusation, 'You are not humane,' Mao answered:

> That's true. When dealing with the reactionary activities of reactionaries we are indeed not practising humane politics. Only among the people do we apply humane politics.[11]

Who was classified as belonging to the people and who to the reactionaries was determined by Mao from now on. *I intellectuals were an instructive case.*

For the time being Mao did not want to scare off the few economic carthorses that the country still had at its disposal off. In Shanghai he promised the remaining business people, 'We want to do business (...). We are only opposed to those domestic and foreign reactionaries who want to keep us from doing business. Apart from that, we're not opposed to anybody.'[12] A few business people pinned a lot of hope on these declarations:

> The more business as usual is coming back to China, and the more the country recovers, the more obvious is the necessity to co-operate with the Western World. Even the most stubborn dogmatist must see that. Those foreigners who have stayed behind in Shanghai are hoping the situation will improve once the communists are in control.[13]

Under the KMT, 'it was difficult to deduce the value of land, houses, warehouses and other property, as one could not find any buyers. Many financiers referred to Shanghai as being a rat trap.'[14] Overseas technicians and engineers were paid court to assist in the building up of China. So too Chinese business people were able to continue trading for the time being. In order to bring the backward economy on to an international level, Mao pragmatically stated, 'we must join together with the national bourgeoisie for a common battle'. China was to 'make use of all aspects of capitalism in the cities and the country which were useful in securing the livelihood of the people'.[15]

Mao needed one thing above all else in the founding year of his bankrupt kingdom: capital. The only country from whom he was willing to accept it was Russia. In December 1949 he embarked on his journey to Moscow. It was the first overseas trip of his life and was to be a sobering experience. Josef Stalin first of all left his Chinese comrade waiting in the hotel room for several days, until he had the time for a meeting. Just before Mao's arrival he had banned the Russian translation of an extravagant biography of Mao that had been written by an American socialist. This action was to clearly state in advance who was in control in the socialist world.

Mao had no other choice but to grin and bear it. In order to curry favour with Stalin, he was prepared to put on a show. In front of Stalin's liaison officer Kovalyov Mao suddenly leapt up from his chair, stretched out his arms and exclaimed, three times, 'Long live Stalin!' In the run-up to the Moscow-trip efforts were already made to disperse the big Soviet brother's doubts concerning China's resolution to firmly root herself in the socialist bloc. The new Chinese government burned all diplomatic bridges to America, and had the US Consul General Ward arrested and expelled.

However the negotiations between Mao and Stalin became a drawn-out process. Mao had to remain in Russia for two months until he could eventually reach a consensus with Stalin on a Chinese–Russian friendship agreement.[16] Upon his return Mao was under no illusion that their friendship was not going to go very far. 'Stalin called me a cabbage (head) communist', he complained, 'red on the outside and white on the inside'.[17] Also Mao was annoyed by the fact that Stalin had always made himself out to be bigger in the official photos, although actually Mao was the larger of the two. On the other hand, that Stalin enjoyed playing the role of the generous benefactor of the leaders of the small socialists states and had made an all-out effort to totally humiliate Mao, proved his secret respect for the social riser. 'A lot of hostility and a lot of honour', also applied to Mao. He would of course have been aware of the fact that a Chinese leader was once again being taken seriously by another powerful country for the first time in at least a hundred years.

However Mao could not really meet the costs of this feeling of superiority. He had been coerced into making some hard concessions during the negotiations. So he had to come to terms/with the fact that the Mongolian People's Republic was no longer a part of the Chinese empire, but instead was now on a satellite of the Soviet Union.

Mao had not accepted the deal entirely without opposition. When the US Secretary of State Dean Acheson in 1950 accused the Soviet Union of pulling not only Outer Mongolia but also vast portions of north China into its orbit, Stalin demanded that Mao immediately reject Acheson's speech. But in his official address, Mao not only referred to Xinjiang and Manchuria, as Stalin had demanded, but mentioned Outer Mongolia as well. This seemed to imply that China did not accept the de facto annexation of Mongolia by Moscow.

Stalin gave Mao a severe dressing-down and accused him of 'Titoism'. In order to make the humiliation even more bitter, Stalin made sure to castigate Mao in front of his loyal vassal Zhou Enlai. It was still a relatively mild punishment, because Mao considered Zhou his personal eunuch. To be caned under Zhou's eyes, and Stalin didn't know that, was far less painful for Mao than a humiliation in front of any other top cadre.

But it had been clear from the start that Mao's recalcitrance couldn't have had any real consequences. The Great Helmsman knew just as well as Stalin that China was in no position to oppose the Soviet claims to power – for the time being. Finally Mao not only had to accept that the People's Republic of Mongolia was no longer a part of China but also that he had to cede the juiciest piece of economic sovereignty over Xinjiang and Manchuria to the Russians. For a period of 14 years he had to concede a monopoly on 'surplus' natural resources in the northern territories to the Soviet Union. That meant losing control over 90 per cent of all internationally marketable Chinese natural resources until the mid-sixties. The Chinese did not forget this. As late as 1989 Deng Xiaoping told Mikhail Gorbachev that of all foreign powers which had bullied China since the Opium War of 1842, none has had taken more advantage of China than Russia. In 1950, however, China was not yet in a position to give the Soviet Union a talking-to. Instead, the young People's Republic had to play by the rules of the big brother.

In return Mao received a loan of 300 million US dollars (in converted value) as well as the promise that the Russians would return both of their colonies, the cities of Lushun and Dalian in 1955. At any rate through this move Manchuria, which had been dominated by the Russians and Japanese, was at least formally re-integrated into the Chinese empire. But this deal did not exactly conceal who was the one that had to come begging.

Within a few months China was able to establish a type of central taxation system as well as issue a series of state bonds with the help of the Russian loan. The army was given the task to look after itself and soldiers became farmers, landowners or traders. But the new momentum only gave Mao a few months of breathing space: in June 1950 he was dragged into the whirlpool of international politics.

A civil war had broken out in the partly communist neighbouring state Korea. The 'red' North Koreans had rumbled over Seoul and had managed to take control of half of South Korea. To at least halt the spread of communism on the Korean peninsula the Americans had seen to it that they had a mandate from the UN, which had been newly established in 1949, to enter with support of England and France the Korean War. Simultaneously, the USA revised its policy of non-interference concerning Taiwan. It is due to this engagement that neither Mao nor any of his successors could capture Taiwan.

Mao, whose power base was still quite shaky, realised that the North Koreans were fighting a losing battle unless they were assisted from the outside. Beyond this he also saw a possible danger for China, if the Americans, who had vigorously supported the KMT in the final phase of the Chinese civil war, were to march up to the Chinese border. His predecessors had faltered, as they had not taken the foreigners seriously. This was not going to happen to him. On the other hand China did not have the strength to again let itself be pulled into a huge war. Mao therefore tried it with clandestine support. Without the allies being aware of it at the time, he allowed ten thousand Chinese to fight in Korean uniforms. This however did not suffice. By November 1950 the Americans had almost managed to bomb their way forward up to the Chinese border. The only possible way to contend with their superior weaponry was with huge numbers of troops. As the Russians were prepared to deliver weapons, which Mao had to pay for with the money that had been granted by Stalin, he saw no other option but to urge his people into war so as to reach a quick end to the conflict. In return Mao received the transfer of military technology that he had bargained for in vain during his visit to Moscow.

His decision had devastating consequences for his soldiers, but ended up as a good result for China. When the war ended in July 1953 with a ceasefire at the 38th parallel, with the Americans having lost 60,000 soldiers and the Chinese over one million, amongst which was Mao's son. However Mao was relieved; North Korea now acted as a buffer zone between China and the American troops. And Mao had given the USA a sturdy dressing-down. President Truman declared a state of national emergency in a radio broadcast – this hadn't happened even during the Second World War, and would not occur during the Vietnam War either. Truman in his address declared that the American nation was in great danger. This fact no doubt played up to Mao's ambition to make China once again a world power.

As for internal politics, the campaign 'Resist America, help Korea' added fuel to the feeling of Chinese nationalism, and through this the communists gained new supporters. The Chinese victory certainly had unintended consequences: China found itself more isolated than ever. As feared, the Soviets had not proved themselves reliable friends. After the war when Zhou Enlai urged Stalin to grant a dramatic expansion of military assistance the answer was a lukewarm notice of intent that never materialized.

So too the anti-communist Western world wanted nothing to do with the Chinese. Whereas Mao would have liked to develop closer ties with the West even if for external appearances he continued to uphold the Soviet Union. 'Now and then it was suggested that I should study Russian, but I don't want to. I'd rather learn English'.[18] he confided in his trusted companions. And he also did this over the decades in the hope that would one day be able to use the language. In this respect Mao had a clear vision: 'In fact, I don't want to learn from the Soviet Union; I want to learn from the United States'.[19] He even expressed his longing to be able to measure up against America in poetry: 'With cold eyes I now survey the world beyond the sea', proclaimed one line.[20] Occasionally he cloaked his desire in easily decipherable metaphors: 'In my opinion, there should be a fusion of Chinese and Western medicine. This merger could give birth to a new science. That would be a significant step'. Whilst he officially denounced capitalism he privately trusted American products: 'Even though I think it is right to promote Chinese medicine, I personally do not believe in it. I never rely on Chinese remedies'.[21] From his huge bed, which had been set up on the edge of a swimming pool, in an area that resembled a ballroom, and clad in a bathrobe he was in the habit of performing his official duties.[22] He would ruminate over the fact that Chinese culture had been exhausted and that it could only be given new life by learning from overseas and adjusting foreign ideas to the Chinese world. The result, he thought, would be neither Chinese or foreign, neither horse or donkey, but instead it would be more like a mule.[23]

That did not keep Mao from flirting with the idea that China could develop into the leader of the socialist camp after Stalin's death in 1953. When the East German SED-dictatorship was confronted with a revolt in June that same year, Mao's China treated the GDR like its client state and offered support worth 50 million rubles.

'The East Germans are worse off by far than we', he pontificated. 'We should make it our concern to take care of them', as befits a great power.

Due to the aid from destitute China the GDR in 1958 was able to abandon its food coupon regime.

Dealing with the mini state from the West, Mao acted magnanimously. 'You don't have to copy us in excessive detail', he told SED-chief Walter Ulbricht during the latter's China visit in 1956. Yet, there was a Chinese model that, Mao thought, might well be worth copying for the East Germans – the Great Wall. Such a wall, he instructed the ill-bred SED-leader, can be very useful in keeping certain people off one's own territory, for instance the Fascists.

But Mao's flirt with the role of a socialist protective power was merely a bauble, and also his admiration for the USA would not have any consequences for the time being.

Mao dreamt globally but he acted locally. As far as his position of power was concerned he was not prepared to take any risks. He mistrusted the foreigners who had stayed behind in China. His original promise that, 'in the national economy the capitalist sector (…)', would, 'play an indispensable role'[24] was retracted in silence. Through such measures he prevented the possibility of the global division of labour and trade. He nationalised foreign holdings in succession, amongst which was the China business of Shell Oil in 1951.[25] The last remaining foreign –and also many Chinese – business people who had trusted Mao in the beginning, fled to Taiwan or Hong Kong. China would miss this elite. The Western world shook its head and turned its back. When Prime Minister Zhou Enlai stretched out his hand to greet John Foster Dulles, the Secretary of State of President Dwight Eisenhower's cabinet at an Indo-China conference in 1954, Dulles only said, 'I cannot', and left the room.[26] The USA was in fact a model and yardstick for Mao, but he wanted to make it on his own and not have to come to an agreement with other nations.[27] He had unified the country. Now all of it belonged to him.

It is difficult to decide if stubbornness won over reason in regards to Mao's relationship with the Soviet Union.[28] This would have meant that it could have been possible to have a working relationship based on an equal footing. Or did caution win over good faith? It is actually perfectly possible that the intentions of the Russians had been to turn China into a giant vassal. In any case the chemistry was not right with either Stalin or his successor Nikita Krushchev. Mao still had a resentful respect of Stalin but with Krushchev he felt challenged to a measure of strength. When he complained about the deceased Stalin's (1953) claims to absolute power and his crimes in a speech at the 20th anniversary of the KPdSU in 1956, the alarm bells went off for Mao. Particularly because out of all people his adversary (and eventual successor) Deng Xiaoping was also present at the Party's anniversary in Moscow and so he was concerned that his own claim to absolute power could come into question. He suspected that Deng would sing to the tune of collective leadership so as to weaken Mao's power and increase his own. 'May the Soviet Union criticise Stalin', he stated categorically, 'we are not going to do it. But not only that: we will continue to support his policy'.[29]

Krushchev the pragmatist did not succeed in winning Mao over, the passionate theorist as well as power-obsessed visionary. The Soviet leader had realised that his own authority would never be able to match that of Stalin, and for this reason he had to govern with an alliance and wanted to create international coalitions. Mao felt powerful in comparison. This success gradually went to his head. In 1957 he declared that he would be prepared to sacrifice half of his population in a war. It would not be a great detriment to China as the remaining half would again be able to produce a massive population.[30] Even the hardened Russians were shocked with such immense heartlessness. Mao was still riding on the last waves of euphoria from the founding of the republic. The Chinese thought the world of him:

> What counted was Mao's will alone. Still, I admired him. He was China's guiding star, the saviour of our country, our highest peak, our leader. In my eyes China was a single huge family, and a family needs a patriarch. Chairman Mao was that patriarch. I wanted to serve him and the Chinese people.[31]

Krushchev was prepared to turn a blind eye partly out of respect and partly because he was being pragmatic. In the meanwhile, Mao increased the pressure on the Russians to support his superpower plans for China and come to the aid of the Middle Kingdom's nuclear arms programme. In March 1955, the People's Republic shelled a number of small islands under KMT-control which provoked the USA to declare that they would be prepared to make use of their nuclear arms. Kruschev, who did not want to get dragged into a nuclear conflict with the USA, reacted as Mao had wished: He granted China technological aid for the construction of an atom bomb. Mao was happy. Without an arsenal of nuclear arms, the Chairman opined, 'people simply won't listen to you'. It helped that in this situation Moscow, for a change, needed help from China. The festivities for the 40th Anniversary of the October Revolution, the largest summit-meeting ever in the socialist camp, was scheduled for 7 November 1957 in the Soviet capital. Moscow had to have Mao on board to make the event a success. Mao declared that he would only come if the Russians would increase their

support of the Chinese nuclear programme. On 15 October Moscow signed
the historic agreement in which it agreed to delivering a model bomb.
Kruschev issued the directive 'to place at the disposal of the Chinese
whatever they need to build their own bomb'. When Mao arrrived in
Moscow three weeks later, Khruschev handled him with kid gloves. He
arranged for two aeroplanes to pick him and his followers up from Peking,
personally guided him to his quarters in the Kreml palace and offered him
his Datscha for relaxation. 'Just look how they are treating us now!', a satisfied Mao said to his Peking comrades. 'Even in a communist country they
differentiate who is powerful and who is weak. These snobs'.[32] At last he
saw himself as being in the position of being able to negotiate with the
Russians on an equal level, as the Chinese urgently needed their industrial
and economic know-how. However it never came to that. Did Mao gamble
away this opportunity because of his overriding need for the recognition of
his position or did he provoke Krushchev to see how he would react under
pressure? Mao had, as he himself had said, decided to 'stick a needle in the
arse',[33] of the Soviets. When Krushchev came to Peking for a secret meeting
in July 1958, Mao did not go to welcome him at the airport but instead met
him at his swimming pool in his swimsuit. Krushchev did not show his
feelings. After he suggested that they should build up a fleet together, Mao
retorted cheekily, 'We can build a fleet together: with your ships and our
captains'.[34]

Krushchev left outraged and attested that Mao had global political vision
of, 'a frog who is gazing up at the sky from a well'.[35] Mao had gone too far.
When several months later he authorised for a group of Taiwanese islands to
be fired at, Moscow refused to give him political support. In June of the
following year the Soviet Union stated that they would not be furnishing
China with nuclear weapons or the corresponding technological requirements, which China assessed as a political affront. One month later when
China and India engaged in an armed border dispute Moscow openly
assisted the Indians with the provision of loans. At the end of the year
Krushchev once again travelled to Peking and Mao met him displaying the
same arrogance as he did the year before. Mao did not trust Krushchev. He
only trusted himself.

The eventual public rift between the Soviet Union and China came in
July 1960. More than 11,000 Soviet engineers and economic experts, who
had established 150 industrial enterprises, that included 7 steelworks and
26 electric power stations, were recalled. They took the blue prints for
600 planned major projects with them. Mao was now home alone.

If the Soviets had expected Mao to soon start obsequiously asking for
help, then they were mistaken. Mao went even further with his foreign

policy. In 1961 he supported Albania which had rebelled against Krushchev. In 1962 China openly criticised the retreat of the Soviet missiles during the Cuban crisis and again in 1963 Moscow's nuclear test ban treaty with the USA and Great Britain. In 1964 he published an article laying down the principles of 'Krushchev's Psuedo Communism'.[36]

While Mao still had the goal of 'overtaking'[37] the USA he was however dependent on international trade agreements. Until now France was the only major Western nation that maintained diplomatic relations with China. In May 1964 Mao began to lobby Germany, the miracle economy. Through discussions in Switzerland he suggested a trade agreement.[38] The Germans were exceptionally interested as the proposal implicated some good business opportunities. But the aspirations of the economy were in conflict with the overall political climate. The Chinese would have been prepared to overlook the complications in the political dealings of the day. 'We will continue our business relations with West Germany, as we are particularly interested in German precision instruments', the Chinese Foreign Minister Chen Yi expressed this ambiguity in words. 'But we are opposing a policy which has begun with Adenauer and been continued under Erhardt, which relies on the USA in order to realize a reactionary policy'.[39]

The Germans however were not in a position for this type of pragmatism. As soon as the USA had got wind of what was going on they blew the whistle on the German Government. During a visit to Washington, four weeks after the start of the negotiations, the Federal Chancellor Ludwig Erhard had to deliver an emergency lie to the press: 'We never would have thought of finalising a trade agreement'.[40]

The withdrawal was not a huge problem for Germany, but for Mao it was a bitter defeat. His attempt to separate the economy and from the politics, which had been born in the hour of need, had failed. In this respect Mao was ahead of his time. It was only a good ten years later that economic globalisation had advanced to the level that his successors were able to work together with the West economically whilst at the same time being able to stand at a distance, on opposite sides of the political stage. Now Mao's only connection with the outside world were a few developing countries that needed more help than they were able to offer to China.

His wounded ego needed a shot in the arm. On the 16th of October 1964 he let China's self-developed atomic bomb be exploded for the first time – a popular step. The population, which only now was informed that China had developed its own nuclear weapons, was genuinely elated that China had come a good deal closer to be counted among the great powers again. Mao's attitude to the new weapon, however, might have curbed their enthusiasm somewhat: 'One does not need to fear the atomic bomb,' he had already told the Indian Prime Minister Jawaharlal Nehru ten years previously.

> There are many people in China. They cannot all be annihilated by a bomb. If somebody else is able to drop a atomic bomb, so am I. The death of ten or twenty million people will not frighten me off.[41]

The fact that Mao could now actually make this a reality did not increase his appeal for the rest of the world. He was now even further removed from any form of collaboration, and the USA, than ever before.

Even more imposing and comprehensive was that his economic and social mass movements had to be cancelled. In this respect it is hardly surprising that he was obsessed with the idea of trying to find a revolutionary short cut to the modern economic and political age, which guaranteed prosperity for China and allowed all Chinese to have a share of the wealth. He ranked the most equal distribution of growth that was possible, as the most important foundation for the unity of the empire. China was to become a modern socialist nation. 'Our country has never been as united as today', he explained in a speech, 'and an even brighter future lies ahead of us. The state of national fragmentation which our people abhor is forever over'.[42]

For the time being Mao and his loyal followers could still depend on one skill that they had learnt on the long march and during the war against the Kuomindang that followed. They were very skilful at being able to reconcile different groups such as cadres, the army, farmers and administrators. Across the country the Chinese joined the communist party and submitted themselves to its rigid organisation. It was above all the agricultural reforms in the first years which gave Mao wind in his sails. A good 40 per cent of the farmland was confiscated. The landed gentry had to relinquish estates to farmhands who then became self-employed farmers. About 60 per cent of poor farmers benefited from this.[43] The saving rates climbed dramatically. If the saving rate was under 5 per cent before 1949, it reached nearly 25 per cent in the 1950s.[44]

Therefore Mao could still dare to take a radical step in the 1950s, which made it possible for him, following the model of the military, to gain formal control over the rural population. The farmers were bound together into co-operatives. These were organisations combined production and administration. It was initially a popular measure with large sectors of the population as the communes promised farmers a social security, that never existed before. But a fateful combination of administrative chaos and draconian disciplinary measures quickly changed optimism into abhorrence. Mao was even flirted with the idea to rob the people off their names and replace these with numbers.

At the same time Mao acted brutally against his opponents, who were referred to as 'counter revolutionaries', 'corrupt cadres' and 'capitalists'. Twenty-eight thousand people were murdered in the southern Chinese city of Canton alone.

'On the whole, the violence during the reforms does entirely seem to be on the proportion of that during the cruellest episodes of the struggle against the Japanese and the Kuomindang', Spence sums up the situation.[45] In fact there are no reliable statistics to indicate how many members of the former large land-owning class managed to survive Mao's brutal actions. Estimates vary between 200,000 to two million victims. Mao consciously took the many dead into account as a deterrent for his enemies. Entrepreneurs, who had been aligned with the nationalists, also belonged to this group. In April 1954, as was previously mentioned, the private economy was totally abolished. With these decisive fundamental changes of society Mao managed to rob the economy of its newly gained strength. The first five-year plan (1953–57) had begun implementation with great expectations lost its steam. It is true that the standard of living in Shanghai in 1956 was higher than in 1930.[46] But things were not able to progress. The pioneering atmosphere gradually ebbed away. The farmers in particular were unable to deliver what Mao expected of them.

It did not take long before the death penalty was enforced. Mao's internal party opponents around Deng Xiaoping used, as he had feared, the aforementioned Krushchev speech against him. On the day of the 8th party anniversary the idea of collective leadership became firmly anchored in the statutes of the party. Mao lost the autocracy of the communist party. In 1954 Deng was already nominated as the party's General Secretary and as the acting Prime Minister. Mao was only to serve as the honorary Chairman in the party. It was one and a half decades later that Mao managed to once again regain autocratic power. At a point in time when Germany discovered that one could ignite an economic miracle through integration into the global economy, Mao had the bitter experience of the disadvantages of globalisation. He had not succeeded, as he had intended, to build up his personal power with the help of foreign countries. To the contrary, Deng had used the Russian development of collective power to curtail Mao's power. China had learned from foreign countries, but this was not at all what Mao had in mind.

Mao had to get himself back into the limelight with ambitious political campaigns. At least he still had one important resource at his disposal – his charisma with the people. With the slogan, 'Let one hundred flowers bloom, one hundred schools of thought contend', the 'communist poet'[47] appealed to the country's intellectuals for constructive criticism and suggestions for the reconstruction of China on the 27th of February 1957. This sounded like progress. Although the old emperors had also gathered highly educated officials around themselves, there had not at any time been the free intellectual environment Mao had promised. The intellectual spring certainly did not last for very long. This was because Mao had not started the 'hundred flowers campaign' without an ulterior motive. Through the campaign he had also wanted to find out who was with him, and who was against him. 'How can we catch these snakes if we don't let them come out of their holes? We want that these bastards worm their way into the open, that they sing and fart. Then, we can catch them', he very openly explained to his trusted companions. 'My strategy is to let the poisonous weeds grow for a while, and then eradicate them one by one. That's how I turn them into fertilizer'.[48]

In his power-intoxicated state he had hoped to pick out a few harsh words among the general praise for his politics. He was bitterly disappointed: the criticism of his politics was devastating. Professor Ko Pei Shi at the renowned Peking University warned with clear foresight:

> If the Party does not begin reforms and make an end to degeneration, it will inevitably dig its own grave. (...) But the downfall of the CP by no means equals the downfall of China.[49]

A former young cadre even questioned the claim that the party represented the interests of the people: 'The CP has twelve million members, less than 2 per cent of the population. Should six hundred million Chinese become the obedient subjects of this 2 per cent?'[50] If Mao still had the analytical and self-critical astuteness that had distinguished him in his earlier days, then the protest storm would have made him realise that he was going down the wrong political path. Instead he hit the emergency break five weeks later: between 300,000 and 700,000 intellectuals were sent to the countryside for re-education; for most of them this was the end of their career. China's intellectual energy became frozen solid, and it managed to slowly thaw and free itself only after Mao's death. Mao on the other hand celebrated the failed campaign as a victory. Never again would the intellectuals dare to stand up against him or the party.

They had been easy prey for Mao. The opposition in the party that had formed itself around Liu Shaoqi and Deng Xiaoping, which had stood up against Mao's course of isolation and had demanded greater international integration, was certainly more difficult to disband. 'A spiritless bunch with the mentality of slaves',[51] as Mao referred to them disdainfully. The new solution was that only a powerful and presentable China was to reappear on the international stage.

Mao's greatest concern now was that disappointment could spread throughout the population because economic accomplishments had failed to materialise. He classified every form of open protest as a danger to the stability of the recently unified country. In order to keep the population on the go he developed the concept of the 'permanent revolution'. From now on, one mass campaign was to follow the other. Everything was to continually be improved even further or to at least be kept in motion. Slogans that could have come from the American industrialist Henry Ford appeared in the national newspaper: 'More, better, quicker, cheaper!'[52] However whilst Ford built up a highly successful car group, Mao ruined the country.

In January 1958 he set off on the 'great leap forward' (1958–60). It became 'more a social vision, than an economic plan', said Roberts.[53] As calm as a board member, who is trying to divert from his immediate problems by looking into the long-term future, he promised, 'It is possible to catch up with Great Britain in fifteen years time'. The slogan was by far more sappy than the concept that he had thought of in order to reach his goal. He divided China's gigantic population into small units of 'people's communes', which were each supposed to generate their own economic boom. At the same time he let huge infrastructure projects be constructed through mass movements. Whilst automation made headway in other countries and companies created more sophisticated notions of the division of labour, the Chinese had to accomplish great tasks with primitive tools. As the first feat of strength China was to establish a modern infrastructure through the construction of bridges, roads and canals. In Peking in May 1958 Mao himself picked up a shovel and dug around in the dirt at a dam for half an hour, until his white shirt was dripping with sweat. This was the last time that he publicly exerted himself in such a manner. But the performance in front of the cameras had been worth it. 'Never before in history had such a simple symbolic act released such enthusiasm for manual labour among the entire population', contemporaries who were critical of Mao had to admit.[54] Mao was a genius in the generation of self-esteem, but he failed in his attempt to catch up with the economically advanced countries through a mass movement of 'breaking rocks'. The gigantic irrigation projects lacked in both planning and execution to the extent that they actually caused damage rather than benefits. On top of this the government was no longer capable of assessing the actual economic situation because Mao had set a process of decentralisation in motion at the same time. Mao had thought to himself that if one divides large tasks into many small ones China would be able to grow faster. The co-operatives were therefore supposed to manufacture and satisfy their own demand for products. Each village had its own small blast furnace, was meant to survive on its own produce and build its own roads. In order to supervise the growth of the country Mao declared the planned targets of output, whose non-attainment resulted in such severe punishment that the people even melted their pots, pans, doorknobs and pitchforks in their small furnaces just so that they would not fall behind the requirements. Steel production did actually rise, but the steel was unusable and there were no longer any spades to work the fields. The managers of the state enterprises falsified the production statistics. The still undeveloped industry collapsed and the failures in the agricultural sector resulted in a famine, which according to the estimations of Western researchers cost between 20 to 30 million lives. 'Never in its history had China experienced such a terrible famine', is how the British author and journalist Jasper Becker who resides in China summed up the disaster in his book 'Hungry Ghosts'.[55] China had once again fallen far behind. So as to not lose face in front of Krushchev, who had vehemently spoken out against the commune system, Mao even delivered a large portion of the Chinese grain to the Soviet Union during the famine, so as to repay his debts. He was not willing to sacrifice his independence at any cost. It would be better for China to starve than to be on its neighbours drip.[56]

Also China went on to supply food aid to East Germany. During his trip to the GDR, Marshall Peng Dehuai, who would soon risk and lose his life raising his voice against Mao's disastrous policy openly, had to listen to Walter Ulbricht's long-winded remarks on the fantastical rates of growth in Chinese farming. While in China people were starving to death, Ulbricht actually asked his guest to increase meat-supplies from China in order to help the GDR compete with the West German per capita consumption of 80 kilogrammes a year. At that time the meat supply in China had dwindled to a few pounds per year even in the most privileged cities. When Ulbricht was through, Peng let a few moments pass without saying a word. Then he informed the East German Party Chief that China in fact was suffering from a catastrophic food shortage.

The Great Leap was the greatest failure in Mao's life. In 1959 his comrades forced him to pass on the post of state president. In 1960 the campaign was aborted. The great chairman had shrunk to the position of parliamentary leader and was fully aware of his shame: 'They treat me like an old relative at a funeral', he complained.[57]

The balance between central steering and economic dynamics had leaned too far in the direction of steering and was in the process of suffocating the feeling of self-esteem. The country was on the verge of collapse under the command economy. When it became clear at the beginning of 1959 that Mao also wanted to introduce the commune system in the cities, Peking immediately turned into a gigantic flea market. Everyone tried to sell all of their possessions in the hope that they would at least be able to keep the money. Mao realised that he had gone too far and quickly dropped the plan. This was not associated with an admission of his fundamental mistakes. His tenor went more along the lines – if only we want to, we will be able to get it done. He said at a session of the politburo:

> If our production has increased strongly, then why is the food supply so deficient? (…) Since we cannot explain the situation, we shouldn't even try. Instead, we should weather through the crisis and continue our work with even greater determination and energy. Next year the supply will be better, and then we will explain everything. Our general assessment is that the situation is indeed excellent. At present, there are still many problems, but a bright future lies ahead of us.[58]

Economic experts like Deng Xiaoping, stood in and increasingly decided the course the economy was to take. In a speech, which Deng Xiaoping gave at meeting of the communist youth league in this period, he used for the first time what was later to become his famous motto: 'It doesn't matter whether it's a yellow or a white cat. As long as it catches mice, it's a good cat'. He was more pragmatic than Mao.[59] Eventually the pressure became too great. Mao had to take a step back in order to take a new run-up. 'I am responsible for all errors that have to be attributed – directly or indirectly – to the central authorities', he declared, 'Afterall, I am the Chairman of all central authorites'.[60]

It was after the Great Leap that the realisation sunk in within the party that the mobilisation of masses of people with simple tools was not a solution to crank up economic growth. Agro-technology was therefore introduced into the agricultural communes, but despite this agricultural production in 1965 only reached the level of what it had been in 1957. Industrial growth only once again churned into motion in 1963, after new industries such as petrochemicals had been set up and heavy industries in the three north-eastern provinces of Liaoning, Jilin and Heilongjiang had been centralised and reorganised.

Mao had frightened off the intellectuals for good, the trust of the farmers and workers had suffered, and within his own ranks he had lost his shine. He was not going to regain absolute power through his own vigour. He needed a new allegiance that had the necessary energy and dynamics to be able to propel him to the top once again. Thus he immediately became involved when a youth movement began to organise itself in the big cities in the mid-sixties. Whilst the older generation was exhausted and disillusioned, the youth wanted to drive China's construction with new vigour so that it would become a recognised power within the world. This group was absolutely perfect for Mao: it was full of life, had force and until then had not had a leader who had realised how one could convert this youthful creative drive into political activity. 'It has always been the young and uneducated who developed new ideas and founded new religions', Mao explained. 'Confucius was 23 years old when he lay the foundations of his teachings. And what education did Jesus have?'[61] Then there was also Karl Marx who had written his 'Communist Manifesto' at the age of 30. Additionally the youth was political, hot blooded and belligerent enough to put up a fight with Mao's opponents for the party leadership. 'Since times immemorial the great scholars have been challenged by the young and the uneducated', he said. 'Their youth and ignorance didn't matter. What counts is only to see the truth and promote it with courage'.[62]

At the beginning of 1966 Mao placed himself at the head of the youth movement. He surrounded himself with the myth of the long march, the revolution and the first euphoric years of the People's Republic. He played the role which he knew best: he was the pop star of the new Chinese feeling of self-esteem. He hardly ever spoke to his young fans, and just stood there, winked or shook hands. The famous little red book appeared in May 1964, which was to go down in history as the 'Mao bible'.[63] In it Mao had – right in the style of the national Chinese philosopher Confucius's 'Analects' – packaged his revolutionary wisdom in crisp bonmots and banal observations, which his followers learnt by heart. He cleverly covered up the fact that he was already 70 and no longer had full control of his mind or bodily functions.

In order to appear as robust and youthful as possible he let himself drift down the Yang-tze River for an hour in the summer of 1966. He had only learnt how to swim when he was over 50 and always used his victory over the water as a political metaphor, that anything was possible with a strong willpower. The pictures of Mao in the Yang-tze that appeared in the Chinese newspapers the following day did not fail to have the desired effect. In the meantime public sentiment had been stimulated by theatre productions criticising corrupt and autocratic cadres, so that huge debates ensued. It was time for Mao to return to Peking. Soon after he autocratically proclaimed school holidays on a national scale so that the youth could be put into the service of the national interest and give the establishment a severe jolt. 'Schools are to be closed now', he said. 'But we will feed the young people. With food they get energy, and what they want is turmoil. They've nothing else to do except causing riots.'[64] It was the beginning of the 'great proletarian Cultural Revolution'.

An unprecedented personality cult emerged. And so for example in one of Peking's most modern textile factories, a mango which had been touched by Mao came to be worshipped like a relic. An alter was built for the fruit in the factory's assembly hall, and when the fruit began to rot after a few days, the factory's revolutionary committee ordered that 'the mango be taken down from the altar and peeled. Its flesh was boiled in a large pot. (…) Finally, all the workers drank a spoon of the water in which the sacred mango had boiled. Afterwards, the revolutionary committee had a wax-model made, and every day, the workers reverently paid homage to the sacred object' an eye witness reported.[65] Mind you, the workers had acted on their own initiative and without external pressure.

Mao was at long last once again exactly who he wanted to be. 'Everything has been turned upside down', he triumphed.[66] The official government was unable to counter this force in the streets. Whereas in fact it had originally been Mao's opponents who had supported the youth movement, the so-called 'Red Guards', and had wanted to use them for their political agenda. Mao enjoyed destroying the system, which he felt had humiliated him so thoroughly: 'A great chaos will lead to a great order. It's coming to full circle every seven or eight years'.[67] He was soon to have more chaos than he would have felt comfortable with. Under Mao's directive not to respect any authority, the Red Guards at first terrorised teachers and literary men, and then sacristans and managers. When eventually even their alleged benefactors, even the party officials were not safe from random attacks; and public order fell apart in many localities. On 21 January 1967, the first ranking functionary – the minister for coal industry – was tortured to death. In August that same year, more than 10,000 rioters torched the British embassy and did not allow the staff to leave the burning building.

Within a few weeks the Red Guards had caused the total collapse of the state apparatus that had so arduously been assembled. Anarchy spread throughout the country. The state's monopoly of power was systematically destroyed.

The Red Guards wanted to drive 'four old things' out of the country: old ideas, old culture, old customs and old habits. Of the 6843 historical monuments in Peking that had survived Mao's urban development policies, 4922 were now razed to the ground.

A large portion of the economic elite that thought more progressively than Mao was sent into the countryside. Zhu Rongji the later Prime Minister and economic reformer had to tend pigs and Deng Xiaoping had to work in a tractor factory. In January 1967 the whole country plummeted into chaos. The Guards stripped the Shanghai city administration of their power. Liu Shaoqi the 69-year-old state president, whom Mao regarded as his adversary, was beaten to a pulp on the grounds of the seat of government and later taken into custody. He died in prison in 1969.

Now that there was a lack of competent managers, decentralisation led the industrial sector into an unplanned future. The movement escalated and several months later China threatened to fall back to the development level of the forties. Mao's uncontrollable desire to find his way into the modern world and to overtake the West on his own accord had brought the isolated country to the brink of civil war. Rivalling factions of guards engaged in street battles.

Mao had released a dynamism that he was unable to control. He ordered the rivalling factions to unite, but nobody paid much attention anymore. The street fights were clearly more fun for the young men than their dull regular routine. They claimed to crush reactionaries, went on fighting, and ignored the ordinances of the Great Helmsman.

Only in the army was Mao able to maintain obedience. 'He is still clinging to the dreams of his youth', the *Spiegel* commented at the time, which had a picture of Mao on its cover with a dragon hanging round his neck that was biting its own tail and the inscription 'Mao's last stand'.[68] 'A state which has to govern 700 million people – and in a few years probably one billion – and a nation that is building up a nuclear arsenal and testing missiles is not able to take the first step into the technological future with an all-purpose people who have been forced into line and whose spiritual know-how originates from Mao's treasure chest of quotes'. The West was to underestimate Mao. For the third time he had to re-establish order in the country, which he himself had earlier put at risk. He achieved it with the help of the army. Mao was at the same time the destroyer and the saviour.

Economic life went back to normal. People went back to work, shops and banks opened their doors again. The postal system, hospitals and transport facilities were back in operation. Only the students who had facilitated Mao's putsch did not find their way back into their old lives so quickly. For the majority of these young people, university gates remained closed until after Mao's death ten years later. Uncounted numbers of them were deprived of higher education. They had done their bit.

In April 1969, at the ninth party anniversary, the paragraphs concerning collective leadership were removed from the party statutes. Mao was now also formally an autocrat. However in order to be able to hold on to this position he also had to share his power with the military. At the beginning of the seventies more than half of the members of the politburo were high-ranking officers. His dependency on the army put Mao in a precarious position. It took him two years until he was able to again curtail the power of the military.

With his last strength Mao – in the meantime seemingly a great deal wiser and more disillusioned – did the only right thing to do; he opened China to the rest of the world. Whilst the official Chinese newspapers were full of angry attacks against the USA, Mao put on the right face for his new world and fulfilled his desire, which had remained with him ever since he took power – he built up diplomatic relations with the USA. 'The United States never occupied Chinese territories. America's new President Richard Nixon has always belonged to the right and is a leader of the anti-communists. I like to negotiate with members of the right. They say what they think – not like the left, who say one thing and mean another', he now argued.[69]

His rapprochement, however, was not solely motivated by his newly discovered fondness for right wingers. While Mao was contemplating détente with America, Sino-Soviet hostilities were reaching a dangerous crisis. To sharpen his profile at home against the 'revisionistic' Russians, Chinese crack troops ambushed Soviet army units along the Ussuri River on Maos's orders on 2 March 1969. There were 32 casualties on the Russian side, and fifty to hundred Chinese soldiers were killed or injured. But the Soviet answer was more vehement than Mao had anticipated. A series of immediate retaliatory strikes made it quite clear that the Soviets took the matter seriously. Finally long columns of Russian tanks crossed the Chinese border in the north-west of the country, routed the far inferior PLA units, and penetrated deep into Chinese territory. In this situation, Mao remembered the ancient rule of thumb of Chinese foreign politics – form alliances with distant countries while feuding with your neighbours. Consequently, China stretched its feelers to the West.

The first rapprochement took place at the side of a Warsaw fashion show in 1969. With a cocktail glass in hand the American ambassador suggested a meeting to his official Chinese colleague. The Chinese man was in agreement. Less than a year later China took up diplomatic relations with NATO members Canada and Italy. In October 1971 a simple majority of the UN expressed their approval for the admission of China.

During this period of slow rapprochement a convenient occasion was created by the insubordination of Chinese table tennis champion Zhuang Zedong. Before flying to Tokyo to take part in the table tennis world championship the Chinese team had been sternly advised not to shake hands with or talk to members of the US team. But when the American player Glenn Cowan took the liberty to simply walk into the Chinese team bus, Zhuang decided to talk to him. Mao was delighted and called Zhuang an able diplomat. Soon afterwards China invited the American table tennis team to a match in Peking. In April 1971 Prime Minister Zhou Enlai welcomed the players of the class enemy. The term ping-pong diplomacy was born. Three months later the American defence advisor Henry Kissinger arrived on a secret mission to Peking and negotiated the terms of the official state visit of the US President. His visit coincided with the annual vote in the UN concerning China's seat in the Security Council. On 25 October the People's Republic entered the highest body of the United Nations, replacing Taiwan.

In February 1972 Richard Nixon eventually left for China in order to normalise relations between the two states. Nixon met an elderly but nevertheless quick-witted Mao. And so it is rumoured that Nixon had asked Mao what the course of history would have been if not Kennedy but instead Krushchev had been the victim of an assassination. Mao promptly answered, 'I don't think that Onassis's wife would have married Krushchev'.[70] Mao had barely given in to the pressures of globalisation when it began to wash like a wave over the country. The Japanese Prime Minister Kakuei Tanaka followed in the autumn of 1972 and took up diplomatic relations with China. In October 1972 Germany also sent their ambassador to Peking.[71] In the following year the French (state) President Georges Pompidou visited China.[72] Admittedly, the Chinese still had to wait another 15 years for a visit from the Russian leadership.

In the meanwhile, the good mood in Peking subsided somewhat. On 22 June 1973, Nixon and Brezhnev signed an agreement concerning the prevention of a nuclear war, undermining Mao's hope that the Chinese-American rapprochement had put an end to the bi-polar world order of the post-war period for good. A further hefty blow was dealt to Mao's ambitions when Henry Kissinger, by then served as the Secretary of State, relativized the American position concerning Taiwan. Initially, Kissinger had promised Peking that the USA would seek full diplomatic relations with the People's Republic. But now he declared that Washington was not willing to stop relations with Taiwan 'immediately'. This, however, was precisely Peking's condition for the establishment of diplomatic relations. Mainland Chinese ambitions to rule Taiwan were once more frustrated, and Peking was still lacking full diplomatic recognition by the USA. In spite of these annoyances, Mao's initiative had greatly increased China's options in foreign politics.

The Chinese diplomats who Peking now dispatched throughout the world were instructed to act as worldly and urban as possible. Wang Shu, China's first ambassador to Bonn was urged by Prime Minister Zhou Enlai to from now on wear a Western suit instead of his Mao suit.[73] In the (German) Federal Republic the feelings towards China swayed between disillusionment and a spirit of victory. Those who believed that the Western way was the only right way felt that their opinions had been verified and were glad about the fact that China had now finally swung after decades of economic standstill. The free market economy had asserted itself; capitalism therefore really was irresistible. Good had triumphed and a ramshackle China was now to beg the rest of the world for forgiveness. The wall through Germany was still standing tall, but communist China had already opened itself to the Western world. The Soviet Union could now be put under intense pressure with this development. Certainly not everyone trusted Mao's advancement. Their conviction was that communists would always be communists and they were afraid that the West would have a high price to pay for giving their trust.

The 68-year-olds and the other young representatives of the postwar generation, who had witnessed a model for a more even distribution of a county's wealth in Mao's China, were disappointed. The more that gruesome details of life in Mao's China became public throughout the world, the more quiet became the voices that still wanted to make out that one or another aspect of Mao's politics was progressive. Only a few stuck stubbornly to Mao's theories and continued to stand at the factory gates in order to convert German workers. Only the disappointment that China had now also succumbed to the temptations of capitalism were keeping the old Maoists together.

While the analysis was bound in the categories of victory and defeat in cold war confrontations, there were only a few who recognised an astonishing fact: China had not only suffered during Mao's era it had also matured. From the first day that China returned to the global community the West had the tendency to underestimate its strength.

In 1976 at the end of the Mao era the world was confronted with a China that possessed three huge strengths and three dangerous weaknesses. First since the founding of the People's Republic China had once again become a stable state. Despite all the strains that the country had been exposed to in the second half of the twentieth century it had been spared from further collapse. The huge separation movements that could have shaken China did not. Besides this there was the prospect of shortly being able to attain the colonial enclaves of Hong Kong and Macao without military conflict. The leases that had been settled for a period of 99 years were to run out in the last quarter of the century. So too Taiwan's economy was moving closer to the mainland and recognition of it as an independent entity was decreasing amongst the community of nations. Because the Chinese had to endure the extreme ups and downs of their society for decades, they still take the personal burden that result from the reorganisation of society with great patience. This end result of the learning process should not be underestimated. We Germans find it difficult to handle changes after the long period of peace and stability.

Second despite the turbulences the communist party had managed to establish lines of command, with which it was possible to steer the country; which had not happened for centuries. Even if many considered the policy of the central authorities to be arbitrary and filled with unreasonable demands, it was of inestimable importance for society's development and the struggle for power with other nations that the country could be governed efficiently. In the West however one is used to measure the progressiveness of a nation: the degree of individual liberty that citizens enjoy. But this is the next step. First the state must have a stable central control. In this phase of the development of a nation the strong leadership of individuals achieves more than a system that is characterised by individualism.[74] China's further development in the eighties and nineties would not have been conceivable without the strong power structures that Mao had created.

Third against all expectations Mao had managed again to give the Chinese people a strong feeling of self-esteem. The Chinese were proud of their country and its independence, despite the never-ending suffering that they were made to endure. For a long time this independence was based on isolation after the West had imposed an embargo on China as a consequence of the Korean War and Mao had fallen out with the Soviet Union. What is even more surprising is that China did not cave in under Mao's social experiments and become, as before, the easy prey of more powerful countries. When China opened itself up to the world again at the beginning of the seventies it was a self-sufficient and independent country, which was obviously so important for the world that it was visited by one of the two most powerful men in the world, the American President. Mao did not have to travel to the USA, but instead was able to hold court in Peking. Only a good hundred years earlier it would have been below the dignity of every Western ruler to pay an official visit to the weakened Qing emperors. From now on no one talked about China in the foolish and derogatory manner that the German emperor Wilhelm II had once done. Neither did Chinese rulers have to feed the wives of foreign diplomats as the widow empress Cixi had done in her time. China had become far too important economically and strategically partner to put up with that.

However China was to pay a high price for the three negative developments of the Mao era. First the gap between China and the developed countries was greater than ever before. China's economic strength had again reached a low point at the end of the Mao era. The crushed people were no longer willing to endure further social experiments. In fact the official Chinese historical records insist that this slow and laborious development was necessary in order to establish stability, independence and the ability to direct. However since China did not try an alternative this may appear to be begging the question.

On the other hand one thing is certain: the huge reforms which would reduce the distance from the most powerful and most developed nations still needed to be undertaken. To find its real strength China had to accept the challenge of not only opening itself up but also competing with West.

Second China was to a large extent isolated despite the international interest. Official visits and diplomatic politeness could not hide the fact that indignation and contempt dominated the collective consciousness of the Western world in view of the millions of people who were sacrificed in order to bring about Mao's social experiments. For countless Chinese families the first decades of the People's Republic had been a succession of bitter personal setbacks. A whole generation was cheated out of their lives, had to starve and were not educated. Families were torn apart and scattered all over the country. It was not possible for them to live a normal life in peaceful and stable circumstances. The fluctuations between good and bad times had not been as great in previous centuries. Euphoria and depression were unlikely bedfellows. As much as leading world politicians of the world may have been fascinated by the Chinese leaders, they did not trust them. This trust needed to be built up.

Third, China's unity was based on an unusually charismatic leadership. This longing of the population for a strong leader concerned the potential successors and reminded them to be cautious. Any politician – even Mao's megalomaniac wife Jiang Qing who was in a world of her own – was only able to pass the water to Mao from a respectful distance. Would China only be able to function with a strong man at the top? Mao's successors therefore did not dismantle the Great Chairman after his death. The charisma of even the deceased Mao partly contributed to the solidarity of the country. Even today, according to the internal evaluation of the party, two-thirds of Mao's achievements are considered worthy of praise and one third of them miscalculations. If one were to take down Mao's portrait from the Gate of Heavenly Peace now, it would mean questioning of the legitimacy of the communist party.

If one regards China's power balance at the end of the Mao era in light of the competition between nations, then this balance is positive. Mao certainly cannot take all the credit for this success by himself. The forces of globalisation asserted themselves and saved him.

Quite apart from the fact that an integrated China served Western security interests against the Soviet Union, the world economy needed the huge market. As the dependency was two-sided, China did not have to come begging to the West. For all those individuals who wanted to see Mao punished for the way he ruled, there remained only a sobering realisation: globalisation does not judge. It has little to do with moral values. It is not just and does not necessarily reward the competent. Mao would just as gladly have been able to steer it. However the currents of globalisation are so powerful that we can only swim with them. Only gradually we learn about its peculiarities and to control individual currents. China under Mao shows that no country can place itself outside of the community of nations for any length of time, as it can only determine its position in relation to other nations. New constellations arise in the interplay between nations that cannot be planned, but they do force all participants to adjust to one another and fine-tune accordingly. One of the most important tasks facing every nation is to recognise new groupings and alliances as early and accurately as possible. Even if the West still feels morally superior to China, what is decisive at the end of the day is who most skilfully manages the existing global political constellations.

The fact that economic engagement seemed increasingly suitable for nations, in order to exist in the global competition, is one of the major changes of this era, which resulted in the decline of centuries-old traditions. In view of the danger of a nuclear war the states increasingly backed away from military conflict. Now the art consists most importantly of being able to reach the markets and consumers of other countries, and thereby acquiring the biggest possible world market share securing this in the long term. The avantgarde of this development were Germany and Japan, who after the Second World War had been robbed of the possibility to measuring themselves with other countries by the victorious forces. They therefore concentrated themselves much earlier than the others on the construction of an efficient economy, with which they wanted to conquer the world: 'Goods instead of weapons'. Japan in particular succeeded in doing this. In only three decades the East Asian country rose to be the second biggest industrial nation of the world and even became the leader in electronic entertainment innovations. Through this Japan also gained political influence. Germany ascended in a similar way to being the leading industrial nation in Europe, with an exemplary automobile industry and a solid middle class. At the beginning of the seventies the leading world power, the USA was forced to look for new possibilities of economic expansion because of the rapid ascent of Japan. Of all things, forming a friendship with China and thus being able to open a new market in the direct neighbourhood of the Japanese was not immediately self-evident. Added to this China's social system had been developed on the other side of the iron curtain. America had been inflicted with heavy losses in the Korean War because of Chinese troops. Added to this China's bankrupt planned economic system did not extend an invitation for co-operation. The extent to which the American leaders were torn back and forth in the epoch of this transitional phase was shown in the results of the negotiations which Henry Kissinger at first conducted in secret with the Chinese: On the one hand China remained America's military opponent, from whom Taiwan had be protected. On the other hand the US was ready for economic co-operation. Even today not much has changed in this respect. China continues to be America's military opponent and at the same time its economic partner, and simultaneously its competitior.

The shift of the competetive global heavyweights made the integration for China easier in two respects. Because of its size it had already gained in importance, and not despite, but exactly because of its backward economy which promised the developed nations new room for growth. And also within the economy the parameters shifted and favoured the large realm. In every epoch of economic development there is one factor that come to the fore in the accumulation of value. After property ownership had for a long time been considered the largest factor determining success, British economic theory had already observed in the middle of the eighteenth century, that increasingly workers produce a higher surplus value than land. Whoever had the greatest number of cheap labourers at their disposal hardly needed land and still became rich. About one hundred years later with the industrial revolution the machine became increasingly important. Those who developed efficient production equipment no longer had to get annoyed with the workers. But this advantage diminished in the same measure in which everybody else processed similar machines and could produce to similar margins. Again a good hundred years later the world economy had reached the stage where enterprises primarily earned more with new products. Because cycles of development followed increasingly quickly on the heels of each other, new markets that were able to take the pace out of the business gained more and more importance. It was the start of the epoch of the market share and with it marketing which until today exercises noticeable pressure on enterprises and nations. This presented China with its population of 1.3 billion with undreamt of possibilities. It could offer the world a deal that China's economy determined in the following decades and will still be relevant in the future. The rules are simple: China exchanges a share of its large market for Western technology and investment. It is a deal that was also to change Germany.

# Chapter 6

## REFORM ROULETTE

> The door was opened and everyone went wild with excitement. The economy reared itself like an unbridled horse. I have to say that we lacked experience.
>
> Deng Xiaoping

Deng Xiaoping always wore a Mao suit but was not a Maoist. In this uniform he demonstrated continuity and managed to organise himself to manoeuvre so that he could be different from his predecessor, fighting companion and adversary. Mao unified China and exercised authority over his people – and he did both with the same reckless abandon. Deng on the other hand set free the business savvy of the Chinese, although he did keep a tight reign on it in times of political necessity. Mao placed his bet on the power of the group. Deng placed his on the economic obstinacy of the individual. Mao strived for autocracy. Deng searched for the protection of collective leadership. Mao was self-righteous, Deng self-critical. Mao raised himself above the law and ruled as an arbitrary tyrannical reformer according to the motto, 'my wish will become a reality'. He could afford to do this as he was a cult figure, was idolised by the people and was painted by the pop art artist Andy Warhol. Deng on the other hand was only admired, sometimes even hated, and it was only 25 years after he had opened China to the modern world that he was able to oust Mao as one of Chinese public's greatest idols. All his life Deng exhibited his down to earth nature and so even in the presence of photographers he spat like a farmer and chain-smoked – pictures which never existed of the mystically transfigured Mao.

In this respect the break between Deng and Mao appears even greater than the one between Mao and the last emperor. As a good communist Mao was actually what he should not have wanted to be – the very last son of heaven, even if it was without a yellow dragon throne. Deng on the other hand was China's first modern leader. Their association with the world varied accordingly; Mao alternately quarrelled with it until shortly before his death and then chose to ignore it. In him there was still to a great extent the belief of infallibility of the old Middle Kingdom, a pride that ignored the world instead of forming a kinship with it. If he were alive today Mao would be an opponent of globalisation. Deng in comparison was a man of the world.

The somewhat provincial Mao had made his first trip abroad at the ripe age of 56. Deng on the other hand, born in 1904 in Sichuan province, went to France as a student when he was merely 16 years old. Back in China he nostalgically compared the French cafes to the teahouses of his home province and indulged in reminiseences of a small café on the Place d'Italie that he had frequented as a young man. Later in his carreer he also visited the USA on numerous occassions.

It therefore comes as no surprise that it was not Mao, but Deng who carried out change, which had been overdue for centuries; Mao opened the gate with his last strength. Deng led China through the gate and out of its isolation. His critics accused him of selling China. Looking at it from today's perspective exactly the opposite has happened; Deng laid the world at China's feet.

Although they did not warm to one another during their lifetime, Mao and Deng were unified by a strong conviction and a huge weakness. Both believed that the only way that China would be able to accomplish something was under the leadership of one party – the communist party. Of course through this they also secured their own power, but most of all they had both learned from China's history that their massive country was full of contradictions and would descend into chaos without a strict central leadership. With total rigidity they demonstrated that this position was irrefutable. Just like Mao, Deng was also – even though more restrained – prepared to sacrifice the freedom of the individual for the great project of China's re-ascension. And just like Mao, Deng also overestimated his room to manoeuvre. Despite their abundance of power they did not succeed in getting the most populated country in the world under control, and they were similarly surprised by the consequences of their actions. With Mao things went topsy-turvy. And Deng, who is nowadays regarded as a great economic visionary, had no idea of the necessary characteristics that China's economy needed, so that it would be able to exist in the world. He knew just as little about how one was able to balance the domestic economy.

He only knew that China had to swim in the current of globalisation and that it was possible to use it to one's advantage. Impetuously he let go of the ropes and was nearly washed away by the massive tide of the global economy.

Deng had no idea that it was going to be a rough ride when in 1978 he initiated his market economic policy of the 'four modernisations'. He may have been 74 years old, but he knew his enemies, who he was only able to keep under control when he could show tangible results. Already twice in his lifetime he had almost climbed to the top of the Chinese political ladder and at both times he had fallen and been humiliated. In his third attempt he wanted to be more successful.

In 1952 Deng became Vice Premier for the first time and in 1954 he took up the newly created position as Secretary General of the communist party. A thankless job, as he had to sweep up the political pile of broken pieces that Mao's heave-ho economy had left behind in the early years of the People's Republic. The two men clashed with one another. 'I couldn't bear his imperious manner', Deng said in retrospect. 'He never wanted to listen to other people's opinions that differed from his own. It was detrimentally feudal, the way he behaved himself.'[1] During the 'one hundred flowers' campaign he tried in vain to prevent Mao from frightening off the best brains of the country for good.[2] And when in 1961, at a central working conference of the party Deng independently decided on the corrections of the Mao line, he was warned by Mao with the angry exclamation, 'Which emperor has made this decision?'[3]

Deng was occasionally considered a capitalist. Already in 1953 he had drawn attention to himself through his remarks, which did not fit in with Mao's canon: 'The Chinese capitalists have moved forward after having been through hard struggles. They are capable people. As some of them have studied in America they have a better understanding of management than we do'.[4] Mao was annoyed: 'Even though Deng Xiaoping is hard of hearing he always sat far away from me during the session. (...) Nie Rongzhen says that the lad is lazy.'[5] When it was of all things Deng's 'half capitalist measures of revival'[6] that eased China's economic situation at the beginning of the sixties, the tone became harsher. There were now two 'independent kingdoms' in Peking, Mao disseminated as a warning. The second kingdom was on the capitalist road.

The start of the Cultural Revolution gave Mao the opportunity he had been waiting for. Deng deliberately kept himself in the background in Mao's darkest hour, when in 1961 the latter had to take the responsibility for his erroneous policies in front of seven thousand cadres.[7] At the beginning of the Cultural Revolution Deng had even wanted to save himself by joining the side of the Maoists. Mao's confidant Chen Boda had described him as 'very cunning'. 'He is the spearhead of the wrong line. It is easier to go to heaven than to have a discussion with Deng Xiaoping.'[8] The shocked Deng surrendered:

> I, as a flawed person have to learn from comrade Lin Biao with full conviction, and after his model uphold the red banner of Mao Zedong's thoughts, as well as study the works of the Chairman from a practical point of view so as to apply them. (…) This is my first self-criticism and therefore it has not delved deeply enough. I hope that the comrades will criticise me and point out my mistakes. Long live the great proletarian Cultural Revolution! Long live the great victorious Mao Zedong thought! Long live the great teacher, the great helmsman, the great commander in chief and the great leader, Chairman Mao.[9]

This was in fact the tone that was music to Mao's ears, but he did not trust him. The 64-year-old was branded as a 'capitalist roader second only to Liu Shaoqi'. In 1967 he was put under house arrest; his children and mother in law were driven out of their home, and in October 1968 he was relieved of all his official posts. It was the height of a typical witch-hunt: already in March the victimizers of the Red Guards had driven Deng's young brother Deng Shuping to suicide. One month before Deng's degradation the Red Guards had locked Deng's son Pufang, a budding nuclear physicist, into a laboratory that was radioactively contaminated. During the attempt to escape from the deadly radiation he climbed out of the third floor and plunged to the ground. He still sits in a wheelchair today. Deng and his wife learned of their son's paraplegia only when they were granted a brief visit to their children before they were banished from Peking in October 1969. Deng's brother-in-law Pu Desan died in prison at the age of 65. Deng on the other hand was taboo for the Red Guards. Only Mao himself was allowed to punish him. He banished his rival to the city of Nanchang, 1700 kilometers from Peking, to serve as a machine fitter in a tractor factory. The location had been chosen with care: this is where the long march had started, during which Mao had taken over the leadership of the communist party. The assigned work had also been maliciously selected: the fitter's trade, which Deng was to perform for three and a half years he had learnt at Renault in Paris in 1925–26.

However the more the Cultural Revolution thinned out the personnel of the political leadership and the economic problems took the wind out of the sails of the political campaigns, the more vividly people remembered the expelled economic reformer. Particularly Zhou Enlai, who was suffering from cancer – probably the only one who was allowed to criticize Mao without being punished – was convinced that Deng was more useful in the central headquarters than in a car workshop. In 1973 Zhou recalled him with Mao's approval to be his replacement. Thereupon Deng was once again Vice Premier. 'Your advantages and disadvantages can only be evaluated at the ratio of seventy to thirty', Mao greeted him, to which Deng retorted, 'Wasn't the supreme Marxist Stalin assessed at seventy to thirty?'[10] He made a sobering evaluation of his position; 'they thought, "that I could once again make myself useful, and that's why they got me out of the grave" '.[11]

At first everything went well. In April 1974 Deng travelled to New York instead of the ailing Zhou Enlai to give a speech at the UN. In it he not only wanted to explain the aim of Chinese foreign policy to the world, but also to attain a more advantageous position in the internal party struggle for himself in matters concerning the best economic path and the relationship with foreign countries. 'Self reliance in no way means that one has to cut oneself off and decline foreign assistance', Deng declared/proclaimed.[12] The speech went down well – at the UN and at home. On his return he was welcomed at the airport by all the top brass of the party, and one month later on the 11th of May 1974 he ascended to the position of Prime Minister. He immediately used the new authority to form a large coalition for a new economic birth. For the first time since 1966 he again summoned China's parliament, the National People's Congress in January 1975. In order to not immediately leave his still-sheltered position he convinced the critically ill Zhou to position issue the new direction. The programme was called the 'four modernisations'. At the top of the list were agricultural and industrial reforms these were followed by defence and then education and science. The farmers were supposed to be able to sell a portion of their harvest on the free market, and industry was to modernise itself with the assistance of foreign countries. And the industry managers were to take on more responsibility themselves. The army was to be reduced in size and modernised. Research was to orientate itself according to international standards. Education was to be de-ideologised. Deng's suggestions were accepted; and with it his room to manoeuvre increased in size. In the summer he succeeded in rehabilitating one hundred and twenty of his adherents who had been degraded during the Cultural Revolution.

Unlike other top cadres Deng began to deal with Mao in an increasingly self-assured manner. When the Great Chairman ordered Deng to draft a Party resolution to immortalize the Cultural Revolution, Deng did not simply refuse, but did so under the eyes of 130 rank and file officials – a clear sign that he was willing to take Mao on.

Yet before Deng could consolidate his power base and point to the first results of his economic reforms, the labouriously created political equilibrium started to loose its balance. Between April 1975 and September 1976 five of nine members of the permanent committee of the Politburo died. When Zhou Enlai passed away in January 1976 Deng lost his most important ally. Only a third of the central committee stood behind him.[13] The spontaneous demonstrations of mourning for the popular ex-Prime Minister in the square of Heavenly Peace and in over one hundred cities grew into month-long mass demonstrations, and it was easy for Deng's opponents to use these against him. The reactionary 'Gang of Four' around Mao's wife Jiang Qing,[14] who had increasingly edged her way into the limelight as Mao became weaker, stuck up wall newspapers in which Deng once again was antagonistically referred to as a 'a capitalist ruler being resistant to improvement'.[15] Deng was 'a needle wrapped in cotton wool',[16] and it was rumoured that Mao stayed away from the funeral of his long-term companion, Zhou because he has annoyed with Deng.

When the rallies increasingly turned into demonstrations of support for Deng Xiaoping, Mao had his competitor arrested and ordered his deportation to a part of Peking far removed from the rallies.

His reforms – as cautious as they may appear from a Western perspective – were then slapped around his head in internal meetings with the same malice with which one nowadays grumbles about Manchester capitalism in Germany: to discredit all those who consider Germany's social system impossible to finance. Deng was considered a bungler, who was accused of not understanding the world and wanting to drag China down. Mao's impulsive wife Jiang Qing resented him as he had publicly contradicted her contention that the Chinese deep-sea fleet was the best in the world. Even the state enterprises were confrontational, ever since Deng had returned from a trip to France in May 1975 with a sophisticated twenty-point plan after a visit to modern Western companies. State enterprises were to orient their operations less on ideology and more on profit. The workers were to receive material incentives through a piece-rate system and the managers were to establish contacts with foreign enterprises – an unpleasant thought for the leading cadres who usually spoke Russian at the most as a foreign language.

At the same pace as the demonstrations grew in size, so the tone intensified. The conservatives accused Deng of not only risking the financial independence of the country with his new course, but was now also of endangering the state's hard-earned monopoly of power. The argument had historical clout: At the beginning of the century China had already been ruined on account of its foreign debts. Whereafter the country had destroyed itself through civil wars that lasted decades. So too it was not Deng's fault that his first attempts to open the country had taken place at the same time of the oil crisis. China, which barely extracted its own oil and so suffered like the rest of the global economy due to the escalating oil prices which were increased twenty-fold by the OPEC cartel during the seventies. The communists who were accustomed to fixed prices got the shock of their lives, when in 1973, as soon as they had opened China just a fraction, they were hit with a trade deficit of 150 million US dollars. In the following year it rose, just like a spring tide, by more than four times to 760 million US dollars. Deng faced his opponents as if he were a magician's apprentice. His power base had already received a heavy blow when the demonstrations were violently brought to an end by the military on the 5th of April. Two days later Deng was relieved of all his official posts. Whilst the pale and opportunistic party soldier Hua Guofeng became Prime Minister, Deng fled to Canton in Southern China where the powerful marshal and friend Ye Jianying granted him protection.

Taken from today's perspective this may have been an advantage, because he had just left Peking as a series of catastrophic events unfolded. In July an earthquake that claimed 250,000 lives shook China. It was thus a bigger tragedy than the tsunami wave that hit South East Asia at the end of 2004. This earthquake made it painfully obvious the system how backward was in terms of logistics and the supply of medicines. Mao died on the 9th of September 1976. The struggle of succession, which had already been smouldering for months, now broke out in full force. Prime Minister Hua Guofeng announced his claim. He enjoyed little support but he could use the party's and the people's hatred of the so-called 'Gang of Four' to his advantage. Hua placed everything on one bet: in October he had the four arrested.[17] He also tried to create an anathema around Deng Xiaoping, his adversary from the reform camp who was still in hiding: 'You have made mistakes and therefore have to be criticised further'.[18] Hua had not reckoned on the fact that the people thought highly of Deng. The mourning ceremonies for Mao turned into demonstrations – at first against the 'Gang of Four' and then in support of Deng Xiaoping. Poems appeared in which Deng Xiaoping was referred to as being the man who Zhou Enlai trusted and loved: and one could see that there was something in the works.

Between the 6th and the 15th of January 1977 one million people demonstrated in the bitter cold for the rehabilitation of Deng Xiaoping. Also within the party there was increasingly of the opinion that the power vacuum could only be filled by a leadership personality who radiated charisma and the power of persuasion. The economy had stagnated. China in the meantime had amassed debts of 1.8 billion US dollars. Hua managed to stand his ground for a further six months and then had to throw in the towel. In July 1977, about 15 months after his removal from office Deng once again became acting Prime Minister and – more importantly in terms of political power – General Chief of Staff of the People's Liberation Army.[19] Deng had learnt a lesson from his setbacks; from now on he wanted to keep himself in the background and pull the strings from behind the scenes rather than leaving himself open to attack in the front row. For outward appearances he modestly called himself 'the assistant of Chairman Hua' and entrenched himself behind a shield of propaganda: 'we must renew and develop the practical tradition which Chairman Mao had founded for our party'.[20]

However from now on the Martin Luther King of the Chinese communists made the market economy his cause. Through hundreds of backroom discussions he began to forge the coalition with which he would eventually be able to enact the crucial change in course. He first of all wanted to establish 'a system of responsibility within the agricultural sector'. The farmers were to freely cultivate a part of their land and were to be able to sell a portion of their harvest on the free market. Additionally he wanted to open China for Western technology so as to be able to catch up with the West.

Deng explained to his adherents that to break the resistance of the conservatives in the party would be similar to orchestrating the collapse of a wall. Instead of wasting their strength by chiselling away at the hard wall, they should concentrate their energy on the loose stones. Gradually the brickwork would be so riddled with holes that it would cave in. But first he had to generate enthusiasm for the innovations. At the first conference of the fifth People's Congress in February 1978 he outlined the prospects: 'with certainty we can build China into a modern, powerful, socialist country in the next twenty years and definitely within this century'. That he wisely concealed that he wanted to achieve this through processes of the market economy although – his opponents would realise this soon enough.[21] He therefore left it to Hua to lay down this course in a marathon six-hour speech, and to promise the people who were pressing for tangible improvements, that the gross domestic product would increase annually by at least 10 per cent over the next eight years. The archetype Maoist work brigades served as his model. Deng wanted 120 large-scale projects to liberate China from its backwardness, however this time it was not to be done through the mobilisation of the masses rather with the help of the West. The transformation was prepared and the fundamental philosophy was thought out. In summary Deng's theory was: 'The planned economy as the main component and the market economy as the supplement'.[22]

He was aware of the scepticism that he unleashed with it; for the Maoists who still believed in China's strength to heal itself, the theory went too far.

For the intellectuals who demanded a structural change in tandem with economic freedom had also hoped for political slackening, it did not go far enough. It is for this reason that he sought an escape. He found an enemy that people could complain about collectively and which had been on the rapid rise since the beginning of the seventies: corruption. 'Before one used to go through the small backdoor for only two pounds of pork or two pounds of sugar, two tickets or purchasing slips or for three meters of cotton material. Nowadays everyone uses the large backdoor. Nowadays it is a matter of the relationship between enterprises. As corruption is more varied and coupled with theft the national economy is being undermined on a grand scale.'[23]

Deng did not know how to integrate (free) market-orientated national economies into globalisation. He tried to steady a huge ship into the middle of the river, without knowing the river. He persisted energetically and sent his confidants on the search of foreign partners. It did not matter whether they were Americans, Germans, French, English or even (from a Chinese historical perspective) the hated Japanese; anyone was suitable. The main thing was that they could supply machines and industrial plants as favourably as possible, so that the Chinese were not forced to reinvent the wheel.

Heinrich Weiss, at that time an entrepreneur in his mid-thirties, was among the first Germans with whom the Chinese negotiated in June 1978. Weiss, who was later to become the head of the most influential German business association BDI, had just a few years before taken over the running of Schloemann – Siemag AG (SMS) from his father, the Dusseldorf-based steel plant and construction company. SMS had already delivered a rolling mill to China in 1965; a second one had just been completed. When Deng's chief negotiator explained what they had in mind Weiss saw the chance of a lifetime: they wanted to buy a foundry complex, including a coal-fired power station with an annual output of a 1000 megawatts for 18 billion marks. This came as a big surprise for the West.

With the promise that the Chinese would not negotiate with another German steel plant construction company, Weiss formed a joint venture including among others Thyssen and Siemens. In addition he succeeded in acquiring a grant of credit to the value of 28 billion marks from a banking consortium led by the Dresdner Bank for a period of ten years – a huge sum, that in fact corresponded to 2 per cent of Germany's gross national product at that time. It was not only the enterprises, but also the banks who dealt with China as a market of the future. Hans Friedrichs who at that time was the chief executive of the Dresdner Bank, travelled to Peking during Mao's lifetime, in 1974 in his capacity as the Secretary for Economic Affairs. Jurgen Pronto, his predecessor at the Dresdner Bank had mentioned during this in his capacity as CEO visit that he would immediately buy Chinese shares if this was possible.

Despite this prominent backing there was still considerable mistrust in Germany: 'The people labelled me as mad', Weiss remembers. 'Particularly because Chinese business people intrinsically have a legendary reputation, it is nowadays surprising', commented Germany's biggest daily newspaper, 'with the speed the new rulers in Peking are driving the industrialisation of the Middle Kingdom.'[24] This pace led to a new phrase doing the rounds at the meetings of the German business elite: 'China euphoria'. The global competition of displacement had begun. The sceptical commentators were to be proven right: The Chinese rediscovered their old talent for trade and studied the strengths and weaknesses of their potential suppliers. The hated Japanese were cheaper than the Germans, but there was no way that they wanted to become dependent upon them. The Brits were considered unreliable suppliers and the Americans too powerful and too capitalist.[25]

To gain a better understanding of the working style of Western enterprises Deng allowed the establishment of Special Economic Zones in 1979 near Macao, Hong Kong and opposite Taiwan. These were so to speak small capitalist islands, in which international enterprises were able to settle. Additionally Deng invited foreign experts to lecture at Chinese universities as well as in corporate groups. He also sent thousands of students to the West on state scholarships – knowing that many would not return to China. In 1981 the Wella AG set up the first Chinese–German joint venture. It produced hair care products for the Japanese market. The pioneering euphoria of the Chinese was so great that they actually forgot about the limitations of their own capabilities. 'The door was opened and everyone went wild with excitement', Deng explained later. 'The economy reared itself like an unbridled horse. I have to say that we lacked experience.' Another cause of the problems according to Deng was that, 'there was not enough time and we were only able to prepare ourselves inadequately'.[26]

This situation was not to change. As much as the leadership strived, their economic learning curve remained lower than was required for the rapid development. In all the excitement hardly anyone noticed this at first. Many things that sounded reasonable soon turned out not to be unworkable and were retracted out of fright. Too much happened too soon. If for example the price of 10,000 consumer products were released in November 1979 then these would already be frozen a good year later because although essential goods had increased in price by around 13 per cent there was no adjustment in wage levels.[27]

The huge German steel plant order suffered a similar fate. In February 1981, after the National People's Congress had counted their worldly wealth during their annual convention, China cancelled, under the slogan 'readjustment policy', purchase orders in the value at that time of 20 billion marks which it had assigned to French, Japanese and German companies. Among these was also the German cold rolling mill Bao Shan, the first stage of the SMS order that was supposed to bring in 1.3 billion marks for the consortium.

At one fell swoop international enterprises were sobered up. A Japanese steel plant manufacturer, whose order had also been stopped likewise, insisted on a contractual cancellation fee of 44 million US dollars. An amount that hurt the Chinese, but was nevertheless paid. Weiss on the other hand advanced from the status of business partner to friend, when he informed the Chinese that he would not be demanding a cancellation fee from them: 'We will wait patiently until such time as you have money'.[28] A few years later it turned out that Weiss had correctly read the prevailing conditions.[29] The contract was signed again on the occasion of the Federal Chancellor, Helmut Kohl's visit to China again. In addition the Germans were awarded the order that had previously been allocated to the Japanese. It is true that the Chinese were now more experienced in their negotiations and demanded a significant discount from their patient friend. Even on eve of the Chancellor's visit Weiss had to concede to improvements. The Chinese obviously gained immense satisfaction from the fact that they now had global concerns at their feet. China was once again being taken seriously.

In other industries China also did business with the giants of the global economy. Whilst the Chinese learned which conditions one could request from the foreign corporate groups, the latter realised that China was not just any developing country. The classic concept of the rate of return that the West had for Third World Countries, whereby outdated and already written-off factories were being shipped overseas, so that they could there once again be brought to life with a cheap labour source, was soon reached its limitations in China. This was definitely the case in the automobile industry. At the beginning of the reform period there were practically no modern cars in China. China's first car assembly plant had been opened in 1956 in the northern Chinese city of Changchun with the help of the Soviets. Since then little had happened, apart from the fact that factories had been established in different regions, by the advocates of the planned economy, which manufactured trucks, tractors and cars that ran badly. Yet the state and the fast growing internal Chinese transportation (network) needed new vehicles urgently – in fact vehicles that were simple and durable, suitable for China's bumpy roads, inferior gasoline and inadequately trained mechanics. The American producer, American Motor Corporation (AMC) manufactured such a vehicle: the Jeep Cherokee. In January 1979 negotiations began with the Chinese car manufacturer Beijing First Automotive Works that built the military jeep B212 in Peking. The American managers were sure of themselves and demanded, exactly in the style of an old colonial power, that the Chinese had guaranteed that AMC would be the sole foreign vehicle manufacturer in the whole of China. The negotiation partner Rao Bin, the Vice Minister for mechanical engineering listened to the excessive demand and pointed out that the word 'exclusivity' had a negative and restricted connotation in Chinese. After a few friendly words about cultural understanding the negotiators agreed that for the letter of intent the Chinese expression 'bu fen xin' would be used, which meant that the Americans could be sure of the 'undivided heart' of the Chinese.[30]

To the surprise of the Americans nothing happened for the next two years. Lucian Pye, the American-Chinese sinologist and scientist advised the AMC managers not to be concerned and explained the strange behaviour to them: 'the Chinese believe that patience is a merit of power in negotiations, particularly with the impatient Americans. This is why they often employ delaying tactics.'[31] His evaluation was found lacking. It was only years later that the Americans found out that immediately after the Chinese had signed the letter of intent they had disclosed their undivided heart to the Japanese competitor Toyota. Just like all good managers they wanted to have a counter offer for their first international car enterprise. Still the Americans were in luck; the Japanese in fact wanted to sell cars to the Chinese, while refusing to supply China with technology. In May 1982, a good three years after the start of the negotiations, a contract was signed. AMC shares, which for years had been making a loss, rose by 40 per cent within twelve days. For the first time the expectations on the Chinese market boosted a foreign share value dramatically. Twenty years later nearly every large listed enterprise has tried to improve their rates with their commitments in China.

If Toyota and AMC could have predicted at the time the significance of the Chinese market was going to be at the end of the century, then they would surely have bargained differently. But at the beginning of the eighties the Americans in particular saw China as a country of low wages. In their global strategy they were still completely fixated on the three-way contest with the Japanese and German competition. One therefore read reports in the *New York Times* that AMC intended to export the Chinese-manufactured jeeps to other Asian countries and so begin to compete with the Japanese four-wheel drive vehicles that dominated the Asian market.[32] The Japanese on the other hand regarded China as a potential economic and political competitor, who could only be kept in its place by refusing it access to modern technology. It was not within Japan's power of imagination that their economy would enter a period of stagnation, which it would only be able to overcome with and in China.

Yet the room for negotiation was still limited for the Chinese. When they started to set up the first modern Chinese car production facilities with AMC in Peking they had demanded that one should develop a totally new jeep for China. AMC was only prepared to let the latest American model, the Jeep Cherokee be assembled in Peking.[33] The first jeeps rolled off the conveyor belt in October 1985. The goal of selling 4000 jeeps in 1986 was not reached, let alone the planned sale of 40,000 units in 1990. The joint venture had committed itself to buying the kits of the jeeps in US dollars, however most of the vehicles were paid for in the local currency. After 2500 kits had been bought the foreign exchange ran out to finance further imports. The enterprise's Chinese managers banked on the fact that the American managers would continue to supply AMC's kits in the future even without immediate payment. But the Americans felt that the wool was being pulled over their eyes and turned to the press. The *International Herald Tribune*, the *Washington Post*, the *Wall Street Journal* and even *Time* picked up the topic and examined to the extent to which risks in the Chinese market were greater than the opportunities: 'Sweet Becomes Sour', was *Time* magazine's headline.[34] When even James Baker, the American Secretary of the Treasury spoke publicly to Prime Minister Zhao Ziyang during a visit to Beijing about the fact that American enterprises, 'had serious problems doing business in China',[35] the Chinese government assigned the Vice Minister of the National Economic Commission (and later Prime Minister) Zhu Rongji to solve the problem in the spring of 1986. At the last moment – the Americans had already announced that they were leaving the country – China committed itself to buying 12,500 kits in the value of 120 million US dollars from the Americans up until 1990. Zhu solved the foreign exchange problem in the following way: Beijing Jeep placed yuan from the car sales at the disposal of Peking's Sheraton Hotel, and in return it received foreign exchange from the hotel business, with which the parts could again be paid for in the USA.[36] From then on AMC earned brilliantly – and two scores: on the sale of the parts and on the sale of the vehicles. With an initial investment of 16 million US dollars AMC was able to transfer profits of altogether 400 million dollars home until the end of the nineties.

China also profited. Deng's negotiators became more skilful in the handling of foreign managers. The success of the AMC joint venture, which was celebrated by the media and share analysts, attracted hundreds of

= $960 per kit

international enterprises to China. The Peking leadership now no longer needed to mould themselves according to foreign demands. The next international car manufacturer that gained a foothold in China had to be content with less favourable conditions. There were no longer any purchase warranties. Between 1982 and 1984 Volkswagen (VW) assembled two cars in the country on a daily basis to test the market. In October 1984, Volkswagen AG's Chairman Carl H. Hahn, who had made China a top priority, signed a contract for a joint venture in Shanghai in the presence of the Federal Chancellor Helmut Kohl and Prime Minister Zhao Ziyang. The laying of the foundation stone took place on the following day in the presence of the Vice Prime Minister Li Peng. Volkswagen wanted to produce the Santana in China, which was then its most modern medium range car. A rumour that still persists is that VW transferred plants to China that had already been written off as the Santana had not been a huge success in Europe. To produce the first 30,000 units, all the parts were manufactured in Germany and then transported to China. There were therefore no old plants that were transferred. 'We set up an assembly plant locally, and later with newly acquired presses a pressing plant, and we also equipped with local welding apparatus to construct the shell', comments the former Audi Chairman Martin Posth.[37] He was appointed together with his technical colleague Hans-Joachim Paul to Shanghai VW's (SVW) board of directors in March 1985.

The concept began to work. Production started in October 1985. And already in 1986 VW made a good 10 million marks profit from the production of 6000 vehicles – a major portion of the costs had already been met in the previous year, the completed vehicle parts came from Germany and the joint venture charged a fantasy price for the car. They were given guidelines by the Chinese government, who had a huge interest in ensuring that the project would become a success.

The Chinese had admittedly committed themselves to localising production, in that they wanted to establish a supporting industry in the country to lower the costs, but they hardly had an idea of how to manage this. When Posth took over the factory the workers still chased the fenders out of the (sheet) metal with a hammer. 'Negotiating with the Chinese was about the same as negotiating with the German trade unions', the former VW Chairman explains the then state of affairs.[38] And as the ex-board member responsible for personnel at Audi he had a lot of experience in this regard. 'One has to find a way so that they can yield, without loosing face.' The Chinese were proud however they did not have any knowledge of modern manufacturing and were extremely annoyed about the fact that one foreign manager earned as much as a hundred Chinese managers put together. Fifty per cent of the personnel expenditure went on the wages of twenty to thirty 'expatriates' and the other half was divided among 1800 Chinese workers. There was nothing that could be done about this yet it did stir up mistrust among the Chinese. Were they being exploited by the West once again? The only way of easing this situation was to supply the Chinese with the necessary know-how and to assist them with the establishment of a supporting industry. 'But this was also not easy', Posth notes of his experiences. Nonetheless it was helpful that China already had a functioning light industry. 'They were so stubborn, that sometimes the only option was to let them run against the brick wall for so long, until it dawned on them that something was not right.'[39] However Volkswagen's ambition and the pressure of competition ensured that the Chinese got everything that they urgently needed under favourable conditions. And what they were not supposed to get, they managed to procure themselves. The plans of the fields of production, as for example the paint shop, were secretly pilfered over the weekend, copied and then put back by Monday.[40] Posth tried to join forces with his competitors Peugeot and Beijing Jeep and so be in a better position to assert himself with the Chinese. However from the get-go the competitive thinking between the Western manufactures outweighed all else – an opportunity that China used to its advantage in the ensuing years. After ten years at the most the Germans were the decided winners in the competition with the French and the Americans. Until the end of the nineties the vehicles manufactured by VW especially the Santana gained a market share of 50 per cent. Volkswagen lives on this triumph of its image to this day. However the Chinese did everything to make the overwhelming power of VW more relative.

Thus the reformers around Deng Xiaoping succeeded in the first few years in arranging a series of business transactions that caused quite a stir, and which gave the Chinese the feeling that finally something was happening in their country. The measures were however not completely sufficient in order to integrate the enormous country into the global economy. Negotiations with foreign companies were mostly part of a learning process; often the completion of a deal was not the actual interest of the Chinese. For example the Chinese leadership invited a delegation from the Salzgitter AG, primarily to find out from the Chief Executive Ernst Pieper how to operate state enterprises within a free market economy.[41] At the time the Salzgitter AG belonged to the state of Saxony.

Zhu Rongji the Vice Minister of the planning commission came across as particularly curious and persistent. In the nineties, first as the boss of the central bank and then later as Prime Minister Zhu had to solve such questions. As the Mayor of Shanghai he had time and again also helped the

VW joint venture non-bureaucratically with difficulties and established a medium-sized support industry.

Despite all this dynamism a rather large element of uncertainty still existed within the party at the end of the seventies. Although Deng outwardly gave the impression of the indefatigable reformer, the truth was that he considered his reform project highly risky. He was therefore disproportionately hard in the way that he dealt with any form of public rebellion – even that small independence movement of students who had come out in the demonstrations for his rehabilitation. In the autumn of 1978 a kind of small Prague spring had broken out in Peking. In the centre stood the 'wall of democracy', a wall onto which everyone could attach a note bearing their thoughts. At first Deng tolerated the new form of the free expression of opinions. When the students became more courageous, questioned the legitimacy of the leadership and reminded people of the fact that the only alternative was between despotism and democracy, which was being pushed by a small group as the 'fifth modernisation', it had suddenly gone too far for Deng. He allowed the movement to be suppressed and the leaders of the movement were sentenced in show trials. One of the figureheads, Wei Jingsheng was condemned to 15 years in jail because of his 'secret betrayal' and his call 'for the fall of the dictatorship of the proletarians'.

Deng was afraid of losing his monopoly of power. It should not fall into the hands of the Maoists nor a democracy movement, as he was convinced that both currents did not have support of the population as a whole. In his opinion economic reforms that were barely controllable mould, if coupled with an unpredictable democracy movement, be too great a burden for the country that was still rebuilding its strength after the Cultural Revolution. He certainly did not want this to be confirmed through elections.

His tough actions also provided him with more room to manoeuvre when dealing with the Maoists, particularly as the state and party chief Hua Guofeng had been politically severely damaged in the power struggle against the Gang of Four, and with whom he had for a long time acted in unison. This strengthened Deng's position in the People's Liberation Army, after he had promised the old soldiers that Mao's achievements would not be trodden on. He used the trust of the officers to carefully curtail their power. At the same time a 'more independent' legal apparatus was to help Deng to better balance his power and to place the stability of the country on a firmer foundation.

The key to the power equilibrium that Deng had created between his adherents and diverse opponents was that he himself could not be attacked while at the same time he could pull all the strings. It took about three years for Deng to establish his power system to the point where he was no longer dependent on his second rate post as Vice Prime Minister. In August 1980, more powerful than ever, he resigned. As his successor he installed a closely trusted companion, who was not only a proven economic reformer but also extremely popular with the people: Zhao Ziyang. Then Deng succeeded, after some effort, to dismantle the overly cautious Hua Guofeng, by putting the responsibility for the economic woes on his plate: inflation soared, and the national debt had again increased by 52 per cent between 1982 and 1984.[42] Many of the large-scale investments, which had only just been celebrated, proved to be a waste of money in the shortest period of time, as for example the steel plant Baoshan in Shanghai that had cost the state 10 billion yuan showed. Admittedly a few years later the steel plant earned decent money. Hua still tried to defend himself with a clumsy reference to Deng's credo of 'free competition'. But at the twelfth Party Congress in September 1982 he had to hand over the Party Chairmanship and the Chairmanship of the Military Commission. Deng became a member of the permanent committee of the politburo, took over the politically influential position of power as Chairman of the Military Commission, made Zhao Ziyang Prime Minister and entrusted a further reformer, Hu Yaobang with the party leadership. After three attempts Deng who liked to refer himself as 'bu dao weng', the skipjack,[43] now firmly sat in the saddle. It is true that he preferred to operate in the backrooms of power, so that not he but his front men intercepted the harshest blows and that he would also be able to sacrifice them if necessary. 'In five years I will no longer be here', he coquettishly referred to his age whilst speaking with the Japanese Prime Minister Yasuhiro Nakasone. 'But if the sky falls down Hu Yaobang and Zhao Ziyang will have to carry the weight.'[44] Actually the sky did threaten to fall down five years later – but it was to be Deng who had to bear the weight all on his own.

At first he had a tail wind. The 'socialist market economy with Chinese characteristics' delivered good growth figures and allowed Deng to increasingly free himself from the ideological straight jacket of the communist system and to publicly make statements such as 'one can not expect the compositions of Marx and Engel's to be able to solve today's problems'.[45] In 1983 China had a trade surplus of 5.2 billion US dollars. Foreign direct investment rose to 910 million US dollars. The new era was noticeable throughout the country. Between 1978 and 1985 it was possible to lower the number of people living below the poverty line from 30 to 10 per cent.

For the first time in the history of the People's Republic more than 400 million tons of grain were produced in 1984. Between 1981 and 1986 industrial production nearly doubled.[46] The private sector also obtained more room to manoeuvre. In 1979, for the first time since 1956, private craftsmen and small service providers were allowed to operate. A Central Committee resolution dated October 1984 permitted private enterprises to employ up to eight workers. With this resolution the party had to yield to reality. Already two months later a prominent party paper's report was full of praise for a camera and lens factory in Fuzhou that had been founded by three brothers and employed over three hundred workers.[47] As the shadow market increasingly determined economic activities the price controls were also eventually lifted and replaced with a dual pricing system. Farmers only had to sell a part of their harvest to the state at fixed prices and the rest they were able to offer at the market price in the newly created markets.

Competition with foreign countries was only to exist where it was of use to China. The republican US President Ronald Reagan experienced this when he travelled to Peking in April 1984 with the intention of getting the Chinese to commit themselves to a basic principle of the market economy – the guarantee that all profits which had been made by American enterprises could be transferred to the USA. But already one month before Reagan's visit the Chinese insisted that this formula should be determined on a case-by-case basis.[48] They only wanted to permit the export of profits if it meant that they would lose out on important business. Reagan, a staunch anti-communist and who with his economic advisors, pioneered neo-liberalism, travelled to China in spite of this defeat. This was because the English Prime Minister Margaret Thatcher,[49] as well as the French Presidents Valery Giscard d'Estaing and Francois Mitterrand[50] had already built up trade relations for their enterprises in China and the Federal Chancellor Helmut Kohl followed several months later.[51]

The managers of the first foreign–Chinese joint venture in particular felt the effects of the new regulations on their cost of living. A family of five had to pay 125,000 US dollars a year for a three-bedroom suite in a Western standard hotel, and, added to this was a laundry bill of 400 dollars a month.[52] In Peking, China International Trust and Investment Corporation (Citic) build the first office building for foreign companies, and still known as 'chocolate house' because of its shape and color. Its rents were twice as high as Hong Kong and four times as high as Paris.[53] The Chinese state enterprise managers in the Beijing Jeep joint venture demanded 40,000 US dollars per annum.[54] Make as much money as possible, as quickly as possible, was the motto by which the Chinese traded to the annoyance of their foreign business partner. The Chinese did not yet believe in stable economic progress. The cadre had learned to love the bird in the hand instead of believing in the two birds his leaders had claimed to spot in the bush.

Large sections of the population remained sceptical and were not quite so sure how many liberties they were allowed to take. 'Don't be afraid of prosperity', Secretary General Hu Yaobang encouraged them on his provincial trips. Whereas during Mao's time prosperity consisted of the 'four must-haves', a bicycle, a radio, a clock and a sewing machine, it was now about 'three high things': a high salary, a high education and – as a sign of good nutrition – high body stature.

The Chinese leadership still knew nothing about how to establish and regulate functioning market mechanisms, and so it slowly began lose control over its reforms. This was because the main economic actors of the eighties were not the state enterprises but rather the party and administrative cadres in the villages and the communes who in a short period of time had established over 700,000 medium-sized enterprises employing almost 30 million workers.[55] 'Reforming China is like crossing a river', Deng described his policy, 'one has to look for stepping stones'.[56] This sounded ominous to many comrades. Indeed the river proved to be flowing increasingly rapidly and the stones becoming increasingly unstable. Manchester capitalism prevailed. Many products were overproduced and because of this others were not even produced at all. Corruption exploded, which led to massive losses. Economic growth sagged to under 8 per cent – which was too little to support the upswing of the huge country.

Foreign countries were content that China had swung onto the path of Western development, but hardly recognised the enormous problems that are brought about when a gigantic developing country is to be integrated into the already highly developed global economy. In 1984 *Time* magazine chose Deng as the man of the year. Even the leaders of the most progressive 'socialist brother countries' became envious: 'From an economic perspective this country was for me the better DDR', admitted Gunter Schabowski a DDR Politburo member.[57]

Added to this Deng's successes had not by any means eliminated the tensions within the communist party. The conservative camp still feared that they would become dependent on foreign countries. In particular the growth in imports was seen as a danger by the hardliners. In 1984 imports were only covered by foreign exchange reserves for seven months, although these had risen between 1980 and 1985 from 2.26 billion US dollars to nearly 14.5 billion US dollars. As quickly as the cushion had grown it disappeared. A 15 billion US dollar trade had deficit built itself up in 1985, which was the highest in the history of the People's Republic. The biggest problem was consumer goods that were bought overseas but frequently not even used. The state traders with import licences still lacked the experience of adapting to the demands of the market. They used their gut feeling to buy anything that they fancied. The few entrepreneurs who had done business with foreign countries before the founding of the People's Republic were not yet reinstalled in their positions. And so the times were favourable for inconsiderate gamblers who secured their living from the open policy. They used their lead to create large enterprises. State enterprises were converted. Many of them, as for instance the household appliance manufacturer Haier, who had shaken off their former joint venture partner Liebherr Holding, still exists. However they still suffered from casual expert knowledge and only rough commercial structures with which they were established. In the eighties though, they accumulated a considerable trade deficit. The Government lost control over imports[58] and got itself into debt overseas. These debts grew on a monthly basis between 1 and 1.5 billion dollars, and between 1984 and 1986 by 35 per cent to 21 billion US dollars.[59] As there was not enough money at hand the Government printed it. Thus the value of the yuan decreased further and further. The salesmen followed and put up the prices and so the divide between rich and poor widened.

The penalty came quickly. In December 1986 students took to the streets in the province of Anhui. While earlier demonstrations were frequently organised by cadres and were instrumental in internal power struggles, these demonstrations happened, for the first time in the history of the People's Republic 'without the request of high ranking Party officials'.[60] The conservatives were alarmed: China's recently gained esteem in the world and thereby its national feeling of self-worth was at risk.

Deng stepped on the brake in 1986. He did what developing countries usually do in such a crisis. He devalued the currency in order to make China's products cheaper so that it was easier to sell them overseas. In only one year the trade deficit dropped by nearly 70 per cent. So at first Deng was able to calm down the anxious comrades, however it was not possible to steer the unleashed market economy with the levers of the command economy. For most people devaluation meant an increase in the price of imported products. They began to hoard, and so the products became scarce and even more expensive. The central bank once again had to print money to meet the need for cash. Deng had provoked an inflationary spiral. The indignation of the people rose with the prices. The author Zhang Jie aptly depicts the atmosphere in her novel *Leaden Wings*. She lets an old cadre declare: 'Blind reform mania! Nobody knows if the new stuff even works. If it fails, one has nothing left in the pocket. You'll have to rely on yourself in order to survive. Is this still a planned economy? Where can you now find the superiority of socialism?'[61]

What started as a small demonstration in a provincial town spread itself out to Shanghai and Peking. On the 20th of December 1986 about 10,000 students demonstrated in Shanghai. Three days later 23,000 students protested in Peking and broke through the barriers around the square of Heavenly Peace. The foreign press noticed increasingly that everything was not running smoothly in China. Deng bet on a hard approach and the fact that the Chinese market had in the meantime become so interesting for foreigners that they would not be frightened off by a few arrested demonstrators: 'We have put Wei Jingsheng behind bars. So what? Has it harmed China's reputation? Under no circumstances! In fact the opposite: we have not released him and nevertheless China's reputation grows on a daily basis.'[62]

Deng was unable to dispel the concerns of the conservatives with such statements. The memories of the chaos of the Cultural Revolution returned with the demonstrations. Deng had to present an offering before he himself became a victim. At a sitting of the Politburo on the 17th of January 1987, in shortened proceedings that were against the rules, he gave up his best man. Hu Yaobang, whom he had actually chosen as his successor had to give up his office as the party's Secretary General as the conservatives considered him to be to compliant and liberal. Hu was very popular among foreign politicians because of his unconventional openness, liveliness and sense of humour. Prime Minister Zhao Ziyang took over the party leadership and passed his office onto the conservative Li Peng, who had been educated in Moscow. Throug this Deng had lost an important position to the conservatives. It was a painful defeat for Deng as Hu had already served under him as a faithful top cadre in the civil war. Nevertheless Hu was partly rehabilitated at the 13th Party Congress in the following autumn as a result of Deng's pressure and was again taken in as a full member of the Politburo but without portfolio. Deng hoped that he would be able to install him several years later. He himself left – true to his belief not to be on the foremost frontline – the Central Committee in 1987 and only maintained control over the state's monopoly of power, namely the Chairmanship of the Military Commission.

The internal party power games however did not solve China's economic problems. Foreign debt rose until the end of 1987 by a further 50 per cent to over 30 billion US dollars. Imported goods were only covered by foreign exchange reserves for six months. In their helplessness the Party sought refuge in a discipline, which it commanded like no other: give names to the developments and hope that reality will subordinate itself to their iron will. If the 11th Party Congress had still decided that the market economy was to be developed within the planned economy, at the 13th Party

Congress in 1987 it was decided that it had to develop itself next to the planned economy. The new Secretary General Zhao Ziyang claimed that there would be a reduction in 'class contradictions through economic development'.

The reality looked quite different. The salaries of the state employees and the wages of the workers were unable to withstand the price increases. The recently filled shelves in the department stores were of no use because everyone had to spend nearly all income on food. The chaotic markets resulted in absurd incentives; taxi drivers earned more than university professors and waiters more than teachers. In this phase of adventurism young people decided to forgo their education so that they could make money as quickly as possible. The number of secondary school students had dwindled by 25 per cent since the end of the Cultural Revolution. Rampant corruption did its bit to thrust the developing economy in an unhealthy direction. The fact that 150,000 cadres were excluded from the party because of corruption between 1983 and 1987 proved to be a drop in the ocean. The administrative machinery ballooned, as there were always new cadres who wanted to enrich themselves with the new flow of money. Smuggling and the black market were stronger than the markets. In 1988 out of the 2200 tons of raw silk mostly from national silk factories, which had been assured to the national textile industry, only 13 tons were delivered. The rest was illegally relocated; the money disappeared into the pockets of the state managers. The economic consequences were enormous; out of Shanghai's 1600 weaving factories 1400 were inactive; nevertheless the wages still had to be paid.[63]

Grain production also declined. Even though farmers in 1984 had brought in 407 million tons of grain – so much that China could even export grain – in 1987 the country had to once again import 6.7 million tons; in 1989 this figure was at 16 million tons. A further problem was population growth. The Government gave warnings of a 'national catastrophe'[64] as the number of inhabitants had doubled since 1949. The one-child policy that had been introduced at the end of the seventies could admittedly slow growth down, however the population will only shrink in the third decade of the twenty-first century.

Business on the black market flourished, as people changed their money into US dollars or other foreign currencies. In 1989 the dollar's black market rate was twice as high as the official rate and it robbed the leadership the possibility of controlling the development of the economy through the revaluation and devaluation of their currency. Inflation resulted in a diminishing purchasing power and so the Chinese believed less and less that their currency was actually worth what the official rates promised.

Political chaos was nothing new to the Chinese. But this time it was somewhat different: for a brief moment an alternative had been visible on the horizon. The removed and now deceased Hu Yaobang seemed to have pointed out a better direction. The willingness to unresistingly tow the authoritarian course of the party line decreased because of this, along with ever-increasing numbers of Chinese who had travelled overseas praised the high standard of living in Western countries and Japan. Between 1978 and 1988 65,000 Chinese studied overseas. Joint venture companies who invested approximately 10 billion US dollars in China between 1979 and 1988 did their bit in pointing out to the Chinese the difference in quality between their own and the Chinese products. To prevent social resentment Deng had actually been cautious by limiting the establishment of most of the factories in the four Special Economic Zones. With barbed wire fences separating them from the rest of the country one was only allowed to enter with special permission. However this did not prevent the exchange of information. Particularly in the metropolises of Peking, Shanghai and Canton that attracted a multitude of tourists and business people, people found out about the standard of living behind the Chinese wall. And the more the Chinese had access to money, the more they wanted to surround themselves with the objects of Western affluence. The first German pub was opened in Peking's Lido Hotel in 1988, with the advertisement: 'Our German chef prepares plump rural sausages next to the bowling centre.'[65]

The dissatisfaction of the majority of the Chinese population, who did not share in this new wealth, was increasingly vocalised. The intellectuals, who had gained the least from the upswing, had however become aware of the growing dissatisfaction within the population; and very early on they saw their opportunity. In January and February 30 writers, scientists and artists demanded an amnesty for all political prisoners. At that time Soviet President Mikhail Gorbachev had apparently brought the dissident Andrej Sacharow out of his banishment to Moscow. Even if China was far ahead of the Soviet Union in the matters of economic reform, the Chinese leadership was supposed to learn from Moscow's new political tolerance. Nevertheless the comrades remained hard. When US President George Bush Snr travelled to China at the end of February and wanted to meet Fang Lizhi, an astrophysicist and critic of the regime, the Chinese security forces did not permit it. Party chief Zhao explained to Bush that all those who demanded democracy according to the Western model would only play themselves into the hands of the conservative breaks of reform: 'In the best case they will ensure that the reforms experience difficulties, and in the worst case they will let the reforms fail.'[66]

When Bush thereupon wanted to enlighten him about democratic values Zhao appeared offended and answered proudly, 'We don't export our system, but we also don't want to copy the system of other countries.'[67] With this he coined a phrase that Western politicians were to hear often thereafter.

In the course of spring 1989 the tensions rose even further. Hu Jintao, the former provincial party secretary and current state and party chief ordered that a violent rebellion by separatists in the Tibetan capital of Lhasa to be crushed after one week. There were twenty to thirty fatalities and several hundred were injured. A state of emergency was imposed on Lhasa.[68] When the National People's Congress met in Peking in March 1989 the situation had not been as tense as this since Mao's death. Deng Xiaoping surprisingly stayed away from the meeting, obviously with the intention of avoiding criticism. Two weeks later the 84-year-old told the Ugandan Prime Minister Yoweri Museveni, that he was undoubtedly healthier as a result of not having exposed himself to the stress and added: 'It is even more important that I gradually retire from the stage and leave the control of the work to others. The "new leaders" should not have the feeling that there are still certain powers standing over them.' The new team were, 'full of energy and will do a better job'.[69]

Deng's designated successor actually seemed to have understood the seriousness of the situation. On the 20th of March Prime Minister Li Peng analysed the economic situation in a two-hour speech and criticised the fatal tendency to begin new modernisation projects without taking the scarcity of resources  into account. In an unusually open manner he mentioned leadership errors and a lack of understanding 'for the difficulties and complexities of reform'.[70] He went on to bemoan the leadership for missing the opportunity to create an apparatus to steer the overall economy parallel with decentralisation. Along with the price reforms, which had been stopped, 'not properly judged the strain on the state, enterprises and population'.

As the most serious symptoms of the crisis he singled out the high rate of inflation which stood at nearly 20 per cent and the stagnation of the production of basic food. The population was growing so quickly that it was endangering food security and China was becoming increasingly dependent on imports. The price increases had lowered the standard of living of a substantial number of urban dwellers and had also adversely affected social stability and the population's confidence in reform. Like all Chinese leaders Li was also concerned about maintaining the feeling of self-esteem and the monopoly of power. By no means did he want to halt the reforms, but he did want to slow down the pace. He also stressed that the Government was resolved to, 'not by any means returning to the old economic model that was characterised by excessive centralisation and exaggerated rigid controls, but also to lessen the inroads into privatisation, which the socialist social order rejects'. Towards the end of the conference Li even responded to Western journalists' questions regarding democratisation. This would have to be built on a firm foundation of social stability; otherwise it would undermine the economic reform process: 'in China one should not pursue political democratisation in too great a hurry or with excessive force'. China would have to pursue other ways so as to improve the population's standard of living.

Although Li Peng and Deng Xiaoping were prepared to personally take on the responsibility for the economic problems, they were however not willing to resign. Deng spoke of 'personal mistakes' and 'a lack of experience'.[71] Li explained that he was as a member of the Permanent Committee of the State Council, 'both involved in the decision making and also the execution and therefore I cannot shirk from my responsibility'. And even the party's chief ideologist Hu Qili admitted: 'the reforms have got out of control'.[72] The leadership had hoped to calm down the anxious masses, particularly as there were sufficient anniversaries in 1989 which offered the opportunity for very symbolic demonstrations: the 70th anniversary of the 4th of May Movement, a little later the 200th anniversary of the French Revolution, and on the 1st of October it had been 40 years since the founding of the People's Republic.[73] But the confidence of the people had already been lost. And this was to develop itself at an event that no one could have predicted.

When the former Party Chief Hu Yaobang died of a heart attack on the 15th of April, posters, wall newspapers and banners appeared only hours later at numerous universities that mourned the death of the despised Hu. On the following day approximately 4000 people gathered on the square of Heavenly Peace in Peking, demonstrated against corruption and bureaucracy and demanded a re-evaluation of Hu's historical achievements. 'We are asking history how many unselfish people it knows', was written on the bow of a wreath, which the students had laid down in the square. 'He died too early, but the others ...'. Other banners complained: 'China is again standing at the crossroads',[74] or referred to the economic crisis thus: 'we are being criticised because we are allegedly destroying the national stability and unity. But we have sky rocketing inflation, corruption within the party and growing chaos. Now who really is responsible for this instability?'[75] Many of these views coincided with Deng's opinions, but internally he distanced himself from his deceased companion: 'his stance in regards to the economy was not right. His beginnings of a two digit economic growth will only entail higher rates of inflation. (…) Let us not elevate him too high, just because he has died.'[76]

The demonstrations gave Deng, who had already experienced the risk of many mass movements, grave concern: 'This is not a normal student movement, but a riot. (…) We cannot permit them to continue doing what they want. (…) We have to do everything we can to avoid a bloodbath, but we should also take into account that it will perhaps not be possible to completely avoid the shedding of blood.'[77] Even with foreign visitors Deng outlined this position:

I told (the American President) Bush that there couldn't be stability in China if we permit demonstrations of so many people in our country, which is so enormous. And if there is no stability, we cannot achieve anything. (…) Currently we have a few people who proceed in the same old way as the rebellious parliamentary group during the Cultural Revolution. They will not be satisfied until everything has descended into chaos. In this way they would let China's hopes burst like a soap bubble and prevent us in continuing economic development and the open door policy. That would be our immediate ruin.[78]

These opinions were published in the party's mouthpiece, the *People's Newspaper* on the 26th of April. But the demonstrations continued to grow. On the 70th anniversary of the 4th of May Movement there were already parades that had not been officially approved passing through the streets of Peking and other cities. The protests gradually became the central focus and the leadership had to deal with them.

Not all politicians agreed with Deng's stance. Importantly his faithful Party Chief Zhao Ziyang increasingly became his opponent. On the day after the 4th of May demonstrations he used a meeting with the Board of the Asian Development Bank, without arrangement with the Permanent Committee of the Politburo, to publicly present another view of the situation:

Because the judicial system is imperfect, there is a lack of democratic control. Because there is a lack of openness and transparency there is an unrestrained spread of rumours. The problem of corruption definitely needs to be solved. But the problem must and can only be got to through the connection of reform measures such as the completion of the judicial system and the extension of transparency.

The speech was widely disseminated, and thereby the conflict within the party became public. Zhao tried to radiate peace: 'there will not be the

occurrence of a large riot in China. That is my firm conviction.' He was to
be mistaken.

The differences became more and more marked. In the fifty days
between Hu's death and the fateful 4th of June, approximately 20 million
people took part in demonstrations across the country. The centre of the
movement converged at the Square of Heavenly Peace, the 'cult centre' of
the country and the communist party, on which the People's Republic had
experienced its greatest triumphs and defeats. When Mikhail Gorbachev
became the first Soviet head of the party and state to have visited for
30 years, the official parade of honour had to be cancelled on the square and
instead Gorbachev had to be led into the Great Hall of the People through a
back entrance. The visit of Shanghai's city centre was aborted altogether. As
his journey drew near he had made surprising concessions in the face of the
newly strengthened China: he gave his troops at the north Chinese border
the marching orders, relinquished the occupation of Afghanistan and
promised to exert pressure on the Vietnamese, so that they would withdraw
their troops from Cambodia.

These issues had long been points of dispute, some reaching back to the
falling out between the two countries at Mao's and Khruschev's time. Not
before the early eighties did positions slowly begin to change. The first step
to a rapprochement was taken by Leonid Brezhnev in 1982. On the 24th of
March he delivered a speech in Tashkent, the capital of what was then still
the Soviet Republic of Uzbekistan. Although peppered with the usual
attacks on China, in his speech Brezhnev recognized China as a socialist
country, acknowledged the People's Republic's sovereignty over Taiwan,
and expressed the wish to improve relations between the Soviet Union and
China. Finally, he proposed consultations between the two countries. The
first round of talks started in Peking on 5 October 1982. Deng Xiaoping,
convinced that time was on his side, instructed his diplomats not to be too
anxious to accomplish anything. Almost four years later, at the eigth round
of consultations, no substantial progress had been made. The fronts didn't
move until Mikhail Gorbachev made a long speech in Vladivostok on
28 July 1986, in which he announced that the Soviet Union would pull
troops from Afghanistan and Mongolia, and indicated his willingness to
reduce the number of troops along the Sino-Soviet border. In addition, he
was the first leader of the Soviet Union to speak favourably of Chinese modernization efforts. Gorbachev's visit to Peking was to cap the détente
between the ailing Soviet Union and a reinvigorated China. At that moment
however he did not encounter an ascending super power with stable leaders.
Instead, what he saw was a huge realm that had been shaken by crises and had
helpless, bickering leaders. Party Chief Zhao had not as usual lectured him on

the decisions of the collective leadership, but had stressed instead that he needed to obtain Deng's approval regarding all-important questions. In short, Zhao blamed Deng for everything.[79] For Gorbachev this was an irrefutable sign of the disorder at the leadership level. Before departing Gorbachev let the national press agency TASS report that the Chinese government had lost their control over the demonstrations. This was not a false impression. Increasing numbers of people, and now not only students, were out on the streets complaining about the deplorable state of affairs in the country. Memories of Chiang Kai-shek's last years of rule became vivid.

Now Deng's overhasty decentralisation policy took its revenge. The economic crisis had snatched the power out of the hands of the leadership. Since the 3rd Plenary of the Central Committee in November 1988 Party Chief Zhao Ziyang had been frustrated in his attempts to get the reform policy under control again.

The banks in the provinces, special zones and large cities were no longer allowed to make independent decisions. The city of Peking imposed a provisional building ban for more than eighty large-scale building projects in order to examine their financial viability. Most of them were postponed for two to three years. With such measures in place the leadership tried to lower the industrial growth rate that had plummeted from 25 per cent in 1988[80] to around 10 per cent a year later. These good intentions did not match the complexity of the situation. The economy continued to stumble its way forward. In 1988 grain production fell around 3 per cent so that it was again below the 400 million ton limit. The growth figures in the spring of 1989 indicated that the economy had again grown by 11.2 per cent between 1988 and 1989. However inflation rose twice as fast in the first half of 1989 to over 25 per cent.[81]

On the 17th of May more than one million workers, employees and students demonstrated against the Chinese leadership in Peking. They occupied the square of Heavenly Peace and demanded the introduction of democracy, without really knowing what they imagined it to be. According to enquiries, which the university administration had conducted in 1987 and 1988, the students no longer wanted to be considered as belonging to the working class, but as a separate social class attaining more intellectual and political freedoms. At the head of the country a government characterised by neo-Confucianism with new authority hovered in front of them. Many of them dreamt of studying in the USA.[82] It was only years later that they realised how unworldly their demands were. According to the former demonstrator Qian Ning 'I left high school at the end of the Cultural Revolution. We had learnt that China would only ascend if we followed one model, one ideological plan of construction', when he returned to China after a 10-year stay in the USA. 'So we demonstrated at the end of the eighties and wanted to improve the world. We thought that we would only be able to change the world through a large political mass movement. That of course is nonsense.'[83] But this self-realisation only came later.

On the 8th of May party Secretary General Zhao Ziyang and Prime Minister Li Peng made a last ditch attempt to meet with the students. They went to a hospital to personally speak with those who were exhausted from a hunger strike. Some rejected the visit and others talked to them.[84] The Prime Minister acknowledged the demonstrators' 'patriotic sincerity' in front of the rolling cameras. In this way the people were able to observe how the mediating smile gradually disappeared from the face of the Prime Minister. The student leader Wuer Kaixi rejected his suggestion that the Red Cross should bring all the hunger strikers to hospitals. 'I have a clear conscience', he said and pointed with his finger at the Prime Minister, 'because the student movement has made the party notice the real opinion of the people'.[85] Li was shocked. All at once his government had also lost face domestically. In the presence of the Soviet President he had explained: 'we are not of the opinion that liberty, democracy and human rights are a patent of capitalist countries. Socialist countries should also be free and democratic and fully enjoy human rights'.[86] Now the front liners hardened their positions.[87]

On the 20th of May a state of emergency was imposed in eight districts of the city. Party Chief Zhao Ziyang who right until the end sympathized with the students had lost the internal party struggle. 'I have come too late', he said in his last discussion with the demonstrators on the square of Heavenly Peace. Shortly afterwards the 70-year-old was placed under house arrest because he had voted against the imposition of martial law, and thereby against Deng Xiaoping at the crucial Politburo session. On 24 June the CP Central Committee officially relieved Zhao of his post. He was accused of 'very serious mistakes' and 'splitting the party' but was not labelled a counter-revolutionary.

Weeks later, DDR Politburo member Gunter Schabowski, who during a visit to Peking had asked about the reasons for Zhao's removal from office received the following information: 'He (Zhao) had, as was reported to me, begged the students to leave the square with tears in his eyes, because he probably suspected the imminent disaster. Jiang Zemin the new Party Secretary told me that the betrayal or the faithlessness had consisted of the fact that he had said in an interview that everything that happens in this country is not subject to the authority of the Secretary General. Rather in this country there is one person who has the highest authority, and that person is Deng Xiaoping. Or expressed in a more simple and harsh way: with everything that happens from now on, I Zhao, have to wash my hands in innocence, as this is Deng's doing. (…) It was Henry Kissinger who then remarked that after this attempted slandering attack Deng had indeed no other option but to drop the man.' Nowadays Zhao is still under house arrest and is not able to express his political views.

In order to hold on to his own power, Deng had to sacrifice the second of his long-term companions. Deng summarized that Hu Yaobang and Zhoa Ziyang, 'are unable to stand on their own two feet'.[88] Immediately other cadres sought to prove their loyalty to Deng. Prime Minister Li Peng, also a pupil of Deng's, declared that the 'successfully' implemented reform and open door policy in the past ten years came from Deng, and 'from no one else'.[89] Thereby it was clear who had the last say and under whose leadership the party was going to re-seize control in the country. Outwardly Deng let his Prime Minister maintain the impression that the party had the situation in hand: 'the Chinese government will adopt measures in a responsible manner so as to re-establish social order and to pursue the smooth continuation of the reforms and the opening of China.'[90] Nevertheless internally he had already taken a hard line for a long time.

He was concerned about the main direction of the reform policy, although he was as convinced of its correctness as before. Therefore he had to prove that in the crisis, he too – like Mao before him – could become the master of the central power and prevent the break up of the country. 'If we (in respect of the students) give way, then up to which point are we going to do that?' he asked on the evening of the 22nd of May, during which the party elders (with an average age of 80 years) discussed the situation in an informal meeting. With this question he wanted to test his room to manoeuvre. Yang Shangkun, who had been installed by him as the (State) President at first answered metaphorically: 'that is the last stone in the dam. Everything will collapse if we take it out.' Two days later Yang was more precise: 'if we do give way, we will loose the power. The People's Republic of China will loose its power; capitalism will be re-introduced. Just like the American (John Foster) Dulles hoped, our socialism would transform itself into liberalism.'[91]

On the square where tens of thousands of students continued to demonstrate, the uncertainty began to grow. In the last days of May the protest slackened off and was not as well organized as at the beginning. When the portrait of Mao above the square was showered with paint bombs the student leaders immediately distanced themselves. Nobody wanted to be responsible for this type of provocation of the system. The huge Mao portrait was draped with cloth, as if he should not become the object of further ridicule.

On the 3rd of June 1989 Deng, under the strong influence of Li Peng, decided that on the following night the demonstrators were to be forcibly driven away by the army. Under his orders a huge contingent from the army had moved in from the province(s) for this purpose, as the Peking military had already partly allied themselves with the demonstrators. The worst thing that could have happened – a long civil war – did not materialize. And yet the 4th of June 1989 was one of the darkest days in Chinese history. In fact, it did not come to a bloodbath on the square of Heavenly Peace, but in the adjacent roads there were in all likelihood over a thousand dead. The demonstrators were crushed by tanks or shot by soldiers.

The pictures of the bloody suppression of the democracy movement caused worldwide shock and indignation. The consequences for China's position of power in the world were devastating. Numerous Western enterprises withdrew their workers from China. Prime Minister Li Peng's trip to Germany that had been planned for the autumn was called off by the Federal Government. Deng did not shirk away from clearly reiterating his position, even if it meant being snubbed by world's public: the suppression of the 'counter-revolutionary rebellion', he said a few days later, was not only 'a victory of socialism and the people in China but also a contribution to the healthy development of the international communist movement'.[92]

Why had the leadership decided to proceed with this brutal action without direct provocation? The students had not for example tried to storm Zhongnanhai, the seat of government, had not plundered the shops of valuables or to set buildings on fire. They had even been in the process of subsiding. Obviously the leadership did not want their monopoly of power contested under any conditions on the square of Heavenly Peace. They did not want to expose China to any more experiments. To this extent their behaviour could not be considered surprising, even if the tanks were not primarily directed against the demonstrators, but against local military units that had allied themselves with the students. Why and how exactly the situation got out of control is still not clear. It is obvious that Deng and Li were not the unscrupulous butchers who used the first ideal opportunity to massacre their people, as was reported in the Western media. It however changes nothing about the fact that the responsibility for the bloody clashes sticks to them to this day.

The shock went straight to the heart. Deng now urgently needed a man who was not involved in the power struggle but was nevertheless moderate and balanced. He chose Jiang Zemin, who had succeeded as the Party Chief in Shanghai to end the demonstrations peacefully, although he would not be formally elected to his position for another three weeks. During this time, Deng prepared a smooth transition. On 16 June ten days after the bloody incident on Tiananmen Square, Deng met with eight senior party leaders to explain why the next generation of collective leadership should have a 'core', and to affirm that this core should be Jiang Zemin. When the announcement came on 24 June everybody was nonplussed. Jiang himself claimed that he wasn't prepared. His family was worried, and their anxiety was understandable. Since the founding of the People's Republic, the anointed successors of Mao Zedong and Deng Xiaoping had an unblemished record of coming to grief. Liu Shaoqi was hounded to death in the Cultural Revolution. Lin Biao had to flee and died en route. Hu Yaobang and Zhao Ziyang were removed dishonourably and remained in disgrace. Only Hua Guofeng did not experience a dire ending – only an embarrassing one.

Virtually all of Jiang's new colleagues were more experience than him. Several thought they should have had his job, and some continued to believe they might snatch it away. Jiang was alone and not yet established at the top. The government was controlled by others. He had no network of senior support, and no personal staff. He had no guanxi with the army, who seemed to ignore his leadership. And China's elders, some of whom were at best lukewarm about his appointment, would continue to exercise their power behind the curtains.

The East German Politburo member Gunter Schabowski who had met Jiang in July described him as follows:

> he was upset by the angry condemnation that struck them from a world which for years they had been pampered by as the best communists.[93]

For him it,

> (had been) uncomfortable, to talk about it. There was no tone of triumph or justification involved. (…) I hope that I am not reading too much into it, but I believe, that for him there was a feeling of guilt, at least uneasiness about what had occurred. He did not discriminate (against) the students. Rather, they were more remarks, which amounted to the young people not knowing what a revolution entailed. That was also a question of education. (…) He did not speak of a counter-revolution, control from the outside or the like. He was so uneasy that despite my instructions, I declined to deliver the (promise of the) solidarity of the DDR to him.[94]

Officially the Chinese leadership portrayed another line. Still barely a year later Jiang said: 'I do not have any regrets about the way we dealt with the events that occurred in Peking during the last year.'[95] Deng referred to the freedom movement as 'social dregs'.[96] He also completely rejected the foreign critics: 'we are not scared of being isolated by the foreigners. Even if they break off all relations, it's all the same to us. If the state had collapsed, then of what purpose would the investments be, all the assistance and the extensive foreign trade have served?' he said during an internal speech, five days after the event. 'As soon as the political situation has stabilized and the economy is brought back on course, the foreigners will come back and knock on our door.'[97] Yet only a few weeks later, on 9 August he reauthorized the sale of foreign newspapers, banned since June, at hotels catering to foreigners.

In the meantime the conservatives around Prime Minister Li Peng dealt vigorously with the most important figures of the democracy movement. On the 16th of June three workers were sentenced to death in Shanghai. In the north Chinese city of Changchun the police presented 26 workers on a stage, who had been shaved bald. Some of them had huge placards hung around the neck with the message that they were going to be condemned to hard labour in re-education camps.[98] Several thousand people were arrested. Despite all the assurances that those who had only participated in the demonstrations did not have to fear any punishments, fear spread widely throughout the population. Those who had completed their degrees at one of Peking's leading universities in 1989 had great difficulties in finding positions, as employers were afraid of disadvantages for their enterprises. Most significantly the intellectuals perceived the party as their enemy. In August a film about China's revolutionary history was shown at Peking University. When in it, a communist tried to win an independent officer over to the communist party and got the answer, 'they don't tell the truth', there was thunderous applause in the dark hall. In a later part Mao was seen with the words, '(those) who oppose the student movement, will lose the country'. The next day a banner with this sentence hung in the refectory.[99]

On the 9th of July Deng presented a four-point plan, that outlined the economic programme of the nineties: in first place was the complete suppression of the protest movement, then the 'improvement of the economic parameters and alignment of the economic order; even better implementation of the reform and open door policy; continuous, stable and co-ordinated development of the economy'.[100]

In the opinion of the conservatives, the first thing that needed to be tackled was corruption. This fitted in with the demands of the protest movement. The individual steps for this were passed in a seven-point plan. The television reported that the CP Chief Jiang Zemin and Prime Minister Li Peng would in future act with 'absolutely rigorous measures' against nepotism 'in the ranks of the party leaders and members of cabinet members'.[101] The supply of special foods and price privileges for cadres were scrapped and journeys in official cars and foreign trips were strictly regulated. The family members of high-ranking leaders had to give up their positions in businesses. As one of the first companies, one of the country's biggest foreign trading enterprises, Kuanghua Trading, which belonged to Deng Xiaoping's eldest son was closed.

Admittedly most of the large-scale enterprises of the top leadership's family members, such as the investment conglomerate Citic, continued to do business in October 1989. Even the computer manufacturer Stone Corporation, whose Chairman Wan Runan had sided with the students, still continued to produce unabated even when Wang went overseas as the Secretary General of the Chinese opposition movement.[102] Reform-orientated economic specialists in the Ministries were however only able to remain in their positions if they practised self-criticism. 'Many that one meets prattle on about the official line like parrots, and grate on the nerves of foreigners with advice during business meetings', reported Peter Seidlitz, who was the first accredited German economic correspondent in China.[103]

In the West the prejudices about the Chinese and communists were again the order of the day. *The Financial Times* printed a caricature, which showed Deng amusing himself by picking up corpses from the square of Heavenly Peace with chopsticks, as if they were shrimps.[104] The commemorations of the 40th anniversary on the 1st of October were the most pathetic in the history of the People's Republic. The Russians did not even attend. The USA at least sent the former Secretary of State Alexander Haig, who found himself in the company of a member of the Czechoslovakian Politburo, the North Korean Vice President Li Jong Ok, a party cadre from Cuba, Pakistani Ministers and the German member of the Politburo, Egon Krenz.[105]

China was hit hard by the Western sanctions. Foreign investment came apart at the seams. Economic growth began to lag. The foreign exchange reserves dropped by about two-thirds. China was only able to pay for its imported goods for another three months. In December 1989 it had to devalue its currency by 21 per cent. Despite this the yuan and even the foreign currency the FEC were traded at double the official rate on the black market.[106] The conservatives were now apparently in the right. At the beginning of November Deng officially withdrew from all of his positions and handed the power over to Jiang, who became the State and Party Chief as well as the Chairman of the Military Commission. Part of the reason why he stepped down was because of his age and the other part was that he was forced to as his position had become so unstable. This time he had underestimated the complex economic rules of globalisation. It was not easy to integrate China into the world so that it was beneficial for the country.

However, the 85-year-old had not reached the end of the road. The global economy did give Deng impetus. As the progress of China's opening was now in jeopardy the West realised that it would miss out on the huge market. Deng sensed this and publicly made it known that China was, 'not afraid of the economic and political sanctions that have been decided upon'.[107] The Prime Minister Li Peng expressed similar sentiments: 'If the capitalists want to loose the Chinese market they can do so, that is their problem.'[108] Chinese enterprises were not even allowed to give discounts in order to attract Western partners. China's industrial plants were rather supposed to save face and persevere with 'business as usual'.[109] This was playing with high stakes, but obviously set the right tone. Certainly after the German wall had fallen and the Soviet Union had been destabilised China had to remain stable, and the best possible way to do this was through economic co-operation. Besides the competition for shares of the world market became so important that the foreign governments and enterprises could hardly afford to restrict their manoeuvrings by taking a political and moral stands. The former US Secretary of State lent support with the tactical argument: a withdrawal from China would only put the ball in the court of the hardliners.[110] Three and a half months after the bloody suppression of the democracy movement the Chairman of the Asian Committee of the German economy, Otto Wolff von Amerongen was one of the first foreigners to pay Prime Minister Li Peng a visit.[111] A little later he was followed by the SMS's Chairman of the Board, Weiss – the first German entrepreneur who had bought into the motto 'change through rapprochement' from Willy Brandt. Weiss indicated to Prime Minister Li that the German economy wanted to stick to its commitments in spite of the shock.[112] On the other hand he tried to make it clear to Li that China had at least learnt one thing; in the meantime they had ordered ten water cannons from England. In fact one month after the bloodbath, the Bundestag decided to suspend all national capital assistance and guarantees until further notice. But the Germans were under particular pressure because, amongst others, the construction of the underground in Shanghai, involving Siemens and approximately one hundred and twenty medium-sized German enterprises had been delayed.[113] The World Bank gave the Western managers a rational argument for support: 'there are 1.1 million poor people in China. We cannot cut the contact,' noted the Head of the World Bank Barber Conable. Besides it was good to see that the economic policy emergency programme was making an impact. In September 1989 inflation had dropped to 13 per cent. Even the World Bank had an interest in getting a foothold in the Chinese market and thereby increase its influence. Since 1978 it had assured China of loans to the value of approximately 8.5 billion US dollars, from which however only four billion had been claimed by the cautious Chinese.[114]

From the middle of October 1989 Cathay Pacific's Boeing 747s, which flew in three times a week from Hong Kong, were booked out in all classes. So too the seats on flights from Japan and other Asian countries had high bookings. Peking's most important business hotel, the Lido, had an occupancy rate of over 70 per cent. The Palace Hotel, a five star palace in the neighbourhood of the Square of Heavenly Peace that had been opened at the beginning of 1989 was already 50 per cent occupied. Only the tourist hotels still remained empty, which signified a harsh slump for China as the country had realised a foreign exchange income of 2.2 billion US dollars from tourism in 1988.[115]

The evaluation of many local Western business people and the official Chinese (line) coincided when it came to one point: it was primarily the Western press that had spoiled business for them. 'This is not a single voice,' wrote the Handelsblatt. 'For the local representatives of the German economy, who are anyway restricted in the scope of their work and have to struggle with local difficulties on many fronts, the political disturbances came as an inconvenience: projects cannot be ratified, the executive committees are concerned about the increasing credit risk and the continuous political uncertainty.'[116] Harmut Heine the China boss of Coutinho, Caro & Co and later the representative of the ThyssenKrupp AG said in retrospect: 'it was tragic that the leadership did not have water canons and that the demonstrators did not know their limitations. But after half a year everyone was grounded again. I stayed and did good business.'[117]

At the beginning of November the Central Committee publicly addressed the economic difficulties for the first time.[118] How the transitional problems were to be addressed individually however remained nebulous and only the framework was marked out: a re-centralisation in many industries was to serve the purpose of 'stabilising, perfecting and improving' the reforms of the previous years. At the same time it was not a matter of, 'negating the necessary decision-making powers of enterprises and institutions'. China could in fact not do without the market and competition but these had to be, like a bird in a cage, kept under the control of the planned economy. Jiang only responded very vaguely to the question of how much of a planned and how much of a free economy there was to be in the future. In fact he ruled out that interfere with everyday decisions by the party but that should ensure that the management keeps to the socialist order properly.[119]

The Chinese leadership argued about the details because to a large extent it consisted of cadres who were inexperienced when it came to economic problems. However, they were certainly much more modern than the West believed. Whilst the foreign media still reported on the communists in terms of the framework 'planned economy – market economy', the leadership had struggled for that middle road for a long time already. 'Peking returns to the command economy,'[120] read a four-column headline in the international press in December 1989. In the German weekly *Die Zeit* one could read the following rough analysis at the beginning of 1990: 'After the fall of the last Stalinist bastion in East Europe, Communist China stands completely isolated – apart from North Korea and Cuba. (...) Whilst the reformer in the Kremlin unwaveringly holds on to his programme of economic and political renewal in defiance of all resistance and setbacks the Chinese leadership, after a decade of having opened up is looking for their remedy in the recourse to the orthodoxy of the fifties. The economy again has to obey the commands of the central (authority), and private businesses are refused credit and raw materials. China is turning back the hands of the clock.'[121] Even Erwin Wickert, a diplomat with considerable experience in China saw the situation too pessimistically:

> The way into crisis began two years ago, when the supporters of the old socialist planned economy gained the upper hand. They did not want to release the economy from their control and leave it to the peculiar forces of the market. Since the downfall of Party Chief Zhao Ziyang, the leadership is consistently following the course of planned economy. Private entrepreneurs are being slandered, harassed and pestered. Two years ago the Party's interference into industrial management had been outlawed; now they may meddle with it again. Business once more is to be subordinated to the rigid bureaucratic regime which Deng had set out to liberate it within his reforms.[122]

The more that observers had an understanding of questions of economics the greater the chance that they were able to realistically evaluate the course of events realistically. They were under great pressure and came to the sober realisation that China was in fact weakened but would not collapse economically. The only sensible reaction therefore was, out of economic egotism, to take up work in China once again. It would have been too risky to force China on its knees.

On the 10th of December US President George Bush Snr, who himself had been the director of the USA's liaison office in Peking from 1974 to 1976, sent his security advisor Brent Scowcroft and the Deputy Secretary of State Lawrence Eagleburger on a secret mission to Peking. Deng Xiaoping, who despite his official retreat still had the greatest power, received them and set the tone of the conversation: 'the matter at hand is the common desire on both sides to end the disputes between China and the United States, which have continued since June as quickly as possible, so that our relations can make renewed progress'. Scowcroft shared this position and stressed the important role of economic relations.[123] The grain deliveries to China were resumed.

On the 10th of January Prime Minister Li lifted the state of emergency after almost eight months.[124] The economic situation however continued to be dire. The macro-economic control mechanisms with which the central (authority) could effectively steer the economy were still missing. 'After ten years of economic reforms we still seem to be unable to understand the principles of the social market economy. We are still at the stage that got Deng onto the formula: "first find a stone and then cross the river" ', said the current affairs commentator Zhou Derong.[125] The retreat of the Western economies and the policy of limited finances had mutually reinforced each other. Economic growth had fallen to the lowest level since the beginning of the reforms. Out of the 15 million small private firms in the cities, two million had to give up or had closed down.[126] Inflation had not decreased by even 1 per cent and remained at almost 18 per cent. Unemployment had risen as fewer loans were being granted to the construction and manufacturing industries. The foreign exchange reserves melted away as China had purchased abroad for more than 6.6 billion US dollars, than it could sell in the world.[127]

The Special Economic Zones that attracted about one quarter of direct investments[128] had to concede 20 per cent of their income in foreign exchange in return for yuan. At least the level of interest and debt that China had to pay back to foreign countries stood at approximately 10 per cent of export revenue and was so was well below the critical level.[129]

While the Western media still debated whether the leaders should be punished for the brutal suppression the economic race had already begun. The Taiwanese in particular took advantage of the situation that the Chinese were critically dependent on investments. The cry of indignation had not yet died away when they travelled to the mainland to secure the best business deals. The leading Taiwanese entrepreneur Yung-ching Wang, the Chairman of the Board of the Formosa Plastic Group, the biggest petrochemical group on the island announced at the beginning of 1990 during an American trip in *Time* magazine: 'This is the best time to invest in China.'[130] He had already negotiated with high-ranking politicians and had received concrete offers from different provincial governors for a project to the value of 3.8 billion US dollars. The Bank of China wanted to advance a third of the construction costs. Additionally the enterprise would be able to produce tax-free for a period of two years and then for the three years following that at half the tax rate.[131] Wang was not alone in his commitment to China, but only announced what had for some time been an everyday occurrence. The trade between Taiwan and China had risen by 30 per cent in 1989 to 3.2 billion US dollars. Five hundred and fifty-two Taiwanese enterprises invested nearly 440 million US dollars. In the economic arena it was impossible to stop the rapprochement between the two Chinese states.[132] This trend continues.

At the end of February 1990 the Head of the World Bank announced that he would again grant China a loan of 60 million US dollars. At the same time Japan's Prime Minister Toshiki Kaifu decided to release a credit of 8.9 billion marks. In the US President Bush Snr vetoed a law with which Congress was to have enabled an extended stay for Chinese students in the United States, who did not want to return to their homeland because of the fear of persecution. The mechanisms of free market competition gained full force. Every Western country hoped that it would receive some kind of a bonus from China for carrying out the inevitable before other competing nations.

The American government was particularly quick to move. As early as 21 June 1989 – a mere two weeks after the bloody suppression of the Tiananmen Revolt – President Bush wrote a secret letter to Deng Xiaoping asking to send a special envoy to China to have a frank talk. As mentioned on 1st of July Bush sent the national security adviser, Brent Scowcroft, accompanied only by Lawrence Eagleburger, and a secretary. The United States took more stringent security measures to keep Scowcroft's visit to China secret than it had done when Kissinger flew from Pakistan to China on his secret diplomatic mission in the early 1970s.

Scowcroft would meet first Deng Xiaoping, and then Li Peng and Foreign Minister Qian Qichen would have talks with him. Deng briefed the two, 'We will talk only about principles today. We shall not talk about specifics. We don't care about the sanctions. We are not scared by them.' The meeting didn't bring about any tangible results, but on 28 July Bush wrote a second, extremely carefully worded secret letter to Deng. 'Please understand', wrote Bush, 'That this letter has been personally written, and is coming from one who wants to see us go forward together. Please do not be angry with me if I have crossed the invisible threshold laying between constructive suggestion and "internal interference". When we first met, you told me you had turned more and more day-to-day matter over to others; but I turn to you out of respect, a feeling of closeness, and, yes, friendship. You have seen it all – you have been up and down. Now I ask you to look with me into the future. This future is one of dramatic change. The United States and China have much to contribute to this exciting future. We can both do more for world peace and for the welfare of our people if we can get our relationship back on track.'

The international Cambodia conference held in Paris on 31 July 1989, provided another opportunity for the US to improve relations with China in spite of the sanctions. Before the conference, the United States had proposed that Secretary of State James Baker meet the Chinese Foreign Minister Qian Qichen in Paris to discuss bilateral relations. During the conference, Qian was in touch with 11 other foreign ministers, including Britain's John Major, Mitsuzuka Hiroshi of Japan, and Charles Clark of Canada. Later that year, on 6 November Bush again wrote to Deng, this time to inform him that a forthcoming US–Soviet summit on Malta would not impair Chinese interests. Further, Bush wanted, again, to send a special envoy to China to inform Deng of his meeting with Gorbachev and discuss ways to normalize Sino-American relations. It so happened that Henry Kissinger was visiting China at that time. Deng agreed to meet Kissinger, and asked him to convey a 'package solution' of the impasse to Bush. Deng proposed that China would permit Fang Lizhi, a critic of the government involved in the Tiananmen Revolt, to leave the US Embassy in Peking and go to the United States. Secondly, the United States should make an explicit announcement that it would lift the sanctions on China. Also, both countries should make efforts to conclude deals on one or two major economic co-operation projects, and finally the USA should extend an invitation to Jiang Zemin to pay an official visit the following year. On 10 October 1991, Bush decided finally decided to send Secretary of State James Baker on a visit to China – and without attaching any conditions. Bush said this was his own decision. Baker arrived on 15 November, more than six months after his Japanese counterpart had paid a visit to Peking to prepare for the visit of Prime Minister Kaifu Toshiki to the Chinese capital.

Moral public opinion increasingly concentrated itself again on Eastern Europe. In the meantime, Jiang managed to use the worldwide crisis in Communism to his advantage, solifdifying the authority of both the party and himself. This was bemoaned by the Chinese dissidents living overseas: 'The Chinese exile movement is facing a great danger: it will end up in oblivion. In the West one only talks about the revolution in Eastern Europe, about Gorbachev and about the surprising end of communism. No one any longer talks about the massacre on the square of Heavenly Peace about the 4th of June 1989.'[133] Their disappointment was even greater, as they had the feeling, according to their former leader Wuer Kaixi in Peking, that 'with their blood cleared the way for fundamental changes in the societies in Eastern Europe'.[134]

The Government in Peking argued the other way round: 'Whatever happens in the world, socialist China will continue to solidly exist in the East', is how Li Peng underlined the stability of the People's Republic. In April he travelled to Moscow. The Foreign Minister Qian Qichen flew to India. These were important signals as China traditionally had bad relations with both countries and there would have been plenty of reason to postpone the visits. Particularly as the Chinese did not speak well of Gorbachev after he had abolished the monopoly of the communist party at the beginning of February and thereby kindled the democracy debate, which did not come at exactly the right moment for the Chinese. Peking accused Gorbachev of having plunged his country into 'hopeless chaos'. A judgement on the part of the Chinese within which they were later proved to be right. While China had simply cut the contact 15 years earlier, the political differences now could not be considerable enough to warrant a decline in economic co-operation.

Slowly the Chinese leadership gained a foothold. State and party Chief Jiang Zemin did not believe that there would be a repetition of the unrest: 'we have a proverb in China: A fall into the pit, a gain in your wit,' he pontificated.[135] One had made preparations for the strengthening of the police and stored 'non deadly weapons'. 'In this respect I am prepared to learn from all civilised Western countries', he told Barbara Walters of ABC Television.

When she inquired about the crackdown, he explained, 'The People's Liberation Army exercised maximum restraint, as proven by the fact that nearly a thousand military trucks and armoured cars, including tanks, were burned at the time,' adding, 'Had we failed to adopt resolute measures, the entire capital of China would have been thrown into chaos, resulting in a national disaster.' He paid his respects to those PLA soldiers who were killed in the revolt. 'We cherish their memory', he said. 'At the same time', he went on, 'our government at all levels has shown great concern about those people wounded or killed by accident'. Referring to the famous photograph of the lone man staring down a line of tanks, he said, 'That picture is a case in point. How could the tanks have been stopped by a young man? Because they would never roll him over, that is how! I am convinced', he went on, 'that the American people will gradually come to understand what really happened in China last year and support our joint efforts towards the restoration of normal bilateral relations.' The President explained that there had not been any executions in connection with the unrest; the students who had fled overseas could return without fear of punishment. One month before the first anniversary of the Tiananmen Revolt, Jiang sought reconciliation with China's intellectuals. 'We should welcome those comrades', he said,

'Who made some wrong remarks and did some inappropriate things at that time when they were not clear about the truth, but now have seen things in a new light and learned a lesson. As for those comrades who still fail to find new understanding of the issues, we should continue to help them warm-heartedly and wait patiently.'

Also the party Chief Zhao Ziyang who had been removed from office was not to be punished, but only placed under house arrest. The leadership's fear of Zhao, the figure of integration was so great that his arrest was not to be revoked for the rest of his life. Zhao died in Peking on the 17th of January 2005 at the age of 85. In addition China used the media focus of the first Gulf War, to sentence student leaders to imprisonment nearly two years after the Tiananmen revolt.[136]

Which ever way the Chinese government acted, the German economy pushed its way back into the market. In April 1990 Carl Hahn, VW's Board Chairman travelled to Shanghai and explained that China was the 'emphasis of our Asia policy'.[137] He had every reason in the world. The VW joint venture that was established in 1984 was still the smallest concern in the VW group. Nevertheless it had the capacity for producing 70,000 Santanas a year. Admittedly in 1990 it only produced 17,000 vehicles. The factory had to be used to full capacity as VW had re-invested 250 million marks in the plant.[138] However in November of the same year Hahn signed a contract in the north of China for the largest Chinese car plant for the production of the Jetta. A further 750 million marks were invested; the contract had a duration of 25 years.

Heinrich Weiss who in the meantime had become the Chairman of the Asian Committee of the German economy used this model to increase the pressure: 'we do not want to neglect the economic presence we have managed to build up over the last ten years. The Federal Republic has to avoid slipping from being China's most significant trading partner within the EU and being outstripped by the competition.'[139] The Government had approved a loan of over 230 million Euros for the construction of the underground in Shanghai, which was not released on the grounds of political concerns. For the licensed production of trucks 120 million Euro had been estimated. In November 1990 German engineers assisted with the construction of China's first nuclear power plant. Their ingenious justification was, 'we have to prevent a Chernobyl in China'.[140]

Helmut Schmidt, as the ex-Federal Chancellor and co-editor of the *Zeit* had at his disposal the best combination of reputation and room to manoeuvre in order to take up political contact again. In May 1990 he travelled to China as a 'private citizen' and met for detailed talks with

Deng Xiaoping.[141] 'We are not advocating a complete economic boycott,' said Wan Runan, the Secretary General of the dissident group, 'we are only against long-term government loans at low interest. However we support cultural and scientific exchange. This door should not be slammed shut'.[142] The Taiwanese President Lee Tenghui proposed discussions with the Chinese for the first time since 1949.[143]

When the first anniversary of the bloody suppression took place on the 4th of June 1990, the board global economic mood and the Government's hard actions meant that there were only isolated protests. About 2000 students demonstrated on the campus of Peking University. However in Hong Kong around 100,000 people went out onto the streets. In the USA, France, Japan and Great Britain tens of thousands protested. In Germany it was merely 2500 people who drew attention to the anniversary in Peking's twin city, Cologne.

The world went back to the competition agenda. In the middle of September the Secretary of the General Agreement for Tariffs and Trade (GATT) appointed a committee to look into the admission of China. A delegation travelled to Peking. In October the EU's Ministers of Foreign Affairs largely lifted the economic sanctions. The French and the Italians had already turned a blind eye to the boycott for some time so as they could secure the first new orders. China was again considered as the market of the future.

As such, China was in a position to exercise economic pressure on the very countries that had imposed sanctions on it. The second anniversary of the Tiananmen had not yet arrived when China put its economic weight in the balance to prevent France from concluding a US dollar 2.7 million deal over six Lafayette-class military escort vessels with Taiwan. It was too late to stop the business, but responding to Chinese pressure, the French government, when announcing its authorization of the sale, issued a communiqué in which it restated its fidelity to the 'one China policy'.

When only a year later France once more sold weapons to Taiwan – this time 60 Mirage fighter jets worth US dollar 2 billion – the People's Republic offered to purchase French commodities of equivalent value. In addition, it produced a list of 50 co-operative projects with a total value of US dollar 15.4 billion. The French sold the aircrafts all the same, but not without announcing that the fighters had been modified so that they were purely defensive. The Chinese government was not appeased, and so cancelled a number of large-scale joint ventures with France, such as the Guangzhou subway, the second phase of the Dayawan Nuclear Power Plant Project, and the purchase of French wheat. There would be no further talks about significant new economic cooperative projects with France. This time, Paris had learned its lesson. In 1993, the new conservative government declared, 'The French government promises that it will not authorise French enterprises to participate in arming Taiwan from now on'. In spite of the sanctions, the prospects of the Chinese market continued to strengthen China's influence in the world.

Actually the business world was convinced that the opening up of China's market would take decades. However the pressures of competition do not ease in the name of patience. Those who have the best contacts will get tomorrow's orders and control the market the day after tomorrow.

Slowly the impressive achievements that the Chinese leadership had accomplished over the previous 10 years came into the limelight: 'It can not be estimated positively enough', commented Peter Scholl-Latour at the beginning of 1991, 'that the Middle Kingdom is able to feed its enormous population by its own means, that the food markets in most provinces are excellently supplied and the department stores are bursting with consumer goods, whilst Russia has to save itself over the winter with charitable dona-tions (…) And that the central authorities are frightened off from the idea of hastily privatising the heavy industry that was preferred by Mao, has also become more comprehensible to the Germans since they have had to plague themselves with the unravelling of combines in the former DDR'.[144] His arguments are plausible because he does not just reason economically but also sees the sense of responsibility of the politicians. The provision of food for the population is at certain stages of development of societies more impor-tant than the permission of greater political liberties. It is improbable that both would have been possible. To avoid embarking on a shock therapy during reforms – which, as Russia shows, may cause imeasurable dislocations – is not simply an economic course or even a strategy in internal power struggles. It is a responsible approach motivated by genuinely caring for the welfare of the people.

The developments in Eastern Europe seemed much more unreliable and threatening to the Western industrial nations. On top of this there was the Kuwaiti crisis in August 1990. That the Iraqis attacked their small neighbour was quite convenient for the Chinese leadership. New opportuni-ties for negotiation presented themselves. On the afternoon of 31 August the American embassy in Peking passed a letter from President Bush to Deng Xiaoping. Bush wrote that the United States would not lower the level of Sino-American relations, which he considered to be of strategic importance. America appreciated China's position regarding the Iraqi occupation of Kuwait. But what precisely this position would be was not quite clear yet.

As a permanent member of the Security Council, China could have blocked a resolution against Saddam Hussein, and for its abstention it could have demanded a dismantling of sanctions.

During the crisis, Qian Qichen visited Iraq in an effort to persuade Iraq to withdraw its troops from Kuwait. He was the only foreign minister of a UN Security Council member-country to do so. On learning of Qian's mission, the United States proposed a meeting with Secretary of State James Baker in Cairo to 'synchronize' the steps of the Security Council regarding the Gulf crisis. So the Chinese foreign minister encountered the Secretary of State 'by chance' – the American sanctions against China were still in place, and meetings of senior officials of the two countries were still banned, however the fact was that this meeting in Cairo was the fourth contact between China and the United States since June 1989.

With the support of the Egyptian authorities, Baker and Qian met in the VIP room at Cairo airport on 6 November 1990. Baker said that if China voted for, or at least did not veto the US draft during the Security Council meeting scheduled later that month, the American government would create an opportunity for Qian to visit the United States. Later Baker modified the deal in an attempt to create a more lucrative bargain. Only if China voted for the American draft would there be no impediments for Qian's visit. On 27 November the day before the meeting of the Security Council, George Bush wrote letters to General Secretary Jiang Zemin, President Yang Shangkun and Premier Li Peng pressuring China to vote for the American position. But the Chinese were too sure of their bargaining position to give in. Eventually they abstained from the vote.

After the communists had determined the goodwill of the West they signalled that they wanted to integrate themselves further. This course meant cementing very symbolic but socially low-risk decisions. At the end of 1990 the stock exchange was opened again in Shanghai after more than 40 years. With this the mayor Zhu Rongji wanted to create new sources of capital for the modernisation of the port and to advance the reform of the financial system. This was a big step for China. Just 15 years earlier the quite open-minded Chinese ambassador in Bonn had refused to visit the Frankfurt stock exchange as well as meet the managers. 'Shares, future commodities and such like I also saw as "capitalist things". If I think about it these days, I think it's a great shame – and ridiculous', Wang wrote in his memoirs.[145] Ambassador Wang was not the only Chinese leader left clueless by such outlandish things as a stock exchange. As late as 1991, Jiang Zemin asked a possibly baffled Liu Hongru, who would later become the first chairman of the China Securities Regulatory Commission 'When stock prices go up, who makes the money, and who suffers the losses?'

The Shanghai stock exchange was admittedly not integrated into the arena of international financial markets. Until today foreign investors have only limited access and even the opportunities for Chinese enterprises are limited. The open economic policy began to entrench itself. In 1991 Prime Minister Li presented the new slogan in his annual government statement: 'Economically open the gate to the West, in order to raise the standard of living in the most densely populated country'.[146] At the beginning of April, Deng Xiaoping arranged for the enterprising Zhu Rongji, an English-speaking, cosmopolitan economics professor and the then Party secretary of Shanghai, to become Li's substitute.

For the world the new vice Prime Minister became the face of the new China. His sense of humour and pragmatic understanding made him popular with the Chinese as well as with foreigners. To the journalist's question, 'Are you China's Gorbachev?' he gave the quick-witted reply, 'If I were I would now be facing huge difficulties'.[147] China again had a bearer of hope with a clear record and who in addition understood the market economy better than all his predecessors put together. Several weeks after his coming to office the first high-ranking politicians travelled to Peking to meet him. This included Jurgen W. Molleman, the Federal Minister for Economic Affairs, Foreign Minister Hans Dietrich Genscher and Minister in the Chancellery Rudolf Seiters.

Simultaneously, China began to stretch out its diplomatic feelers in its home region. On 8 August 1990, it restored diplomatic relations with Indonesia after more than 30 years of silence. In the same year China also exchanged ambassadors with Singapore, and in 1991 with Brunei. That meant that China had now diplomatic relations with all six members of the Association of South East Asian Nations. In July 1991, ASEAN sent an unprecedented invitation to the Chinese foreign minister to attend the opening ceremony of the ASEAN Ministerial Conference, advancing China's integration and influence in the region. In August 1992 the People's Republic established diplomatic relations with South Korea. Three months later, Emperor Akihito of Japan made a historic trip to Peking, it was the first time a Japanese monarch travelled to the People's Republic of China.

The political state of affairs among the leadership was certainly more unstable than it appeared to the outside. The ultra-conservative forces that had suddenly gained in weight in 1989, and where now again losing ground. They were ready for their last battle and did not shirk from risking everything in the process. One of them was the Long March veteran Deng Liquin: 'If we do not decisively fight against liberalisation, capitalist reform and the open door policy our socialist system will be ruined'.[148] The orthodox faction pushed for the fact that the party should under all circumstances hold onto the 'four basic principles', therefore the socialist system, the dictatorship of the proletariat, the leadership of the communist party and

Marxism-Leninism with Maoist characteristics. It was possible that the 'four basic principles' could still have a motivating affect in the country, but in the large cities this would be difficult. Here hardly anyone felt that they belonged to the proletariat. But even these conservative politicians had to register that the theory was more fiction than reality. The texts were like shells that could sometimes serve one purpose, sometimes its opposite. The fight against 'civil liberalisation' for example openly contradicted everyday life, which after the suppression of the freedom movement had Western characteristics and continued to further liberalise. Coca Cola and miniskirts were no longer excluded from the cityscape. The intellectuals continued to have their own concerns, even if they had become more careful with whom they voiced these. The market women grumbled about the government as loudly as before.

Deng had got into difficulties often enough because he had underestimated the counter-movement. This time however he overestimated the faction that was trying to apply the brakes in the Politburo and underestimated the pressure of globalisation. China found itself in an unstoppable current. Foreign investment again rose substantially. Globalisation would already ensure that the country would further open itself up, and the Chinese leadership would only have to make sure that nothing was too rushed. In the documentation for the eighth five-year plan the party had found quite a reasonable compromise. 'The guiding principals are not reform and the open door, but a constant and coordinated development.'[149]

Deng however, was fed up. With little support in Peking, he decided to go to Shanghai to give some talks, which were then summarized in four articles that appeared in *Liberation Daily*, the Shanghai Party newspaper, between February and April 1991.

The Paramount Leader, who was 87 years old, wanted to be on the safe side. The same old man who had permitted the shooting down of demonstrators, was two years later fighting for the cause that would ensure that no more doubt would ever again arise about the economic opening of China. He wanted to force Jiang Zemin into a clear declaration of his belief. Jiang however, who had seen exactly how Deng had worn out his predecessors and had shifted the blame of the Tiananmen debacle onto the unpopular Li Peng, would not let himself be orchestrated but rather be a man of reconciliation. Thus Deng, supported by his daughter, boarded his special eight-car train at Beijing's central railroad station on the morning of 17 January 1992, and travelled to the south of the country for five weeks – into the part of China that had much better interconnections with the world than any other region. In front of economically aligned cadres and particularly in front of the military he criticised Jiang's government for the fact that they were not opening the market quickly enough. Deng demanded that one has to deal with progress in the world: 'This also applies to progressive working procedures and managerial methods that other countries, capitalist included, have developed'.[150]

In a verbal message, sent through the Hubei Party chief, to the Central Committee in Peking, Deng drew a line in the sand. 'Anyone who is against reform', he warned, 'Will be put out of his office'.

Almost for three weeks the journey was hushed up in Peking. But garrison after garrison became enthusiastic, cadre after cadre was convinced, special economic zone after special economic zone sided with him. In Shenzhen, a birthplace of China's economic miracle, Deng spoke to an enthusiastic crowd. 'The success of Shenzhen clearly proves that there was no need to worry whether we are following "socialism" or "capitalism." Only suspicious people raise this question, and they are self-defeated.' For the comrades in Peking, he had this warning: 'If we don't continue to improve people's standard of living, if we don't continue to build the economy, there will only be a dead-end road for our Party'. He was also fending off objections against the boom in Shenzhen and other southern cities that were being fuelled largely by foreign investments. 'These [foreign joint venture] firms make profits under our laws, pay taxes, and provide out workers with jobs and pay', he added. 'What's wrong with that?'

Deng's message was enticing: wealth through pragmatism. 'Where the local conditions permit it, development should proceed as quickly as possible. We should not be concerned about anything as long as we stress efficiency and quality and develop an export-orientated economy. Slow growth leads to stagnation or even a step back. ... Guangdong should catch up with the four small Asian dragons in 20 years time.[151] Deng was to win his last battle as he had the global economy behind him.

The resistance in Peking cracked in March, shortly before the annual conference of the National People's Congress. In a two-day, all-member Politburo meeting, Deng's speeches from his southern tour were studied carefully, and the Politburo agreed to endorse his ideas. The next day, on 11 March, six weeks after his trip to the south, the official Xinhua News Agency finally reported what had occurred. It was the lead story. Deng's Southern Tour had become the policy of the Party. Jiang had to follow Deng's opening rhetoric and advocated the 'use of all the productive forces and outstanding cultural progress that the capitalist forces have created'.[152] Also Prime Minister Li Peng let it be known that 'we must take a bolder approach with reform and the opening (of the country)'.[153] The state television showed a documentary about Deng's 'Great Journey to the South' and the People's Daily printed his most important ideas.

By the time the Party met for its 14th congress, Deng had cleared the way for his reforms. His keenest opponents, such as Yang Baibing and Yang Shangkun who had a strong foothold in the army, were relieved of their influential posts. The Party congress, held in October, established as its guiding principle Deng Xiaoping's slogan that the country should 'build socialism with Chinese characteristics'. Second, it made clear that the country's goal in reforming its economy was to build a 'socialist market economy'. Finally, it assured people that the Party must focus on economic development.

In the end Deng was like a surfer. At the right moment he rode the right wave. The wise old tactician had managed to win the population over and sensed that even he, as a strong leader was not able to challenge the forces of globalisation. He left behind a pragmatism for his successors that was new in Chinese history. It was quite clear to him that, 'nobody has gone down this road. That's why we have to tread carefully.'[154] It is exactly for this reason that ideological impartiality is necessary: 'a planned economy is not to be equated with socialism, because even with capitalism there is planning. … (and) also with socialism there are markets. Planning and the market are both means with which one can steer the economy.' To find the right relationship for China was the task of the following generation.

# Chapter 7

# DICTATORSHIP FOR THE COMMON GOOD

China is an island of stability in Asia.

Robert Rubin, US Secretary of the Treasury, 1998

The overview of routine Chinese life became clearer in the nineties. In the course of the decade the communist party had become more composed and convincing in their major political policies than ever before.

The rules according to which the new China was to function were developed and accepted without any huge opposition. The unwritten social contract between the leadership and the people now was clearly defined. Whoever wanted a career in politics, the public service, in the field of law and also in research in the arts and humanities could only do so within the structures that had been set up. One could also succeed in the economy without a party book. Public interest stood way above the interest of the individual. In an interview with the *New York Times* Jiang Zemin summed up the attitude of the party at the end of the decade:

I can tell you with certainty: Should China apply the parliamentary democracy of the Western world, the only result would be that 1.2 billion Chinese people would not have enough food to eat. The result would be great chaos, and should that happen, it would not be conducive to world peace and stability.

Sects and religious communities that could have kindled competing mass movements were firmly suppressed. The communist party continued to rule unchallenged and used its power to create the conditions in which everyone could become affluent. The party's positive attitude regarding the private economy became official when the sixteenth People's Congress in 2002 made the resolve to permit private entrepreneurs as party members. 'What we insist on doing', Jiang elaborated, 'is a combination of the fundamental tenets of Marxism applied to the real conditions in China. But we have to know that Marx and Engels lived more than 150 years ago. The Communist Manifesto was published 153 years ago. It is impossible to apply every single word or sentence they wrote at that time to today's reality. When I was young', Jiang mused, 'I thought Communism would come very quickly, but now I don't feel like this'. Within a socialist wrapping, Chinese life in many areas even more was determined by capitalist competition than in the Western industrialised nations.

During the period of Jiang Zemin's leadership Chinese people had more personal freedom than at virtually any other time in their history. 'China did not achieve political pluralism', comments Nicholas Kristof of the *New York Times*, 'but it did move toward economic pluralism, cultural pluralism, and social pluralism'. This idea, as little as it coincides with our democratic standards, holds true. The agreement also applies to the losers of the reforms. Many farmers who are hardly able to do more than support themselves from their small plots and workers whose fate hinges on outdated state enterprises have been waiting for years so that they can also have a share of the wealth. Their patience and hope feed themselves – for us difficult to understand – on the pride that they are a part of their country which is on its way to becoming a Middle Kingdom once again. It means a lot to them to be a part of it. And within the family networks, many are being looked after by those who are on their way up.

The majority of the Chinese population is rather apolitical and are happy to let themselves be pulled along by the upswing. Property ownership and an improved standard of living remain their goal and education and knowledge their means of attaining it; enjoyment through performance is their creed. Most of the people in this huge group, who are no longer solely found in the coastal cities, do not have the feeling that they have to fight against the state. On the contrary: they have the impression that the state smoothes the way for them, provides them with infrastructure and opportunities that they need for their own advancement. They feel free, as in most cases the interests of the state coincided with their own private interests and still consider the common influence of the state to be normal. In areas where this is not yet the case they can appreciate the slow progress and the successes when they take their problems into their own hands and solve them informally. This contradicts with our perceptions of freedom, but one is reminded of the period of emergence of the German economic miracle when one observes Chinese life today.

Germany already was a democracy. But one could only trust it conditionally as the nationalist socialist personnel not only sat at the middle level but also in decisive positions. Besides either oneself or close relatives were involved with the Third Reich. Only very few tried to shed light on history within such parameters, and those who did it anyway, did not have the silent majority behind them. Their self-confidence was strengthened with every new jacket or skirt that the people could afford. They planned and lived for the first car or at least for a better motorbike, for holidays, new furniture, perhaps even a private flat.

The demonstrations and economic crises of the eighties were a warning to the Chinese leadership: a gigantic economic ascent would be the only compensation for political freedom – at least for the time being. To be able get those who had their doubts onto their side and to keep them there was crucial for the stability of the country. The ambitious ones from the intellectuals whose conventional routes of ascent had been blocked after 1989 looked for career opportunities in the economy. The gates were wide open for anyone who wanted to become rich and contribute to the strengthening of China's economy. Even some young painter who had made an entrance in the eighties with high ideals was overwhelmed by the new desire for wealth, and began to paint 'pop art with slanted eyes' for the Western market.

Song Gang was one of the young intellectuals who was very successful as a businessman.[1] To a certain extent he owed his prosperity to the suppression of the democracy movement. Originally Song was a political scientist. In 1989 as the chief editor, he created the reform-orientated *Newspaper for Foreign Policy*. The paper was closed down in the weeks of June 1989: 'Actually I still had a desk, but no longer had a chair', he recalled. 'It was clear to my friends and me that the political door had been shut on us.' Ten years later he came to be wealthy by trading in camera bags and now belongs to the wealthy upper middle class. 'The more dissatisfied that one is as an intellectual the more one needs economic success', according to Song. 'And when all the signs are pointing to the economy, one is then just pulled along.' The leadership under President Jiang Zemin had established a system in the nineties in which one was allowed to do many things but some things were very dangerous, summarises Song. One was allowed to earn money and also to spend it and one could even openly grumble about the leadership. However it is strictly forbidden to question the autocracy of the communist party and to demand political freedom.

Even at the beginning of the twenty-first century those Chinese who form their own party or call for democratic reforms are punished with several years in prison. In this way Ouyang Yi a 35-year-old secondary school teacher was arrested in December 2002. He belonged to a group of 192 Chinese democracy activists who had published a petition for democratic reforms on the Internet in November.[2] In February 2002 the renowned journalist Wang Binzhang was sentenced to life imprisonment because of 'espionage and the preparation of an armed rebellion'.[3] In the spring of 2004 Jiang Yanyong, a high ranking 72-year-old military surgeon, who had been celebrated one year earlier as he had contributed to uncovering the SARS crisis, was arrested for a short while after he had demanded coming to terms with the Tienanmen crisis. He is once now to move but is not allowed to talk to the Western press.[4]

Those people, whose statements are sanctioned by the state, however belong to a minority. Many are only able to publicly air their displeasure without being punished if their position within society allows them to do so. Pan Shiyi the building contractor from Peking gave up a secure mid-level job in the oil Ministry at the beginning of the nineties and went to seek his fortune in the real estate industry on the southern tropical Chinese island of Hainan. Nowadays he is one of the most prominent building contractors in Peking where he has built several dozen luxury high-rise blocks in the best locations. Now he can afford to openly criticise the government's town planning, without having to feel like a dissident, but rather with the authority of a successful specialist: 'Big mistakes have been made. China's town planners are not conscious of how far reaching the consequences of their decisions are. Every time the politicians plan too much, there is a disaster – just like in Shanghai's Pudong.'[5]

Others on the other hand do not identify themselves with the official party line but nevertheless have adapted outwardly. Song Gang belongs to this group. When he visits his bag factories, which are located a good three hundred kilometres from Peking, he takes in a lot of the far-off atmosphere of the modern metropolises. He often talks to the mostly young women who sit behind their old sewing machines in long rows and fight with the unwieldy plastic material. Through this he has observed that the question of political freedom may have disappeared as a topic of public discussion, but it has not disappeared from the minds of the people. It is not a question of the large theories he says. The people do not spend a great deal of time thinking about whether they can vote for the president or not. Neither do they care about the dissidents who have been locked up. Yet they do want to be able to have more of a role in decisions regarding their direct surroundings; they want legal security. In times of rapid economic development this is particularly important. Young workers demonstrate because they no longer receive their wages and see no chance of success through the legal process. There are tens of thousands of protests in China on a yearly basis. Song knows about the tactical tricks of the demonstrators and the police: 'They learn how to deal with one another'. Because the police always drive the young agitated workers apart they have in the meantime mobilised their parents and grandparents. The police complain to the old people: 'Go home!' They retort back, 'We old people are also suffering'. And the police are hesitant to physically attack the frail pensioners. Song smiles to himself: 'the demonstrators have created an equilibrium of power. Now they can negotiate.' Sometimes the police loose their patience and then it gets very brutal. The victims have no chance of being compensated for the mistreatment.

Song considers a multi-party system quite sensible at the local level. 'Its also good for the economic environment that the cadres have competition.' He certainly does not want to become politically active himself. 'I lack the rebelliousness.' Also a scientific career aboard was never a consideration for him. 'I can only judge China in China', he said. But it would have been easy for the English-speaking scientist to have gone to Europe. In 1987 he spent a year conducting research at the university in Rotterdam. In the difficult times after 1989 he stayed in Peking and managed to survive with a small shop in which he sold stationary and business cards. The business ran well but it bored him after some time. Then he traded in computers. In the middle of the nineties at the height of the economic boom he opened his own company and specialised in the production of camera bags. Soon he was able to afford a VW Jetta and pay for it in cash – as also for the cost of the repair of the dents that he managed to get in the beginning. Prosperity put him at ease. And political enlightenment had its limitations: 'I better not tell my workers what the camera bags cost in Germany.'

The leadership for the time being accepted the gap between the rich and the poor as a necessary evil. 'When Deng Xiaoping initially decided to let one segment of the population get rich first', Jiang Zemin explained, 'everyone knew that income disparity would be a natural by-product – it was inevitable. But our expectation was that entrepreneurs, by creating new products and starting new businesses, would lift the entire population by providing more jobs with better pay and by offering an increasing variety of goods and services that would be available for everyone. It is the government's role to take care of the less fortunate, to redistribute income, to find a better balance between rich and poor, and to stop illegal moneymaking. The system is hardly perfect, but it does work. I don't know what's better – certainly not the old way where nobody had anything.' *U've never had it so good.*

Disillusionment characterised the mental climate. Now the leadership had to show that it was capable of guaranteeing prosperity in all circumstances.

* Cp W.S. Churchill on W.l. dmcy.

Economic experts were necessary but these were rare in the nomenclature. One of the few exceptions was Zhu Rongji who already as the Mayor of Shanghai in the second half of the eighties, and had seen through the macro-economic mechanisms. In 1991 Deng made him Vice Prime Minister: 'Zhu Rongji is the only one who understands something about economics', was Deng's opinion.[6] Zhu needed two years to be able to anchor himself in the hierarchy of power in Peking. There were not easy times: growth was like a roller coaster ride; the economy alternatively sagged or overheated.

In 1992 China's GDP grew by an unprecedented 12.8 per cent, a number that far exceeded the officially estimated 6 per cent. By the end of that year, China's economy was starting to overheat, threatening to unleash inflation. The business world was beginning to notice China's surging economy. 'The numbers are indeed dazzling', reported the *Asian Wall Street Journal*. 'In 1976, 80 per cent of China's production was directly owned by the state. Now it is about half. The economy is growing at a sizzling 12 per cent, easily the fastest in the world. Foreign exchange reserves are brimming. And the system is delivering the goods to the emerging middle class. In 1980 the masses bought 600 washing machines a day; today they're soaking up about 40,000. Thirteen years ago some 10,000 televisions were sold daily; today it's about 70,000. These are facts no sceptic can ignore.' ✳

At the same time inflation was spiralling out of control. The banks hardly had cash reserves after they had, as Zhu called it, financed excessive real estate projects with 'chaotic credit'.[7] Finally he sat behind the wheel and took up the position as the head of the central bank in July 1993. This was not a month too soon. Inflation had reached a new record high of 21.7 per cent. In June 1993 he announced a 16-point plan, which was the first macro-economic concept in the history of China that corresponded to modern, globally established economic methods. Zhu introduced rules for the granting of loans, a policy of money supply, increased interest and froze the price of goods, which particularly fuelled inflation. He fought the black market and ensured that the banks had cash reserves so that account holders could withdraw their money whenever they wanted and did not get the impression that the state was insolvent. The state's indebtedness was now to take place in a more controlled manner.

He needed money for the implementation of this concept. It was not possible to do this through conventional methods such as a better system of tax investigation. And so he reached back to the old levers of the command economy and introduced the so-called Tanpai system, which meant just about the same as 'put your cards on the table'. State employees and enterprises were forced to take up national bonds according to quotas. This did

✳ Unless they are not ~~so~~ materialistic.

not correspond with the ideals of the market economy, but it did work as a transitional phase and it did allow China to retain a high degree of independence.

Parallel with this the state also had to fight inflation primarily because it could not expect people to be asked to go to the till by the state, whilst their savings melted away at the same time. This would otherwise only have resulted in them spending even more money or secretly exchanging it into US dollars. The population stayed amazingly calm, partly due to rationality and partly because they could still feel the shock of 1989's unrest in their bones. But their patience had limitations.

In 1994 rumours of grain shortages led to panic buying and food-hoarding frenzies, spiking prices by as much as 50 per cent. The national inflation rate was 22 per cent, the worst since the People's Republic was founded. Urban inflation, driven by quick-profit real estate construction, was higher still. In order to take the power out of the black market and to diminish speculation on the international capital market, Zhu increased the foreign exchange reserves. This was possible as the export machine was once again running at full steam and bringing foreign exchange into the country.

Zhu knew that when Hong Kong once again returned to Chinese rule in 1997, China's stability would be put to the test by the international financial industry. The Hong Kong stock exchange, one of the most developed in Asia, could not be placed under state control. The Chinese had promised the English in the handover agreement that Hong Kong would maintain its status as the most free market economy in the world. The world would be observing to ensure that China stuck to this settlement. In addition the communists not only wanted to overcome the colonial humiliations with their takeover of power, but also wanted to demonstrate to everyone that they knew how to manage a modern economy. China had to be stable enough in order to do this.

Zhu already used the run-up to the handover of Hong Kong to tame intractable top officials. The middle layers of the administration he kept in check with high, almost unattainable demands. At the same time the noticeable success of his policy took the wind out of his opponents sails. At the end of 1996 he succeeded in giving the economy a soft landing. Inflation now stood at around 6.1 per cent whilst growth amounted to 9.7 per cent. This he owed particularly to the high foreign investment as well as the export boom.

Thus Zhu was able to stabilise the condition of the patient but the illness was far from vanquished, because the Chinese economy suffered as before from a rampant ménage a trois: the state gave the order for growth, the enterprises borrowed money and produced goods with it, which frequently nobody needed, were of an inferior quality or were manufactured in excessive numbers. In all three cases the result was the same: the enterprises had a limited income, could not pay their suppliers and therefore had to again ask the state for credit. With such a going-on there was hardly an end in sight, as this oversupply of credit was just the right thing for many local cadres. In any case, Deng's motto that false growth is better than none, was still valid. At this time Deng was so frail that he was no longer capable of making political declarations. But he still was alive and Zhu was not yet powerful enough to give out an opposing slogan without being accused by his opponents of betraying Deng's ideas. Jiang Zemin the state and party chief whose power gave him more room to manoeuvre wanted to remain a man at the centre and not to place himself too clearly on Zhu's side.

So to get something rolling Zhu at least needed a fitting Deng quotation. 'Production must be of quality', from now on read the truism that the economic reformer now carried in front of himself like a shield.[8] Those who were unable to make profits out of the state loans had obviously produced bad quality. This was new: under Mao the enterprises had received money and with it fulfilled plans; under Deng they had received money in order to increase the turnover; now they were to receive money only when they at least did not make a loss from it. This new guideline had already been announced at the annual economic conference of the state council in the spring of 1992, before Deng's journey to the south: 'Whoever invests, pays or goes bankrupt.'[9] But there remained a huge gap between theory and practice. The state entrepreneurs had been quick to relax with the justified hope that they out of all people would not be hit by the shots that went into the thicket of the indebted state enterprises. From their point of view there was even a certain logic in producing more bad loans, because the more loans you were unable to pay back, the more the stability of the country was endangered – and the less likely the Government would be able to assert itself. 20 to 40 per cent of the state loans could not be paid back in 1997; 70 per cent of these had been given to state enterprises.[10] In fact while there were individual successes,[11] but the situation was not under control. And the half-a-dozen reductions in the interest rate between 1986 and 1986 did not help much.

The Chinese were only educated in free market thinking through increasingly closer ties with foreign companies, because entrepreneurs who managed their business badly thoroughly disgraced themselves in the industry, and so eventually the chaff was separated from the wheat. Those who worked together with foreign partners could improve the quality of their products, could learn about modern business structures and thereby for example lower the cost of wages. In many operations the separating out went right through the enterprise. Some departments improved themselves, whereas others were left behind.

One could not think about a fundamental reform of the economy as long as China did not possess a functioning financial system, which distributed capital efficiently according to free market criteria. Putting the banks back on their feet was easier than the modernisation of the state enterprises. Four major national banks had been established in 1994, which were to become the pillars of the national financial system: the Bank of China (BoC), the Agricultural Bank of China (ABC), the China Construction Bank (CCB) and the Industrial and Commercial Bank of China (ICBC). The economic planners hoped that the competing banks would quickly shed their enormous personnel apparatus of 150,000 to 600,000 people to a healthy size and make it more professional. 'Banks will only support businesses that make a profit and can guarantee the repayment of their loans', announced Wang Zhongyu, who at the time was the Minister of the National Economic and Trading Commission. This was to remain wishful thinking. The banks were not strong enough and the market was not developed enough to balance out the bad loans with profitable business.[12] According to official statistics, 25.4 per cent of all loans could still not be paid back in 2002. The investment bank Goldman Sachs estimates that in reality the mountain of debt is at least twice as high. And this after the Government had taken debts to the value of 170 billion Euros from the banks in 1999 and handed them over to be wound up by national debt managers. 'Actually this should have been the banks' last free lunch', the Minister of Finance, Xiang Huaicheng declared at the end of 2002. 'But to be honest – there are going to have to be a few more.' Since the end of 2001 international investment companies have also taken part in the disposal of inherited burdens. At that time a consortium under the directive of the investment bank Morgan Stanley bought the first package of securities, mostly shares in Chinese companies, with a paper value of 100 million US dollars for 1.2 billion US dollars. So to the Deutsche Bank AG took over a package to the value of a good 300 million Euro.

In order to reactivate the competition and to experiment with an alternative to the state system, the leadership approved of Minsheng in 1996, the first private Chinese bank. 'State bankers don't understand private customers', explained Jing Shuping the chairperson of the bank's board and founder of the enterprise. 'We on the other hand also try to educate our customers to becoming better business people.'[13] In 2002 the enterprise already made a profit of 108 million Euros. Jing's bank is also considered the most modern in China. Its market share is admittedly so small that it only has a minor significance for the national economy. Western banks still hardly play a role in the Chinese market. So far the 181international banks that have taken up residence in China have a market share of 1.5 per cent; they also do not calculate more than 3 per cent in the medium term, despite the agreed opening of the market through the membership of the WTO. At the same time there is huge pressure to open up the market. 'China is growing so quickly, the global market so slowly', as a Western banker formulates it.[14] China's small, half national banks have certainly already been able to test co-operation with foreigners for several years: five per cent of the Pudong Development Bank belongs to the American Citigroup; The Royal Bank of Scotland holds 10 per cent of the Bank of China; the Hong Kong Shanghai Banking Corporation (HSBC) owns 8 per cent of the Bank of Shanghai. The Shenzhen Development Bank lets itself be completely managed by foreign bankers.[15] There is a strategy behind this that has worked satisfactorily in other industries: China's banks are to get international credit institutes on their team – and let them do all the hard work. For their capital and management know-how the foreigners receive access to the market as junior partners.

First experiences with international public offerings of the smaller banks show mixed results. The Bank of Communications, almost 20 per cent of which belongs to the HSBC, was one of the most successful IPOs in 2005 and obtained more than 1.6 billion Euro. The Minsheng Bank on the other hand had to call off its initial offering. The leadership, however, concluded that the strategy is sufficiently successful, and wants to promote still more partnerships between foreign and domestic financial institutions. The beginning is maybe very promising but economically it has hardly any weight.

A further strategy of the banking reforms involves the co-workers of the Chinese enterprises learning about international business practices in the overseas branches which they then transplant back home. The BoC is currently represented in 23 countries and does 50 per cent of its business outside of China. At the beginning of the decade, 90 per cent of the Chinese trade in foreign exchange was handled by the BoC. In Hong Kong it is the second largest local banking house after the HSBC.

But even these progressive measures did not bring convincing success because the communist party would not budge on central issues. 'The tradition of letting party organisations manage the national financial sector has to be broken', the influential Chinese economic magazine *Caijing* demanded. As a first step the Government had after all separated the supervision of the banks from the fiscal policy tasks of the central bank, the People's Bank of China.

The competition among the four major banks and the small, more agile private banks, the overseas business of the Bank of China, the asset management companies, the foreign involvement and the new organisational structure did however move the financial system forward. Still the bad loans continued to mount and the Chinese banks could only be as good as the Chinese enterprises. The reform of the state enterprises therefore set the momentum for the banks. Meanwhile the private economy increasingly delinked itself even further from the state banks. The private sector accounted for approximately a third of the Chinese economy, but less than 1 per cent of the loans came from the state banks.[16] Private businesses acquire their money from illegal private financial institutions, which have become increasingly efficient in the last few years. The leadership had to learn that only partial success can be gained if one tries to reform individual isolated industries and in the process one neglects the reciprocal effects on the interwoven economic components. But as long as the road may be to an efficient modern economy, Zhu had at least stabilised the economic system to the extent that it withstood all of the shocks of the late nineties.

As had been expected for a long time, Deng Xiaoping died during the night of the 19th of February 1997. It was conceivably an unfavourable moment in time, several months before the handover of Hong Kong. China held its breath, as the death of emperors and prominent politicians had frequently resulted in unrest. But it was quiet on China's streets; demonstrations as well as passionate displays of mourning did not take shape. The feeling of self-esteem was solidified and well-being and suffering of the people was less dependent on a ruler than ever before. The succession had been sorted out long before, and Deng had personally seen to it that no cult had developed around his person. He had expressly forbidden a Mausoleum for himself and had instructed that his ashes should be scattered from a plane above the sea. Only his closest family and Hu Jiantao, Jiang Zemin's successor whom he had personally selected, were allowed to render him the last honour. With this Deng had made provisions for personnel for at least the next 15 years. Additionally he was clearly no longer a positive figure with whom to identify. In the end when he had ordered the protest movement to be violently disbanded that he became regarded as a person with as much of a dark as a light side.

Nevertheless it still took several weeks before the leadership could be sure: Deng's death would not overshadow the handover of Hong Kong. Since the start of the open door policy there was no other event that was so important for the Chinese feeling of self-value. It represented the end of colonial humiliation and at the same time the increasing integration into the global economy. It was the first time that China possessed a first class international stock exchange; and the first time that the international financial community could reward and punish China in seconds; it was the first time that China had one of the most important ports in the world and one of the most modern airports at its disposal.

When choosing a chief executive overseeing the administration of the city, Peking made sure to appoint a man of clear loyalties: in December of the preceding year, Jiang had already met with the Hong Kong shipping magnate Tung Chee-Hwa who was to become head of government in the Special Economic Region. In 1986, Tung's business had been bailed out by a 120 million US dollar loan backed by the Chinese government, and many Hong Kong citizens had serious doubts where Tung's allegiance lay. But even the prospect that China could only grant the city the status of playing second fiddle to the self-created metropolis of Shanghai, had not shaken the confidence in the Hong Kong economy. The stock exchange and the real estate market boomed – although the leadership in Peking and many analysts had been suspicious of the high growth.

The handover on the 30th of June went according to plan. It rained incessantly. The British Governor Chris Patten and his family wept movingly as they left behind England's last important colony on the Britannia. Around midnight the Chinese soldiers moved into the former British barracks. They avoided materialistic gestures. The major Chinese entrepreneurs, the so-called tycoons, who for decades had been the engines of the Hong Kong economy, had already made arrangements with the leadership in Peking as well as with Britain. On the outside everything appeared as in the old days.

But it was only to take a few days before Hong Kong and China were dragged into an economic whirlpool, the waves of which sloshed all the way to Germany: the Asian Crisis. 'The financial storm came suddenly, without any warning, like a natural disaster, sweeping away every tree and destroying every building', recalls Qian Qichen, the former Chinese foreign minister.

One day after the handover ceremony Thailand had to free its currency, the Baht which had for along time been firmly pegged to the US dollar. Within one day it fell by 20 per cent; in return Thailand's US dollar debts rose by 20 per cent as well. The Tiger nation had overdone it.[17] On the 28th of July Thailand asked the International Monetary Fund (IMF) for help. Two weeks later a rescue plan was agreed upon with a credit amounting to a value of 17 billion US dollars. And the Asian economies, which at the time had seemed sure of their global supremacy and forecasts of 'Pacific' twenty-first century, not been so strongly interconnected with each other, the problem could have been solved. However everywhere in Asia there were investors who had thoughtlessly gambled in Thailand and now found themselves in difficulties. Added to this Thailand could all of a sudden sell its products so much cheaper than the surrounding countries, whose currencies were still being traded at a much higher rate.

The day of horror, which actually rang in the Asia crisis, was the 14th of August 1997 – six weeks after the handover of Hong Kong. The region's economies collapsed into themselves like houses of cards. Indonesia's Central Bank had to float its Rupee; five months later it only had a seventh of its original value. In October the Government in Jakarta had to ask the IMF for assistance. On the 22nd of December the US rating agency Moody's agreed upon the credit worthiness of Indonesia. At the beginning of November Sanyo Securities, the first Japanese securities house after the Second World War, filed for a petition in bankruptcy. On the 20th of November the South Korean Won fell to a record low; on the 15th of December it was floated. One day later South Korea asked the IMF for emergency aid in the value of 20 billion US dollars. On the 8th of December 56 out of Thailand's 58 finance companies went bankrupt, after it was made public that the country's foreign debt with 90 billion dollars had reached 50 per cent of its gross national product.

Hong Kong was also sucked into the whirlpool. On the 15th of August a massive wave of speculation had already started against the Hong Kong dollar. Hong Kong was able to fend off several waves with Peking's assistance. The real estate prices could certainly not be saved. They fell by two-thirds. So too the Hong Kong stock exchange collapsed dramatically; on the 23rd of October alone the Hang Seng index plunged by over 10 per cent. As the Hong Kong stock market was considered the last bastion of Asia, the large stock exchanges of the world reacted severely and likewise gave way.

The Chinese leadership was gravely concerned. Would their half-reformed national economy be able to withstand the strain? Now they reaped the rewards as they had not been so rash as the governments of other South East Asian countries who, in the euphoria of the upswing, had indebted themselves overseas in the short term, heavily and at high interest. Because many investors wanted to have a share of the growth of the Asian tigers, the countries were offered plentiful amounts of money and many Asian banks declined with the belief that things would always continue in this way, with appropriate reserves. In their households the governments also planned with a grossly uneven relationship between their own capital and loans. The state, businesses and private households lived on the flow from overseas.

At the same time most of the currencies were firmly pegged to the US dollar. The state guaranteed therefore that one could exchange the local currency at a fixed rate into US dollars at any time. So if no one in the financial market wanted to do the deal, the state would carry out the exchange. When suddenly an enormous amount of Thai Baht was to be changed into US dollars because the investors had lost their confidence in the currency, the state had to make immense quantities of US dollars available. However the reserves quickly dried up and the state was unable keep up with the fixed rate of exchange. The ones who had not yet saved in the US dollar realised the problem, the currency collapsed. Companies who had their income in the local currency and debts in US dollars could become bankrupt within a day. The former gushing springs of credit ran dry, money became scarce and consumption collapsed. The heart of the economy stopped beating.

In their exuberance the countries had wanted to enjoy the advantages of the liberalised financial markets and so the seemingly endless flow of credit, without having to be conscious of the disadvantages such as currency fluctuations and over-indebtedness. Those who venture into financial dependence on overseas credit can no longer act independently. National economies that get themselves into debt overseas, both heavily and in the short term, are therefore well advised for their own benefit to make the currency freely convertible, so as to get a constant feedback on their own credit worthiness and the sentiment of the global economy. Only those that have huge foreign exchange reserves at their disposal can afford to firmly peg their currency to the US dollar.

The Chinese government had already recognised these mechanisms of the international financial world in the eighties and had decided, for historical reasons too, to remain independent from foreign countries. In the interest of investment and long-term growth it declined the option of quick money. Foreign countries should not put their capital into speculative businesses but into machines and factories that could not quickly be disposed of in times of crisis. With this huge wall China succeeded in protecting itself from the invaders of the modern (world), the international financial speculators. However the weak points in the Chinese system also became visible during the Asian crisis. The South East Asian currency landslide had hardly begun when Prime Minster Zhu issued directives to frantically look for the cracks. He found them in the economically progressive southern provinces. Particularly Hong Kong's neighbouring province of Guangdong felt that it was a tiger state and acted accordingly.

It was the biggest beneficiary of Deng's open door policy. In 1979 he had assigned the Deputy President Rong Yiren in establishing investment houses, which were to attract foreign capital. 'You will manage an enterprise that will be an open window to the outside world', he warned Rong at the time, who was known as the 'red capitalist' and had already been a successful entrepreneur before the founding of the People's Republic. 'You find the personnel, manage the business and are responsible for everything. Do not build up a bureaucratic enterprise. Accept what is rational and reject what is irrational. You will not be punished if you make mistakes. You are to manage the business with the methods of the economy and conclude contracts according to commercial criteria. Only sign if it brings profit and foreign exchange. Otherwise don't sign.'[18] There is hardly another document that shows more clearly the mixture of the down-to-earth nature, craftiness and tremendous naiveté with which Deng groped his way forward. Nevertheless the concept worked for a period of 20 years. The China International Trust and Investment Corporation (Citic), which was established in October 1979, operated its business very successfully and in the middle of the eighties built the first high-rise building next to the International Diplomats Club in Peking. The concern's offshoot in Hong Kong, which is run by Rong's son Larry Yung, is one of the most successful Chinese conglomerates.

The Guangdong International Trust and Investment Corporation (Gitic), an investment house that was set up according to a similar model in the booming most southern province of Guangdong was especially ambitious. It levered the control mechanisms of the central authorities in that it forged coalitions of interest with foreign investors against Peking. Just like Thailand and Indonesia it borrowed a lot of money in the short term without the central government in Peking being informed about it. The province of Guangdong hardly felt the risk. Although it has a gross domestic product which is larger than Thailand's it could assume that the central government in Peking would give it support with fresh credit in case of an emergency.[19] The fact that it had so far covered all of the province's debts out of consideration for the stability of the country was sufficient for the international banks to lend Gitic money under favourable conditions, because the Western financial institutes, and above all the Germans, had come to know the Chinese state as a reliable borrower since the opening of the economy and became involved in business without demanding a written guarantee from Peking. It was sufficient for them that it 'was commented on with a nod'[20] when they mentioned their provincial business dealings during discussions with the central authorities in Peking. Between 1986 and 1998 Gitic alone started up almost twenty different offshoots in Japan, Hong Kong, the USA and Europe, whose dubious investments that mostly went to the dogs.[21] A subsidiary company of Gitic, a so-called red chip was listed on the Hong Kong stock exchange. The shares were oversubscribed by 892 times and managed to fill the coffers with a converted amount totalling 8.5 billion Euros. The managers from Canton were proud of their coup. They now wanted to be told less of what to do by the central government in Peking. Their arrogance decimated Peking's power. At the beginning of 1997 Gitic already controlled 4.5 per cent of all the Chinese banks' and the financial sector's assets. This was a critical amount capable of shaking the whole country, and definitely enough to start rocking the pegging of the yuan to the US dollar. A gateway had been created for foreign interests that became dangerous for the whole country during the Asian crisis, as the creditors could now unite and put the Cantonese government under pressure to pay back the borrowed money at short notice. China suddenly saw itself as being in a similar situation as the Tiger states. Also other provinces, and the tropical island of Hainan in particular, had cleared the way for international speculators.[22] The financial world looked anxiously upon China. A devaluation of the yuan would draw the region even more deeply into the crisis.

The greatest capital, China's stability was at risk, the government acted quickly and decidedly. In July two of the largest institutes were closed down on the island of Hainan. In a sitting of the central committee Zhu elucidated that that biggest problems, 'result from risks that cadres have thoughtlessly taken'.[23] The closure was also meant as a warning for other provinces, particularly Guangdong. 'The mother has no more milk, even if the children continue to suck', wrote the *Jinrong Ribao*, China's national financial paper.[24] But the local cadres who considered themselves to have good economic statistics – Guangdong provided approximately 40 per cent of Chinese exports and pulled in a quarter of foreign investments – were beyond all criticism and did not hear the signals.[25] Yet the danger for the stability of China that had been caused by them was at least as threatening as the suppression of the freedom movement. At the end of September, two and a half months after Thailand had kicked off the Asian crisis, the central bank forbade the provinces 'the authorisation of financial institutions without permission and the illegal operation of financing transactions'.[26] The power struggle between the central authorities and the provinces was historically loaded: the new warlords were now the 'money lords', the powerful provincial princes who fought for supremacy and in the process had won large foreign banks as allies. Both the economic competitive ability and also the ability to control China were now at risk. The international financial community was waiting for a call to order from the leadership. Zhu had to get it straight that, although more power had been given to the provinces through the economic market reforms, it was the central government that continued to determine the rules of the game and also could enforce adherence to them.

Zhu sent a reliable controller as a Vice Governor into the independently-minded province in order to inspect the mountain of debt.[27] His report was devastating. The Cantonese had far more bad loans than Peking had expected: Gitic in the value of 2 billion US dollars and the state enterprise Guangdong enterprise to the value of 4.1 billion US dollars. The collapse of the central government's power had already progressed a long way. Zhu took advantage of the bad news in order to take drastic action. The sudden closure of Gitic in the middle of the Asian crisis resulted in an enormous loss of faith in China as a location for investment and now particularly focused attention on its weaknesses. It was for this reason that Zhu first of all played for time,[28] but on the 6th of October he let Gitic and the Guangdong enterprises be closed down because of over-indebtedness. As a majority of the outstanding debts were owed to foreign banks, amongst them the Dresdner Bank and the Commerzbank, the bankers began a counter-attack and described the closure as 'illegal'. They publicly voiced their doubt regarding the stability of the Chinese financial institutes and threatened to immediately demand the return of a further 10 billion US dollars. A delegation consisting of bankers and ambassadors, lead by representatives of the American investment bank Morgan Stanley travelled to Canton with the demand that the foreign commitments must first of all be served. The chief of the Chinese liquidation committee responded curtly to this: 'the Chinese insolvency laws do not treat foreigners as a matter of priority'.[29] As the foreign creditors did not have written guarantees and the central government had already made it clear in 1997 that it would not vouch for a second-class guarantee, the result of the power struggle was obvious. 'The Chinese government will not take the responsibility for the debts of financial institutions that were not guaranteed at the different levels. The foreign banks have to secure their risks by themselves. This is in accordance with international standards.'[30]

This was a risky game to play. On the one hand the costs and the damage to their image could be enormous. On the other hand the international economy had gone back to the agenda relatively quickly after the suppression of the protest movement. Also after the Asian crisis the world needed a stable China more than ever. It was for this reason that the leadership decided to let the international banks go away empty-handed. Soon it became evident that they had played the right cards. The banks did not want to risk a long-lasting forfeit of their relations with China. The public threats resounded without major consequences. The raising of the interest rate could not seriously press China. In fact the shares of the Chinese enterprises listed in Hong Kong, the so-called red chips, fell abysmally and the Gitic share eventually had to be taken from the market. But as all the Asian shares had already been free-falling for a year, this did not really tip the scales. China dragged out the corruption scandal for so long, until it was inconspicuously ended in March 2003. Out of the debts of 5.6 billion only 2.4 billion were legally classified as free of dispute by the Chinese courts. The 110 foreign banks lost approximately 75 per cent of their capital contributions.[31] Guangdong was left with bad loans to the value of 20 billion US dollars. 'If Guangdong were an independent country it would go down the same path as Thailand', commented Hong Kong's *South China Morning Post*.

The international investors' confidence in Guangdong province returned quickly. Actually in the first three months of 1999 foreign investment still fell by 24 per cent these after it began to rise again.[32] 'Guangdong is back in business', was the press agency Reuters headline. The provincial rulers were replaced and Guangdong was once again firmly led by the central government. Mandarin was introduced as the compulsory language for the whole administration instead of Cantonese. The protective power of the national state had saved the province. Additionally, China had tested its economic and political influence as well as its room to manoeuvre within the world. For the first time in hundreds of years, the Chinese leadership once again dared to put in a word in world political issues and to act according to its own interests. A new power struggle for sovereignty in the Asian crisis had begun. The two Chinese currencies, the yuan and the Hong Kong dollar, became the issue in this power struggle. Both currencies, which were tied to the US dollar at similar rates, played a decisive role in the progress of the Asian crisis. China had the choice to devalue both currencies and thereby adapt itself to the region's rapidly fallen currencies. Through this Chinese products would have become cheaper on the world market and become more competitive. However devaluation would also have had the consequence that the currencies of other countries affected by the Asian crisis would have slid further, placing an even greater burden on the international financial markets.

At first the USA took up the position of autocrats over the crisis.[33] Josef Stiglitz the winner of the Nobel Prize in Economics and at that time the chief political economist of the World Bank, tried to convince Prime Minister Zhu of the fact that the yuan needed to be traded in a wider framework, because China could not possibly hold onto a currency in the long term that did not correspond to real market conditions.[34] However this is exactly what China wanted to prove to the world – it turned out to be right. As matters progressed further the Americans had to acknowledge the fact that the succession of events was determined less by them than by China. The diplomats and politicians of other governments also registered, to their surprise, that they had less means of pressure at their disposal to force China into a direction that was to their advantage. After the Chinese leadership had thoroughly examined the situation they came to the conclusion that two-thirds of China's exports were not affected by the Asian crisis, which however only accounted for 30 per cent of the gross national product, because they did not have any competition worth mentioning. For example China exported more than twenty times as many shoes as the whole of the rest of Asia put together. Entrepreneurs who had cheap products manufactured in China did not wander over to Malaysia or Indonesia without hesitation because of the lower labour costs, because it takes far too long to get a new factory up to the appropriate quality standards. Additionally, despite the devaluations of the other Asian countries, China was still at the bottom end of the scale when it came to labour costs. Numerous foreign financial experts agreed with the assessment that China should hold on to its currency.[35] 'The Asian market is so weak that a thrust of exports would be missing,' was the concern raised by Yukon Huang, chief of the World Bank in China. Investment bankers warned of a political loss of face and the damage for the Hong Kong shares and property market.

The pressure from the West certainly did not ease up. China was gambling with a bad hand.[36] The earnings from the crisis-battered global economy sank noticeably and was again reflected in the reduced growth. Politicians in the USA in particular became more nervous by the day, and in January 1998 sent a delegation to China at short notice under the supervision of Lawrence Summers, the Secretary of the Treasury who hailed from a dynasty of Harvard professors.[37]* Prime Minister Zhu who had just been on a inspection of tour the desert province of Gansu did not hurry towards his guests, but instead let them make their way into the hinterland. Towards the end of the discussion Zhu let his final decision be known: 'China is not going to devalue'.[38] The financial world celebrated China as the last stronghold of stability. China immediately used its newly gained reputation to extend its influence in the global economy.

President Jiang Zemin relished the fact that at least in one respect, he finally was on the same level as the USA. In an American newspaper interview he stressed the huge burden that China had taken upon itself in order to secure the region: 'China and American have common interests when it comes to stabilising the national economies of Asia. We want to continue our dialogue with the USA so that we can mutually promote the stability and development of the Asian economy.'[39] The international financial world was interwoven to such an extent that solutions now had to result from a common dialogue. Robert Rubin, the Treasury Secretary in the Clinton Administration preceding Summers, answered: ' I have already said this and can only say it again. China is an island of stability in Asia.'[40] Actually there had hardly been an acute danger of the devaluation of the yuan. The Chinese had recognised globalisation's logic of integration and had placed the right bets. It is more amazing that this gain in world political power was heard in camera, because although the international power struggles were increasingly shifting themselves to the economic arena, the media

*Subsequently ousted from Harvard presidency following incandescently M.C.P. remarks.

as before primarily focused on military and political conflicts. Only with historical distance will the significance of the devaluation battle unfold and in hindsight possibly even be dealt with on a higher historical level than the protest movement of 1989, because neither the demonstrations nor their bloody suppression changed the course of China's development. However since the Asian crisis China is able to have a say when it comes to the world's economic and political issues. Dai Xianglong, the head of the central bank, put forward new demands only weeks after the successful trial of strength. He requested that China be more effectively amalgamated into the coordination of globalisation: 'taking part in the work of the international financial system, will better secure the stability of our national financial system'.[41]

On 26 October President Jiang Zenin embarked on an eight-day landmark visit to the United States. Although he had met President Clinton on four prior occasions, this was the first formal head-of-state summit between the two leaders. At Clinton's suggestion, the two leaders agreed that Treasury Secretary Robert Rubin and Executive Vice Premier Zhu Rongji should work together 'to promote financial stability in Asia'. Jiang was determined to show America the new face of China, and next to talking finances, this included facing some uncomfortable questions from the American press. Jiang was up to the challenge.

During a press conference, the temperature rose considerably when a question about the Tiananmen Revolt was asked. After setting the stage ablaze, the reporter launched a verbal projectile at each president. To Jiang, he said: 'Do you have any regrets about Tiananmen?' His question for Clinton was: 'Are you prepared to lift any of the Tiananmen sanctions, and if not, why not?' Jiang talked first, unfolding his often told, carefully scripted explanation. What had happened, he said, was a 'political disturbance' that had 'seriously disrupted social stability and jeopardized state security'. He defended the 'necessary measures' the Chinese government had to take 'to ensure that our country enjoys stability and that our reform and opening-up proceeds smoothly'. Clinton responded with 'a very different view of the meaning of the events at Tiananmen Square', asserting that a 'continuing reluctance to tolerate political dissent has kept China from developing the level of support in the rest of the world that otherwise would have been developed'. He mentioned the lifting of sanctions on peaceful nuclear energy, while other areas needed to be reviewed 'on a case-by-case basis'. Jiang was ready to counter. 'I would like to speak a few words, in addition, to this question', he said in English. His argument was highlighting the differences between China and America – 'Different historic and cultural traditions, different levels of economic development, and different values'. He added, 'It is just natural for our two countries to hold different views on some issues. The concepts of democracy and human rights and of freedoms are relative and specific, and they are to be determined by the specific national situation of different countries'.

His next stop was the New York Stock Exchange. Standing on the balcony that overlooked the trading floor, he was given the honour of ringing the opening bell. He did not anticipate that this was the place where big Chinese IPOs would take place just a few years later. Less than two weeks after Jiang's return, China offered a good-will gesture to the Americans and released Wei Jingsheng, the most eminent political prisoner, from a labour camp and put him on a flight to Detroit.

The US President's first visit to China at the end of June 1998 became the litmus test of the new relations. From large political gestures to small physical reactions the visit was characterised by the new world political constellations. Clinton's China trip, his longest overseas tour as president, would be a special one: he was not stopping in any other country. Such exclusivity was a tribute to China's importance, and both sides were eager to make things proceed smoothly.

On the one hand the USA wanted to solidify their status as the only global power, and the Chinese on the other hand wanted to make it clear that they once again belonged to the elite group of nations. Already the first contact at the airport showed how the tectonic plates had shifted. Clinton was received by Hu Jintao the Deputy President and Deng Xiaoping's chosen crown prince. When leaving the airplane Clinton did not wave with his hand and instead left it on the railing. He only greeted Hu briefly, then got into the car and slammed the door shut. For almost a minute Hu had to stand on the red carpet on his own and smile into the tinted windows before the convoy set off. American human rights activists had put Clinton under pressure, as the Chinese government had deported thousands of migrant workers from Peking before his visit. Additionally dissidents had been arrested. Clinton called the incident 'disturbing' and his security advisor Samuel Berger reacted strongly: people 'are not debris which one can clear away when a visitor comes'.

Nevertheless Clinton could not get away from showing China respect when it came to the topic of devaluation: 'China behaved firmly and statesmanlike and had thereby done a lot for the entire region', he praised Prime Minister Zhu Rongji, who once again publicly assured him that China would not devalue. The real trial of strength was however at the meeting with the head of state Jiang, who Clinton challenged to a mutual press conference to be broadcast live on television. Jiang left it open until minutes before the discussion if he was going to take the risk and let the Americans wait for him, whilst the 'Eagles Take it easy' came out of the speakers in the Great Hall of the People. As a sign of the new sovereignty he then declared to be ready for it. Clinton bantered in a friendly way, whilst Jiang often during particularly hard attacks stubbornly held his head back and his chin up. Then he showed himself to be quite a match for his American counterpart. 'He even seemed to be enjoying it', was the *International Herald Tribune*'s assessment. He could only win, as the human rights debate increasingly provided a welcoming pretext for him under which the actual power conflicts could be hidden.

It was no coincidence that Clinton was the first foreign statesman who could demand a live broadcast, because for the USA such symbols of power are important, and the more relative their own power becomes. At his departure it was clear that China and the USA were more dependent on one another then ever before. Towards the end of his presidency, China's integration into the global economy and the WTO were some of the few praiseworthy events with which Clinton had been able to secure his entry into the history books.

As had been the case with Clinton's China summit, the tension between the democratic aspirations and economic pressures determined the China debate in the nineties. Federal Chancellor Helmut Kohl was the first Western head of state after 1989 to visit a unit of the People's Liberation Army in 1995. He was accused of ignoring human rights standards by currying favour with the Chinese leadership in order to obtain orders for the German economy. Kohl insisted that the People's Liberation Army was an important element of power in China, which one could not ignore if one wanted to maintain close relations with the country. Moreover the unit had not been involved with the suppression of the 1989 movement.

Things came horribly to a head in 1996 when Otto Graf Lambsdorff, the former Chancellor of the Exchequer and Chairman of the Friedrich Naumann Foundation tried to use the topic of China to hatch a domestic political plot against his party colleague Klaus Kinkel. In the spring of 1996 he let the Dalai Lama, in his role as the representative of the Tibetan government-in-exile, be invited to a conference in Germany, although no country in the world recognised the Tibetan union that had taken up residence in the Indian Daramsala as a legitimate government. The Chinese government protested bitterly and demanded that the term 'government-in-exile' be taken off the invitation. Unusual for an ambassador, the former ambassador Konrad Seitz intervened in the public debate with an interview: 'a realistic politician would say that one would have to exclude human rights. You know Henry Kissinger's statement: "Moral crusaders make dangerous politicians." But pure real politic is not possible for a democracy.

A dialogue over human rights is an essential component of our China policy. But here concrete matters can only be achieved through quiet diplomacy. If one publicly talks about human rights in China one has to do this in an appropriate tone. The topic cannot be misused to get domestic recognition or for oneself to go about playing the moral hero. We want to achieve something, not to compromise China.'[42] Lambsdorff was not ready to compromise and instead arranged a resolution of the Bundestag against China, behind the Minister of Foreign Affairs' back. Kinkel, received the Dalai Lama as a religious leader a year before without huge protests from the Chinese, let the national subsidies for the meeting be cancelled and the resolution of the Bundestag was to the effect weakened to 'Tibet's status under international law has remained contentious among the experts'.[43] The SPD and the CDU however assumed that Tibet belonged to the Chinese federation of states and that there was no reason to move away from the one-China policy. At the same time the parliamentarians were fully aware of China's position of power: 'The Chinese (…) have indiscriminately taken advantage of their position as a contested market: for economic development as well as for interests in regarding foreign policy', according to a member of the Bundestag during the debate. 'They know that Western states and enterprises compete. They skilfully play states off against each other as well as entrepreneurs against their government. The economic competitive struggle takes place anyway. But do we also have to take part in a race of political favours?' On the following Sunday ambassador Seitz was summoned to the Foreign Ministry. He had not counted on the fact that the Chinese would remain tough, and so had let his driver have a day off, Seitz was thus forced to let himself be driven without a national flag in his translator's old orange camping van. There he was informed that the planned visit of Foreign Minister Kinkel could not take place. This was the first time that a German Minister had his invitation cancelled. The representative agency of the Friedrich–Naumann Foundation in Peking has remained closed until today. While the parliamentarians had shown where they stood, they also substantially reduced Germany's possibilities to influence Chinese human rights issues. The Minister of Foreign Affairs who was well known for his quiet commitment to human rights issues had to start off his next visit from a defensive position and to once again build up the confidence of the Chinese. Germany had to acknowledge that the Bundestag resolution did not have any effect as a political tool in relation to China. In the following years one discovered more supple methods of controlling political and social influence, such as for example the German–Chinese dialogue on the rule of law.

The ways and means the leadership dealt with the Falun-Gong sect provides an insight into China's level of development in this issue: On the one hand China is no longer the all-encompassing police state. On the other hand the leadership can use extremely tough measures against individual groups. The biggest surprise was that 6000 to 100,000 Falun-Gong followers from different parts of the country were able to demonstrate on 25 April 1999 in front of Zhongnanhai, the area of government administration, without the state security having noticed them marching up. 'How could it be?' Jiang Zemin exclaimed, 'That in one night the Falun-Gong just appeared? Did they come from under the ground? Where was our Ministry of Public Security? Where was our Ministry of State Security?' And this had happened despite the fact that the day before there had been unrest in the neighbouring port of Tienjin. In this respect the leadership were able to apply full force against even harmless sympathisers of the sect. *The People's Daily* reported in an agitated leading article that it was a matter of a 'serious ideological and political battle', yes about 'the future of the party and the state'.[44]

The biggest challenge related to domestic affairs since 1989 was followed barely two weeks later by the biggest challenge related to foreign affairs. On the 7th of May NATO put the sovereignty of the Chinese, but also their national pride, to a hard test. In the Kosovo war American rockets destroyed the Chinese embassy in Belgrade. In a May memo, shortly after the attack, Jiang had wryly observed, 'If the Falun-Gong masters can foresee everything, why didn't they predict the bombing of our embassy?' Three people were killed and several were injured. They apparently only had older city maps on which the new Chinese embassy building had not been marked – not a very believable reason in view of the high standards of secret target attainment and the accuracy of American guided weapons, which the USA always has always prided itself on. At the same time there were rumours that China had supported the Serbian government with a (radio) communications station on the embassy grounds, which the Americans had wanted to shut down. Peking's first reaction was accordingly severe: 'The Chinese leadership maintains every right for further action'.[45]

Such an attack would most probably have resulted in a war several decades earlier, particularly as NATO was acting in Kosovo without a mandate of the UN Security Council, which as permanent members China and Russia had refused to give it. Peking left it at protests – certainly very hefty and threatening for the USA and Great Britain. For this the Government unlocked a value of indignation and bitterness of the population, not least of all the students, while at the same time they tried not to let the frothing anger boil over. There were violent demonstrations in front of the American and British embassies in Peking. Demonstrators threw stones and Molotov cocktails and caused substantial damage to the buildings. The police let the demonstrators have their way, however at the same time ensured them that they did not storm the US grounds, and so avoid a bloody showdown with heavily armed marines. After US President Clinton had personally expressed his regret, the Chinese government channelled the protests, by blocking off the embassy area and thus having an overview the number of demonstrators.[46] The indignation of the people and the feeling of having been challenged by the USA were genuine and long lasting. Over a period of weeks the students visited a memorial on the Peking University campus, without having been requested by the leadership to do so, and laid white carnations, apples and small Chinese flags in front of a board on which the three photos of the killed Chinese had been stuck. And Vice President Hu Jintao spoke of the 'strong patriotic feelings of the Chinese people'. For the time being there was no dialogue with the USA to reduce the dangerous tensions.

Matters were further complicated by the release in Washington of the Cox Report on 25 May 1999. 'The People's Republic of China', the Cox Report claimed, 'has stolen design information on the United States' most advanced thermonuclear weapons ... including the W-88, a miniaturized, tapered warhead, the most sophisticated weapon the United Staes has ever built'. According to rumours President Jiang Zemin refused to engage in President Clinton's attempted discussions. Nevertheless Peking did not wish for an escalation of tensions. After some time the Chinese leadership finally ended the demonstrations with a call from President Jiang Zemin to return to their jobs and work even harder, so to become even better at confronting future American aggressions.

The new Federal Chancellor, Gerhard Schröder's first visit to China took place in this period of dangerous tensions between China and NATO. The date had been confirmed long time before – during the term of his predecessor and fell in the time of Germany's presidency of the EU, which further increased the political weight of this visit. Peking looked to the Chancellor's Red–Green coalition, about which one still knew very little in China, with great interest. And now the bombs in Belgrade – five days before the date of the visit – resulted in a complete change of the situation. While Germany was not the cause of this action, as an important NATO partner it shared the responsibility. It was inconceivable that that China's government could greet the German Federal Chancellor with military honour and officially receive him together with a huge economic delegation, so that he could take part in a reception that he wanted to host as the President of the EU. It was also inconceivable that the Federal Chancellor could view the Forbidden City or the Temple of Heavenly Peace while only a few

kilometres away the embassies of NATO partner countries were being
stoned by agitated demonstrators.

Yet after the humiliation in Belgrade by the USA, a German cancellation
of the visit had to hurt China and lead to an unnecessary burden on the
traditionally good German–Chinese relations. This was in no way in the
interests of Germany. From the Chinese perspective they made it known
that the visit would only be called off reluctantly, as one did not want to
make Germany liable for the strike on Belgrade. So the issue was to find a
formula that was acceptable to both sides to carry out the visit at the
intended time, and in a way that would take both sides points of view into
account. The German ambassador Hans Christian Ueberschaer, who
through his long service in the Chancellor's office was entrusted with crisis
management, succeeded in coming to an agreement about the procedures of
the visit with Ma Canrong who was the Director of the West European
department and who is nowadays the Chinese ambassador in Berlin. There
was agreement to a one-day working visit of the Chancellor having the
common goal of promoting an end to the Kosovo conflict under an appropriate mandate of the Security Council of the United Nations.

Regardless of this compromise formula, which appeared to be able to
bear the burden, the ambassador had to point out to the Chancellor that there
was not an insignificant residual risk associated with a visit at this time:
could they be sure that Schröder was able to come without there being a
political scandal? Could one trust China's politicians as before, even after
this humiliation by the most important NATO partner – a humiliation, the
extent of which one only becomes aware of if one considers the history
between China and the West? Would Peking not be tempted to let its bitterness and anger out about the 'US-led NATO' on its representative Schröder?
And because the Chancellor's plane due to technical reasons was to land
shortly after the aeroplane that was carrying the coffins of the victims from
Belgrade: wouldn't it be possible for Chinese protocol to let the Chancellor
drive into town at walking speed behind the coffins?

Fully conscious of the risks Schröder decided to embark on his first trip to
China – a visit in which he had to prove his statesmanlike skills with great
empathy and which within 16 hours was to become a sensational success for
foreign policy both for himself and for Germany. The Chancellor landed in
Peking in the early hours of the morning. The Chinese abstained from confronting him with the recently arrived coffins. At the Kempinski Hotel he
informed the Foreign Minister Tang Jiaxuan that he had come to formally
apologise to the Chinese not only as the German head of government but also
on behalf of NATO. This he not only wanted to do privately in the company
of Prime Minister Zhu Rongji but also in front of the Chinese television

cameras for the Chinese people. It was the first time that a leader of a Western nation had apologised to the Chinese. Prime Minister Zhu was so impressed by the impending gesture that he went against the customs of protocol and picked Federal Chancellor Schröder up at the entrance of the Great Hall of the People, after he had only minutes before given his condolences to the survivors of the strike and a last honour to the dead. In the discussion that followed the two heads of government gained each other's trust. During the farewell Zhu asked half jokingly when Schröder now wanted to repeat his official visit to China. The Chinese were never to forget the Federal Chancellor's important gesture, which had not been forced upon Schröder diplomatically. Both the economic ties of both countries, and the common concern of securing peace in the world in a difficult and unclear situation had ensured a close German–Chinese alliance.

For Jiang, the crisis over the Belgrade bombing had meant walking a thin line between not straining relationships with America too much and not appearing too soft on the issue in the eyes of a patriotic Chinese public. Ironic though it was, ten years after demonstrators on Tiananmen Square had erected a Statue of Liberty, many Chinese in 1999 accused their president of being too lenient to the Americans.

Now it was the Chinese people, not their leaders, who were growing more anti-American. In May 1996, a rousing new book called 'China Can Say No', written by five young Chinese intellectuals, declared that it was time for China to stand up for its rights. The book was published only weeks after a Chinese–American confrontation over Taiwan. Briefly before the presidential elections on the island, the People's Liberation Army transferred the main force of its First Army to Fujian, just across the Taiwan Straits, to stage a large-scale military exercise, clearly intended as a warning to the Taiwanese independence movement. President Jiang Zemin was not altogether happy with the operation. But unlike Mao and Deng, who could issue decrees and expect everyone to follow them, Jiang had to build consensus. His way was to bring the appropriate leaders together and float a new policy, then allow discussions, and make the new policy official only when he and his staff were highly confident of its acceptance. But this also meant making compromises on serious issues. Even though Jiang, ever following a temperate course, had managed to scale down the size of the military operation, he was not entirely in control of it.

The USA did not allow the challenge to pass without a reaction. The Seventh Fleet's USS Independence carrier battle group, with one hundred Tomahawk missiles and more than fifty state-of-the-art aircrafts plus a flotilla of advanced warships and a nuclear submarine, began patrolling the Straits, and soon afterwards, a second carrier group entered the theatre of operations – a force whose combined firepower far exceeded that of China's entire navy. With eloquent understatement, US Secretary of State Warren Christopher said that the ships had come only to observe and 'cool tempers' and to 'be helpful if they need to be'. In spite of this show of military might, President Clinton publicly elaborated America's 'three nos' policy regarding Taiwan during his first visit to the People's Republic two years later: No support for Taiwan's independence; no support for 'two Chinas'; and no support for Taiwan's entry into any international organization of sovereign states.

Eventually, the Taiwan crisis of 1996 subsided, but with patriotic sentiment boiling up in China, and an ongoing presence of American military in the region, similar problems continued to haunt US–Chinese relations. In April 2001, two Chinese F-8 fighter jets took off to track an American plane that flew a surveillance mission along China's southern border. One of the Chinese jets was piloted by a veteran named Wang Wei, a pilot with a reputation – the Chinese called him fearless. The Amercians thought he was reckless. After a collision, the Amercian aircraft declared emergency and landed, without permission, at the nearest airstrip – on China's Hainan Island.

'I have visited many countries,' Jiang said in the heat of the spy plane confrontation, 'and seen that it is normal for people to ask forgiveness or say, "Excuse me", when they collide in the street. But the American planes come to the border of our country and do not ask forgiveness. Is this behaviour acceptable?' But soon Jiang returned to a measured approach, against public opinion. 'Given the importance of our countries', he concluded, 'I think we should find an adequate solution to this problem'. Jiang clearly had no intention to allow the incident to escalate. There were more important issues at hand than feeding popular patriotic appetites.

The Asian crisis had not brought China to its knees, but had subjected it to great strain. In order not to risk the stability of the country further Prime Minister Zhu, lowered the pressure of reform in his government address, barely a year after the outbreak of the Asian crisis. Foremost, growth should amount to at least 8 per cent, inflation should be below 3 per cent and the yuan continued to be devalued. Secondly it was a matter of attaining achievements and to give even more influence to the macro-economic structures for steering the economy, such as the Central Bank in particular, which he had built up in the first half of the nineties. State enterprises were to be reformed further and the administration was to be slimmed down. In only third place was the reform of grain distribution, housing reform, reform of medical supplies, reform of the taxation system and the development of new sources of capital.

The Asian crisis had also confirmed to the Chinese leadership that it was advisable to continue to protect itself from the outside world. If the capital markets were opened too quickly then they could easily destroy the national economy, according to Zhu.[47] Modern economic steering mechanisms work only to some extent in China. In the two years after the Asian crisis the Central Bank had by reducing the interest rate three times attempted to make saving less attractive as well as loans cheaper in order to encourage people to consume more and entrepreneurs to invest more. Admittedly this classic method did not have the desired effect for numerous reasons. The population had already acquired their basic goods such as refrigerators, televisions and mobile telephones in the previous 15 years. Now people adapted themselves to the fact that previous social benefits they received from their employers such as housing, minimal rent, pensions and affordable medical care would soon be abolished and be replaced by a new central social system. It was for this reason that most of them hesitated to spend money. From experience they already knew that making provisions for worse times could be vital for survival. As low as the interest rates might go, people saved.[48] The biggest problem for state enterprises was not to access capital, but to use it efficiently. The rule of thumb was now as follows: only when the Chinese population and entrepreneurs react to a lowering of the rate of interest, will China's economy be a market economy.

Neither did the international situation act in favour of the policy of lowering interest rates. Because of the Asian crisis less business people from the neighbouring countries were making purchases in China. Additionally after most countries had devalued their currencies Chinese products had become comparatively expensive. Exports stagnated and the increasing foreign investments did not suffice to keep growth at 8 per cent.

In view of the tense situation the Government had no other choice but to invest itself. Fortunately the building of roads, canals and railway tracks promised a substantial economic value in the still backward country. The funds also had to reach the place they were intended for, and the building projects had to be swiftly put into action. The Peking leadership had to prevent the managers of the regional offices, the state banks and the provincial government from continuing to use the funds for their purposes. They therefore introduced a system that had already successfully helped Mao in controlling local army units. He had appointed eight regional military commanders who in each case had several provinces under them. They were regularly moved around so that they were unable to establish a network against the central government. Following this tradition nine offices of the central bank were now opened, whose bosses rotated in a similar fashion. At the same time the four large banks were inspected by the National Audit

Office a combination of a Court of Auditors and an anti-corruption Ministry. The authority found billions in unaccounted income, tax liabilities and undeclared accounts. Altogether 800 million Euros had disappeared from the Bank of China during the nineties. At any rate this figure corresponded to a percentage of China's private savings. A key figure of the scandal was Wang Xuebing, a vassal of Prime Minister Zhu who first of all chaired the Bank of China and later the China Construction Bank. At the beginning of January 2001 he was placed under house arrest and later sentenced to a long period of detention. The Government even had luck in their misfortune. The people believed that they would be made responsible for the damage. Even though the Chinese press reported the incident, queues of small time investors trying to rescue their savings did not form in front of the banks. 'If our cadres become indifferent and undermine the interests of the people, then we will lose the support of the people', Jiang Zemin warned the comrades.[49]

Also in the field of corruption there were particularly serious cases that had resulted from foreign business dealings. The smuggling ring around the businessman Lai Changxing was responsible for the most spectacular scandal. In the nineties Lai had channelled cars, oil, mobile telephones and computers to the value of approximately 6.4 billion US dollars through the southern Chinese city of Xiamen and had alone provided one-third of the Chinese oil supply.[50] The tax losses amounted to 3.6 billion US dollars. Within half a year the national oil company PetroChina had lost 360 million US dollars as it had to reduce its production due to the over-supply in the country. Around two hundred representatives of various authorities in the city of Xiamen were connected into Lai's network, among them the Chief of Police, the Director of the Customs Authority and the Vice Mayor. When Lai realised in 2000 that the lid was going to be taken off his empire of corruption he made contact with Prime Minister Zhu Rongji. He admitted to the tax evasion and offered Zhu 400,000 US dollars if he did not charge him in return. When Zhu wanted to have the smuggling king arrested, Lai was able to flee in time over to Hong Kong and on to Canada because of an insider tip-off.

'We must use our fist, and not our ten fingers, in order to deal a blow to the law breakers', Zhu raged.[51] Jiang spoke of a 'tumour that is jeopardising the stability of the country'.[52] With Deng's words in their ear, the central leadership had for too long allowed a wildly rampant growth. The party and its cadres had used the boom for their personal enrichment; yes, even the authorities that were actually supposed to uncover the corruption. One group of civil servants from Peking's Ministry of Finance for example siphoned a multi-millions from the treasury in order to establish their own technology investment business.[53] In Shanghai high-ranking officials built the Jinlong Tower in the Special Economic Zone of Pudong. The high-rise was auctioned off at a loss. Thousands of Chinese managers who were working for the 1800 Chinese state enterprises in Hong Kong were replaced on orders of the central authorities. The media was encouraged to report cases of corruption vigorously. Wei Jianxing the head of the party's Central Monitoring Commission for Discipline spoke of the media as a 'a form of mass monitoring that is irreplaceable'.[54] A 3000-man special unit were given the task of supervising the 1.5 million policemen.

But the guardians could not be everywhere. The leadership had to set its weapons on scattered fire. 'One is executed, so as to frighten one hundred', ✶ said Prime Minister Zhu as to the point of the strategy. The Deputy Mayor of the eastern Chinese city of Ningbo was sentenced to death because he had accepted the equivalent of 55,000 Euros in bribes. However enforcement of this punishment was suspended for two years. It did not fare any better for this General Manager of the International Trust and Investment Corporation of Hunan province who had allowed himself to be bribed for three years to the tune of 25,000 Euros. The death penalty was even imposed immediately in bribery cases involving approximately 12,500 Euros. 'The consciousness about the rule of law is hardly pronounced within the population', stated the Head of Parliament Li Peng. 'If people want to charge someone they are more likely to turn to an influential person than the court.'[55]

This was the price of the boom. China had carried out a technical-economic modernisation in 20 years, compared to the several hundred years it had taken Western nations. Consequently the Chinese did not get to form reliable structures of conscience, so too the ability to hold themselves back in relation to others in order to attain a larger measure of liberty. This form of far-sighted egoism is the basis of every modern economy. Even today China is still a long way from this. Added to this legal parameters change constantly. The faster the pace of modernisation, the more control and self-control limp behind.

The leaders had wasted the first half of the 50-year history of the People's Republic in proving the opposite. Mao had failed with the attempt to re-educate people. Deng Xiaoping had to find out how wild rampant economic reforms could let people get out of hand. With the reorganisation of the country Prime Minister Zhu and the State President Jiang Zemin had, not only the losers of the reforms against them but also the winners who made a lot of money through corruption. They considered themselves to be modern entrepreneurs and cheekily cited the free market postulation, that the economic development of a country functions only if it is accompanied

✶ par encourageur les autres

with the freedom for people to choose what they would like. The pressure of globalisation alone stood up against the erroneous trend. The problems were greater than had been assumed, and the reforms progressed more slowly than had been planned. The goals that they had set were not achieved.

China was more stable at the end of the last century, and despite the Asian crisis the central leadership was able to further develop its internal and external influence. To have saved themselves from a major collapse through this transitional phase of the unstable conscience is the biggest burden that the economic power of China moves forward with the twenty-first century. Here Jiang Zemin can demonstratively wear his Mao jacket as often as he likes. More freedom means less order. The new leadership has to live with this dilemma.

# Chapter 8

# THE CONCUBINE ECONOMY

The emperial concubines were subject to a hierarchical order of precedence, and the most able and favoured among them enjoyed special recognition. They competed fiercely for the grace of the emperor or at least the empress dowager. Whoever was the favourite of the hour found a thousand ways to fuel the envy of her rivals, since her elevated rank was not outwardly apparent. (…) She was brought in to give birth to a son after her predecessor had not lived up to this expectation. (…) As soon as the emperor had lost interest in her, she was merely counted as a maidservant.

Sterling Seagrave 'The Concubine on the Dragon Throne'

China is the undisputed future location for the automobile industry – more attractive by far than India, Russia or South America. It is for this reason that the Chinese leadership can specify the conditions under which it allows international automobile manufacturers into the country, even if these are conditions that would never be accepted under any circumstances in the Western free market economy. Also global players like Volkswagen, General Motors or Toyota have to comply with these mechanisms of power. Today they are treated similarly to the former concubines at the imperial court.

What makes the 'concubine economy' attractive is its simplicity. Manufacturers, who would give each other a wide berth in the game reserve of the market economy, let a Chinese parent company with whom they have to establish a joint venture company be forced upon them. The extent of freedom that the central planning commission allows them is dependent on how high their investments are in China, in other words the admission fee for the Chinese market. From the beginning the foreigners compete for the opportunity to be allowed to pander to their Chinese partner and thus in the long term be able to acquire an influential position at the court.[1] They risk a lot in the process. The conglomerates, that develop in this way, look for their own kind in the modern economy: Chinese capitalism has developed one of the most effective ways of strengthening one's own position using foreign money and the know-how of global players.

The role of the emperor is played by the three most powerful car manufacturers: Shanghai Automotive Industry Corp. (SAIC), First Automotive Works (FAW), and Dongfeng Automotive. Formerly the playmates of the emperor were chosen by the emperor's mother and high-ranking officials of the court; sometimes they were also a tribute or a gift of reconciliation from foreign rulers. The choice was based 'not primarily on the criteria of sexual attractiveness: a girl did not necessarily have to be beautiful, but kind, healthy, well educated, emotionally balanced, buxom and well formed'.[2] Nowadays the choice of partners in the automobile world is settled by the national development commission, whereby its criteria for choice noticeably resembles the above-mentioned selection criteria.

Generations of concubines were under great illusions during their stay at the court. They not only hoped for security and a stable life, but also strove for power and influence. Whilst doing so they often forgot that they basically only had one function, 'to strengthen the manliness or the yang of the emperor'.[3] The international vehicle manufacturers' ecstatic hopes are not far behind those of the concubines, however there certainly is a substantial difference: the probability of bearing the emperor a son and through that eventually becoming the influential mother of the ruler was higher then than the chance of becoming decisively influential in the Chinese automobile market. This is because the big Chinese manufacturers have their own interests. They want to see their name among the world's biggest corporate groups, in the famous 500 largest enterprises, which is compiled by the American economic magazine *Fortune*. They want to become independent from foreign companies and regulate the market with their own cars. These notions in no way match those of the big international automobile groups. Yet just like the concubines, they also do not have any power over the rules of the game. They only have two options: to play along or do not play along.

How did it get to the point that these self-confident organisations of enormous standing in the international automobile industry are letting themselves be treated like the emperor's concubines? There are two reasons: China had – once again – luck and sensibly used its opportunity. Luck was responsible for presenting China with favourable global economic conditions. As the sales volume have stagnated nearly everywhere in the world, the European, American, Korean and Japanese manufacturers are dependent on a huge new market. That's just the way it is that publicly listed enterprises survive from growth and are judged by their share of the world market. And where else are more market shares opening up than in China, where only one out of a hundred families owns a car? In Germany almost every family has at least one passenger car in a country with 88 million residents. China, in contrast, only two million cars are produced annually in a country with 1.3 billion people. Even in the capital of Peking just 12 per cent of families own a vehicle. Its size makes China a market of the future. This is China's massive competitive advantage, and the economic planners in Peking are doing everything they can to remain at the wheel. This is why the development of the market is carefully planned within the corridors of power.[4] As in Japan, Korea and Germany, where the automobile industry with all its suppliers and service providers is a central component of the economy, this industry is likely to become a supporting pillar of China's economic system.

Since the opening up of the country the automobile market has played a pioneering role. China's first industrial joint venture manufactured the Beijing Jeep in Peking. The first comprehensive easing up of import restrictions involved Japanese vehicles. The first Chinese enterprise that was listed on the New York stock exchange was Brilliance China Automotive, a mini bus manufacturer with a 40 per cent market share.[5] At the end of the eighties influential politicians such as the former mayor and later President Jiang Zemin as well as the former party chief in Shanghai and later Prime Minister Zhu Rongji were both significantly involved in the establishment of the first Volkswagen joint venture. Jiang paid several visits to the VW parent plant in Wolfsburg, most recently in the spring of 2002. Zhu, as we already have discovered saved the deadlocked Beijing Jeep joint venture.

The car industry can also serve as a model for the change from the planned economy to the planned market economy. The economic planners applied the car industry success formula to other sectors as well. This is why the industry is ideal for observing how Chinese policy and Western industry interact with one another and what kind of elbow room the foreigners have in asserting the international rules of the market economy in China.

The concubine economy has only crystallised gradually. 'This is a fitting picture, yet no one has invented the system. The market has created it', explains Xu Kuandi the Chairman of the national trade association and former mayor of Shanghai. 'It is an efficient means for Chinese enterprises to get onto a world market level quickly, as we learn from the foreigners. In addition there were so many foreign companies that wanted to invest in China that there was no other option.'[6] Foreign car manufacturers are only allowed to produce in joint ventures, in which the Chinese are the majority share-holders. Even in the latest joint ventures with a 50:50 share the Chinese actually have the majority. 'They're always the ones who have more pull', is the opinion of Jorg Blecker the former German boss of Shanghai Volkswagen. Blecker's official title reflected this balance of power: Deputy Managing Director.

The Chinese were quick to realise that such an arrangement gave them the opportunity of making the best use of their advantages. They were better traders than manufacturers and were skilful at playing off future partners against one another during the establishment of joint venture companies. 'We can not be too careful when it comes to foreign investors, as they affect our self-sufficiency', Deng Xiaoping had already warned.[7] The central planners took this warning to heart. 'There is no other nation that can dictate the international automobile manufacturer's access to the market in such a manner due to the market potential', as an analyst summarised the situation.[8]

In fact there were several failed attempts to put the Chinese car industry on its own feet. For instance the manufacturer First Automotive Works (FAW) was unsuccessful in producing the Audi 100 independently, after it had had a fallout with the German partners in the autumn of 1996. The model was legal as the carmaker from Ingolstadt had given FAW a licence, however with the assumption that they would manufacture the successor together. The FAW merely exchanged the motor with a Chrysler engine and stuck a red flag on the bonnet with which they wanted to continue the bulky Chinese limousine in the Russian style, in which Mao had let himself be driven around in.[9] However FAW were unable to maintain the quality standard without German support and the 'red flag' soon had the reputation of being a vehicle of rather inferior quality. Barely 3000 cars were produced in 2001.[10] In comparison, FAW's real success was to be the A6, which it manufactured together with Audi.

Ironically it was the German car manufacturers who supplied the Chinese with the idea for the concubine mechanism. Because the VW AG frequently had conflicts with their Chinese partner SAIC in their working routine, Carl Hern the chief executive of VW at the time reached the conclusion that one could only exist in the Chinese market if one was not exclusively dependent on one manufacturer. And so VW founded its second joint venture with FAW in 1990. The existing partner SAIC was furious about the loss of face – with VW and just as much with the Peking planning commission that had approved the joint venture in the interest of new investments. However VW's joy was fraught with risks. As the state purchased the largest share of the annual production, lethargy spread among the managers. The outdated cars could be bright (wine) red and expensive, but nevertheless sold themselves. Volkswagen was the unquestionable market leader and in 1992 doubled its production to 35,000 vehicles and took in tasty profits. In this the Germans overlooked the fact that it was not their superior strategy that was responsible for their success, rather the Chinese supply market where there was hardly any competition and cars as a commodity were not produced in great numbers.

This was not likely to continue for long. Especially the American competition realised that a business for private customers would also soon develop in China, for which VW was badly set up. At the end of 1991 Jack Smith, who was later to be the boss of General Motors, travelled to Shenyang in the north of China conduct his first discussions with Jinbei Automotive.[11] Smith was under huge pressure to succeed, as with their North American manufacturing plants GM had suffered losses of 12 billion US dollars in the preceding three years. Only the profits from Latin America and Europe kept the head of the biggest car manufacturer in the world above water. The negotiations dragged on,[12] and when eventually the Peking government made the development of the supply industry the highest priority in 1994, Smith was immediately at their disposal. Through their subsidiary Delphi, GM invested 350 million US dollars in 15 companies over a five-year period.[13] 40 million US dollars alone flowed into a technical development centre alone. The American's enthusiasm was noticed by VW's displeased partner SAIC.[14] If VW had two partners, then why should SAIC not look for a second one? In October 1995 GM and SAIC came to an agreement, without VW even having a say in the matter. From that day onwards SAIC began to play off the two manufacturers off against one another. The concubine economy was born.

One thing had become crystal clear: the Western manufacturers needed the Chinese market more than the other way round, and this is why China could demand huge investments. GM paid 750 million US dollars for a 50 per cent share and construction of a production plant with the capacity of 100,000 vehicles a year. This was for example double of what GM had been prepared to pay for a one hundred per cent subsidiary in smaller developing countries such as Poland or Argentina. In the meantime Shanghai GM, with investments of more than 1.5 billion was the largest American joint venture in China. The time had come for VW AG's rude awakening. Production of the Buick started in 1998.[15] Already in the first year the American manufacturer continuously seized more and more of the market share – at Volkswagen's expense. In order to expand more quickly in the

Chinese market, Smith also tried to take over Peugeot's unsuccessful joint venture in Guangzhou. Here the French had only sold a few hundred cars in 1996, and were apparently making a loss of a million US dollars per week.[16] In the meantime the Japanese car manufacturers had also put out their feelers towards China and were faster. Honda was awarded the contract. In 1999 the Japanese manufacturer was already producing around 10,000 vehicles in its facilities.[17] VW's market share slid to under 50 per cent in 2001 and three years later it had only 35 per cent.

By 2005, the share had dwindled further to 18 per cent, while GM's sales soared 35.2 per cent last year to a record 665,390 vehicles last year, slightly boosting its share of the country's increasingly cutthroat car market form 9.4 to 11.2 per cent. In the meantime VW is dramatically cutting costs to heave its share up to 20 per cent again by 2008.

The Shanghai plant was scheduled to axe its spending by 570 million Euros until the end of 2005, and VW's joint venture with FAW in Changchun had to cut costs by 300 million Euros in the second half of 2005 alone. This, however, will not suffice. Problems for the German carmakers are growing faster than profits. Under the pressure of competition and over-capacities profit margins are slumping rapidly. The cost reduction hardly helped. Shangai VW ended the accounting year 2005 with a loss of 119 million Euros. Volkswagen's sales in China nosedived by 13.8 per cent – while the market grew almost by 27 per cent. With about 560,000 vehicles sold the VW Group in China reached a market share of merely 17 per cent. Neither did the business year 2006 have a promising start for VW. In the first quarter of 2006 VW's sales grew 20 per cent less than the market.

The Chinese manufacturers have profited more than anyone else from the competition among the foreigners, and so are now all acquiring international partners, who had to help them with the modernisation of their enterprises and took care of investment and turnover. Increasingly the Chinese played the foreign manufacturers against each other and put them under pressure. Seldom has the cliché of the agile global corporate group from the free market getting the lethargic state enterprise from the planned economy moving been in reality so completely turned on its head.

At the turn of the century the regulatory authorities in the Chinese automobile industry introduced a wave of mergers that nowadays are yet to be finalised. The manufacturers had merged into three main groups: in the north FAW, the middle SAIC and in the south Dongfeng. In addition to these there are still some medium-sized enterprises.[18] This was a way for the communist planners wanted to prepare their enterprises particularly for the free market requirements of the WTO. The number of Chinese enterprises with which the foreigners could co-operate shrank – and the concubine mechanism at the same time became more marked – VW and General Motors serve SAIC. It also merged with Fiat's Chinese partner, without the Germans or the Americans having had any influence over the action. FAW plays VW, Toyota and Mazda off against each another. In the southern Chinese Guangzhou Auto Group Corp, a purely Japanese duel takes place between Honda and Toyota. In the far west, Peugeot Citroen and Renault share the partner Chongqing Changan Automobile Corporation with the Korean manufacturer Kia and the Japanese producer Nissan. Chongqing Changan is also closely connected to with Beijing Automotive Industry Corporation (BAIC), in which DaimlerChrysler and Hyundai compete with each another. Mitsubishi, in which the Germans are still involved with a 35 per cent share, also co-operates with BAIC.

In this period the international car manufacturers have in the meantime invested 30 billion US dollars in China. Until the end of the century the manufacturers will have invested a high two-digit amount in billions. The Volkswagen AG will double its production capacity of 750,000 vehicles, Peugeot and Honda will do likewise. Nissan aims to manufacture four times as many cars, Toyota and Kia six times as many, Ford seven times and Hyundai ten times as many. Added to this the Chinese manufacturers are increasingly successful in bringing their own cars onto the market. Whereas five years ago, the market had been entirely in the hands of foreign brands, domestic manufacturers today boast a market share of more than 25 per cent.

According to all predictions, this is far more than the Chinese market will be able to absorb. This overcapacity in production is fine by China, as it will force the car manufacturers to turn their Chinese plants into locations for export, at first to the surrounding Asian countries, but eventually to the whole world. 'It's completely open, who will be at top at the end of the day', concludes Blecker, Volkswagen's former joint-venture boss in Shanghai.[19]

Already since the beginning of 2002 China is the single most important market for VW. According to a study by the investment bank Goldman & Sachs the corporate group currently derives, including the parts supplied from Germany, 80 per cent of its income from China.[20] Just by itself the joint venture with SAIC with 16,000 employees is alone as big as the VW subsidiary Skoda or Seat. Saying this, Shanghai VW has not yet reached its optimal size.

And so the Chinese market becomes the most crucial location for the companies, even before it has unfolded itself to its full size. In 2004 only relatively few vehicles were sold, barely totalling two and a half million cars. If the market triples in size up until 2010 – one of the more cautious estimates – China will be, after the USA, the second biggest market for cars in the world. To what extent will the foreigners have a share of this market? 'The Chinese', according to Blecker, 'have the advantage at all times. You can only beat the foreign competition, not the Chinese'.[21] So the ultimate winner in the is already certain.

Only two heavy weights in the industry undertook serious attempts to extract themselves from the system of the concubine economy: the German car manufacturer BMW and DaimlerChrysler. Both were to pay dearly for their attempts to outwit the Chinese system. BMW was assisted by Horst Teltschik. In the Kohl era he was regarded as the Head of the Department for Foreign and Defence policy as one of Germany's most influential political officials and one of the most knowledgeable on East–West relations. From 1993 to 2000 he was BMW's Chairman for business and policy. However even he came to grief with China. The German–Chinese steering committee for integrated transportation projects, which he initiated in July 1994, and to which enterprises such as DaimlerChrysler, ABB and Lufthansa belonged managed to achieve very little.[22] The Chinese only wanted to buy against soft loans. However, even Teltschik was not able to obtain these. More consequential though was that he had rejected the advice of the Peking planning committee's report that BMW should team up with one of the biggest national car manufacturers. If one could not get round forming a joint venture with a Chinese car manufacturer, Teltschik rather wanted to work together with a private, preferably market-orientated enterprise. Out of this he expected extensive control over routine business, less difficulties, lower costs, more flexibility and above all minimal interference from the authorities in Peking. This was a good strategy, but not one of Chinese making. Admittedly a potential partner was found quickly: Brilliance China Automotive, a mini bus manufacturer from Shenyang in the north of China. Brilliance had been built up by the former state manager Yang Rong and managed strictly according to free market principles. Due to its huge economic importance for the remote and backward province of Liaoning, the Chinese Siberia, the enterprise over time been able to a large extent emancipate itself from the state planners' attempts to regulate it.

However they had no intention of also letting Brilliance pull out of the centrally controlled concubine system in their co-operation with foreign companies, and in so doing thereby set a precedent. Teltschik stubbornly ignored the signals from the planning authority. At a meeting the planning boss Zhang Guobao, one of the brightest members of the leadership, told Teltschik clearly and explicitly: 'we informed you on numerous occasions that this is the wrong partner. We do not want this one.'[23] Even after this warning Teltschik threw caution to the wind. He banked on the fact that because of his outstanding contacts he would be able to by pass the planning commission and gain approval for the joint venture. In the first place and understandably he wanted to close the deal before he resigned from office in June 2000. Secondly he was convinced of Brilliance as a partner, even though the Brilliance boss Yang Rong now pressed the methods of the concubine economy on the man from Munich: as he was simultaneously reaching a co-operative agreement with General Motors and Toyota. Teltschik did not succeed in solving the political difficulties of the (business) deal, which were increasingly piling themselves up in front of him, during his term of office. Joachim Milberg, the former Chairman of the board's praise at Teltschik's retirement probably came somewhat too soon. He stressed at his leaving party, 'that we are completely indebted to Mr. Teltschik's judgement that we are nowadays set up so well in Asia, especially in China'.[24]

At any rate the Bavarian carmaker and Yang Rong reached a deal. The Germans promised firstly to lend technical support with the development of their own vehicle in the upper-mid range. The car by the name of 'Zhonghua' cost 20,000 to 30,000 Euros once it had been fitted and was thus not in direct competition with the BMW models. As far as BMW production was concerned they came to the agreement to only assemble 30,000 vehicles jointly in the third and fifth production line in China. However just as before, the planning commission saw no reason for deviating from its policy. It was for this reason that BMW and Brilliance went in search for political allies and found protective support from Bo Xilai, Liaoning's ambitious provincial governor.[25] Bo, who as mayor had built up the formerly decaying port into a modern show case city in the early nineties, wanted to secure the investments, jobs, and the BMW joint venture's technology transfer for his backward province at any cost. He knew that there was only one member of the Chinese leadership team who could push such an unusual project through against the protests of the planning committee: that was Prime Minister Zhu Rongji who had already overridden the complex power structures within the leadership often. When he invited Federal Chancellor Gerhard Schröder to a dinner for a small group in the northern Chinese city of Dalian, Bo, used with the opportunity to address the project. Thereafter Zhu promptly gave his single-handed approval for the BMW joint venture.

It now almost looked as if BMW had cracked the concubine economy. But the enterprise had – obviously just like Prime Minister Zhu – underestimated that the Chinese leadership was already so complex that an order given by only one no longer necessarily had authority. The project was as before not to the liking of the displeased national planning commission. When Joachim Milberg, BMW's Chairman of the Board cancelled a meeting with the Directors of the planning committee in March 2002 'because of delays',[26] and instead only went to Prime Minister Zhu Rongji, he added insult to injury and the planning commission dragged on the proceedings for months until it was presented to the state council for approval.

The affair started to become unpleasant for governor Bo Xilai. On a trip to Germany in June 2002 he had actually intended to celebrate the signing of the contract in Munich. Instead he had to be content with a plant inspection. Admittedly Bo knew well that the BMW limousine would only start rolling off the assembly line in Liaoning once the effects of the levers of the concubine mechanism were firmly set in place. With a composed sense of power he therefore delivered to the economic planners in Peking, what they needed for their approval. He demanded that Yang Rong, the founder of enterprise, should from now on pay more taxes. He fought back tooth and nail and threatened to relocate to a neighbouring province under more favourable conditions. A warrant for arrest was issued against Yang in June 2002. The accusation was tax evasion, used by an accusation authorities against every Chinese entrepreneur who tries to oppose their control. It was only because of an insider tip that Yang, who had a Hong Kong passport, was able to forestall his arrest and flee to the USA. The trade in Brilliance shares was suspended in Hong Kong and New York. Using the argument that Yang had merely run the enterprise as a state manager, the provincial government of Liaoning took over its controlling majority – at a fraction of the market value.[27] Since then Yang has been trying with the help of a prominent Washington lawyer to take legal action before an international court for his confiscated shares.

Brilliance was now a state enterprise and thus under the control of the planning commission, who eventually issued a licence to BMW's new Chief Executive Helmut Panke on the 12th of July 2003. The agreed allocation of duties in the joint venture contract was unfavourable: BMW had to leave the two most important functions, personnel and finance, to the Chinese. The planning commission was hardly able to hide its malice: 'The virgin proved herself to be a widow twice over on the wedding night', as was accidentally mentioned by one of the Directors.[28]

Since then the car manufacturers from Munich have had to fight against a strong head wind. At the official opening of the production facilities in May 2004 there was – different to the usual procedures – neither anyone from Peking nor the new provincial governor present (Bo had been promoted to the Chinese Minister of Trade at the beginning of 2004). Additionally, the Mayor of the city of Shenyang cast a cloud over the event by demanding that BMW should double its production. Also financially the state let the joint venture learn that one could not count on a great inclination to co-operate, if one previously had tried to undermine the concubine economy. Customs used an unclear legal situation to tax BMW on car-part kits as well as imported vehicles. Additionally it turned out to be very difficult and expensive to lure suppliers to the charming Siberian location for the production of a small numbers of items.

Consequently, Shenyang BMWs were too expensive compared to already established competitors such as Audi and Toyota, and in December 2003 BMW was forced to reduce prices by an average 15 per cent or up to 10,000 Euros per car. And BMW had negotiated for so long, that just in the year when it was finally time to get moving, the Chinese leadership instructed the state banks to turn off the credit tap for cars.[29] All carmakers were hit by Peking's attempts to cool off the overheating economy. The government had, among other things, communicated to the banks to allow less credits for aspiring car buyers. For BMW, however, this was even more painful than for its competitors, because the Bavarian carmaker had only just begun to build up its distribtution network. Production targets in 2004 had to be reduced by 50 per cent from 18000 cars – in a plant that is designed for an annual production of 30,000 vehicles. Problems were growing faster than profits. In 2004, Standard & Poor's relegated BMW's partner Brilliance to the status of 'strong sell'. The share price dwindled, and so did the sales. The Bavarians were punished in four ways: they no longer had a private partner, the central government was against them, they had a production location in China's Siberian north and began production in a weak market.

For over 15 years the managers of DaimlerChrysler avoided the Chinese market than get involved with a partner who threatened to create difficulties from the word go. An understandable beginning, which however did not ultimately work out. Because when the Stuttgart natives finally dared to come out of their shelter, they had to take what was left. Actually they had had enough time and opportunity to learn the Chinese rules of the game, in which there are hardly any exceptions. At the beginning of the nineties Mercedes lavishly developed plans for a family car that was specially tailored to Chinese needs.[30] When these discussions evaporated into thin air, they decided to compete with General Motors for the licence to build a top-class car in Shanghai. The contract was eventually awarded to the Americans. Whereupon the Benz managers planned a top-class carrier, the first so-called multi purpose vehicle (MPV). This time Edzard Reuter, the Chairman of the Board at that time succeeded in asserting himself in difficult negotiations (among these the Chinese demanded production facilities in different locations) – against the competition from Ford and Chrysler.[31] In 1995 the deal was publicly announced during the China trip of Klaus Kinkel, then Minister of Foreign Affairs. Daimler Benz wanted to manufacture 60,000 vehicles per year and invest over a billion US dollars. But it never came to that, because the Mercedes managers could not agree on a common course of action with their Chinese partners. The project faltered.

With the next attempt Daimler Benz actually got a step further, but then got itself into serious difficulties. In Yangzhou, located in the southern Chinese city of Jiangsu, Daimler Benz's bus branch, which was with an almost 20 per cent world market share a strong enterprise unit, wanted to produce 7000 buses and 12,000 chassis for the Chinese market annually.[32] The contract, which was worth over one hundred million US dollars, was signed in July 1997 during President Jiang Zemin's visit of Germany. Almost a year later on the 18th of June 1998 the first bus left the production hall of the joint venture Yaxing Benz; 'the first luxury bus of international standard that has been made in the country', raved the managing director Ju Baocai.[33] The elation did not last for long. The sales did not take off and the product did not find its market. Importantly, Chinese partner took over the German know-how and built a plant in the immediate neighbourhood and manufactured buses independently. Instead of the planned 7000 buses, several hundred buses rolled off Yaxing Benz's assembly line in 2000, in 2001 more than a hundred and in the first six months of 2002 only about several dozen buses. In comparison the Chinese partner Yangzhou Yaxing Motor Coach Co. Ltd. manufactured 8000 luxury buse annually. In April 2000 the German deputy general manager of the joint venture and his family were even murdered under mysterious circumstances in his villa in Nanjing. A connection never was ruled out.

A short time later the utility vehicle branch of DaimlerChrysler, the huge corporate group that had merged in the meantime, pushed into China. Negotiations for the production of heavy trucks began in 2000. At first the discussions were very promising. In October 2000 a Mercedes Manager announced that 'up to the end of the year' there would be an outcome. But only one month later the Chinese broke off the discussions. After the Chinese New Year in February of the following year the two concerns were admittedly once again talking to one another. Mercedes again promised a contract to its shareholders. 'The discussions with our partners are running smoothly and we assume that we will be informed about the outcome in the course of this year,' explained Eckhard Cordes the Chief executive of the utility branch in March 2001.[34] A few months later this announcement also was overshadowed by reality. As FAW refused to assure that it would exclusively co-operate exclusively with DaimlerChrysler in regard to heavy trucks, the Germans were 'calm and collected' in their search for another partner, as Cordes declared in January 2002. In July 2002 he said, 'the discussions with FAW will be concluded within this year'.[35] In February 2003 he finally announced that the talks would be broken off. The Chinese market proved itself to be treacherous. The DaimlerChrysler managers were careful. This strategy had a disadvantage.

After negotiations that had gone on for several years DaimlerChrysler still stood there empty handed. Thus the German enterprise hauled a project that had already failed ten years previously to the surface. Through the involvement in Mitsubishi[36] the Germans had access to a mainland joint venture of the Taiwanese China Motor Corp. (CMC), 15 per cent of which belonged to Mitsubishi. The new partners finally came to a commercial agreement. The plan is to produce around 40,000 units of the Mercedes Benz Sprinter and the van family Viano/Vito from 2006 onwards, in a new plant in Fuzhou, located in the province of Fujian. It took an unusually long time before the state council gave DaimlerChrysler the licence in November 2004. The competitive products from General Motors, Honda, Fiat and Mazda have already been on the market for quite a while.

At the same time the managers had to worry about an inherited deal. Through 1998's Chrysler merger the Germans were all of a sudden involved in the first foreign–Chinese joint venture. This enterprise had seen its best times a long time ago. The sales figures dropped and with them so did the image of the car. Due to the pressure of the Chinese the modern Jeep Grand Cherokee did in fact roll off the assembly line in Peking from 2001 onwards. But as the Germans wanted to spend as little money on marketing as possible, only over a hundred vehicles were sold in January 2002. In February it was down to 70. The economic planners were not willing to accept this. Whilst other countries try to bring ailing industries back to life with tax exemptions and subsidies, Peking delivered an unconcealed threat. For DaimlerChrysler there, 'would be no further chances in the Chinese market',[37] if the Beijing Automotive Industry Corp.'s (BAIC) joint venture was not put back on its feet. The warning was accompanied with detailed reports in the national media that wrote about the problems with the quality of the imported Mercedes vehicles and readily reported the case of a disappointed customer who in September 2001 and March 2002 smashed up his limousine with a sledgehammer in front of rolling cameras. The Director of the Wuhan safari zoo complained that DaimlerChrysler treats the Chinese as second-class customers and palms off defective goods and bad service on to them. The Mercedes owner's anger was probably genuine: the extensive reporting was however an industrial-political and ploy an old trick. Already in 1985 the government tried to slow down the wave of Japanese imports by reporting about 'angry' customers of Mitsubishi trucks who wanted to have their money back: 'there are quality problems with all of the 31 trucks'.[38]

This plain language was understood in Stuttgart: within a few weeks DaimlerChrysler came to an agreement with their Chinese partners. A marketing campaign improved the image of the Grand Cherokee and the Mitsubishi off-road jeep Pajero was introduced.[39] In addition it was decided that a Mitsubishi should be rolling off the assembly line in Peking as quickly as possible. However the Chinese planners did not want to let themselves be fobbed off with second-rate American and Japanese technology in the long term. They sent a high-ranking delegation to Stuttgart in June 2002 to persuade Jurgen Schrempp, the Chief Executive who in contrast to his colleagues in the industry had not been to China since 1997, to build the E and C class in Peking. The Chinese actually succeeded in convincing Schrempp, who stated, 'In this year the concrete course for the further development of the business (...) will be set. After long negotiations the company's plans are now taking shape for the future market.'[40] And he added, what one had already heard quite frequently about the DaimlerChrysler CEO, that he would in this year travel to China to sign contracts.

However it actually took more than another year until Schrempp finally signed these contracts during the Chinese Prime Minister Wen Jiabao's visit to Germany. It was not until November 2004 that the state council approved of the project. The laying of the foundation stone took place in December in the presence of the Federal Chancellor Schröder. Schrempp excused himself. The VW boss Bernd Pischetsrieder naturally flew in the next day for the inauguration of a new VW plant. In the middle of 2005 Mercedes produced the C and E class in Peking. DaimlerChrysler also plans to start a new joint venture for trucks. Currently, the world market leader is negotiating a deal for the production of heavy utility vehicles with Beijing Foton, a 30 per cent subsidiary of BAIC.

The long wait had however not been worth it. The entry fee into the Chinese market had in no way been reduced since the beginning of the negotiations in the early nineties – in fact the opposite was true. DaimlerChrysler was worldwide the last large car manufacturer that did not yet have a substantial production in China. It had an accordingly weak bargaining position. With pressure being brought to bear on them by share analysts, who were accusing the Germans of snoozing while losing in the Chinese market, the DaimlerChrysler managers only had a restricted room to manoeuvre, reported the top managers of BAIC.[41]

'Our partnership is looking at investing one billion Euros and the mutual production of Mercedes passenger cars as well as utility vehicles', Jurgen Schrempp described the business on the other hand. 'Our medium-term goal in China is to manufacture approximately 25,000 passenger cars in the

C and E class from kits. To me it utterly depends on the quality of the partner and the contract, not on the speed. Especially in China it matters to breathe slowly and attain the long-term security of the business model.'[42]

DaimlerChrysler could also not escape the concubine system, because the partner BAIC had already been producing upper-middle range sedans with Hyundai since 2002. DaimlerChrysler had a 10 per cent share in Hyundai. Hyundai on the other hand was indignant about the contract as BAIC had apparently closed an exclusive contract with Hyundai. The South Koreans therefore publicly challenged DaimlerChrysler to cancel the contract, or otherwise they would reserve the right to legal action.[43] The companies fell out with each other, after which Stuttgart broke off its participation. The winners of this power struggle were again the Chinese. For them the collection of prominent car manufacturers was now complete and everyone danced to Peking's tune. And the European manufacturers on the whole do not cut fine figures in this dance. While the Japanese carmakers extended their market share from 19 to 24 per cent between 2002 and 2006, and the Koreans improved from 2.4 to 12 per cent, the market share of European manufacturers plunged by more than half from 48 to 22 per cent. Even the Americans managed in this time period to increase their share in the Chinese market from 5.5 to 15.5 per cent.

The system of the concubine economy differs from all other economic growth models in history. Japan (and the Tiger states which copied its model) tried to conquer the world without the assistance of foreign countries. Until the beginning of the nineties there was hardly any foreign participation in Japanese industry. India also tried to seal itself off for a period of time, but nowadays has to conditionally let foreigners into the country, who harm the underdeveloped home industries. Differently from the Japanese and the Koreans, the Chinese do not have to develop their own technology – it is supplied. The market economy is the engine driving this system. Globalisation's huge competitive pressure puts the Chinese planners in a powerful position. The foreign car manufacturers not only have to support and develop the Chinese competitors with new technology, but they also have to count on the fact that their intellectual property will be copied. In the first half of 2004 alone, 42 new Chinese models came onto the market.

Just how large the Chinese room to manoeuvre is, is indicated by the fact that 60 per cent of the suppliers of the joint venture Shanghai VW belong to the Chinese partner SAIC. It is for a good reason that the Chinese oppose the worldwide trend that the manufacturers can sell their supply share, so that they are freer to drive the costs down. SAIC is thereby able to skim off a majority of the profit already in the production process, without having to share it with the foreigners. They are thereby forced to help sustain expensive and unprofitable supply companies. Additionally they have to pay above average wages and buy machinery which is of inferior quality or does not work at full capacity. It is for this reason that the production costs of manufacturers like VW are still above the world market level.

Many of the foreign car manufacturers do not have any access to the sale of their vehicles. This is taken over by the Chinese, or they hand it over to trusted agents; either way the foreigners have their hands tied when it comes to the development of their own markets. Too, now and again foreigners have to occasionally accept unfavourable locations because the government in Peking wants to promote underdeveloped regions. Audi is for example settled in Changchun in the north of China and Citroen in the central city of Wuhan, which is a sticky, humid industrial pit.

The Chinese partners are in a comfortable position and this can still be improved. They want to develop cars themselves and sell them under their own brands. The foreigners then have the same fate as the concubines – once the emperor had lost interest in them, they were only maids.[44] At the end of November 2004 it had got to that stage. SAIC, the Chinese mother (company) of VW (with an annual turnover of approximately ten billion dollars) took over 70 per cent of the British car manufacturer Rover for 1.4 billion Euro.[45] Now SAIC has cars from VW and GM at its disposal from which it earns 50 per cent and a brand from which it earns 70 per cent. The question, on which vehicle they would put all their energy into in case of any doubt, is easy to answer.

Already nowadays it appears that many vehicles, which are successful in the West are too expensive for the Chinese mass market, because Chinese customers are not prepared to pay a lot for technical finesse that is not obvious and visible. It is also for this reason that the more simple American cars, at which the German car builders turn up their nose, are becoming increasingly successful.

Moreover, all of the manufacturers are to some extent dependent on the macro-economic strategy of the Government, which is unknown in the West. When the auto market grew by 70 per cent in 2003, the Government put their foot on the brake and instructed its national banks only to grant a quarter of the previous car loans. An economically sensible decision, which however foiled the manufacturers' production planning into disarray.

The biggest restriction of the concubine economy will in future hit the foreign manufacturers even harder in future: they are hardly able to do a de facto transfer of the profits that they have gained in China, out of the country. The majority of the joint venture would have to approve of such a transfer, and the majority is always the Chinese side, which naturally has no interest in letting capital out of the country. So far this has hardly been a problem since the manufacturers wanted to invest a lot of money anyway. Volkswagen can for instance completely finance all of the six billion Euros that the corporate group intends to invest in China until 2007 from the profits that it has gained in the country. But what is going to happen when one of these days the market is saturated and it is no longer worth making further investments? There are only two possibilities: the enterprises can create new production facilities for global export in China, whereby other manufacturing locations such as Germany would suffer. Or they could invest in another industry. The winner in both cases is again China's national economy. But perhaps the concubine economy is a temporary form of economic control, which will no longer be possible in a more complex, highly developed economy. Will China be forced through its WTO membership to adhere to the international rules and open its markets for foreign countries? Will the foreign manufacturers' position of power improve through this?

The concubine mechanism that China has developed in the automobile industry, have in the meantime also been applied in other industries by the economic planners. This upholds the Chinese belief that they have learned during the colonial times that they are only allowed to integrate their country with the world to the extent that it is appropriate for their interests and abilities. Or it can be put another way: if a foreigner makes money in China then a Chinese must make more money through the same business. No large foreign enterprise – be it in the steel, chemical, pharmaceutical, banking or insurance industry – can take in a direction in China with which the government is not in agreement. If it concerns attracting highly developed technology to China and so modernising one's own backward industries the Chinese government pulls no punches. As for example in the aircraft industry, China needs a fleet of medium haul aircraft, to which the domestic direct traffic between the provincial centres outside of the main traffic junctions will be transferred in the future. According to their estimates China will need approximately 8600 planes to the value of 180 billion US dollars in the next 20 years.[46] If possible one does not want to buy these airplanes from overseas, but rather build them on one's own. In fact this is to be managed by the huge but backward native aircraft industry with – free if possible – foreign assistance and technology. The interest of those responsible also focused, among others, on the German–American joint venture Fairchild Dornier in Oberpfaffenhofen near Munich. Fairchild Dornier was in the process of building one of the most modern medium haul jets, the Do 728 Jet, which had created interest in the European airlines, not least of all with Lufthansa.

The company had already delivered 19 32-seater regional airplanes of an older and smaller model the D 328 Jet to Hainan Airlines, the southern Chinese airline. Hainan Airlines, a half national joint venture, in which the billionaire George Soros was also involved, were so delighted with the Fairchild Dornier aircraft in their regional operation that it ordered a further

21 jets. However despite having a valid contract of sales agreement for these planes they did not receive the necessary import licence from the Chinese government.[47] Zeng Peiyan, who at the time was Chairman of the powerful National Planning and Development Commission and is now in the meantime the Vice Prime Minister, made it clear to the Germans that Fairchild Dornier would only be allowed to deliver further aircraft to China if it was prepared in return to share its technology with China and mutually develop an individual regional aircraft with the national Chinese aircraft industry.

Fairchild Dornier was financially in a difficult position because of the high development costs for the Do 728 and urgently needed the income for the series of jets that had already been completed for Hainan Airlines. In November, during the Air Show China 2000 that took place in Zhuhai, Fairchild Dornier signed a declaration of intent with the China Aviation Industry Corporation (AVIC I and II), to investigate the possibilities of involving the Chinese industry in the 728 jet programme.[48] Despite intensive negotiations with the Chinese aircraft industry in the summer of 2001 the project did not move forward, as the Chinese side did not want to enter into a deal involving a mere declaration of intent and an import licence and even more did not want to lose their means of applying pressure. The original plan to make a German–Chinese declaration of intent for the mutual development and production of a German–Chinese regional jet during the Federal Chancellor's visit to China in November 2001 was cancelled by the Chinese a few days before the date without a reason. They had obviously found out that Fairchild Dornier was in bigger difficulties than they had expected, and now probably hoped that it would be possible to get at the technology even more cheaply in the event of the company's bankruptcy.

The banks providing credit to the enterprise thereupon asked themselves, whether China's retreat also meant that Fairchild Dornier had lost their most important growth market for regional airplanes. This risk evaluation had a negative result. Five months later Fairchild Dornier was forced to declare bankruptcy. Those responsible in the Chinese aircraft industry – at first pleased – soon had to determine whether the almost free acquisition of the Fairchild Dornier technology would be too expensive and probably too difficult to now build the aircraft themselves, and so dropped the plan. The Chinese conglomerate D'Long – a Shanghainese company without any experience in aircraft construction – took over the most interesting parts of the enterprise for a negligible sum in order to begin a new attempt in German–Chinese aircraft construction. However it soon became clear that it would take a financially strong enterprise and above all one related to the industry to further develop the highly complex Do 728 up to the production stage. D'Long did not pay and so Fairchild Dornier had to be liquidated.

The last German enterprise of the airline building industry with an almost fully developed ultra modern regional aircraft, extensive know-how and enormous experience in the construction of regional aircraft, as well as a staff of highly qualified workers was lost. This was not a problem for the Chinese. A year later they signed an agreement of the establishment of a joint venture with the Brazilian manufacturer Embraer.[49]

In 2005 Gustav Humbert, the German boss of the European concern Airbus, also got to feel the icy wind of Chinese negotiation tactics. During the state visit of Chinese Prime Minister Wen Jiabao to France in 2005 he could sign the biggest China-deal in the company's history alright: The Chinese bought 150 passenger planes of the A320 type. But there were conditions attached to the deal. Humbert had to commit himself to start negotiations with the Chinese aviation industry about the development of a production line in China. Humbert's wording in public is careful so far: 'We are pleased to enter talks with our Chinese partners about possible next steps,' he said after signing the declaration of intent. Humbert praised the Chinese for having built 'a real industrial competence' in recent years; Airbus could profit from that. But in fact it will not be easy to evade the Chinese desire for their own Airbus production. The Chinese certainly know how to profit from the competition between Airbus and Boeing. Since the Americans hesitate to start production in China for reasons concerning their security policy, Humbert now has the chance to leave Boeing far behind in the long term. This, however, will be at the expense of Airbus' European facilities in Toulouse and Hamburg. China will be the largest customer in the aviation industry and will order an estimated 2500 new planes until 2020. A business that beckons to the company that grants the Chinese the best conditions for technological transfer and production shares, because the Chinese certainly want to see the aviation industry create jobs in their own country. In recent years China has already bound supply contracts to the condition that Chinese supplier firms can participate. It is agreed that the supply of components from the People's Republic will rise to an annual 60 billion US dollars, and will double to 120 billion US dollars by 2010. In the meanwhile, Airbus receives supplies from five Chinese companies. Among these are 5 per cent of the airframe for the A350. As early as July 2005, Airbus opened a technology centre in Beijing, employing 54 Chinese engineers. From the Chinese perspective, assembly of aircraft is the next logical step. They have already negotiated a pilot project. Airbus' mother company EADS will develop a helicopter in co-operation with Chinese companies.

Heinrich von Pierer, the German manager who had endeavoured in the Chinese market like no other and had built up contacts in China since the beginning of the eighties, yet had to contend with the fact that one cannot be sure of China's friendship. When a top Chinese politician visits Germany, von Pierer will sooner or later step out of the back row to shake his hand. Committed/involved, but never persistent/pushy, he is publicly the Chairman of the Asia Pacific Committee of the German economy, but internally he is always the top employee of the Siemens AG, Munich. Whether in the company of both former Federal Chancellor Helmut Kohl or Gerhard Schröder, he has been a prominent member of the delegations from the nineties to the present. And if the Federal Chancellor does not have time for a background discussion with journalists, von Pierer is allowed to take over the role.[50] He does this so well and so discreetly that one does not miss the Chancellor and nevertheless does not get the impression that von Pierer would want to take over Schröder's remaining tasks. For a long time the Chinese returned von Pierer's solidarity with China; in particular since the nineties when Zhu Rongji became Vice Prime Minister and then Prime Minister, the doors in Peking were open for von Pierer. Only a few enterprise leaders had the privilege of being able to clarify their concerns and needs with Ministers over the telephone. The Chinese leadership knew that they could rely on von Pierer. He was considered to be one the most important Germans in this regard. Always in January, just before his birthday, when the politicians and top managers of the Western world are on skiing holiday, Pierer would travel to China. Then the Chinese leadership had time to discuss everything with him. In between these occasions he also dropped in numerous times.

However the good times when China's (early) reformers and the German pioneer of the Far East had faith in one another and exchanged views about China's modernisation did not last forever. With the change in government in the spring of 2003 von Pierer came to realise that he was a friend of the old government. Although the new and the old government consist of the one and same communist party, the new members of government did everything completely differently to the old. The new leadership under President and Party Chief Hu Jintao and Prime Minister Wen Jiabao is rather more interested in social balance than spectacular high-tech projects. Von Pierer adjusted his managers to this: now it was electrical and medical technology instead of the ICE and Transrapid. Even so the new government initially presented its reserved face. It became more difficult in the country where everything had gone without a hitch before. The increasing competition in the market had slowly made Siemens's position more competitive in the previous years. Von Pierer had good contacts but the competition got the contracts. Between September 2001 and September 2003 alone the turnover of Siemens's Chinese business had fallen by 15 per cent to 3.3 billion Euros.

Even if one deducts the losses determined by currency fluctuations on the grounds of the strong Euro, this was a painful fall.

Von Pierer struggled onwards but nothing turned to success. The mobile telephone business halved itself in 2002 and in 2003 it had reduced from 8 to 4.6 per cent of the market share. Also in the energy sector things were no longer running at their best: von Pierer's negotiating partners seemed unusually distant also in 2003 when it concerned a 1.52 billion Euro contract for a gas turbine system. The German friends are too expensive, was the message from the Chinese side. Wolfgang Clement, the Minister of Economics and Labour tried to intervene but without success. The new government had only just been in office when the deal went to the competition. Nine gas turbines worth 620 million US dollars were delivered by Mitsubishi Heavy Industries and their Chinese partner Dongfang Electric. The other part of the huge order, 13 turbines for 900 million US dollars, went to the American group General Electric with its partner Harbin Power Equipment. Both enterprises not only had the better price, but also had offered a new joint venture with a high transfer of technology. The same applied to transportation technology. The ICE was obviously not desirable on the prestigious route between Peking and Shanghai. One would choose a more mature technology with good financing for the long distance route, was the laconic answer of Parliamentary President Wu Banguo, whom von Pierer had already known for a long time. There was likewise no licence from the planning commission for a joint venture to produce 120 underground carriages in Peking. The low point came in July 2003 when von Pierer returned to Germany from a secret trip more annoyed than he had been for a long time. With 1.5 billion US dollars, General Electric had so far invested much more than double the amount of the Germans. 'The competition in China is getting increasingly harder', said von Pierer, 'even for China's good friends'.[51] The German's problem was that they considered their technology to be so valuable, that they showed little flexibility with their pricing.

In these situations the former Siemens boss functioned like a gas turbine. He converted pressure into energy and anger turned into ambition. At the celebration of the 100th day since the opening of the first Siemens representative office in China in May 2004 von Pierer wished for a new vision for the Chinese market. Siemens had to show the Chinese that the corporate group was prepared to get heavily involved in China. The concubine mechanism functioned magnificently.

Up to the end of decade the enterprise wanted to invest more than one billion Euros in China. Siemens would buy more in China: in 2005 already for as much as five million Euros, three times as much as in 2004. Although China only covers 4 per cent of the world economy, Siemens wants to sell

10 per cent of its products there as quickly as possible. Additionally Siemens wants to employ a thousand new engineers in the fiscal year 2005. In order to optimally manage the new Siemens-China a new company quarters is currently being built in Peking for 100 million Euros. Von Pierer also gave the ailing Mobilfunk a breath of life. As Siemens had problems in both getting its mobile telephones to its customers quickly, and in covering as much of an area as possible, the corporate group went into partnership with the Chinese market leader Ningbo Bird. It owns 30,000 shops in China. Mobile phone production in Shanghai is supposed to grow from 14 to 20 million units in 2005. Even then there will be more than 300 million mobile phone customers in China. Already in 2003 Siemens sponsored the first Chinese football league. The Germans paid approximately 8 million US dollars for one year, thereby replacing Pepsi. In spite of their efforts, the Germans finally had to throw in the towel. In 2005, Siemes had to sell its mobile phone business. The Taiwanese manufacturer BenQ took over – but not before Siemens paid them a US dollar 300 million dowry.

The case of Siemes can serve as a warning for other Western companies. Whoever invests in China under the delusion that their products are irresistible will wake up to an unpleasant surprise. The Munich-based company for too long had dreamed that Chinese consumers were willing to pay more for a German high-tech product than for other cell phones. And they refused for too long to adjust their products to their customers' expectations. Fold out designs were popular in China, but for a long time the Bavarians ignored this. Added to this it turned out that local competitors were able to copy the technical edge of the Siemens gadgets within just a few months. Finally, the Germans had to realize that the Chinese market can quickly turn into a trap. In early 2004, however, it had not come to that, and von Pierer could again take a slow deep breath. In March that year Siemens sold underground trains to Shanghai Metro to the value of approximately 270 million US dollars. However Siemens only got the order after the company had given the assurance that at least 60 per cent of the trains would be manufactured locally. It is quite certain that the local share of production with future projects will become even larger. The German colleagues are not happy to hear this. Now Siemens already has three times the turnover overseas in comparison to Germany, and since 1997 the group has employed more people outside Germany. 'China offers a series of cost benefits that we have to use for our global competitive ability', von Pierer describes the pressure of the concubine mechanism.

But there were also cases where Germany and China were after the same thing – at least the two governments. No large-scale German–Chinese project has ever been more strongly supported by both governments than the electro magnetic levitation train, the Transrapid: China wants Shanghai to be the most modern city with millions of inhabitants in the world, the symbol of its economic upswing, a globally unique transportation system of high-level technology. Germany – developer and promoter of this outstanding technical feat of German engineering, has still now not been able to start using it – it at least needs a reference project in order to spread and market it throughout the world. And so the Shanghai route became a dream and a prestigious project for both sides. It was supposed to become the crowning of the German–Chinese high-tech partnership. As China's government is planning a countrywide network of high speed trains it considered using the Transrapid on long routes as well, for example between Shanghai and Peking.

The project was from the outset a political top priority. Prime Minister Zhu Rongji visited the test section in Elmsland during his visit to Germany in the summer of 2000 in order to try out the Transrapid. On the 31st of December 2002, a few weeks before the end of the Chinese Prime Minister's term of office, Prime Minister Zhu Rongji and Federal Chancellor Gerhard Schröder were supposed to go on a test run together. The interest on both sides was so great that China eventually even declined the subsidised trade credit, which is otherwise usual with such deals. On the other hand, Germany in return transferred the countrywide licences for the construction of the Transrapid's track without cost and provided the necessary know-how so that it could be built. In January 2000, just before the Chinese New Year celebration, the Siemens boss von Pierer managed during an six-hour visit to Peking, to seal the contract through negotiations with Prime Minister Zhu Rongji. Zhu topped it up with another 50 million Euros, whereupon von Pierer gave in to his demands of 50 million Euros. In a general feeling of merriment von Pierer turned his jacket pockets inside out. He let the Prime Minister know that he now had nothing left.

The two governments had built a good launch pad with German tax funds. But the rocket failed to operate. As it turned out, the German consortium and particularly the ThyssenKrupp AG, was not capable of using the opportunity to establish a countrywide Transrapid network. The construction of this 37 kilometre Transrapid route between the airport and the financial centre of Pudong provides excellent insight into the condition of German industry, as it also shows how the world changes: uncertainty, arrogance, inflexibility and tactical ineptitude on the German side; sovereignty, pragmatism, flexibility and tactical shrewdness on the Chinese. 'The Germans don't treat us like customers, but like employees', was how a senior staff member of the Shanghai City administration summarised the relationship.[52]

The biggest mistake on the part of Thyssen Krupp was that they underestimated the Chinese. Thyssen Krupp suffered its first major setback when the group wanted to sell a huge amount of steel for the track at an inflated price. The justification was that it was patented, special steel. The Thyssen Krupp managers had not only lost a lucrative contract, but also their bond of trust to the Chinese. At any rate, back then it was still a question of whether the 1300 kilometre stretch between Peking and Shanghai should be built with the German electromagnetic levitation system. After this incident the Shanghai operating company rightfully issued the rule to order as little as possible from Thyssen Krupp.

They were not only inept at trying to cheat their customers, but also delivered inferior quality. They produced, according to a staff member of the Shanghai city administration, with the attitude, 'for the Chinese it's not so important'. The list of defective parts was long and this caused substantial costs and eventually eroded the Germans' profit. It was only after about half of the approximately 2.4 million earthing seals had already been delivered by Thyssen Krupp-Casting Techniques that it emerged that they had a fundamental manufacturing defect.[53] The Thyssen Krupp managers let too many weeks go by until they finally admitted to the mistake. The parts had to be manufactured again. The Chinese still evaluated this production fault as an exception to the otherwise world-renowned German skills of production and engineering. Even with the manufacture of the Stratorpakete the core technology of the suspension technique no quality assurance was undertaken. They had the wrong measurements. It was annoying for the Chinese that despite the enormous time pressure, they again did not get an answer to their complaint for several weeks. In order not to lose time they consented that the packages that had already been produced did not have to manufactured again but could be re-treated instead. This saved Thyssen Krupp a lot of money. Whilst there were no problems with this in Shanghai, as the Chinese controlled the processes, the parts were so unprofessionally polished by German workers, so that they began to rust just after having been put in place.[54] Replacements for the defective parts eventually had to be flown in by airfreight at great expense. The Chinese were speechless over this excessive negligence.

But things were to get even worse. Also the hundreds of kilometres of cable that had been delivered had to be exchanged after weeks of negotiations. The word on the construction site was that even the German's six automatic cable-laying machines were not operational. The semi automatic devises manufactured by the Chinese on the other hand did not cause any such problems. Also the railway engine switches that had been delivered from Germany were too weak, which meant that they sometimes worked and sometimes not. And the pressurised carriages manufactured in Hanover had even greater defects: the air conditioning systems were not suited for

Shanghai's stiflingly hot weather. The rivets of the pressurised cabins began to rust before the vehicles had even started their normal operations. The Chinese are convinced that they could have manufactured vehicles of this quality by themselves. Wu Xiangming, the project manager on the Chinese side, who was nicknamed 'Commander Wu', asked Prime Minister Zhu Rongji to mediate. Ekkehard Schulz, the Thyssen Krupp AG's Chairman was informed through the Chinese–German diplomatic channels that he had an audience with the Chinese Prime Minister on the 8th of March 2002. The Prime Minister had fixed the meeting despite the annual conference of the People's Congress in progress at that time. Zhu openly addressed the problems. Schulz apologised, as the participants reported, and assured that they would be responsible for all additional costs. It was however particularly important for the Chinese Prime Minister that the work was finished on time. Schulz made the promise to keep to the 31st of December 2002, no matter what happened.

However little changed as far the problems were concerned. The trial run had hardly begun when the cables started to singe at high speed. Again and again the train came to a standstill on an open stretch. These hundreds of kilometres of cable had to be exchanged and flown into China. The additional costs mounted to millions of Euros.[55] However there was not enough time to exchange the cables before Prime Minister Zhu and Federal Chancellor Schröder's trial run. The probability that the train would come to a standstill on an open stretch in front of the world press was irresponsibly high. However the journey proceeded without problems. Immediately afterwards Zhu and Schröder visited the control centre and followed a further journey on the monitor. About two minutes after the delegation had left the room, the train came to a standstill on an open stretch. It was more then a year later that the Transrapid was eventually able to begin its regular service. Thyssen Krupp was irresponsible in the way it handled German taxpayers' money. The damage to the image of the German economy is inestimable. The long distance stretch between Peking and Shanghai was assigned to the Japanese. The Germans will only receive the contract for the 170 kilometre stretch to Hangzhou under the condition that as much as possible is manufactured locally. And the problems continued for Thyssen Krupp. Shortly after Wen Jaibao had taken over power as Prime Minister, the rolling mill section was not approved for Thyssen Krupp's ultra modern steel plant in Shanghai the company's largest steel plant outside Germany – despite the agreement of the former President Jiang Zemin and even though the German group had already acquired the property for this purpose. The reason given by the Mayor of Shanghai Han Zheng was that the industrial complex was too close to the site of the 2010 World Exhibition.[56]

Meanwhile, the Chinese are increasing the pressure: rust-proof steel sheets worth 300 million Euro are kept idly in stock, because the Chinese partner together with the Japanese competitor Nisshin Steel offers a cheaper product. A planning commission is making sure that in the context of the Transrapid extension everything is working according to Chinese interests. Because negotiations were delayed, ThyssenKrupp's CEO Ekkehard Schulz decided to downsize the Transrapid department considerably at the beginning of 2006. Almost two-thirds of the 270 employees working on the Maglev (magnetic-levitation) project in Germany were laid off. Another 60 had already been axed in early 2004 already. Günter Weckerlein, sent in by Siemens as the chief representative of the consortium in Shanghai was also relieved of his duties, and the ThyssenKrupp executive in charge of the Transrapid, Heinrich Ingelbüscher, already had been sent into retirement tacitly a few months early 'due to health reasons'. Time and again he had clashed vociferously with the Chinese project manager Commander Wu Xiangming. ThyssenKrupp demanded 200 million Euro from the Chinese for the permission to build the train under licence. The Chinese however argue that the maglev train will reach its series-production readiness and commercial potential for other countries only in China, hence they claim the right to build it free of charge. Added to this that the Chinese are arguing among themselves. The Hangzhou administration wants to share the costs equally between the two cities, Shanghai demands to set the new track against the 38-kilometre-long track between the international airport and the financial district Pudong. One thing however is certain: Under each of the options currently disputed, almost 90 per cent of the Transrapid will be manufactured in China.

By the spring of 2006, the Chinese had cooked up a new strategy to exert pressure on the Germans. 'China is planning its own Maglev train', Chinese papers reported. 'We're taking it calmly while avoiding arrogance', was Siemens' comment when the government-owned China Aviation Industry Corporation (CAC) announced its plan to build a test track in July for its own maglev train, named CM1 Dolphin. Until then virtually nothing was known about the Chinese train. Like many recent successes of Chinese development, the maglev train was part of the Chinese high-tech pro-gramme 863, in which the government is focusing on the research and development capacities of the country's universities, institutes and compa-nies. It was claimed that the maglev technology was a product of the Xinan Traffic University and the Beijing University for Defence Technology. The train-sections with a length of 27 metres with room for 60 to 90 passengers each are a product of CAC, an aviation firm founded in 1958, from the central Chinese city of Chengdu. This is where the test train is currently being built. After completion, scheduled in April, it will be shipped to

Shanghai where the Tongji University is laying a 1.7-kilometres-long test track. It seems unlikely, however, that it will be possible to bring the Chinese development to its maturity phase there. The train is supposed to reach a speed of 100 kilometres an hour. But this is not possible on the test track in Shanghai, to say nothing of the 500 km/h the CAC is aiming at.

Even the Chinese admit frankly that the Germans are still far ahead. 'It is as yet impossible for us to build a train that equals the quality of the Transrapid', says Professor Li Fu of Xinan Traffic University. 'It will take another eight years at least before China can solve the relevant problems.'

Either way, the building of the Transrapid will go down in history as an important record of the shift of the world's main economic emphasis from the West to the East.

The concubine economy was able to take shape because the forces of the market and the planned economy converged on each another under the huge pressure of globalisation. It was not the fresh wind of the market economy that managed to assert itself, but it was the planned economy that showed capitalism its limitations. In the free competition of markets China has the most attractive market and has organised this efficiently enough. The surprising part is that capitalism's mechanism of competition is playing companies into the hands of the Middle Kingdom. The pilots of the planned economy are beating the market economy with their own mechanisms. At the same time Western industry voluntarily invests in China, because even though there is limited room to manoeuvre it is worth the effort. Many companies are already tuning in to the worst of all possible success models for the China market. The companies are breaking even – enough to get rewarded at the international stock exchanges for their higher turnover and world market share with increasing prices.

This corresponds approximately to the strategy, which is being discussed in the think-tanks of the state council.[57] Even if the Western and Japanese industries consider the concubine mechanism as harassment it is nevertheless a sensible beginning from an economic point of view. China operates according to its own code. It behaves like a tough bouncer in front of a trendy disco: where many want to get in, there is a strict dress code, so that all (the people) who do get in can surround themselves in a pleasant atmosphere. International corporate groups therefore only have the choice of ignoring the Chinese market and thereby earn nothing, or involving themselves in the market and earn a little with great difficulty. China has no reason for allowing the foreigners to make huge profits, which are then taken out of the country and lost for the national Chinese economy. 'The emperor had to consume his concubines like vitamins', wrote a historian.[58] This is exactly the role that China has in mind for the foreign industry.

# Chapter 9

# CONTROLLING THE WORLD

> The victimisation of countries that are weaker or less pampered through luck by more powerful or richer countries should not remain unpunished.
>
> *Prime Minister Li Peng in front of the International Monetary Fund.*

The International Monetary Fund (IMF) and the World Bank made it easy for the Chinese to play their trump card. They allowed themselves to make gross misjudgements. Instead of looking to the shadows that outline the future world order, and to develop their strategies accordingly, they were caught up in their familiar neo-liberal ideological framework.[1] As American interests are very strongly represented in the IMF, its managers during the 1997/98 Asian crisis firstly ensured that this did not flow over to the USA, and then administered the financial shot in the arm to the affected Asian countries dependent on how far these were willing to open up to the international financial markets and trade. In addition to this they have always paid attention to only letting countries ascend only under condition in which Washington maintain a strong influence, and in which above all American interests of world dominance were assured. 'Sometimes the conditions seemed to be hardly anything more than simple demonstrations of power', is how Josef Stiglitz, the World Bank's former chief political economist describes the situation.[2]

Originally the IMF was meant to be a global institution financed out of public funds, ensuring global economic stability through collective action. It was supposed to have the function of financially supporting countries that were threatened with an economic slump and putting pressure on those states that, 'are not rendering an appropriate contribution to the total demand'.[3] Such international organisations are urgently needed.

Asia (without Japan) only has 10.5 per cent of the votes. The World Bank is frequently headed by an American and the IMF always by a non-American, who however must be much more heavily weighed on the side of the USA than for instance the UN Secretary General. For the Chinese it is therefore an important goal to bolster their influence in the world's economic organisations onto a similar level as that in the UN.

Under the pressure of the Asian crisis China succeeded in substantially improving its position. The world officials of the IMF forced the countries affected by the crisis to open their markets, with the argument that only in this way would they realise how strong they actually were. In other words, only without armbands can one find out how well one can swim. There is a lot to be said for this theory, certainly only under the condition that the countries concerned possess a minimum capacity to bear the burden. Otherwise they simply go under. Russia collapsed (into itself) with this opening strategy at the beginning of the nineties. But the IMF preaches; 'until today with the ideological fervour of the superiority of the market', Stiglitz rages in his book *In the Shadow of Globalisation*, in which he gets even with the international organisations. The IMF 'had forced markets to open before social security nets had been put in place, before there was an appropriate legal framework and before the countries could withstand with the sudden swing of the rules of the market, which are substantial components of modern capitalism. The IMF forced political-economic measures, which led to the eradication of jobs before the most important conditions for the creation of new jobs had been fulfilled. It had imposed privatisation before there was sufficient competition.'[4] The American economist Paul Krugman described the IMF officials as,

> Medieval doctors who kept insisting on venesection and repeated the procedure even when the bleeding worsened the condition of the patient.[5]

Admittedly nobody had forced the Tigers to live beyond their means, In 1986 Thailand already had to borrow 8 per cent of the gross domestic product annually, to maintain a growth rate of 7 per cent. Between 1993 and 1996 the national foreign debt rose by 32 billion US dollars.[6] In the same time period the – mostly short-term – indebtedness of Thai enterprises doubled itself from 38 billion to 74 billion US dollars. The state acted as if it would take the responsibility for this. The American creditors in particular were not well disposed towards their debtors, when they discovered that there was nothing left for them. The international financial world had been deceived by the Tiger states. To describe the collapse that followed in the manner of globalisation's adversaries as, 'brutal economic imperialism with the help of the IMF', or 'the organisation of globalisation along the lines of radical neo-liberalism',[7] is forceful, but a little bit simplistic. No one in the case of the German property fraud Jurgen Schneider, who would accuse the German Bank of 'brutal economic imperialism', because it firstly lent money to Schneider at first and then made sure that he ended up in jail.[8] But Asian countries with nice beaches and friendly people arouse more sympathy in the public than real estate sharks. That the banks in the case of Schneider and the international financial world in the case of Thailand first closed their eyes and then dealt a heavy blow is the other side of the coin. Nevertheless this does not change anything with regard to who the swindler is and who has been swindled. Even those well versed in the subject like the former Minister of Finance Oskar Lafontaine were inclined in the estimation of the responsibility of the Tiger states to create legends: 'The process of opening the market demanded the free movement of capital. But foreign capital needs for example the national economies least of all. The Tiger states and Japan had the highest savings rate in the world. Under the protection of tariffs and controls on the movement of capital they built up export economies and invested in education and infrastructure. Over many years they had enormous economic growth, which not only benefited a few rich people but the entire population. The free movement of capital, implemented by the IMF, destroyed the Asian economic model and consigned the until then rapidly growing national economies to the currents of international movements of capital. It resulted in the well-known bubbles of the real estate prices bursting and the collapse of currencies.'[9]

The Thai government also knew before the cave-in that it had overdone it. A few months earlier the Thai Prime Minister Chavalit Yongchaiyudh had sent a delegation on a secret mission to Peking to borrow 10 billion US dollars. Premier Zhu did not want to become an accomplice of the Thai machinations.[10] It was quite clear to him: the Tigers were to blame for their bankruptcy.

The IMF, however, further weakened them, as the developed nations wanted to secure for themselves the juiciest parts of the bankruptcy assets.

'The hedge funds and speculators were more like a pack of hungry wolves attacking a sick and weakened prey', according to Supavod Saicheu the managing director of Phatra Securities. 'The wolves took advantage of the situation, yet they had not created it.'[11]

China was the only winner of the Asian crisis. The IMF had eliminated the competitive ability of its direct rivals and thereby ironically had greatly assisted its rise to the USA's biggest competitor. China succeeded in taking over the market shares of the Tiger states, an action which it defends this day. Through this course of events the alternatives for investment in Asia were also reduced for German enterprises. The IMF therefore had not only harmed itself, but also the world and had rendered bad services to its American patrons, because the focal point of American interests in Asia, as Henry Kissinger formulated it, is

> to prevent the dominance of one power – especially a hostile one – over the entire continent, to secure the contribution of Asian nations to global prosperity and to cushion inner-Asian conflicts.[12]

South Korea, economically the strongest Tiger state and China's eastern neighbour became the biggest victim of IMF policy. Only months after Thailand had to carry out its oath of disclosure in 1997, South Korea had also got into difficulties. Rumours that the country could not pay back its Western debts led to devaluation speculation. Thousands of speculators exchanged the South Korean Won into a stable currency, mostly the US dollar. To support the national currency, the state had to buy Won with valuable US dollars. Within weeks the foreign exchange reserves were as good as exhausted.[13] Foreign debts amounted to over 170 billion US dollars. South Korea urgently needed money and therefore invited the representatives of the IMF to Seoul. For an aid programme of 58 billion US dollars the South Korean government committed itself in December 1997, to float the exchange rates, open the bond market, permit the sale of Korean companies to foreign enterprises, liberalise imports, approve market access to banks and security houses and to facilitate the purchase of real estate by foreigners. Additionally South Korea had to increase the interest rate, simplify the dismissal of workers, and break up the large conglomerates as well as close several banks. The insolvent government had barely agreed to measures that had been forced upon them in their hour of need when it began to rally the call for resistance against the IMF. President Kim Dae-jung called on the population to lend its private gold to the state so that the IMF credits could be paid back as quickly as possible and free itself from its obligations. The Koreans did actually deliver over two hundred tons of gold within three months from which the government was able to release over 2 billion US dollars. This was certainly little compared to the 9 billion US dollars with which foreign investors bought themselves into the economy in 1998.

Nearly two billion of this amount originated from Germany. BASF took over the animal feed subsidiary of the chemical group Deasang and the Bosch AG bought Mando, the largest auto supplier. China on the other hand used the favourable moment to take market shares away from the Koreans through cheaper and better production, as for instance in the shipbuilding and automobile industry. In order to be able to keep up, numerous South Korean enterprises had to shift their production to China.

The IMF's strategy to put Korea back on its feet under high pressure and in the shortest time with open capital markets, was used by China and left Korea's new flank wide open.[14] It behaved in a similar way with Thailand and Indonesia. Strangely the IMF had acted to its critics' liking, because nothing does a better service to levelling the playing field of globalisation than the emergence of a competitor that can stand on an equal footing with the overly powerful USA. China is the only country that one can believe is capable of this role at present.

The IMF had obviously underestimated the economic strength of China. In fact its managers should have known better. China had for a long time already disentangled itself from its ensnarement as an IMF donor country. It pursued exactly the opposite policy that the IMF recommended. The country was praised for this whereas other Asian countries were criticised. At the Asian European Ministerial Meeting in January 1999 this differing yardstick became glaringly clear. Malaysia had also opposed the IMF strategies and cut a path similar to China's: the country's currency had again been pegged to the US dollar, Malaysian fortunes were not allowed to be transferred abroad, Western investors only had a limited access to the Malaysian market and the foreign debts were not allowed to rise rapidly again. Added to this the country allowed itself a massive budget deficit and set demand in motion through state contracts. In the first six months of 2002 foreign investors transferred approximately 2.5 billion Euros to Malaysia, the stock exchange got moving and growth leapt from 0.3 per cent to 4.1 per cent. The quota of loans that had not been paid back sank to under 10 per cent. Malaysia had quickly regained control of its economic crisis. It had, to put it bluntly, followed China's development scheme, and not the USA's. Through this China's reputation gained enormously in Asia.

The IMF on the other hand classified Malaysia's economy as being weak and made the prognosis: 'The prospects for a lasting medium-term recovery are much more uncertain than they are for other East Asian countries'.[15] Admittedly the financial and enterprise sectors had been strengthened, but the state had through its measures 'gambled with the successes'.[16] Beyond this it warned that 'the investor's confidence has been damaged, (...) the official sources of external financing have been sealed off. None of the two sources will once again gush, unless the policy is modified.'[17] As a counter-move China and Hong Kong were praised for the same classical Keynesian policy: the Chinese had, 'successfully been able to defend their exchange rate regime and (...) had thereby contributed to the stability of the Asian financial markets'.[18] The pressure on the currency had been 'cushioned to an extent'. The increased expenditures, 'by the state are appropriate. In this context it is important that the recently strengthened capital controls do not have a negative influence on legitimate trade and investment activities.'[19]

Whilst the IMF only gives money to countries like Korea or Thailand if they fulfil its hard demands, it restricts its criticism of China to polite appeals, which are mostly also packaged in huge praise. So for instance in August 2001 after the exuberant acknowledgement ('outstanding economic achievements, with durable growth cushioning the deflationary pressure and in a strong external economic position') there was a softly formulated suggestion that China should give up firmly pegging the yuan with a range of 0.2 per cent. 'At the right time the current practice should be replaced by a gradual opening of the pegging and the connection to a basket of curren-cies.'[20] China did not even give an answer. There was absolutely no reaction from the financial markets. 'I'm not sure if an IMF comment alone is able to accelerate China's plans', was the description of the power relationship by an analyst working for the Hong Kong branch of the Bank of America.[21] And another formulated it more cuttingly. The IMF is 'no longer an advi-sory institution as far as China is concerned'.[22] Andy Xie Morgan Stanley's Chief economist for Asia indirectly doubted the professionalism of the IMF: 'a change in policy in this regard is years away. I cannot see anything in the global economy or in the domestic economy which will make it necessary to alter the present course.'[23]

When in the spring of 1998 the Japanese yen fell to its lowest level for almost a decade and subsequently put the yuan under pressure, the Chinese decided to test their new power in the world. Dai Xianglong the Head of the Chinese Central Bank postulated self-confidently: 'we are requesting the Japanese to stabilise the yen'.[24] Dai not only had Japan in his sights, but the USA, too, as only the Americans had enough money at their disposal to help the Japanese. Actually the boss of the Central Bank did not threaten with an automatic devaluation of the yuan, but he also did not rule it out.[25] 'The sinking yen is having a very negative influence on China's trade and its economic reforms', warned Dai. It 'puts China under great pressure to guar-antee the stability of the East Asian economy'.[26] When the Americans and the Japanese did not react, Peking became clearer and let the Vice Minister for Foreign Trade announce that an adjustment of the currency could no longer be excluded.[27] The threat worked. After only an hour the American bank of issue decided to give in and support the yen with a financial boost of 4 billion US dollars.[28]

For the first time in history China was able to force the most powerful country in the world to a billion dollar transaction, in so doing it had clearly stated the new significance of China for the global economy. At the same time Japan's independence diminished, as the Japanese Government had had to make political concessions in return to the Americans. The Chinese had been right in their assumption that the Clinton administration did not want to the American economy to have to handle a massive collapse of China. Especially as Clinton intended – as the first US President after the bloody repression of the protest movement – to visit China in only a few days. 'We hope that the USA and Japan will (under) take further steps to stabilise the yen', commented the Chinese Chief of the Central Bank and affirmed that one would not devalue the yuan.[29] This was to represent a turning point in the relationship between China and Japan, as China had won independence and recognition, whilst Japan became increasingly dependent on China, and still is until today. A good half a year later at a banking conference in Tokyo, the Central Bank chief Dai Xainglong played with the initiative of the IMF like a cat with ball of wool. He let it be known that, 'we are seriously thinking (about a devaluation)'. This not only frightened the IMF. Nobody had wanted a definite devaluation. Soon however it became obvious that this surprising statement was only a warning for the Japanese colleagues, not to let the yen get even weaker. Japan is China's most important trading partner. Only a few days later on the tropical island Hainan Prime Minister Zhu clarified: 'due to the consideration of the interests of the region and our own interests, China continues to insist on not devaluing its currency and to further peg it to the US dollar'.[30] Thereby relegating the IMF initiative as a non-starter.

A few years later the IMF's financial policy clearly leaned in the direction of China. In the official speech of the former Head of the IMF and current Federal President Horst Kohler during a visit to China in September 2002, not one critical word was said about China's economic policy. In fact the opposite: in fine diplomatic nuances Kohler represented European interests, which in this case coincided with those of the Chinese and opposed those of the Americans. 'China's actions demonstrate that it is possible to use globalisation to everyone's advantage, by taking part in global growth and campaigning for international co-operation that bears the legitimate rights of all nations' in mind[31] – and so puts the autocratic demands of the USA into perspective, one might add as an afterthought. When however Snow, the American Minister of Finance visited China, Kohler requested more flexibility with the exchange rate of the country: 'The IMF has already for quite some time been of the opinion that it would be in China's best interest to gradually create a more flexible exchange rate system.'[32] In this way the Central Bank could improve its control over the money supply and additionally more effectively protect the economy from domestic and foreign shocks. Because of the fast growth of the money supply, the risk of inflation is supposed to be relatively high in China. However there were some concerns he did not raise: 'I would advise not to liberalise the flow of capital overnight'.[33] The seeds that had been spread by Kohler began to sprout. The industrialised nations also didn't get round to inviting the Chinese Minister of Finance to the meeting of the G7 Finance Minister's in October 2004 for the first time. And also in this round the topic was addressed in distinct terms, without generating any major actions from the Chinese. 'The stability of our currency is crucial for Asia's and the whole world's economic stability', Jin retorted.[34] The concessions of the Chinese were of rather a rhetorical nature, was how Hans Eichel summarised the situation after a meeting with his Chinese counterpart Jin Renqing: 'It is new that they have merely accepted the free market principal of a freely tradable currency'.[35] Afterwards Eichel also openly criticised the USA: 'I do not consider the solution of the pegging to the US dollar to be sensible. China's economy has to become more stable. We also only floated our currency in the seventies.'

In the following months, however, the Bush administration began to increase its pressure on China's monetary policy. The Americans argued that the yuan would be grossly undervalued, leading to a distortion of competition in favour of the Chinese economy that amounts to doping the Chinese export industries. Finally Peking reacted with an upward revaluation of the yuan by 2.1 per cent. 'This has virtually no economic effects', said Andy Xie, chief economist at Morgan Stanley in Hongkong. The revaluation was merely a symbolic gesture to counter international pressure. China has no intentions to revaluate its currency significantly in the near future. And nobody will be able to force them. China is a special case: No country under pressure to revaluate its currency has ever had so much influence on the global economy, and never before has the global economy been so integrated. Two-thirds of Chinese exports to the USA, for instance, are produced by Sino-American joint ventures. Consequently, punitive tariff duties would be harmful to US companies as well. The interdependence of both sides is so strong that it is in nobody's interest to allow the tensions over the yuan-revaluation to escalate. As a result the exchange rate of the Chinese currency will more or less stay put. This is a new reality: no power, country or institution is currently commanding enough to assert itself in this matter against the will of China. And China and Europe are moving closer together.

China is also trying to establish itself in the IMF as the representative of the developing countries. Already at the IMF conference in Hong Kong in October 1998 the country stood against the powerful in the global institution. Partly out of concern that the country would be infected by the crisis and partly because of the awareness of their own position of power, the former Prime Minister Li Peng openly attacked the IMF managers in a manner that is unusual for the Chinese. 'The free flow of capital over national borders strengthens the development of the global economy. It makes it easier for many countries to access capital. But it also brings financial risks along with it. Developing countries are easy prey for international financial speculation. A financial crisis is no good for anyone.'[36] And he added: 'if the international community is searching for peaceful, stable, economic development then it cannot afford to ignore the reasonable needs of the developing countries'.[37] The IMF should therefore orientate itself according to the following basic concept: 'every country has the right to independently search for its social system, its path of development and its lifestyle. In this respect it is important that the path of development be in accordance with the national conditions existing at that particular time.' This is also absolutely in the interest of the industrialised nations. If the developing countries posses healthy economic growth and social stability, 'they increase the volume of the world market, which creates more work and more business opportunities for all countries'.[38] And without naming the USA he demanded: 'the victimisation of countries that are weaker or less pampered by luck by more powerful or richer countries should not remain unpunished'.[39] The fact that such statements are formulated by a politician who in his own country tolerates the victimisation of the weaker by the more powerful, when this serves the higher goal of stability, may weaken his position somewhat. Nevertheless with this Li qualifies himself as a critic of globalisation. The similarity with the substance of what for example the Chief editor of *Le Monde* diplomatique wrote several months later in December 1997 under the heading 'Disarm the markets', is remarkable:

The tornado which is devastating the Asian money markets, is threatening the whole world. The globalisation of investment capital creates universal uncertainty. It derides national borders and weakens the power of states to secure democracy and happiness for its citizens. The globalisation of financial capital sets up its own laws. It has established a separate supranational state with its own administrative machinery, its own spheres of influence and its own policy: the International Monetary Fund (IMF), the World Bank, the Organisation for Economic Cooperation and Development (OECD) and the World Trade Organisation. The powerful organisations unanimously sing to the tune of market values and the huge media (organisations) of the world are their faithful echo.[40]

The German representatives of this movement pressed home the same argument: 'They were always the single/independent decisions that were not democratically controlled but were merely based on the national interests of the Bank of issue and the financial technocrats of the USA, Japan and the EU, which time and again threw back the development of the world economy and thereby the fight against poverty and unemployment', wrote Harald Schumann in his book, *What do the critics of globalisation want?*, 'but until this day the regents of the money world refuse to recognise this. Instead they transform, of all things the institution, whose task was actually to prevent such crises, into the central instrument for causing and aggravating such catastrophes: the IMF'.[41] Even if the one lacks credibility the others are not so exact when it comes to the facts; one comes to the surprising conclusion that the overlap of positions between the Chinese government and the opponents of globalisation is large. And if there is a power that exists, which is in the position to assert the ideas of the critics of globalisation, then it is the Chinese government. Used to tasks that take perseverance, it will also keep at it in the years to come. In May 2001 the Vice Governor of the Bank of China and IMF Director, Li Ruogo challenged the industrialised nations in front of the International Monetary and Financial Committee, to adopt efficient measures to, 'create a friendly international economic environment for developing countries'.[42] The goal of the Chinese policy is perfectly obvious: the power of the prominent industrialised nations, and above all the supremacy of the USA is to be relativised. The developed countries are to transfer money and technology to the developing countries in the interests of a stable world economy. China also ranks itself among these countries. Additionally the industrialised nations are to raise their development aid to the UN required level of 0.7 per cent of the gross national product. China's IMF representative also demanded the 'full opening' of the developed countries' markets for the developing countries.[43] The Chinese leadership, which traditionally will not put up with an interference in its internal affairs, demanded, without naming certain countries, that, 'the adaptation to certain norms and standards should correspond to a country's level of development at that particular time. Additionally the measures should be voluntary and not be forced upon (a country).'[44] With growing self-confidence the Chinese leadership has become increasingly pronounced in its criticism. The speech of the Chinese Central Bank boss, Dai Xianlong on the occasion of the fifth meeting of the International Monetary and Financial Committee in Washington in April 2002, sounded as if it had been written by the IMF critic Josef Stiglitz.[45] Dai was hard and precise when he said in his first sentence that there is, 'no clear indication of a long-term recovery of the American economy', in order to immediately afterwards demand, 'structural reforms in the Euro zone' and to exert pressure on Japan: 'Japan should strengthen its efforts to free its economy from the current difficult situation.' He was forthright in rubbing salt into the IMF's wounds: 'the systematic irrationality in the international financial system had led to an unbalanced allocation of global resources and to huge fluctuations of the most important currencies, which had once again impaired the development of international finances and trade'. At a later stage he actually named the institution concerned: 'The IMF has to take greater care of the reform of the international financial system.' No other representative from an important country that allowed themselves to render such a clear message.

Only weeks after the USA had closed its steel markets in 2003, Dai demanded, as the representative of a country that protects its markets like no other: 'special attention should be given to protectionism that is once again gaining weight in the weak economic environment'. The analysis was followed by a prescription, which diametrically opposes the goals of the IMF. There should be 'measures taken', he demanded 'in order to prevent these huge fluctuations among the most important currencies, and to thereby create a stable environment for the world economy'. Additionally the developed countries should, 'financially support, transfer technology as well as totally open their markets', to the developing countries. He called for a 'multipolar' world economy that would contribute to, 'a new international political and economic order, which is fair and rational'. So far developing countries have not had the opportunity of participating in the establishment of these new standards and their special needs had therefore not been considered. Developing countries that had got into difficulties should not through the critical comments of the IMF be 'excluded from international capital markets'. They should have no 'unfair burdens' placed upon them and have 'more scope' with the implementation of measures agreed upon with the IMF. Besides the World Bank and the IMF should co-operate more effectively and share the tasks among themselves. A few weeks later the national press agency quoted a representative of the Chinese Central Bank as saying: 'it is necessary to control powerful financial organisations. China is concerned about the relatively slow progress in this field.'[46]

When in turn the Swede Stefan Ingves, who is currently Director at the IMF, spoke four weeks later at the Second China Financial Forum,[47] he held himself back in the presence of the recalcitrant country. He did not even mention that technically China is financially cut off from the outside world; he also did not address the fact that the pegging of the yuan and the US dollar hardly had a fluctuation margin, that a strong regime prevailed with the control of the flow of capital and that international banks hardly have access to the market despite China's membership to the WTO. Instead Ingves began his lecture by listing China's achievements. 'The economic leadership in China is aware of the challenges and has a reliable reform strategy. The fundamental elements of the restructuring of the banks – leadership, institutions, regulations and strategies – are making far-reaching progress or have already been established.' Only then he mentioned the 'important weaknesses', such as the balance between stability and reforms, credit culture and the writing off of bad loans. 'When I do this, I am very well aware of the fact, of how difficult it is to transfer strategies or solutions from one country to another. China's situation is very unique.'

The hard criticism of and the indignation about China, which would conform to the IMF's policy, were left out. Not because one did not take China seriously but because the West did not want to upset China. The Chinese had certainly achieved exactly what they had intended: they wanted the industrialised countries to divide themselves over the question of correct financial policy strategy, and that this should have the consequence that the new positions were closer to their own conceptions. Already in the autumn of 1998 the former German Minister of Finance, Oskar Lafontaine and his French colleague Dominique Strauss-Kahn took up a suggestion, which to this day has not been more clearly advocated by any other powerful country than China.[48] The leading currencies of the world, the US dollar, the Euro and the yen were to be subjected to exchange rate targets. Lafontaine naturally did not refer to China as a precedent-setting case, as this would only have politically harmed the Social Democrat from the left (wing). Even the words 'target zones' were carefully avoided in the suggestion. However Lafontaine's suggestion contained all the elements that are characteristic of target zones: the purpose of a 'new trans-Atlantic dialogue' was to agree upon 'guidelines' for the market trend of prices between the dollar and the Euro, in order to prevent huge speculations with the currencies. The nations concerned would the have to orientate their national economic policy accordingly. The co-operation in monetary policy should at the same time become the pivotal point of a large-scale international coordination of economic policy. The biggest loser of this policy would be the country with the most powerful currency: the USA. Their scope of action would have to be restricted. Whilst Japan showed cautious interest, the West was indignant: 'I did not realise which hornet's nest I had prodded,' Lafontaine said later.[49] The Eighth European Banking Congress on the 20th of November 1998 became the day of reckoning for Lafontaine. Prominent central bankers, bank managers and politicians from Europe and the USA severely warned the Federal Government about its plans. Alan Greenspan Chief of the American Federal Reserve called Finance Minister Lafontaine's intention of introducing fixed exchange rates, 'an illusion. (...) This plan is neither feasible nor sensible.'[50] Similarly Wim Duisenberg Head of European Central Bank refused to tolerate the attack on their independence. 'Our main goal for the Euro is price stability. The Central Bank does not pursue an exchange rate target.' Such a target endangers stability and is therefore to be rejected. Hans Tietmeyer the President of the Federal Bank again challenged: 'The reputation and stability of the Euro depend upon the markets' confidence in the Central Bank, that it can resist political pressure. A condition of a permanent siege through politics awaken doubts in the Central Bank. Who wants to rule out that something like this could happen?' Then he addressed the main issue: 'What is the use of an exchange rate arrangement with the American Treasury Secretary if Congress pursues a policy that is not adequate? Exchange rate targets will be ineffective.'[51] He was to be proved right. In February 1999 at the G7 meeting in Bonn Robert Rubin, the American Treasury Secretary made it unmistakably clear that the world's strongest economic power would not accept interference in its monetary policy: those who want to have stable exchange rates, he lectured Lafontaine, should not manipulate them, but instead must ensure that there are healthy economic structures at home and follow a sensible economic policy. The USA could no longer afford to adopt this tone with China. At this stage one can go too far to discuss the pros and cons of the suggestion, which was thrown into the ring by the Federal Government and continues to be persistently pursued by China. We should however not forget that these questions have not been resolved, but instead are being again raised as China's power increases. And then the USA cannot deal with it as it did with the suggestion of the Federal Government. At the beginning of October 2004 at the annually held joint meeting of the IMF and the World Bank, Zhou Xiaochuan made it clear: 'The economic and structural problems of the most important developed countries have a negative impact on the development of the world economy, the exchange rates and even the stability of the financial markets'.[52] In the autumn of 2004 the UN Organisation for Trade and Development (UNCTAD) ascribed to this point of view. In its annual report it warned of a spiral of currency devaluations that could lead to a new world economic crisis. As a solution it suggested a global coordination of the exchange rates. The main advocate of this demand is a relevantly well-known German: Heiner Flassbeck the chief economist of UNCTAD was Secretary of State under Oskar Lafontaine.

Sometimes it can also be informative to think the less obvious through to the end. If a coordinated effort of the two groups under the Prime Ministers Li Peng and Zhou Rongji was still unthinkable, because one had been morally discredited in 1989 in the eyes of the critics and the other was considered as being too economically liberal, then this is quite conceivable these days. The current Prime Minister Wen Jiabao is considered social reformer. He was the assistant to the Party Chief Zhao Ziyang, who in 1989 had been on the students' side. He was behind his boss, as he announced in tears at the square of Heavenly Peace, that he had come too late. If this information should get around the critics of globalisation, then they would have in the leader of the most powerful developing country, a crucial ally in the fight against the Western industrialised nations. Those who are interested in the debate about the international economic system becoming more multipolar, have to hope for this. The IMF has already moved under the pressure of the Chinese: 'it is test of the reliability of the rich nations. If it is a matter of fighting poverty, then their willingness to open the markets in which the developing countries have a competitive advantage is of crucial importance'.[53] These were not the thoughts of the critics of globalisation and also not the Chinese leadership, but instead Horst Kohler said this in his function as the Chief of the IMF.

The European's leeway has not increased recently due to the ascent of the Chinese. This trend will certainly come to a halt as the interests of China and Europe coincide with one another. It will increase in strength to the extent in which Asian countries manage to speak with one voice on central issues. The most obvious goal is the establishment of a common reserve pool such as regional bonds, because Asia's central banks hold approximately half of the worldwide foreign exchange reserves and so far have as a matter of priority invested in US American national bonds. In 2004 alone the Chinese bought bonds to the value of 160 billion US dollars. With this they finance George W. Bush's rising budget deficit. This does nothing for the growth of the region. As a test the 'Asian Tiger Bond Fund A1' was already floated in 2003 by eleven Asian central banks, a bond with Asian national bonds to the value of 1 billion US dollars. The ABF2, which followed only a year later, already has a volume of 11 billion US dollars. Additionally the governments want to put together a reserve fund to the value of 40 billion US dollars, with which they can lend each other support in future crisis situations. China is therefore well on the way to exerting a decisive influence over the rules of globalisation.

# Chapter 10

# THE GLOBALISATION TRAP

For historical reasons Japan is our biggest importer of energy. But we now want to give preference to China.

Bijan Namdar Zanganeh, Iranian Oil Minister,
on the occasion of the agreement
concerning oil deliveries to the value of over
70 billion US dollars

At the beginning of the twenty-first century the world seems to be turning for China like never before in its history. In this process it is following a logic of integration, which had been brought out by globalisation and skilfully strengthened by the Chinese leadership. The first big surprise of the century was that the world economic crisis drove investors into the Middle Kingdom, as companies are forced to open up new markets and to produce their goods more cheaply. Further surprises were to follow: the Olympic committee entrusted Peking with the most important large-scale event in the world in 2008.

Through the attacks on the World Trade Centre the USA, being the mightiest of China's competitors, suffered the biggest defeat on their own territory in their history. China on the other hand has since then been considered a stronghold of stability, which has made the country more interesting as a location for investment in Asia. The USA was thus forced to change its tone when communicating with China. Within a few days after the September attack Washington redefined the country from being 'a strategic competitor'[1] to being 'a strategic partner'.[2] China and the USA discovered the common interest of fighting terrorism.

China completed its affiliation with the USA and Russia as space powers with its first manned cosmic flight in October 2003. During the

SARS crisis in the spring of 2003, the leadership showed itself to be slow at first, but then tackled the crisis well, proving that it is able to master domestic disasters competently, and in the process is able to count on the support of its population. The most important change for the future of the world however became visible during the course of the third war in Iraq: one can much more strongly influence the world through economic power than through wars, from which no clear winners can walk away. China is aware of this, whilst the USA still persists with outdated power tactics.

The third Iraq war did also uncover China's vulnerable spots. The battle for the world's energy reserves is becoming harder. China is in a particularly difficult position, as it only has 2 per cent of the world's oil reserves at its disposal on its own territories, whilst China's consumption is rising faster than its state planners could predict. Therefore it has to immediately secure as many energy reserves for itself as possible. Through this it is forced to integrate itself even more strongly with the world. The USA's aggressive policy assisted China in this process. As a result of the mistrust of the world power – the USA – China and most of its smaller neighbours affiliated even more closely with one another than ever before. They mastered their reservation with regards to the new world power, which in return restrained its growing arrogance. The Chinese leadership continued in a disciplined and deliberate manner to change the world according to its plans.

China took a large step in this direction in December 2001 when it became a member of the WTO. Right from the outset it could afford to determine how and when it implemented the agreements that it had made with the world. For a long time China's WTO membership lulled German enterprises into a false sense of security. It is now obvious that the Chinese can continue to determine the speed at which speed it opens which markets. This is because whoever has the monopoly of the future market can repeatedly afford to breach contracts. The WTO membership was the most significant step for China's full integration into the economic world. It was not easy for the Chinese to enter the WTO. Because of the principle of consent they had to reach an agreement with all of the countries about the conditions of entry. On the grounds of the most favoured nation clause they also had to automatically grant the privileges that they allotted to a business partner to all the others. One argued most about which time period and the extent to which the country should open its markets to the world, and vice versa. The most important negotiation partners were the USA, Japan and Europe. And China could negotiate patiently: the longer China waited and the more enterprises produced in China the clearer the balance of power became to

the WTO officials. The barriers to entry that the Chinese establish were to
grow over the years rather than shrink. They had not forgotten the trade
agreement that had been forced upon them 170 before by Great Britain,
France and the USA and did not want to let themselves to be taken advantage of again.

'Economical globalisation by no means equals universal harmony', the
former Chinese Foreign Minister Qian Qichen summed up these experiences.
'Only an armchair strategist would believe in that.' Long Yongtu, the Chinese
head of the negotiations therefore had no reservations in dealing forcefully
with the former colonial countries. 'Negotiating with the Chinese is like
hitting a ball against a wall. It rebounds and comes flying back', admitted
EU Trade Commissioner Pascal Lamy.[3] The Chinese leadership still has a
clear idea of what it needs the WTO for; on the one hand it wants access to
the Western markets and on the other it regards membership as an effective means of pressurising its own state enterprises to finally implement
reforms. It took nearly fifteen years before China had agreed on all nine
hundred pages of text with all of the one hundred and fifty members of the
WTO in September 2001.

This step had not been uncontroversial in the CPCh. The conservatives
had warned that a flood of international competition would destroy millions
of Chinese jobs. The supporters, however, gained the upper hand. In order
to conclude negotiations Zhu Rongji travelled to the USA in April 1999, in
spite of tensions over the Kosovo War. Things did not go altogether smoothly.
'We had reached agreement when Zhu was in Washington', recalls former
Secretary of Treasury Robert Rubin, 'But we thought we'd have a better
chance with Congress if we'd wait a few weeks to get out of the spotlight.
But somehow, to our collective embarrassment, our agreement was leaked
on the Internet – we never did figure out how the leak happened, and we
certainly didn't anticipate the reaction in China to the delay in formalizing
the agreement. Later in the year, though, Jiang and Clinton had their
breakthrough.' 'With China's membership the WTO is taking a big step to
really becoming a world trade organisation', said Mike Moore, the
Secretary General of the WTO in a grand statement.[4] However the event
did not release the spontaneous waves of enthusiasm on the streets as the
awarding of the Olympic games to Peking in 2008 had done a good two
months previously.[5] In fact this step had a much bigger significance for
China and should further increase the scope of the Chinese economy.
Later, Jiang Zemin called China's WTO entry 'a real test of our learning
capacity, our problem-solving, competition, decision-making, and innovative capabilities. In our effort to modernize,' he used a metaphor from his
favourite exercise, 'we must go swimming in the great ocean of the global

marketplace. 'We must swim – and swim hard – and do everything we can to enhance our ability to struggle with the wind and waves.'

The still-young Chinese WTO history is rather a skilful sealing off than an of integration. Because the industrialised nations need the Chinese market more than the other way round, they hesitate to criticise China's policies and likewise keep their markets closed. Complaints are only carefully formulated: 'the German economy recognises the extent and the speed of the Chinese reform process as a huge accomplishment', stated for example a report of the Asia Pacific Committee of the German Economy for Federal Chancellor Schröder in November 2003. 'Admittedly decisions are still made in China, which either contradict the wording or at least the spirit of the WTO's regulations. Many WTO regulations are only implemented after postponement. (…) The German economy has a great understanding for the phase of difficult restructuring in which China finds itself. However China must also pay attention that German enterprises also encounter increasingly reliable parameters in the difficult environment of the transformation process.'[6]

That WTO members override agreements is nothing new. Even those who have been members for many years protect their markets. In Japan the Western insurance industry has approximately 4 per cent of the market share, even though the country should have opened its markets.[7] In South Korea not even 1 per cent (of the population) drives imported cars. In 2003 US President Bush protected the American steel industry through tariffs, which were condemned as 'illegal' by the WTO.

What is new however is the extent and the obstinacy with which China deals with the agreements and asserts its own strategy. Also unprecedented is the size of the market and the weak position from which Western countries and enterprises may insist on their rights. If German companies refuse the conditions the Chinese have set, there are at any time French, American or Australian enterprises that agree to them in order to snatch the contract away from the competition. The strategy paper of the German economy which is supposed to, 'accompany China's complete integration into the World Trade Organisation',[8] basically a document of German powerlessness. The field on which China annuls the rules of the WTO is wide. The Chinese shipping industry is so strongly subsidised by the state that even the German and the South Korean shipping industry are no longer able to face the competition. The Germans reproach the Chinese for the fact that such a policy harms ones own banks and thereby the national budget in the long run. They know this from their own experience: the German shipping industry has been subsidised for years.

Particularly serious is China's handling of intellectual property rights. The registration of patents takes up to two years in China. A period of time which is more than sufficient for the Chinese industry to copy the product. Even if one has a patent protection on a product, it means very little in China. Theoretically one can in fact sue in cases of theft of technology, but practically the chances of succeeding in such action are very small. It is much more likely that one has to give a precise description of the technical details on the order of the judge in the course of such a procedure, and in so doing one loses further trade secrets to the competition. German mechanical engineering in particular suffers from this problem. For example textile machine manufacturers found copies of their machines in the catalogues of the competitor at a fair in Peking, which included their logo. Some of the machines were even better than the original – the Chinese manufacturers had already developed them further. Usually however the copied machines only deliver 80 per cent of the output of the original, but at 50 per cent of the price. With some German manufacturers the turnover has already halved.[9] Repeatedly engineers masquerading as customers came to the exhibition booths of German manufacturers in order to uncover further details. Effective international instruments against the theft of intellectual property, such as the so-called enforcement agreements, which file charges in the home country and then enforce the judgements through the authorities of the host country, are not recognised in China, even though although this is customary among the member countries of the WTO. Symptomatic of the handling of conflicts is the argument over Chinese commercial law, which China had to change in the process of its entry to the WTO. When European diplomats saw the first draft in the spring of 2004, three quarters of a year before the introduction of this law, which was to specify the scope for international trading ventures, they could not believe their eyes. 'This contradicts the agreements of the WTO', the European Chamber of Commerce raged in an internal report. 'The market is not being opened, but in fact the opposite, as new and ambiguous regulations are being introduced, which greatly restrict the access to the market.'[10] According to this draft only enterprises that order products that they need themselves were to be allowed to enter without difficulties. The trade for a third party – the norm in trading transactions – was simply declared to be an exception and was not laid down in more detail. Rather the draft comprehensively detailed in which cases the rights of the foreign enterprises were restricted. However procedures for demanding their rights, which were frequently abused by the Chinese competitors and authorities, remained likewise unsettled. After strong diplomatic protest the law was actually partially amended. Adequate legal hold, with which foreign enterprises can protect themselves, is admittedly also missing in the final version that came into force on the 11th of December 2004. Western lawyers are of the opinion that the use of the

WTO regulations for foreign enterprises exists less to guide the opening of new markets and more for the increased planning security for the Chinese economy.

In particular the Chinese export economy profits from the dismantling of quotas and trade restrictions. This situation then also affects Germany where business with China is growing the most. Whilst German exports to the Asia Pacific region only rose by 4 per cent in 2003, the exports to China increased by almost 25 per cent in 2004. With a simultaneous clear increase of German imports at approximately 17 per cent China is consolidating its position as Germany's most important trading partner in the region.[11]

So that the European market's dependence on Chinese products does not grow too quickly, the European Commission shut a small latch on the Chinese growth pressure in the summer of 2004. For the time being it does not want to grant China the status of a market economy. The import quotas will only fall further when China also continues to further liberalise its market further. Yet China also has enough export possibilities without the concessions of the Europeans.

In the branch of the automobile industry the economic planners in Peking don't even consider it necessary to mask their strategies. 'The Government will continue to control the import of vehicles and protect the local manufacturers with tariff hurdles', said for example Ding Hongxiang, the Deputy Managing Director of the official trading centre for automobile importers, in the presence of the national press agency, six months after China had become a member of the WTO.[12] At approximately at the same time an order was issued to China's automobile importers, that offences against import regulations, which had been committed within the past three years, were fineable with back payments. Soon afterwards a Hong Kong Volvo dealer was slapped with a a fine of 9.4 million Euros. The company withdrew from its business in China and the business was subsequently taken over by a native dealer. This sentence was in accordance with Chinese law, but was victimisation nonetheless. This automobile importation business was never established on a legal foundation that would have made it possible for dealers to conduct business legally.

Until 1998 most of the imported cars were purchased abroad in the West and smuggled into the country, after the taxes at the beginning of 1995 had been raised from approximately 80 per cent to 260 per cent. A small car therefore cost 28,000 US dollars instead of 8000 US dollars. In particular the People's Liberation Army earned money from this as the soldiers transported vehicles in their high-speed boats to the southern Chinese coast at night. Around 90 per cent of the Mercedes S classes came into the country in this way, and were thus up to 70 per cent cheaper than a normal tax paid car. Driving a smuggled car was considered a harmless crime; some owners did not even make the effort of scrapping off the sticker of the car dealership from Miami. The import business certainly had its dangers as the former BMW-China boss, Dong Xianquan got to experienced in 1998. On a journey in his silver grey BMW 740 iL from Peking to the port of Tianjin he was stopped by a police motorcycle patrol. The examination of the chassis number concluded that he was driving in a smuggled car. When he had taken up his new posting at the end of 1997 he had not thought of verifying the legality of his private car.[13] However in 1998 the then Prime Minister Zhu Rongji, began an anti-corruption campaign that forcefully cracked down on smuggling.[14] But the predicament of the importers hardly improved. Corruption in their sector was to a certain extent restructured by the state and made professional. Instead of suffering from the competition of the smugglers the importers were now forced to operate in a grey area, in which they received import licences from government institutions, which had been granted these by the Ministry of Foreign Trade for their own purposes. The institutions had been strictly forbidden to sell the licences, but for the dealers there was no other way to obtain the import licences. Their price amounted to, depending on the market situation, between 10,000 and 20,000 Euros.[15] As somewhere between 100,000 and 150,000 import licences were issued annually, there was at least a hundred million dollars flowing through the dark system mostly into the black accounts of a group of approximately two dozen state officials and their sponsors. Even today dealers make themselves punishable with every car that they import. Every Porsche, every Mercedes and every other imported vehicle in China has come into the country through illegal business dealings. This is a practical mechanism for the state to control imports and the dealers.

But the state also has a number of variables that change the parameters so that it can regulate the importation of cars. These so-called tariff barriers are regulations that international tariff and customs treaties do not abide by, with which it is nevertheless possible to restrict the market access. So for example only Chinese are permitted to sell vehicles in China; international dealers are shut out or need a Chinese partner. All vehicles have to go through a licensing procedure, in which it is examined if they conform to Chinese specifications and safety regulations. Even German luxury cars need to first undergo a Chinese 50,000 kilometre endurance test and be examined under the exhaust standard 'Euro 1', although all European cars already according to standard fulfil the much stricter criterion of the 'Euro 4'. Again and again vehicles fail the inspection because the Chinese mechanics are not able to operate the high-quality Western testing instruments properly. In addition the safety regulations require a crash test, which the authorities admittedly often waive and instead resell the car that has been provided under the table. The officials of the authorising agency willingly let themselves be invited to luxurious visits at the parent plants, where they ask inquisitive questions about production speed and work procedures.[16] Occasionally imports are also held at customs for flimsy reasons such as, for example that the wooden boxes in which the cars are packed, need to go into quarantine and be examined for worms. This expenditure squeezes the profits of the dealer's, who with some luxury vehicles have only sold enough cars after a period of two years to cover their expenses of entering the market. And if a new model comes out in the third year they have to tackle the authorisation process right from the beginning. The Chinese government also knows how to steer the market to its own interests without harming the WTO agreements. So for example the WTO requires China to annually make a certain number of new import licences available annually, yet it does not fix, when and according to which criteria they are to be issued to the dealers. Theoretically the Chinese government could award all their import licences within a certain capacity on the last day of a certain year to one single manufacturer. Here too the Chinese are not clear about their strategy: 'China will open the gates to its markets as late as possible. The warehouses are full of cars produced in China', said Ren Qing, the Vice President of the Chinese Trading Centre for the import of vehicles.[17]

There is also a prohibition on selling imported vehicles together with locally produced ones. So the manufacturers are forced to establish new trading networks for imported vehicles. This regulation puts the brakes on the sale of imported vehicles and at the same time promotes the Chinese economy in two ways. New sales centres mean both new jobs and also new contracts for the building industry as well as providing an advantage for locally produced vehicles.

If the realisation of large infrastructure projects is being carried through, as for example the construction of power stations or underground railways, then these massive projects are in fact publicly tendered for contract by the Chinese government. Admittedly from the outset it has already been decided – against the WTO agreements – what and how much has to be awarded to local manufacturers. World corporate groups like Siemens therefore only have two possibilities: either they do not sell their products to China or they establish a joint venture company with Chinese manufacturers and risk losing their know-how. With some applications for tender it is even a condition that technology is transferred. German enterprises that operate joint ventures with their own majority, which in the meantime are permitted in some branches, only get a chance if they hand back the majority that they had so laboriously asserted. Even when the central government wants to ensure that certain standards are adhered to, the provincial governments are inclined to give preferential treatment to their own enterprises.

So too western banks like the Commerzbank or the Deutsche Bank have not gained the access to the market that they expected. Actually the banking sector is supposed to open on a step-by-step basis until the end of 2006. The banks have so far certainly been hindered from doing so. For every branch that a Western bank wants to open in China it has to deposit several million US dollars. If it wants to do business in Chinese currency – and that has to be in their interest – then the requirements are once again raised explicitly. Chinese banks on the other hand do not adhere to internationally accepted regulations. The Bank of International Settlement, residing in Basel, determined in a globally obliging agreement which percentage of their credits the banks have to hold ready as reserves in the case of a crisis. The Chinese, however, ignored this and could not even be sanctioned for it. Western banks on the other hand are only able to sell money in China at certain rates of interest and can only borrow at certain interest rates from the central bank. The margins that result out of purchase and sale are very small. The banks are also not allowed to transfer as much money as they want to China. The Chinese regulators' strategy is obvious: the Western banks should only exercise so much pressure on the Chinese banks through competition, so that they improve, but at the same time do not take any important market shares away from them. The Chinese consider that to be the best way is for the Western banks to purchase expensive minority holdings from the Chinese banks. Firstly the foreigners are never able to influence the business alignment through a minority holding. Secondly they on the grounds of their involvement have to then be interested in feeding the Chinese bank with know-how in order to strengthen their market position. Finally the foreigners make their partner bank more attractive for other investors, if they decide to get in on the act with an initial public offer with 20 per cent in Hong Kong or New York.

The competition among Western banks is so fierce that this system functions brilliantly. The British HSBC was the first bank to join the Bank of Communications in August 2004. It acquired approximately one-fifth of the shares of the fifth largest Chinese banking corporation, which has a market value of 8.8 billion dollars.[18] The HSBC paid the major Chinese bank 1.75 billion dollars for the 19.9 percentage share. It was the biggest foreign investment in the Chinese financial sector. For this the British bank is actually not allowed to take part in decision-making processes but at least grow along at the same time. The risk that China will be overrun by the West amounts to zero. The Western banks cannot attain any high profits through their business in China, however they do increase their world market share in this sector. It is a deal that works in China's favour, yet it is still one of the best that the banks can close in these difficult times in the world. Admittedly the German banks are no longer financially strong enough to be able to bid in this game.[19]

So too the insurance agents, who had already anticipated 1.3 billion new customers, were disappointed by China's WTO membership. Foreign life insurance agents were supposed to be able to operate freely in the Chinese market from the end of 2004, after individual cities and regions had already been opened for foreign enterprises before this date. The implementation of regulations were however delayed to provide a timely advantage for Chinese insurance companies. 'Foreign companies are only allowed into the market, once it has already been bought up', industry representatives complained in a standpoint paper.[20] In 2003 the Gerling group had once again withdrew from its business in China.

China also profits legally from the WTO, at its neighbours' expense. On the 1st of January 2005 trade barriers, that is, quotas in the textile industry were abolished throughout the world. Since then the country, instead of the poorer Asian countries, can produce even more textiles for the world market. The WTO estimates that China's market share in the American clothing industry are likely to shoot from 16 to 50 per cent.[21] KarstadtQuelle alone increased its imports from China from 37 to 43 per cent in 2005.[22] Countries such as Cambodia and Bangladesh are the biggest losers and thus become even more dependant than before on the support of China. For the German customers this is a positive development. There should be a distinct drop in the price of clothes.

China is a developing country that will not let the WTO bring it down on its knees, which is something that will please the critics of globalisation. The country undermines the goal of the WTO, which wants to liberalise trade at any price. It allows itself to place social stability within its own country as a priority. The foundations of the WTO's policy are shaken by this. This is shown by the sobering reactions of the industry representatives in Germany. China justly opposes international economic interests of the West – exactly in the way that the protest movements in the industrialised nations and developing countries have time and again demanded.[23] If there is one country in which the farmers and local businesses do not fall by the wayside in the neo-liberal competition characterised by the West, then it is China. Although there are many who consider the Chinese government to be a regime that shows disregard for its people, it has pulled more people out of poverty in a short period of time than in any other stage in history. It stands its ground against the economic power politics of the dominant Western industrialised countries. It ensures that capital flows from the First to the Third world, in a volume that has never existed before. Neither the USA nor the UN, nor by any stretch of the imagination the WTO can do anything about this new balance of power. China is too powerful and too successful for them: 'in matters of growth China had the best performance among the large countries and by over-coming the East Asian crisis has proven the best management and ability to react flexibly', Joseph Stiglitz, the winner of the Noble Prize for Economics sums up the situation.[24] The country is asserting its national socialism through globalisation.

Just how stable China is in this process showed itself during the global economic crisis at the turn of the millennium, following only a few years after the Asian crisis. After several smaller collapses, the American stock markets suffered its biggest losses between the 12th and 16th of March since the stock market crash of 1929.[25] The NASDAQ sank by almost 8 per cent,[26] the equivalent of 4.5 billion US dollars, the amount of the entire US American national indebtedness or the combination of Japanese and the South Korean national economy respectively.[27] Since its peak in March 2000 it had fallen by 63 per cent. The crisis shook the entire world. For the first time in 25 years the three most important centres of capitalism – the USA, Japan and Western Europe – caved in at the same time. In 2001 economic growth in the European Union only amounted to 1.7 per cent. The number of sold cars in Germany alone sank by 12 per cent. Eight of the nine largest European stock exchange indices sank by more than 12 per cent.

So for the second time after the Asian crisis it showed how clever the Chinese leadership had been not to have lured by the quick money, and so avoided huge foreign debts and short-term credits. Even in the crisis year of 2001 the foreign exchange reserves of over 180 billion US dollars at the time sufficed more than four times to cover the foreign loan commit-ments for the following year.[28] In fact the Chinese stock exchanges had also collapsed, but as the stock markets are not accessible to foreign speculators, it did not result in an outflow of capital.[29] China managed to keep the Hong Kong dollar as well as the yuan firmly pegged to the US dollar. Yet the international financial markets still doubted for quite some time whether the country could withstand this much pressure. But in the course of the crisis it turned out that it at least profited as much, as it had been burdened by the crisis. Exports actually shrank, but at the same time more Western and Japanese enterprises were forced to invest there.

Foreign confidence had become a determining factor for China, and it has remains so. The upswing is again reflected in the rental market: while the rents in the top locations picked up by upto 10 per cent, they fell in the rest of Asia by upto 20 per cent.[30] China had woken up and was amazingly crisis-resistant.

It is with this certainty that the Chinese government conducts its business. In the autumn of 2002 the party changed its leaders. President Jiang Zemin, who in the confusion of 1989 had begun as a stopgap and had, surprisingly, balanced the conflicting forces skilfully and reliably, passed on the party leadership to Hu Jintao. Deng Xiaoping had chosen him as the best worker of the new generation. In the spring of 2003 the government also changed on a rotational basis. The new government under the leadership of Premier Wen Jiabao surprised their people and the world, in that the policy emphasis changed completely. It was as if the Republicans had been voted out in the USA and the Democrats had come to power. If the old government had been one of the booming cities and rapid economic growth, then the new government stands for their commitment to the interior and social balance. Whilst the booming cities of the east coast had already opened up to the First world, characteristically, rural central and western China was, as before, still deeply stuck in the third as before. Six coastal provinces out of the altogether twenty-two provinces, five autonomous regions and four cities directed by the government produce more than half of the gross national product. 'These are figures that concern me', admitted Premier Wen, 'the development of agriculture and the rural regions is among all issues the most important'.[31] Also Zhou Xiaochuan the head of the central bank stated, 'We have to adapt our model of development.'[32] The model 'growth at any price' with which Deng Xiaoping pushed open the gate to the free market economy has served its purpose. And Peking's mayor explained in a hall full of perplexed Western managers, that 'the social climate is now more important than the investment climate'.[33] After the boom in China and the flow of capital had become a fast-selling item, the time had come to place the economy on a wide, stable foundation. 'Economic growth is important,' stressed vice president Zeng Qinghong, 'but it is not the only criteria for development'.[34] The change in policy once again reflected itself in the biographies of the responsible politicians. Before Zhu Rongji came into the central government as the vice prime minister he had been the mayor of Shanghai. Wen Jiabao had ascended from the rural provinces. He was in Gansu for 14 years, where state and party chief Hu Jintao had spent 14 years. He had hardly been in office when he changed its direction. Because the biggest problem of the Chinese upswing lies in the fact that the wealth is developing in the cities, and only slowly trickles through to the interior. When the deadly lung disease SARS broke out in southern China and threatened to bring the whole country to a standstill, even the usually optimistic analysts of the investment banks saw again a gloomy future of China for the first time since 1989. 'Surely a lot of foreign investment projects will be postponed because of the SARS crisis', thought Andy Xie, Morgan Stanley's Asia economist in Hong Kong.[35] Firstly the southern province of Canton was affected, where approximately 480,000 factories in close proximity manufacture and supply the world markets with consumer goods on the Pearl River delta. The virus also brought the economy in the service and the banking sector of Hong Kong to a standstill. In April SARS cases were reported in Peking and Shanghai. 'The world economy which has already been knocked by war and geopolitical uncertainty, could finally be brought to a tilt by SARS', according to Stephen Roach, the chief economist with Morgan Stanley. 'The consequences of the SARS virus focus themselves on Asia – the strongest growth region throughout the world, which up until now has still kept the world economy's head above water.' Huang Yiping, the Asia Pacific economist with Salomon Smith Barney, painted a black picture for China at that time: 'Investors are already considering whether it really is wise to invest so much money in China. I don't think that China will be able to win back, what it has already lost.' The government reacted late, but not too late. Zhang Wenkang, the Minister of Health and Peking's mayor Meng Xuenong were relieved of their posts. Wang Qishan, the provincial governor of Hainan, who had already been Zhu Rongji's problem-solver in Canton, was called to the capital to take over the role of mayor. With strict quarantine regulations and stringent travel restrictions they eventually managed to get the crisis under control – without any noticeable slump in growth.

Next the Chinese government dedicated itself to the great socio-political challenges. According to a study of the OECD, approximately half of China's 800 million country dwellers are in fact unemployed; approximately 200 million migratory workers are drawn to the cities as construction workers, waiters or domestic helpers. Corruption and fraud cases fuel impatience. According to Western human rights organisations, there are roughly 10,000 demonstrations a year against local governments. The concern is growing that the discontent could reach an uncontrollable scale. Who knows how quickly a cocktail of inflation, unemployment, nepotism and disappointed aspirations can lead to an economic crisis and radical change in the country; the demonstrations of 1989 had resulted under such conditions. Wen Jiabao was formerly the office manager of the liberal Prime Minister Zhao Ziyang, who had opposed the military action and as punishment remains under house arrest to this day.

It is therefore a considerable achievement that Zhao's protégé could go onto become Prime Minister. Eventhough there obviously still is a lot leeway, the most important question is how far can the gap between rich and poor widen, without the social tensions making the country ungovernable? The economy may be bubbling, but must not be left to boil over. So to be on the safe side, no matter what happens, the Chinese government makes the effort to dampen the signs of overheating as early as possible.

The eleventh five-year-plan, enacted in March 2005, clearly reflected these concerns. The paper, now called 'program' instead of 'plan', states that it is 'of decisive significance to speed up the adaption to a new model of growth'. The aims are 'sustainable development' and effective macroeconomic supervision. Also the programme differs markedly from its predecessors in that it omitted the rigid production guidelines that had been characteristic of the previous plans.

The credit tap was turned off for the urban middle classes as the policy on interest is not yet functional. If at the beginning of 2004 40 per cent of vehicles were being purchased on loans; this was reduced to only 10 per cent by the end of the year. Also homebuyers now have to raise more of their own capital. Yet the farmers got such high wage increases that in the second half of 2004, there were three million unskilled workers missing from the factories in the province of Canton. Whilst the Chinese government openly publicises the changes in social policy, Peking does not exactly tell the world about the reversal of Chinese policy that has a significant impact on the world economy. China is increasingly becoming a raw material world power. One Chinese person actually only consumes about a tenth of the oil as an American,[36] but if we look at the total amount of consumption, China has been a heavy weight for quite some time. China already burned more oil than Japan in 2004 and is the second biggest consumer in the world with approximately 10 per cent of global consumption.[37] The international Energy Agency (IEA) estimates that global oil consumption will increase by two-thirds up to the year 2030, and that China will already have ascended to being the world's biggest oil consumer in 2020. Even Claude Mandil, the chief of the IEA, conceded that, 'China's rising demand for oil was underestimated by our own organisation'.[38] 'If China's energy policy does not change radically, its consumption in ten years will lie in the range of 14 million barrels per day', estimates Andy Xie.[39]

The Chinese government was also surprised by the exploding demand. It was only after the September 11th attacks of 2001 in New York and Washington that the problem suddenly came to light. At first the Chinese leadership was concerned about Muslim minorities, who live in the far western oil rich area at the border with Kazakhstan and Afghanistan and have time and again rebelled, even though these have not resulted in considerable clashes for quite sometime. But soon it turned out that China had been hit in a much more sensitive spot: it only possesses 2 per cent of the world's oil reserves, and therefore has to import a third of its requirements. 'The September 11th attacks not only affect the price of oil', said Zhu Xingshan, the deputy director of the Chinese Economic Centre for Energy Research. 'China will have to completely reconsider its oil supply and will have to use many different sources, so as to manage the risks.'[40]

Already in 1996 China had begun investing in a three-figure value in billions in oil fields in Sudan, Venezuela, Kazakhstan, Nigeria, Canada and Indonesia. But most importantly the country has been, just like Russia, despite the UN embargo heavily involved in Iraq since 1997, which after Saudi Arabia has the world's second biggest oil reserves at it disposal. Both countries secured themselves oil fields. Even France began to negotiate, but did not complete a deal. Lukoil, Russia's biggest oil company, bought a share of the huge west Qurna oil field for 1.2 billion US dollars, whilst the China National Petroleum Corporation and the industrial conglomerate China North Industries Corporation (Norinco), which also manufactures weapons, secured themselves rights at the Ahab oil field located a hundred kilometres west of Baghdad, for a total of 1.2 billion US dollars. In addition the Chinese negotiated over the exploitation of the Halfayah field. In these negotiations China, Russia and Iraq not only had the oil supply in mind, but also the weakening of the American position in this region. To strengthen long-term relations with Iraq, China had comprehensively taken care of the building of infrastructure at the beginning of the nineties, after the second Gulf war. The wording of the Iraq strategy issued by President Jiang Zemin is 'Opposition against the USA without it being clearly noticeable'.[41] Wu Lei, a renowned Chinese specialist for international relations, expresses it this way: 'we hardly carry any political baggage. This makes it much easier to expand our influence in the region.'[42]

China's economic activities in Iraq have not yet been fully grasped. Between fifty and sixty Chinese companies, particularly from the construction and energy sector were involved in Iraq in 2003. The China Machinery & Equipment Import & Export Suzhou Corp. (CMEC), the Shanghai Electric Corp. and the Dongfang Electric Corp had all signed contracts to a value of a over 2.5 billion US dollars. The CMEC alone had supplied a power station to the value of 785 million US dollars and had largely finished putting it into place before the beginning of the third Iraq war. First Automotive Works, China's largest automobile manufacturer and VW's partner, delivered buses and pick-ups. In this respect, the American crusade against terror and the decision to march into Iraq, were very bad news for China indeed.[43] *And for Europe & UTC + all*.

The Afghanistan campaign of 2001 had already been a setback for China. The fact that part of the American troops had started the invasion from Mongolia, the buffer state between China and Russia, which had declared itself as neutral, was only a pinprick. That China had already built up very good relations with the Taliban weighed much more heavily on them. Although the United Nations had imposed sanctions against the Taliban, the Chinese state enterprises also involved themselves with the reconstruction of infrastructure in Afghanistan. And so Chinese experts assisted, for example, with the repair of dams and the completely outdated telephone system. 'Only the Chinese are prepared to work under such conditions', said Aryanzai Ehsanullah the manager for government contacts with Afghan Wireless Communication Co. in Kabul.[44] The goal was to combine political and economic interests: China only wanted to become the protective power of countries on their own front door and thereby contain Muslim terrorism, in the neighbouring countries, which threatened western China. And China wanted to secure its supply of raw materials and beyond this to become the raw material hub for Japan and Korea.

When Afghanistan fell into the hands of the Americans the Chinese had to make new arrangements. They concentrated their efforts on Kazakhstan, because the oil-rich country (approximately 6 per cent of the world reserves) shares a 30-kilometre border with China and stretches up to the Caspian Sea in the east. So, the ideal area for a Chinese pipeline. Therefore Hu Jintao's first overseas trip in May 2003 also brought him to a country with 14 million inhabitants, carrying 800 million US dollars in his luggage.[45] A joint venture between the Kazakhstanis and the Chinese had already been extracting oil in Kazakhstan for a considerable period of time. As early as 1997, Kazakhstan's Head of State Nazarbayev and Chinese Prime Minister Li Peng signed a treaty concerning what was then China's largest foreign investment, altogether 9.5 billion US dollars.

Likewise in 2003/2004 China began the construction of a 4000 kilometre pipeline, costing 20 billion Euros, from the western Chinese province of Xinjiang to Shanghai, which will connect central Asia with the booming coastal region. Since the nineties Peking had also endeavoured to stabilise the economy in the other central Asian countries. In Uzbekistan China helped with the building of a railway. It is for this reason that in the summer of 2001 the Peking leadership had, still before the attacks, founded the 'Shanghai Six' together with Russia, Kazakhstan, Tajikistan, Kurdistan and Uzbekistan – an international alliance against terror and separatism. For the first time China tried to visibly position itself as a political player in the region. At first this alliance was smiled upon condescendingly by the USA. After September 11th 2001 the co-operation suddenly gained significance.

Months before the third war in Iraq, China and Russia started to worry about their investments in Iraq. Whilst China was outwardly quiet the Russians did not mince their words. A top Russian manager from the oil industry said that China and Russia were both intervening behind the scenes with the US government, and that they would come to an agreement on the occasion of President Vladimir Putin's visit to Peking in December 2002.[46] The Americans reacted severely to the attempt to undermine their power in the region. They had just occupied Iraq when Thamir Ghadhban, who had been appointed as the Iraqi oil minister by the Americans, announced to the *Wall Street Journal* that the contract with China over the exploitation of the al-Ahdad oil field was, 'mutually agreed to be no longer valid'.[47] The president of the China National Oil and Gas Exploration & Development Corp. (CNODC), Wang Shangli countered that 'this is news for us. Ghadhban was only recently appointed. He doesn't know us at all'.[48] According to lawyers the contract for the oil field holding up to 1.5 billion barrels is as stated by international law still legal: 'The Republic of Iraq continues to exist, and thereby also its institutions.'[49] But China preferred not to settle the conflict in public.

For China the third Iraq war was probably the hardest set back in the short history of reintegration into the world economy. There are a few reasons to believe that this will not been the last dispute between China and America over mineral resources. The third Iraq war will possibly go down in history not as the 'clash of civilisations' but as the first Chinese American conflict over the world's oil reserves. To secure the American way of life, the government in Washington was prepared to strain their international relations to the limit and to sacrifice the spilling of a great deal of American blood.[50]

The new competition in the Middle East was just as dangerous for the USA as the threat by Saddam Hussein. The biggest problem is the USA's alliance with Saudi Arabia, the world's biggest oil producer. Its arch-conservative leadership supports both the USA and Arab terrorists. The American oil industry[51] and probably the political hawks pointed out to the government on several occasions that the following scenario was impending: Energy hungry China could go into a similar functional alliance with Iraq, the second most important oil producing country. This would be easily materialised, because the Iraqis and the Chinese are closer politically, than the USA and the Saudis could ever be. And both would be of enormous mutual benefit: China could secure itself parts of the second largest oil fields of the world and Iraq would have a major client, who would not be concerned what kind of regime was in power in Baghdad. 'China has little room for morality', a Foreign Affairs article informed its readers because one pillar of Chinese diplomacy is that one does not interfere in the internal affairs of other nations. Iraq would also have the opportunity of obtaining ballistic weapons from China, which hardly any other country would sell to them. The USA would then depend more on the Saudis than ever before. If this alliance should falter, Washington would no longer have a new 'partner' in the region. The USA therefore had to act quickly. The fight against terrorism was a welcome cause, to free itself from this geopolitical defensive. Even Donald Rumsfeld, the US Secretary of Defence eventually conceded that there was no connection between the invasion of Iraq and the attacks on New York's World Trade Centre.

The Chinese government however, had no interest in drawing the world's attention to their weaknesses. They did not show their anger outwardly, particularly since a public protest would have raised the unpleasant question about why China had not complied with the embargo. Now the country certainly had to look for new ways to secure its source of energy. Originally Peking had wanted to slowly and inconspicuously build up its oil reserves. But now the supply situation had become uncertain, the price threatened to rise. They immediately began to stock up their reserves. Before the Iraq war China was content with having sufficient stocks in order to be able to supply the country for 35 days, although Western countries install reserves for 90 days and Japan even for 120 days. 'The Chinese demand is the driving force behind the rising world wide demand', is how a report of the IEA in Paris summarised the situation. In 2004 alone the price of oil rose by 40 per cent, and put the level of worldwide economic activity, including the German, under enormous pressure. *The Economist* dubbed China the 'hungry dragon'[52] on its front page, and the ZDF (a German television channel) commented: 'China with its enormous growth potential and associated high consumption of raw materials is booming to extent that it threatens to become a global problem. In the entire industrialised world the oil supply is strained. This is not only the cause of the threat of terror from al-Qaida or the situation in Iraq.'[53] China already needs as much oil as Saudi Arabia, Kuwait and Iran produce together.

China is not only buying oil, but is also securing itself other raw material deposits in far off lands. Beside natural gas, these consist of iron ore and copper and most importantly bauxite, which is indispensable for steel smelting, as well as tin needed for the manufacture of tin plate (i.e., cans), plant protection agents and paints. China is currently the world champion in tin consumption, because the booming electrical industry uses it as tin solder. Copper, which is processed, among other things in cables and washing machines, costs approximately 70 per cent more in 2004 than it did in 2003.[54] Nickel that mainly serves the purpose of steel refinement, costs about 50 per cent more in 2004 than it did in 2003. Gold and platinum increased by around 15 per cent. In 2004 the CRB index which indicates the future prices of 17 raw materials, reached the highest level in 23 years.[55] China accounts for approximately a third of the worldwide ore imports and is thereby the biggest importer in the world. However at present the Chinese annually use only 200 kilograms per head, whilst the South Koreans are already at the thousand-kilogram mark.[56] In 2003 China consumed, with 257 million tons, a quarter of the global steel production. It was thus the first country that produced more than 200 million tons of steel annually. This accounted for 23 per cent of the world's production and was higher than the production, which the two greatest economic powers, the USA and Japan manufactured together. In 2004 alone China added on over 20 per cent and thus accounted for almost a half of world's growth in production. At the same time period China used 40 per cent of the worldwide coal production and processed 25 per cent of the steel production. 'The supply can not keep up with the rising demand', said Klaus Matthies, the raw material expert with Hamburg's World Economic Archives (HWEA).[57]

The Chinese government was hardly prepared for this growth. In 2000 it had forecast a steel production of only 140 million tons in the five-year plan. Investments in the steel sector thereupon rose by 96.6 per cent in 2003, and in the first quarter of 2004 by 106.4 per cent. Worldwide, Germany lies in sixth place with nearly 45 million tons of raw steel, behind China, Japan, the USA, Russia and South Korea. By 2007 China wants to have overtaken Europe as the world's biggest producer of high grade steel. 'This is realistic', says Albrecht Kormann, the managing director of Dusseldorf's steel trade association.

This rapid ascent China has created steel producers who are able to compete with the producers of the world's first league. The largest enterprise is the Baoshan Iron & Steel (Baosteel). In 2003 the group with 100,000 employees had a turnover of 14 billion US dollars, with which Baosteel ascended into the list of the 500 largest enterprises in the world. The enterprise managed to rake in 1.6 billion dollars profit – a rate of 14 per cent profit, which presented the Baosteel share being traded in Shanghai with a growth rate of 70 per cent. In China the enterprise has a market share of 10 per cent. Fourteen per cent of the steel is imported, particularly expensive high-grade steel. But China wants to turn the tables and become a steel exporter within the shortest time possible.

The German steel industry underestimated the steel boom. 'We simply knew too little about the expansion plans of the Chinese', said Dieter

Ameling the president of the steel trade association. It was for this reason that the German capacities were not expanded. Whilst the world's steel production rose by a good 9 per cent in 2004, it only grew by 3 per cent in Germany.[58] For example in 2004 the German steel manufacturer Salzgitter AG was barely able to reach 2001's record gain. The ThyssenKrupp AG regards the developments in the steel market with mixed feelings: on the one hand the group's order books are filled because of the high demand; on the other hand the high cost of raw materials cannot be completely passed on to the customers. 'Those who believe that this development will once again disappear like a ghostly apparition, and that raw materials and steel will soon be available in abundance, are mistaken', said Benedikt Niemeyer the managing director of the medium-sized enterprise Schmolz and Bickenbach AG in Dusseldorf.[59]

In view of the rising steel prices even steel scrap iron has become a rare and therefore valuable commodity. In 2004 the price rose by 145 per cent. Whereas a few years ago one still had to pay at least 100 Euros on a German scrap yard in order to get rid of one's old car, nowadays the scrap dealers pay you 100 Euros for it. Only in this respect does China's bulk buying have a positive effect for the German consumers. The German metal industry already complained to Federal Chancellor Schroeder in 2003, before his trip to Peking. The state gave back turnover tax to Chinese enterprises if they bought Vorstoffe and scrap iron for the non-metal industry and steel scrap metal. Because the market is bare, the German industry has to process expensive premium material or reduce capacities.

The strain on the level of economic activity through the rising price of raw materials is also reflected in the financial markets. The rough direction has been indicated for some years: the dollar is falling and the Euro is rising. A few days after George W. Bush's re-election in November 2004 the dollar fell to its historical provisional low of 1.30 against the Euro. Although the budget deficit turned out to be less than what was at first expected, the American economy was unable to give its own currency any momentum. Under this pressure the European currency had already uncoupled itself from its economy. The Euro is too strong for the weak economic growth in Euro country. The fate of the world's leading currency increasingly lies in Asia, and especially in China, which has through the demand-dependent oil price, the pegging to the US dollar and its foreign exchange reserves, a substantial influence on the development of the rates. A country such as Germany, which almost lives only from its exports only, is particularly susceptible to fluctuations that in Asia. It appears that China's shopping list for raw materials will in future decide the scope of Germany's level of economic activity. The USA's economic activity (Germany's biggest export customer) will increasingly experience difficulties, because everything will become more expensive in the long run. There is no change in this trend on the horizon. Increasing numbers of investors on the international financial markets, and especially in London, have speculated on this scenario since the second half of 2004.[60] They gain if the US dollar depreciates, and thereby put the American currency under additional pressure.

But does the scarcity of resources not strangle the Chinese economy also? Just like other countries the giant realm also has to pay a great deal for its mineral resources on the world market. For years now China has been suffering from an energy shortage. The coal-based electricity network reached its limits long ago. For several years there have been power cuts during the summer in the factories of Shanghai and the southern Chinese boom regions, which sometimes last for days. In fact it will only be possible to get the energy problems under control by the end of the decade at the earliest, when China can put a number of new nuclear power plants and more modern coal-fired power stations into operation. But even today the worldwide raw material crisis is more of benefit to China than of harm. The Peking leadership has learned how to exploit the problems of the developed countries for its own purposes. Because less is being bought throughout the world during the crisis, the producers have to increasingly manufacture more cheaply. There is no country that can profit more from this than China.

The investment bank Goldman Sachs takes the view that we are only at the beginning of a cycle, which could take five to ten years. This time period is necessary to build the infrastructure with which one exploit the new mineral resources. At any rate China has reserve levers at its disposal with which it can cushion surprises. The foreign exchange reserves of over 520 billion US dollars work like an insurance, as China can influence the economic situation of its most important trading partners by switching into Euro, yen or US dollars.[61] The pegging of the yuan to the US dollar also functions as an emergency valve, with which China – if necessary within minutes – can take the pressure off the US dollar. In order to decrease the dependence on the USA, China is increasingly turning to its neighbours. It conducts its foreign policy in the inconspicuous garb of a trader. It does not wrestle with its distrustful neighbours on the grounds of political strategies, but instead offers them business deals, which are very attractive for both sides. China assists Kazakhstan, Vietnam, Mongolia, Laos or Thailand with infrastructure and technology transfer for the development of their economies, and instead buys expensive raw materials. With this pact the region is after the same thing. Because the more difficult it gets to deal with the Americans, the more interesting the Chinese offer becomes.

The fact that Kazakhstan has registered the biggest new oil and gas finds in the last few years has proved itself to be very fortunate for China. The nineth largest country in the world in terms of its land area, yet with fewer inhabitants than Peking, possesses – according to its own data – approximately 4 billion barrels, and there are assumed to be at least a further three to four deposits of such volume. At present it has a nearly 7 per cent share of world production. It has very good oil at is disposal, added to which it is difficult to extract. With every dollar that the oil price increases it stands to gain.

Shortly before the outbreak of the third Iraq war the China National Offshore Oil Corp. (CNOOC) and Sinopec bought, within a period of a few days, altogether for 1.23 billion US dollars a 16 per cent share of one of the biggest oil and gas fields that have been found in the last 30 years, from the British BP group. A good 6 months before that China had already secured itself shares of reserves in Australia and Indonesia for 1.1 billion dollars as well as shares of an Algerian oil field for nearly 40 billion US dollars. Never before had the country acquired such huge fields in such a short of time. The CNN tv channel even spoke of 'aggressive' buying. The fact that Chinese firms were regularly outbidding Indian companies in the Middle East, in Africa and in the Caspian region led to tensions between the two great powers from Asia. On 12 January 2006, however, the two governments sealed an agreement over closed communication with regard to their planned bids.

With the acquisition in the Caspian Sea, CNOOC joined an already ongoing project belonging to an exclusive consortium. ExxonMobil, Royal Dutch Shell and Total each own the same amount of shares in the lucrative field. Production is set to begin in 2006.[62] The future plans of the international corporate groups are being foreshadowed. The oil giant Chevron Texaco alone wants to invest 4 billion US dollars in Kazakhstan over the next four years. ExxonMobil is even talking about 40 to 60 million in the next 50 years.[63]

In May 2004 China and Kazakhstan signed a contract for the construction of an oil pipeline over the Kazakhstani-Chinese border. Construction was carried out with Chinese momentum; building started in August 2004. The China National Petroleum Corp. (CNPC) and the Kazakhstani oil group Kazmunaigaz want to have the 1240 kilometre stretch operational at the end of 2005. Its capacity is to be gradually doubled from a start of 10 million to 20 million barrels. Additionally CNPC is investing in the exploitation of oil and gas deposits in the Caspian continental shelf. Since September 2004 a new section of a pipeline from the Caspian Sea to China has been under construction. The 988 kilometre long section between the Kazakh oil terminal Atasu and the Chinese railroad-hub of Alashankou is scheduled to go on-line in 2008. The extremely expensive pipeline is expected to cost more than four billion US dollars, and with its capacity of 10 million tons per year will supply only an estimated 4 per cent of the Chinese import demand at initial operations in 2008.

Nevertheless Nursultan Nasarbajew, the president of Kazakhstan is keeping all his options open and does not lean towards Russia or China or even the USA. 'We are trying to maintain a good relationship with all three and therefore would like our pipelines to go in as many different directions as possible', he said in November 2003, 'we have a good relationship with Russia. We are currently building a big pipeline to China. We are very grateful to the Americans for their investments, and for the fact that they have driven the Taliban out of Afghanistan. We support the United States with the building up of Iraq. We believe that in the end Iraq must solve its problems by itself.'[64] The Chinese however have the crucial advantage that they can support Kazakhstan with the aim of developing it up into the Saudi Arabia of Central Asia. As an ascending world power they are more calm and collected than the USA, which as a declining world power, wants to gain influence at almost any price. And the Kazakhstanis do not have to overcome a difficult past with the Chinese as for example with Russia, whose government to this day have little confidence in the region. 'The Chinese don't want to improve the world. They want to do business', was the point made by Grigori Marchenko, the former head of the central bank and current vice prime minister.[65] And it is exactly in this matter that one no longer believes the USA.

Even Vietnam with its 82 million inhabitants, now has to rub shoulders with its unloved neighbour. With an annual income of 480 US dollars per head, which does not match half of the Chinese income, Vietnam has no other choice but to attach itself to the upswing of the big neighbouring country. This is despite the fact that the two communist countries have for decades been fighting like cats and dogs and have a thousand-year-old history of enmity. Vietnam needs China's help for a lasting development – and will have to pay for this with its most expensive commodity: with mineral resources. Vietnam is Asia's only net exporter of energy resources and food. 'We are not afraid of China', said Prime Minister Phan Van Khai. 'China is a great country. China's competitive ability in the world looks for its own kind, and the country is a huge market for Vietnamese exports. China urgently needs our raw materials in particular.'[66] Vietnam and China are negotiating over a joint venture for the extraction of bauxite. Approximately two billion US dollars need to be invested. They are already discussing co-operation within the oil industry. In return Vietnam is dependent on imports from China's industry. Televisions, refrigerators and countless motorbikes come predominantly from China. 'Our population is benefiting from these cheap products', remarked Prime Minister Phan. Labour costs are actually lower in Vietnam, but international investors nevertheless prefer China. The furniture house Ikea made the calculation with the sample of a new metal folding chair. The pure production costs were in fact around 15 per cent cheaper; however if one includes containers, authorisation and telephone costs, then the calculation came out in the favour of China.

Thailand's relationship with China is also changing due to pressure brought on by global changes. Whilst the USA is becoming increasingly less attractive as a partner, as they stir up the hatred of the Muslim minority in the south of the country, China becomes more interesting. The outcome of a survey conducted at the end of 2003 was that 76 per cent of Thais regard China as their closest friend and ally, whilst only 9 per cent consider themselves to be united with the USA. Ten years ago it was exactly the other round. 'China is making us stronger, because we take on the competition', explained the Thai Prime Minister Thaksin Shinawatra in March 2004. 'We certainly cannot defy China in that we become even cheaper. We have to find our niche instead'.[67] Logistical co-operation in the energy sector is considered to be one of these. In 2003 the two countries agreed upon the construction of a pipeline through the 400 kilometre wide isthmus between the Andaman Sea and the Gulf of Thailand. Thereby the oil can get to East Asia both more quickly and safely compared to the long route taken by tankers through the straights of Malacca between Indonesia and Malaysia.[68] In addition China began to establish oil storage facilities along the pipeline in 2004. China's reserves are to be spread out in different locations for safety reasons.

Mongolia is in a similar way increasingly coming under China's sphere of influence. Whilst the Americans are interested in the country as a strategic base, and a traditional bond exists with Russia, China is again the country's best customer. The Chinese are not only interested in mutton and Kashmir wool, but also in Mongolian copper. In 2003 Mongolia discovered the biggest copper deposits that have ever been found in the world. In the same year Chinese President Hu travelled to the capital city of Ulan Bator, bringing with him 300 million US dollars in development aid. From 2006 onwards the new mine will extract copper and also gold to the value of at least 60 billion US dollars.[69]

Even the hermetic North Korea is being swept along by the global demand for mineral resources. It is not only because the Stalinist country represents a risk for the security of the region, but also because it is loaded up to the brim with mineral resources, that China, Russia and the USA are striving to integrate it into the world for their benefits. North Korea possesses hard coal and 43 other minerals, which are becoming increasingly valuable and is already the second biggest magnesium extractor. It is in a political situation similar to the one China was in at the end of the Cultural Revolution. Whenever it does take place, the opening of North Korea will represent an enormous economic profit for China. In 2003 the trade between China and North Korea amounted to approximately a billion US dollars, a growth of 46 per cent, of which minerals and metals are the largest share. In return the North Koreans receive oil, agricultural products, simple consumer goods and assistance with the construction of infrastructure.

China is also securing sources of raw materials for itself outside of Asia. Because the Chinese commit themselves to long-term contracts at a good price, the Australian corporate group BHP Billiton, one of the biggest enterprises in the world, took up a national Chinese steel group as a partner for the first time, for a 40 per cent share of a new ore mine in 2004. Additionally ore delivery contracts were signed to the value of 12 billion dollars. Half of the future sales volume of BHP's nickel production was likewise sold to China. The enterprise showed, with 3.4 billion US dollars for the financial year 2003/2004, the highest profit that has ever been brought in by an Australian company.

China invested a billion US dollars in a bauxite-aluminium complex in Brazil, and between 5 and 13 billion US dollars in steel plants, gas pipelines as well as in iron and uranium mining; 440 million US dollars in India for the production of aluminium; 500 million for copper extraction in Chile; 650 million US dollars for a 85 per cent share of a nickel field in Papua New Guinea.[70] In Argentina China will invest 15 to 20 billion US dollars in the next few years into oil production before the coast of Patagonia, as well as in iron ore mining and in the railway network. In Brazil it will invest 5 to 13 billion US dollars into steel plants, aluminium-smelting works, gas pipelines and into iron and uranium mining. Three billion dollars flowed to Chile for the development of copper mines and to Venezuela at least a billion into oil production, gas pipelines, refineries and gold mines.

In November 2004 President Hu Jintao and a delegation of 500 managers spent two weeks travelling through South America. In the last days of that year the Venezuelan President Hugo Chavez and the Chinese government agreed that the Chinese would be allowed to develop 15 oil fields and also set up a refinery there. The contracts were at the expense of the USA, who until now has bought 60 per cent of Venezuela's oil.[71] It is above all because of China that South America once again has a current account surplus for the first time in ten years.[72]

China is increasing its activities in Africa as well. Foreign minister Li Zhaoxing visited six African nations between 11 and 19 January including Nigeria, Libya, Senegal and Mali. In the last two years alone more than 100 meetings between ranking Chinese and African officials and business people have taken place. The fact that Peking issued political guidelines for its Africa policy in January 2006 for the first time is a further indicator of China's increased interest in Africa.

Japan and Korea, which until now were the most powerful countries in Asia, are not only forced to fight against China for their share of the world's mineral resources. They are also drawn into an ever-increasing dependence on the country, because their commercial streams are shifting in China's direction. In 2004 the trade between Japan, China and South Korea constituted a volume of two trillion US dollars – a third of the total trade of the three countries. Particularly the Japanese economy, which has stagnated since the beginning of the nineties, owes its recent recovery to Chinese demand. Whilst exports to China rose dramatically, they have shrunk in the rest of the world. Added to this are the profits that the Japanese companies make with their products manufactured in China.

South Korea, which is the eleventh largest economy in the world, has a similar experience. Already in 2003 more Korean goods were exported to China than to the USA for the first time. Together with Hong Kong, China absorbs a quarter of South Korean exports. Approximately 20 per cent of the growth of about 6 per cent is on account of China. China will attempt to relegate the American influence in Asia to the fringe. Those realists who acknowledge that states do not have to strive continuously for maximal power but rather be able to secure their own security by less offensive means are leaning towards a less pessimistic view on the future of Sino-American relationships.

The trend of the greater integration of Asia, however, works in China's favour. In 2004 the exchange of goods among ASEAN countries grew by more than a third; the volume reached the hundred billion US dollar mark. Starting from 2005 China will be a more important trading partner for the Asian countries than the USA. Therefore it is of greater importance for the states of the region to support China, than to promote the American's consumer level through certificates of indebtedness. Asian unity is accelerated through the ASEAN free trade agreements that were reached in November 2004, which are to eliminate all tariffs up to 2010. Additionally the ASEAN countries recognised China as having the status of a market economy. On this occasion Premier Wen did not want to leave it to the quiet political tones, with which the Chinese otherwise tend to move around in

Asia, and spoke of an 'all encompassing strategic partnership for peace and prosperity'[73] in Asia. The USA tried to use its political weight to disrupt this unity. They had been successful with this once before: Japan wanted to set up an Asian monetary fund in 1997, but had to put the plan on hold under the pressure from Washington. Nowadays the USA is no longer powerful enough to be able to do this.

One way to deal with this is further integration of China; the other is containment. This second prong of Amercian strategy amounts to building and increasing co-operation on security issues with various nations in China's neighbourhood. The tightening of American security networks in the region is certainly not solely – and, as far as the public is concerned, not predominantly – motivated by concerns with regard to China. Singapore is increasingly co-operating with America in the field of security policy; Thailand and the Philippines were granted the status of 'major non-NATO allies'. The following initiatives made last year belong in the same context:

- a new security agreement with Japan concerning the deployment of an aircraft carrier and Patriot-missile defence systems (in February 2005, moreover, the American–Japanese alliance for the first time referred explicitly to the security of the Taiwan Straits in a joint address);
- an agreement with India on co-operation concerning civil nuclear technology, aerospace industry, and relaxation of restrictions on arms sales;
- an agreement concerning the admission of Vietnamese soldiers in an American training-programme;
- the re-establishment of co-operation with the Indonesian military and the lifting of all sanctions on arms-sales that had been imposed with regard to human rights concerns;
- the first visit of an American president to Mongolia, military aid (an annual US$ 20 million) for the modernization of the Mongolian army and joint Mongolian-American military exercises designed to reach inter-operability during peace-keeping missions.

In view of the uncertainties in consequence of the rise of China as an emerging power, the two-pronged American strategy is a rational approach. It seems to enjoy a broad consensus within the administration. And in the wider public the Bush administration's China policy has hardly been contested. The reasons for this are as follows:

- After China has been granted regular trading status at the end of Clinton's presidency in 2000, the annual decision concerning the extension of the most favoured nation treatment were dispensed with. Consequentially, China-critical lobbyists and members of Congress lost their central instrument to influence the public debate.

- President Bush's policy to beef up support for Taiwan while simultaneously warning Taipei not to alter the island's political status stole the influential Taiwan lobby's thunder.
- Finally, the 'war on terror' caused other issues to take a back seat – including China. The 'united government' approach may have further subdued the profile of Congress.

In the two remaining years of the Bush administration, America's China policy may move up the agenda and become increasingly contested. Two reasons support this view:

- There are a number of strains on economic relations, such as a growing deficit, the insufficient protection of copyrights, trade barriers and Chinese monetary policy. The American business world seems to be far less supportive of a policy that is intensifying China's integration than it has been in the nineties; small- and medium-sized companies are particularly worried about Chinese competitors and copy-cats; large enterprises, the driving force behind American business activity in China, are anxiously wondering whether China will ever accept open markets.
- The global expansion of China's economic and political influence, as well as the fierce competition of natural resources and Chinese efforts to modernize its military, provide a sounding board for those who wish to see containment on the top of agenda in America's China policy. The strong response in Congress to the proposed acquisition of Uncoal – certainly no heavy weight among American energy-firms – by a subsidiary of the government-owned Chinese oil company CNOOC shows how sensitive the issue of supposed threats to American national security is.

Yet, as long as the administration shows a consistent approach in its China policy, substantial challenges by Congress remain unlikely. Should the constellation of American domestic politics change, however, Congress may try to increase its influence – especially if the ratio of co-operation and conflict in Chinese–American relations should change in favour of conflict.

The OPEC countries Saudi Arabia, Iraq and Iran have remained the centre of conflict. A lot points to the fact that the USA and China will in the near future bump into each other even harder in the Middle East. Both countries are forced to risk a lot in order to secure their future energy supply.

China is actually not in the position nor willing to step into a direct military confrontation with the USA, and will also politically not have the say in the region. But through its strength as an economic partner, or more precisely as a reliable, long-term customer and investor, it will be able to constantly strengthen its political weight. The international diplomacy that concerns itself with these issues will have to learn to view them from a new economic perspective. The political scope of action will be determined even more strongly than before by economic developments – a trend by the way, which countries such as Germany with a weak army and a still influential economy could use to their advantage.

Although Iraq is in the meantime lost for China, the next thrust of these developments is already taking shape in Iran. China attempts to replace the established economic powerhouse Japan, which covers 86 per cent of its oil consumption with imports from the Middle East, as Iran's most important partner in the oil and gas business.

An oil- and gas-pipeline could be laid from Iran via Central Asia to China – an option that is not available for supplies from any other of the four large oil producing countries in the Persian Gulf due to geographical reasons. Several long-term agreements have already been reached, and China's investments in Iran now total 100 billion US dollars. According to an agreement from October 2004, China Petroleum and Chemical Corporation (Sinopec) alone plans to import Iranian oil and gas worth 70 billion US dollars. Since the beginning of the third Iraq war the economic relations between China and Iran have become even closer. In 2004 Iran was the number in of the OPEC states, although the USA intensified its sanctions against the country and has described its nuclear weapons programme as 'intolerable'.[74] The Chinese at that moment acted calmly politically. Soon afterwards Norinco, China's largest trading and armaments group received the contract for the construction of Teheran's second underground railway line to the value of 836 million US dollars.[75] The state enterprise could offer a political price and thereby outdo Siemens amongst others. The Americans had imposed sanctions against Norinco in advance because of suspicions regarding the supply of nuclear technology.[76] In the autumn of 2004 the concealed confrontation between the USA and China intensified. 'We cannot permit that one of the supporters of international terrorism is developing nuclear weapons and delivering them to Europe, Central Asia and the near east' stressed John Bolton, the then US Undersecretary of State for weapon control and international relations in the State Department.[77]

Colin Powell, the then Secretary of State added a little later: 'that's the limit. We will not allow Iran to become a nuclear power.'[78] The magazine *Newsweek* had reported in September that the US government was preparing for a change in government in Iran, which was to be coerced through secret operations and if necessary with a force of arms.[79]

China resisted the American advance with nothing less than the biggest energy contract in its history. The oil group Sinopec signed a preliminary agreement in the autumn of 2004 to the tune of 70 billion US dollars. China will buy 250 million tons of liquid gas over a period of 25 years and will develop the massive Yadavaran field. Additionally Iran has committed itself to selling China 150,000 barrels of oil a day, at the market price existing at that time, for the next 25 years. So far China had not received more than 13 per cent of its oil imports from Iran. The Chinese leadership wanted to close the deal as inconspicuously as possible. The Iranian oil minister Bijan Namdar Zanganeh however expressed himself decidedly:

'For historical reasons Japan is our biggest importer of energy. But we now want to give preference to China.'[80] Whereupon Li Zhaoxing, China's Minister of Foreign Affairs also took a clear position on the question, if the case of Iran, as the USA suggested, should be heard in front of the UN Security Council, "It would make this case more difficult and more complicated to solve it'.[81]

The deal is perfectly obvious: China protects Iran from the USA and in return gains guaranteed access to the mineral resources of the second most important OPEC state. Differently than in Iraq, China's odds in Iran are decidedly better. The USA cannot afford to invade there; both from a military and political perspective. In the meanwhile China also comes into play politically: that the disarmament experts of the three most important European nations, Germany, France and England are to mediate and a way out is already been indicated. The closer the economic relationship with China becomes, the safer Iran feels and so it increases the possibility of the renunciation of its nuclear programme.[82] Although the USA was manoeuvring, they took the pressure out of the conflict. 'We do not have any plans for a change of regime', said Colin Powell, the US Secretary of State in mid-November. 'However we do not welcome this regime.' But it has apparently not planned to invade Iran with the help of the 140,000 US soldiers stationed in neighbouring Iraq. He stressed that it was a matter for the Iranian people to decide over their future.[83] Ayatollah Ali Khomeini, the spiritual leader and head of Iran, accused the USA and Israel of waging an undeclared war on Islam. This war had overshadowed Ramadan, said the religious leader in his sermon at the end of the month of fasting in front of thousands of believers in Teheran.[84]

The confrontation between the USA and China in the Middle East was of no importance for the Western media. In fact this conflict had revealed itself for quite some time. The Chinese had already put Bill Clinton under pressure. In 1998, just before his trip to China, he found himself forced to give in. On the 18th of May the US government allowed Western oil companies to invest in Iran.[85] An indirect apology from the Iranian President and the reformer Mohammed Khatami made Clinton's decision easier. But the economic pressures tipped the balance. China had begun to build a 2 billion US dollar pipeline through Iran and was negotiating with Iran's National Oil Company over the exploitation of the Iranian off-shore oil fields. Washington on the other hand still blocked the construction of an oil pipeline from the Caspian Sea through Iranian territory. In the previous year the Chinese had bought shares in Iraqi oil fields, which they lost in the third Iraq war. The newly gained economic position was also in this case immediately converted into political capital: 'we are very concerned about the fact that the Iraqi civilian population has to suffer in such a manner under the sanctions. I hope that the sanctions will soon be lifted,' gibed Qian Qichen, the former Foreign Minister and Vice Prime Minister at that time in the weeks before the summit. The USA and Iran have not maintained diplomatic contact for 27 years, whereas China and Iran have had diplomatic relations since 1971. The relations between Iran and the USA, which had existed openly since the fifties, became closer until the Islamic revolution in 1979, when the US-friendly but feudal Shah monarchy was toppled and replaced with a religious state.[86] From then on the USA was regarded as the mortal enemy. In November 1979 Khomeini's followers stormed the US embassy in Teheran. They took 50 Americans as hostages for over 400 days with the aim of forcing the extradition of the Shah, who was in the USA for medical treatment. In the course of the continuous eight-year war between Iran and Iraq, the first Gulf war, the USA became friendlier to the Baath regime in Baghdad. Eventually the Iraqi army received weapons, equipment and important military information. On several occasions it came to (military) engagements between the Iranian navy and the US navy, which had also attacked the Iranian drilling rigs. Only several days before Teheran consented to a UN-mediated armistice with Iraq, the US cruiser 'USS Vincennes' erroneously shot down an Iranian airliner. All 290 people on board were killed. The trade embargos imposed by the USA against Iran remained in force up to the devastating earthquake in the Iranian province of Kerman in 2003. Iran and the USA's history is therefore very strained. How this conflict will continue to develop, is difficult to predict. One thing at least is becoming clear – the more powerful the Chinese economy become, the blunter the threat of American economic sanctions will surely be, and the more expensive and more difficult military actions will prove themselves. China is therefore in a favourable position. It can increasingly develop its co-operation with the states of the Middle East, whilst the USA can only make itself heard and gain respect through political pressure. Peter Scholl-Latour used the appropriate description with the title of a book in which he depicts the USA as a 'world power in quick sand'. China on the other hand is circling in the thermals of the hot desert.

# Chapter 11

# THE CHINA CODE

*The Canadian academic C.B. MacPherson would agree emphatically*

> Naturally every country develops its own form of democracy and judicial system based on its needs. The democracies of this world come in a diverse range.
>
> Li Zhaoxing, the Chinese Minister of Foreign Affairs

At the beginning of the twenty-first century the focal point of economic and political power gradually shifted to the East and relocated itself around the new Middle Kingdom. We first have to get used to this because for centuries it had been a part of the foundations of our culture that we feel superior in China's company. Immanuel Kant, the most prominent exponent of this wisdom, believed that only people in the most progressive region in the world – which for him were exclusively the Europeans – were capable of freeing themselves from their self-inflicted immaturity and understanding the world. 'The sovereignty of Europe is justified through its activities, its science and its inventions', is also how the German philosopher Johann Gottfried Herder praised his cultural group in theories for the 'Philosophy of the History of Mankind' in order to immediately afterwards grind the noses of the Chinese in the dirt: 'This human race in this region will never be the same as the Romans and Greeks. The Chinese are and remain a people that was furnished by nature with narrow eyes, short noses, a flat forehead, little beard, long ears and protruding bellies; that what their institutions could produce, they have produced (already)'. China, so read his summary, was so inflexible and non-progressive, 'as a church mouse in hibernation.'[1]

Despite such presumptions products from China were very much in demand in Europe at that time. Particularly the nobility loved Chinese porcelain and Chinese textiles and competed with one another for the most opulent collection, the items of which had made their way to Europe along the Silk Road. Because there were insufficient numbers of original Chinese pieces, Chinoiserie developed into its own branch of art in the Rococo period. It is this trend in the late seventeenth and the early eighteenth century to which the Meissner porcelain manufacturer owes its fame to. There did not seem to be anything Chinese, that the West could not do better. Also still in the early nineteenth century the German poet Georg Wilhelm Friedrich described China's economy as 'degenerated',[2] and for the German philosopher Friedrich Hegel, who was the first to make the attempt to put the history of the world into a meaningful coherence, considered China plainly and simply 'outside of world history'. Even the French philosopher and Foreign Minister Alexis de Tocqueville, who was one of the first Europeans to have a transatlantic perspective, classified the Chinese in the 1830s as being imbeciles: 'the Chinese follow in the footsteps of their ancestors. But they have forgotten the reasons, which have led them (there). (…) The Chinese have lost the strength to change themselves. To improve themselves, has become impossible. (…) The cradle of human knowledge has run dry.'[3]

The judgements of further sections of the intellectual elite characterised the view of the European merchants and diplomats, who expanded their sphere of operation in the nineteenth century, through near and middle Asia, right to China's border and then into the Chinese interior. A British envoy of the embassy hastily cabled the following words home about the 'semi barbaric race': 'The Chinese were one of the first nations in the world, who had reached a certain degree of perfection, (…) but they have come to a stand still. They are still just as civilised as they were 2000 years ago, at a time, when the majority of Europe could still be described as barbaric. But since then they have not made progress in any respect.'[4] It was superficial that such judgements served as a justification to civilise the allegedly backward countries and to convert the heathens to Christianity. They were however the right tools for European imperialism.

Even in the middle of the twentieth century when the colonial empires were winding down and the Europeans were sweeping away their own prejudices, China hardly succeeded in improving its reputation. Although the Americans and the English supported the republican troops of General Chiang Kai-shek, the country eventually fell to the communists. Chiang's 'modern China' only existed on the island of Taiwan, which until then was known among green tea lovers as Formosa. From then on Mao ruled the Middle Kingdom alone against the rest of the world. During the sixties Mao's totalitarian state, which at that time was almost completely sealed off from foreign countries, was idealised by a small but vocal group of young Europeans as a future model. However, as the Western Maoists never succeeded in convincing the local workers of the benefits of Chinese communism, the movement came to nothing and made way for the horror of the educated middle classes over the Cultural Revolution's mania of destruction. It was not because of insight or worldly intelligence, but because China's market became interesting for the West, and because it annoyed the Russians that fascinated condescension turned into condescending fascination. In 1971 Peking was given the Chinese seat as a permanent member of the UN Security Council, which up until then had been held by Taiwan. China for the first time played a role in the world. In 1972 US President Nixon travelled to meet Mao, and the military strategists had only just permitted contact with China, when Western enterprises stretched out their feelers towards the distant land. Economic pressure allowed long-running political and cultural traditions to fade. In the eighties China made an impression through Deng Xiaoping's economic open door policy and in 1985 Deng was even elected as the 'man of the year' in the American *Time* magazine.

All of a sudden the competitive calculations of the global players started to do the rounds, which had already intoxicated the merchants of the nineteenth century: how much would one be able to earn if one billion Chinese were to annually drink one bottle of Cola every week? Nevertheless, the West was suspicious of the communists, even if they had suddenly started to practise market economics. One could do business with them, but one could not trust them. After 4th June 1989 the sceptics considered their fears confirmed: China, so they warned, was being ruled by harsh dictators, who were not concerned about integration, but with unscrupulously remaining in power. But the market that the Western economy so desperately needed was not going to be conquered with condescension. One closed both eyes: 'change through rapprochement', was also soon the motto in dealing with China. The West's prospect of becoming part of the Chinese economic boom gradually caused the unswerving positions to fade. Respect began to unfold, which was increasingly replaced by a certain high esteem. However we have only become really open for a new evaluation of China since the weaknesses of the West have even more clearly come to light.

The fate of a nation depends not least on the resilience and flexibility of it feeling of self-esteem – a feeling of self-esteem that is not as excessive as that of the Americans and not as weakly pronounced as it is for example in Germany. The history of China clearly shows that a people's pride in a country only benefits that county's progress if it engages in global competition. National self-confidence may be a prerequisite, but it is no replacement for open-mindedness to the world at large. This is what China lacked in the nineteenth century, although this was because it was one of the world's leading economies up to the industrial revolution and had no external enemies. China's leadership at the time missed the opportunity of adjusting itself to the new currents of globalisation, as for centuries it had not seemed necessary for China to compete with other countries. The state's monopoly of power began to disintegrate. The self-esteem of the European nations on the other hand, had at that time matured in a climate of competition; it was dynamic economically and had created new political institutions in an enlightened society. China's 'crisis of self-esteem' led to a 'decline of power'. Nowadays Europe sometimes behaves like a kind of moral apostle and the American President believes that it suffices for the country to flex its muscles, for the world to follow the USA's ideology. Countries, which over longer periods of time have become convinced of their economic power, rarely posses the willingness to readjust in time. The belief in one's own abilities will turn into a dangerous self-overestimation. The crisis, even the Chinese thought at that time, could not upset the equilibrium of their prosperous country. After the first major defeat certainly the Chinese should have made a realistic evaluation of the global balance of power, but the strategists of the court became caught up in a fatal mixture of superiority and perplexity. Nowadays the West finds itself in the same position. We are helpless. It was not its lack of technical and economic expertise that prevented China from keeping up with the other nations. The military backwardness could easily have been made up, as Japan successfully demonstrated. There were also progressive Chinese politicians, who wanted to make things happen at court. But the rigid self-esteem of the Chinese was their worst obstacle, which in crisis situations became even more pronounced.

The great opportunity of the West surely however does not consist of perpetuating its self-assurance. Only the confession of one's own weaknesses can open up the possibility, of being able to realistically evaluate one's current position in the world. In order to do this we have to concern ourselves with the world. China's history shows that the state's monopoly of power is in danger when self-esteem is low and global competition is not taken seriously enough. A system may be rapidly undermined by those who no longer feel that they are being represented by their state. France with its street battles is nowadays the unfortunate precursor in this area. When will the losers in other Western nations take to the streets? The development is even worse, because China is making enormous progress, facing up to the competition and skilfully using it to its own advantage.

The Western nations these days do not always need less central authority. In times of huge upheaval it can be quite necessary that governments need greater decision-making power, certainly for a carefully limited period and under strict democratic control. The politicians' scope of organisation and the possibilities of the population's participation in the decision-making process should not mutually paralyse each other. Democracy has great advantages, but we should not forget that it also has disadvantages. The focus of policy on the short-lived media world has resulted in the fact that currently one cannot be frank even discussing unimportant topics, not to mention being interested in a solution. This undermines the trust in policy within large sections of the population. More central authority, with moderate application, can strengthen people's confidence in the policy.

Also this realisation has long historical roots, which also facilitates the way we handle other countries. In crisis situations when the monopoly of power is at stake those who are governing need to offer solutions, which are based on the level of social development, and need to be able to accept that these solutions mostly lag behind the more progressive countries. There is no short cut to the future. If the majority of the people want more political freedom and independence, then authoritarian leaders who demand obedience hardly have a chance of success. If the wish for a strong leadership personality outweighs other considerations, as in China's case in its phase when it was a kingdom without middle, then free elections in certain circumstances might create more uncertainty. Democracy, self-determination and independence are not a cure all, if it is a matter of stabilising the state's monopoly of power. More advanced countries have the tendency to underestimate this fact. The USA's great difficulty in democratising Iraq after the third Iraq war is a testimony of this.

Germany and China have this in common, that their respective governments made the same mistake in this respect in the first half of the twentieth century. They called upon their population, which unlike their neighbours was still unfamiliar with the concept of parliamentary democracy, to choose an elected parliament. When a charismatic leader appeared, the people once again saw themselves in their former glory, but paid dearly for it: a communist terror regime on the one hand and genocide on the other. Whilst Germany was forced back onto the right path by its neighbours and their allies after 12 years, China needed 30 years to accomplish this task on its own accord.

We cannot learn very much from Mao. What we can learn though, is of great significance: with his 'heave-ho' economy he stood no chance against globalisation. He was convinced that his tightly organised, enthusiastic mass movement, offering its services in the spirit of altruism, would develop China more quickly than any combination of free trade, the opening of the market to the West, material incentives and social advancement of the individual. It was only in the final phase of his rule that Mao opened the country to the world. As global competition had begun to shift from military to economic endeavours during the period of China's isolation, China's position was suddenly more favourable than in previous centuries. The world economy needed the huge market. Moreover, an integrated China served Western security interests. And this is why the economically devastated country did not have to eat humble pie. For many contemporaries, who had suffered under Mao's regime and wanted to see him get his just desserts in terms of history's verdict, there only remained the sober realisation that globalisation has little to do with moral values. It is not just and does not necessarily reward the competent. Many consider it to be just as disillusioning that globalisation can hardly be steered or exploited. Its currents are too powerful for us to able to swim against them.

Its determining influence on us is far stronger than vice versa. Nobody can withdraw from its pressures in the long run; no country can position itself outside of the canon of the world's nations for a prolonged period of time. In the interplay between nations, there are always new constellations being formed. These do not allow themselves to be planned, but they do force all the nations concerned to interact with one another and to fine-tune accordingly.

One of the most important tasks facing every nation is to register these constellations as early and accurately as possible, and to make the necessary adjustments. Even if the West feels to this day morally superior to China, it is nevertheless subject to the same pressures. In the end the deciding factor will be as to who deals with this reality the most skilfully. Only in this way will it even be possible, with the application of common rules, to civilise globalisation or at least to increase one's influence over it in the long run.

Mao's successor, Deng Xiaoping, in fact understood that China had to deal with globalisation. He cannot be praised enough for this realisation and his unswerving determination to ensure its implementation. But Deng had a tiger by the tail – he underestimated the power of globalisation. He opened the country to the world economy with all his might, bought the latest technology – particularly German steel plants and power stations – and invited enterprises such as Volkswagen to invest in China. However, he had no idea how to dovetail the nation with the world economy. He was playing 'reform roulette' and thereby brought about a huge economic crisis in 1989 which led to mass demonstrations and eventually to its bloody suppression. The process of integration with the world economy was out of control, and stability had to be restored at all costs. Deng's success at bringing China swiftly back on the course of economic ascent, without any major interruptions, was largely aided and abetted by global pressures that were forcefully moving in the same direction. The world economy was already too heavily dependent on the Chinese market. Above all the Taiwanese, who had been particularly shocked by the brutal course of action taken by the leadership, were the first to go back and invest in China just a few weeks later. They filled the gaps that had briefly been left by Western companies. The Chinese leadership under Jiang Zemin had to choose between continuing the integration process with the world economy and the bleak prospect of inexorable decline.

At first the Chinese were horrified by the brutal suppression of their protest movement, but then they quickly reacted with great pragmatism. People turned away from politics and towards the economy and consumption. Property ownership and prosperity remain their goal and education and knowledge their means of attaining it; enjoyment through performance is their creed. In most cases the interests of the state coincided with those of the people, which helped the government restructure the economy without too much pressure. The challenge for the leadership generation under Jiang Zemin was to develop an economic system that would integrate the country into the capitalist system without exposing it to that system's inherent risks. Considering the crises that the reformed Chinese economy had to cope with – the death of Deng Xiaoping, the handover of Hong Kong and the Asian crisis – the new system proved itself to be extraordinarily stable. China has succeeded in attracting more foreign investment every year, while increasing its exports and making its Asian neighbours more dependent on it – even Japan, the second largest national economy in the world.

The repercussions for the German economy are significant. With the 'concubine economy' the Chinese created an unprecedented economic mixture of a market and a planned economy, which not only integrated China into the world, but, above all, integrated the world into China. It operates in all the main branches of industry: of which the automobile industry was the first to experience it. Because all of the industry's global players were determined to enter the Chinese market, they let themselves be forced into conditions of production that they would never have accepted in any other country. They had to form joint venture companies with Chinese manufacturers, who co-operated with various international competitors simultaneously and thereby were able to play the different partners off against each other. The Chinese are always certain winners. Chinese capitalism has developed one of the most effective methods of strengthening one's own position with the help of foreign money and know-how. The

Chinese are masters of the art: 'Sound principles are one thing', said Kenneth Arrow in 2004, the 83 year-old Nobel Prize winner for Economics and expert in the welfare theory. 'Practice is something else. In this respect China has the best economic policy, although it violates sound economic principles.'[5]

At the end of a chaotic 20th century China was again stable, united, and independent and had opened itself to the world without being at its mercy. However what is more surprising is, whilst the West seems to be giving rise to democracies that have the tendency to block reforms, China, following on from 150 years of crisis, has developed itself, in a certain sense, into a 'dicta-torship for the common good'. Even avid political reformers in a democracy can only react to short-term changes in mood, as they have to win elections and are constantly pressured by lobby groups. This is the dilemma that modern democracies have to work with. 'They have to constantly change a product in the economy, so that it remains competitive', noted Mei Zharong, the former head of the Institute of Foreign Affairs in this connection, 'policy certainly does not improve if it constantly changes'.[6]

On the other hand China's dictators are also controlled by the people and the pressures of globalisation. However, if their goals coincide with the aspirations of the people and the demands of globalisation, they can plan on a long-term basis and implement their policies swiftly. One then comes to the sober conclusion: at present the balance between the monopoly of power and the people's self-esteem appears more favourable in widespread areas of China. And at the same time modern-day dictators like the Chinese ones, have a keener nose for both local and global imponderables, as they are constantly in fear that their unauthorised power will disintegrate, and because more liberty means less order. That again is the dilemma, which the Chinese leadership has to live with.

China's influence on the world economy and its dependence on it have continued to rise, especially in the first years of the twenty-first century. This is an interconnection which nobody invented, but one which the Chinese leadership skilfully reinforces. As a WTO member China is so powerful that it can choose when and to whom it opens its markets. Neither the USA nor by any stretch of the imagination the General Secretary of the WTO are able to do anything about this new balance of power. China's strategy of gaining power through business rather than through values or force of arms is now paying off. Although China has begun the aggressive purchase of mineral resources, both in neighbouring countries and in Australia and South America, it is welcomed with open arms everywhere, as it does not attach moral conditions to its business dealings with the countries concerned. Through this China has set off a kind of global chain reaction.

The nation's economic rise puts the power of the USA into perspective, because their economy is becoming increasingly dependent on Asia. Competition is forcing a growing number of US companies to buy and produce cheaply – especially in China. This means job losses and less tax revenue in the USA. The US budget is under pressure. In order to finance their deficit the USA has to borrow increasing amounts of money from abroad in the form of state bonds. These state bonds are being bought especially by Asian countries, primarily Japan and China. And they earn large amounts of money from the sale of their products in the USA. At the same time the USA are under pressure from terrorism, Europe's new self-confidence and the strong Euro. The more Washington feels its power eroding, the more aggressively it reacts and the greater its concerns for the future welfare of its population. This in turn depends primarily on the ability of the USA to secure sufficient and lasting supplies of natural resources. In this respect China and the USA are standing eyeball to eyeball.

At the same time China's economic power is setting the agenda for global politics. One of the causes of the last Iraq war was that China and Russia had started buying Iraqi oil fields. The USA was able to prevent this with a war. However, they were not able to prevent China securing a large portion of Iran's mineral resources. The global successes have fuelled the self-confidence of the Chinese government. Meanwhile the new government under Prime Minister Wen Jiabao has even abandoned the policy founded by Deng of 'growth at all costs'. Under the slogan 'the people first' they now see the more just distribution of the country's income as their primary task. This also has the consequence that they will do their utmost to assure that China creates jobs in China and not in the West. If China was a victim of globalisation 30 years ago, it now represents a 'globalisation trap' for the West.

The global shift in power can in the meantime also be seen in cultural self-confidence. While human rights were an unpleasant topic at meetings with Western politicians in the past, Foreign Minister Li Zhaoxing made it clear to his German colleague Joschka Fisher at a joint press conference in the summer of 2004, that China would not put up with any such advice and was in no way willing to leave the interpretation of the question of human rights to the West – an experience, which almost other Western politicians have had to face if they took too vigorous a stand.

*Fischer:* 'On the one hand we see the huge progress that China has made with human rights. On the other we also have great concerns about detention, the death penalty and other points we would like to raise.

*Li:* 'The Chinese are a huge people. But every individual is just as important as the entire population. This is why we place just as much importance as the West on the observation of human rights. Democracy goes along with this, and that is not a recent development. Over 2000 years ago one of Confucius's pupils said: "The people are more important than the kings". We have to strengthen our efforts for more democracy and a better judicial system in every respect. But naturally every country develops its own form of democracy and judicial system based on its needs. The democracies of this world come in multifarious forms.'

*Fischer:* 'We represent a one-China policy not only in words but also in practice. On this basis we would like to find a solution within the framework of this one-China policy, to the question of Tibet in a dialogue with the Dalai Lama.'

*Li:* 'Herewith you have thankfully clearly expressed that Taiwan belongs to China. The Dalai Lama however has (undergone) separatist endeavours. That is unacceptable to us. Even our American friends have described him as a political monk. He must first of all publicly acknowledge that Taiwan is a part of China and then our channels of dialogue will be open.

*Fischer:* 'We also believe that with free elections in Hong Kong, the Chinese government can demonstrate that the system of "one country, two systems" actually functions.'

*Li:* 'We are dissatisfied with the position of our Western friends on this point. When Hong Kong was still under British colonial rule, the people had effectively no democratic rights. Then the Western politicians were silent.'

At the end of the media appointment Li even took the liberty of making a cheeky remark at Fischer's expense: 'And now I have to concern myself with an important human right of my guests: I have to invite them for lunch.'[7]

Foreign Minister Fischer surely speaks for many in the West when he calls on China to adhere to universal values. But at the same time he underestimates the strengths of the authoritarian regime: China has created a comparatively stable system, which is able to bear, not only regional, but also global economic burdens. The Chinese politicians have so far been in the position of being able to plan long-term, and to have established functioning macro-economic parameters, which have in an almost surprisingly way managed to restrain the chaos in the transition from a state-controlled to a private economy. The transitional phase from the one to the multi-party rule has therefore slowed down. China systematically and effectively seals itself against the risks of globalisation and at the same time maximises its opportunities.

The degree of stability can be assessed by three variables: foreign debts, the rate of inflation and the currency's black market rate. At present there is no indication that any one of these three units of measurement could present a danger. Actually China's ascent is not without (inherent) risks. But it is just as risky for the West to rely on the fact that China will get into difficulties. Since the beginning of the nineties the West has systematically underestimated China's strengths and through this has given the country the scope to unfold at the expense of the West. The relocation of the focal point of the economy into another region is from a historical point of view, nothing unusual. At first it shifted within Europe, from Spain and Holland to England. Then it moved to the USA and eventually has partly relocated itself in Asia. Japan took the first step in this direction. China will now carry out the change and let Asia become the centre of the world economy.

The Western elites display the usual behaviour of established groups vis-à-vis outsiders. Their self-image is derived from the most progressive of their own members, and the image of outsiders is based on the most backward underdogs imaginable. Stigmatised to this degree, they do not appear capable of posing a threat. 'Even well-known economic professors at the leading European business schools have no inkling of what is waiting for them in China', observed Rolf D. Cremer, the Dean of China's best management university CEIBS in Shanghai.[8]

Western culture would be well advised to adapt to a fundamentally new position. If China's ascent continues as it has, then for the first time in modern history the West will see itself competing with an 'haute culture' equipped with the economic muscle to be able to assert its claims throughout the world. Even in the 'soft' cultural sphere it is already evident, how much not only China has absorbed the Western world into itself in the previous decades, but also how the West has with increasing strength integrated the Middle Kingdom into its culture. At first Maoism and Western pop culture moved closer together. After that it became fashionable to eat with chopsticks and place red Chinese cabinets in one's loft. And for the first time in history, the Chinese are even making names for themselves as global heroes. Chinese sportsmen, writers, musicians and actors now have the opportunity to rise up to become world class stars and lengthen the list of world-famous Chinese personalities, which has been limited till now to Confucius, Mao Zedong and Bruce Lee.

At the awards of the Nobel Prize for literature in 2000 the jury took a long time to decide. Finally a Chinese writer received the prize. Yet it was a 'more progressive' individual, a dissident, who was in conflict with the Chinese leadership. The choice fell on Gao Xingjian, who has been living in Paris since the mid-eighties, is a French citizen and even writes in French. The Chinese leadership snubbed the decision and refused to recognise Gao as one of them. Prime Minister Zhu Rongji commented ironically: 'I am pleased that a Frenchman, who speaks such good Chinese, has been awarded the prize.'[9]

Conversely the actor Jackie Chan, who has dominated the Hong Kong film scene for decades with his action films, is regarded as more Chinese by the Peking leadership, although he hails from the former British crown colony. In 1998 he filmed 'Rush Hour', his first successful Hollywood film, which handles the subject of the cultural competition between China and the USA. Chan, as a Chinese cop accompanies a chaotic US colleague, who is strongly prejudiced against the Chinese through San Francisco and shows himself to be the better cop through humour, intelligence and a few hard kicks.[10] The film brought in 130 million US dollars. In the 2001's sequel the American cop was then in Hong Kong as a guest.

So too in traditionally typical Western disciplines the Chinese are increasingly becoming an even match. The pianist Lang Lang, who originates from the northern Chinese Shenyang, is casting his spell over the world of classical music. In 1999, as a 17-year-old Lang substituted for a sick colleague at an international festival. Since then he has played with all the major orchestras; and his recordings are top of the classical music charts. The American *Wall Street Journal* selected him in their list of 20 teenagers who 'will change the world'. Because classical music follows a high standard, but does not move the masses, it is not Lang Lang who is considered to be the first Chinese international star but instead it is a young man from Shanghai. In 2002 Yao Ming, who was 21 years old at the time, entered the holy of holies of the American sports world, the national basketball association league. Overnight he became one of the most respected stars of the league. His club the Houston Rockets advertise their new player on huge billboards with the slogan, 'Be Part of Something Big'[11] – an allusion not only to Yao's considerable size, but also to his homeland. Not even the Japanese have managed to reach these heights, even though every youth is familiar with Sony and Toyota. One searches in vain for a Japanese national, who has gone beyond the circle of the cultural specialists and enriched the world's pop culture. And who would have thought that a Chinese would win an Olympic gold medal in the 110-metre hurdles in a world record time, like Liu Xiang at the Athens games in 2004?[12] For Western youth China is already a natural component of the contemporary culture.

This success facilitates the next crucial step for China. Just as the Middle Kingdom felt that it was able to determine the values of the world in the nineteenth century, until the West disputed that right, so China now disputes the universal validity of Western values. Although in fact all one needs is the simple justification: different countries, different customs. However, it is difficult for us to accept this; the frequently held notion of the development of China as 'belated modernisation' suggests a development measured by common standards. However as we have seen, this is not the case. The alternative

*specifically
|Chinese,*

will only emerge gradually. Then the multipolar world order, for which Europe and China are fighting side by side against the USA, will become a reality. But multipolarity does not just mean that there is a relative shift in the American's position, but also in ours. The way in which China is already hollowing out our cultural value system is demonstrated in two little examples. In Western bookshops one finds shelves stacked with books that give advice, as to how one adjusts to the peculiarities of the Chinese as a manager. But the Chinese shelves lack works that provide information about how one deals with the cultural peculiarities of the Europeans, although these are even more complex than those of the Chinese. So it is the Westerners and not the Chinese who are careful that their negotiation partner does not 'lose face'.

China skilfully exploits this concern of the West. And so in relation to copyright infringements, the well-meaning explanation often given is that the Chinese have practised the art of copying for centuries and have not had a tradition of copyright protection. In fact the Chinese know exactly what belongs to them, and what does not. The fact that they score points with their arguments testifies their cultural strength. There is hardly another phenomenon that shows this more clearly than the fact that the Chinese are able to steal our technological developments, without us being capable of effectively defending ourselves. Why should the Chinese observe (these rights) and not savour their power?

The first probing attempt to concern the world with the basic questions of Chinese cultural identity was undertaken by the film producer Zhang Yimou with his film 'Hero'.[13] It is about a Chinese ruler by the name of Qin Shihuang, who is a key figure in Chinese history steeped in legend, and it concerns itself with the question as to how a people should deal with its rulers. The film had a great response in the West. 'Hero' was nominated for an Oscar in the category of 'best non-English language film' as well as awarded the Alfred Bauer prize at the 53rd Berlin International Film Festival in 2003. No other mass product has blended Chinese tradition and modern trends as Zhang film. The moral of the story goes, he who topples his leaders puts the unity and stability of the country at risk. The film is set in the third century BC, in the era of warring realms, which was brought to an end by Qin in that he brutally unified the country and thereby became the first emperor of China. Zhang's film is not a simple declaration of dictatorship, but raises questions which also intensively concern the Chinese at the beginning of the twenty-first century. The prospect of more say in the decision-making process is tempting, but in order to be able to do so should one topple the leadership and risk losing the stable framework? Should one risk one's international position in the community of nations and thereby possibly lose one's greatest capital? These are questions to which there are no simple answers. When Prime Minister Wen Jiabao stresses, 'unity and stability are more important than anything else',[14] it is not just a matter of securing the power of his party, but also about historical experiences and cultural peculiarities as well as the right balance between the feeling of self-esteem and the monopoly of power. The strength of 'Hero', the most successful films from the mainland so far, lies in the fact that he lets this ambivalence exist as a peculiarity of the Chinese path of development. He sways between resistance and adaptation.[15] 'It is his first real Chinese film', said the famous Chinese author Feng Jicai. 'He has proven with the mode and content, that one can preserve the peculiarity of Chinese aesthetics with advanced Western technology, and progress within the internal Chinese discussion without paying penance to international attention.'[16]

Only mainstream Western criticism does not want to open itself to this ambivalence: 'Certainly there is talk of peace and non-violence – this however remains a mixed blessing in view of the historical role of the extremely brutal emperor Qin. At the press conference Zhang Yimou declared several times that he had no intention of shooting a political film. Particularly discomforting are the last shots of the film, depoliticised to the monument of self-sacrificing love on the one hand. And the marches of the ruling guard on the wide squares of the palace particularly awaken negative feelings – the way in which Yimou staged the mass as an ornament, is quite similar to Leni Reifenstahl.' (One notices that the critic, who talks of 'Yimou', obviously did not know that the Chinese surnames come first.)[17]

The absolute and yet tactless will of the Chinese leadership to oppose the Western 'haute culture' with something equally weighty shows itself in the way they dealt with Zhang's film. During the summer holidays of 2004 they pulled all the Western films out of the cinemas and instead showed 'Hero'. But the self-confident people in reaction punished the patronising decision with a boycott, which showed how developed a consumer democracy has become in China. As 'Spiderman II' and 'Harry Potter' could only be seen after a two-month delay, the spectators made do with pirate copies that were available for one Euro. The turnover in the cinemas dropped by 40 per cent. The cinema owners made the government responsible for the loss of earnings. It would however be inappropriate to only blame the disastrous action on the bland propaganda methods. The great pride over the fact that a film for the general public using modern methods had succeeded in describing a central element of their own identity was so great that even the state educators' mistrust of Zhang, who had been celebrated in the West as a dissident for many years, faded.

Based on the reactions of the West and Chinese to the film 'Hero', the difference between the new China and the obstinate West becomes especially clear. The Chinese are looking for something new; the West is only able to again find the familiar. But the Western authorities are not a world court. That applies not only to the American army, but also to our values. 'Especially as a "community of values" the West is not a culture, which is exempt from seeing themselves in perspective,' wrote the essayist Mark Siemons.[18]

Democracy is probably the most convincing idea of the twentieth century, which does not mean that in its present form it will be the most successful in the twenty-first century. 'Democracy is only a specific political civilisation, it is not the nucleus, not the central content of a civilisation', observes Helmut Schmidt, the former Federal Chancellor and still the most intelligent German politician when looking at China,[19] Because in the competition for a common global world order both will compete against each another. Whichever power is stronger remains quite open. Actually the market economy and democracy are the key elements of the future ability of a state. But China has the inconveniences of globalisation under better control and has a monopoly in the field of the large, stable future markets. The perceived stability is lower than the actual stability. Through this China profits from globalisation like no other country in the world and creates a favourable position for itself, in order to have a decisive say in the decision-making process concerning the rules in the world.

That the world could agree may seem to be improbable to many people. Historically however this development has worked well in a somewhat smaller, but not less complex framework. The world is in approximately the same position as the 'Holy Roman Empire' between the eleventh and fourteenth centuries when there was still no monopoly of power of the state. In principle anyone who possessed land, on which people worked, could offer to protect them legally and militarily. And as there were only a few workers the lords of the manor were forced to constantly modernise their protective systems, in order to be able to offer the farmers, craftsmen and merchants a favourable basis of living, as they would otherwise have moved on or rebelled. However none of the liege lords succeeded in establishing valid rules for the entire realm.

Conflicts between the liege lords could only, like with nations today, be solved through bilateral contracts. The gentlemen made compromises amongst themselves, formed allegiances, arranged themselves with diverse lobby groups like co-operatives, federations or vassal organisations, until eventually in the eighteenth and nineteenth centuries the most powerful groups could offer a long-term, convincing business: security of rights against taxes. The national states were established. And again out of the national states developed successively a united Europe. This development is taking place slowly but it has a clear direction. A growing number of states sacrifice their sovereignty in favour of binding political decisions, made at a supranational level. So too in Asia and South America states are making the first hesitant moves to form bigger units. There is nothing to be said against this, or that this process will repeat itself on a global level. One of the crucial advantages of a multipolar world order is that one perspective does not prevail in the world, but that instead a consensus has to be reached. That however means that our view of things also has to be put into perspective.

In order for us not to drop back in this development we have to catch up on several things. The west has an inadequate and incorrect integration policy into the rest of the world. We have to learn to decentralize our thoughts. Universalism of a small minority of the world is nothing other than sectionalism that wants to be more than it actually is. We have to concern ourselves at school with the interconnections of the global economy. This is at least as important as English and maths. It will however only work if we develop a desire and a respect for open learning, the same way that it is deeply embodied in the Chinese culture and strengthened through the speed of the upswing. Otherwise our grandchildren may one day demand an explanation: Why did you sleep through China's ascent? Why did you fritter away our future, by upholding China's weaknesses instead of revealing its strengths and cracking the 'China Code'? We have to learn to view the world with the eyes of others. That is the only way for us to understand the peculiar clarity inherent in Chinese strategies; only in this way we can adjust to them and still be able to effectively articulate our own ideas and convictions. That is not simple.

China is for example very interested in the new world order becoming as democratic as possible. With 1.3 billion people China would have a clear majority in the world parliament; Asia would have the absolute majority with 3.8 billion people, followed by North and South America with 870 million and Europe with 780 million people.[20] Europe and the USA on the other hand may have an interest in China becoming democratic, but that the world becomes more democratic cannot be in their interest. In this respect the position of the west resembles that of the European aristocracy at the turn of the twentieth century. They could not imagine that common people would ascend to being top politicians. Some of them needed the entire century to get accustomed to the fact that only tabloid magazines had an interest in them. In the end they had to admit that the fight against such developments does not hold any prospects. At that time the social democrats were on the right side. And what the social democratic movement was for Europe in those days, China is for the world today.

The West will no longer dominate the new world. It will have to find a market niche. With what can one oppose the mighty China? The strategists

Justice has arrived, at last, to all humanity!

of the American investment bank Morgan Stanley point the way. 'Growth should no longer be focus of Japan and Europe', is the opinion of the chief Asia analyst Andy Xie. 'They should concentrate themselves on the quality of life.'[21] How can Europe turn this into an opportunity? And there are always opportunities.

Through its fall China has freed itself of its historical weight and is refreshingly untraditional. It has become a dynamic hybrid culture, which with great agility makes use of what it needs, no matter whether it is foreign or its own. It's all the same to them whether it's Western modernity or Chinese tradition, leftovers of pre-colonial culture or communist organisation, democracy or dictatorship – the main thing for the Chinese is that the system serves increasing prosperity.

It is high time to consider one's own position if the alleged misfits are in good spirits and full of cheer, whilst an oppressed atmosphere prevails in one's own country. The Chinese sense that the superiority of the established countries are dwindling. The balance of power is starting to slide. For a little while an armour of hope may give the young Westerners a cause for debate, in that they hold the beguiling prospects of history giving them the choice of going one way or the other. From China's perspective – and this could soon already be the dominating point of view – we Westerners are already on the way to becoming a people of archivists who lovingly take care of what has already been achieved. Not that the Western societies would not concern themselves with interesting questions about the future. However in the meantime the music is plays on – somewhere else. 'A wise man', according to a Chinese proverb, 'does not cling to any idea'. That this also applies to the West, and it is the least that China will teach us.

Let's imagine the generation of young Europeans when they are fifty. They are living in a mixture of open-air museum, theme park, nature reserve, and Robinson Club Med. The Chinese and their Asian neighbours are Europe's best customers. They are paying well, and they are coming to Europe to take a time out from an economic boom that is going on for generations. There are so many of them that Europe is earning well. The visitors are longing for places that are not constantly changing.

Around the turn of the new century, the Europeans initiated a process of reforms, but they got worked up with it. Only when Western Europe was as thoroughly de-industrialized as the east of the continent at end of the cold war, only after the welfare-state went bankrupt and it was finally clear beyond reasonable doubt that cars and other machines can only be built in Asia did matters slowly begin to improve again. Even the most stubborn Europeans had finally understood that research and development pays off only in highly specialised niches. This may have generated a lot of money, but hardly any jobs. Only after this had sunk in did Europeans begin to think clearly and were ready for innovations. The rise of New Europe could finally begin.

The Europeans focused on their incontestable strengths: their medieval towns, multi-facetted culture and beautiful landscapes. The Volkswagen Car-City in Wolfsburg became the prototype of a modern consumption-facility. The former car-workers now earned their money in reconstructed cityscapes from the last century. Appropriate cars for each epoch were available for pleasure tours at any time – the New York of the twenties, Swinging London of the sixties, German and Japanese scenes from the eighties. Whether you preferred to experience a meticulously staged shoot-out between New York mobsters in a Cadillac, or a scooter race between Mods and Teds, the choice was yours. Shop attendants wore traditional costumes of yore, restaurants were faithful to historical recipes, and hotels painstakingly imitated the past. Particularly the Germans, as thorough and driven by nagging self-doubts as ever, devoted themselves to their new tasks and developed their skills to baffling degrees of perfection. But elsewhere in Europe, theme parks are booked out for months in advance, and no old-town square ever sees a moment without crowds flocking through. In 2050, people have difficulty to understanding how anybody could ever have wanted to disfigure the picturesque historical cities with high-rises. High-rises are not needed anymore in Europe; population has been dwindling for decades anyway. Only the skyline in the City of London and its counterpart in Frankfurt have been preserved. Tourists from China, Malaysia and Thailand contemplate them with the same childlike joy with which we are today strolling through a romantic village in the Highlands. Frankfurt is so neat compared to the 40-million metropolis Shanghai.

Scotland, Tuscany and Bavaria are among the favourite destinations for Chinese tourists. Fairytale castles, beautifully preserved rural communities, and the jolly dances of the Bajuwaric minority are a delightful holiday experience. In North Germany you can even cruise the old Transrapid test-track. There are industry-museums in Shakespeare country, and, just a few miles away, not even as far as Peking is from Shanghai, spine-chilling stories in the haunted house of Nazi horrors in Berlin. Teatime, Bratwurst and Antipasti merge into an unforgettable experience of old Europe, along with Beethoven's Fifth, the Tower of London, and the beer-halls in Prague. Everything is custom-made for the restless visitor from Shanghai. But what a pity, the seasoned traveller may sigh when he worked his way into the less developed hinterland, that Europe does not everywhere look like Bath or Heidelberg. Instead, the Shanghainese human resources manager from China-Volkswagen may find that many a faceless small town tries to make up for its lack of authenticity with kitschy Chinese restaurants. Have they lost all sense of tradition?, he may ask himself. In the urban centres, however, stern EU administrators are guarding the preservation of the town centre of Warwick as well as the Altstadt in Lübeck. The port of London is harbouring the ships that once served the purposes of gunboat diplomacy. Twice a day a William Jardine look-alike is staging the English commercial conquest of the Far East, and Dutch fish-restaurants will sport plump beauties in traditional costumes to keep the Chinese customer happy.

Europe is so popular that there is even a small but not insignificant number of young Chinese who deal in a more sophisticated way with the cultural history of the Old World and dream of a job in the fields of art history or intercultural exchange. Some of them will develop a liking for the wacky sages of old and meditate upon the difficult writings of Bertrand Russell, David Hume and Immanuel Kant. When they enrol in the universities of London or Berlin for a year or two, their anthropological interest may focus on the retro-chic of restaged parties of Swinging London or the East Berliner nightlife-avantgardists of the early nineties. And the German capital can boast a truly unique attraction – the Berlin Wall, complete with historical checkpoints and snarling communist border-guards. 'Making money as natives of a bygone culture may take time getting used to', writes the Frankfurter Allgemeine Zeitung, 'but it does seem to be the only sustainable option'.

The future is already under way. Young Chinese coming home from vacations in Europe talk with considerable enthusiasm about the heartfelt closeness of Europeans to their own tradition and their love of precision. But it is precisely this nostalgia and keenness for detail that is impeding the step back into a reality that's moving at high speed. Even today, the Europeans are picturesque exotics in the eyes of the Chinese, carefully nurturing traditional lifestyles, including excessive detail, devoted to guarding their dear rituals and achievements of yesteryear. 'Very nice', opines Alexander Helsing-Hu, a Chinese who has lived in Germany for sixteen years, 'but there's no kick left'.

*Russell is rarely difficult, except with Whitehead or Wittgenstein in tow.

# NOTES

## Chapter 1

1 In 2003 China's economic growth rate reached 9.3 per cent, outperforming its target of 7 per cent increase in spite of the lethal lung desease SARS. See: Holbig, Heike: Zur aktuellen politischen Entwicklung der VR China, in: Holbig, Schüler, and Liu, p. 8.

2 See: Sinn, p. 67ff.

3 See: www.eiu.com.

4 Ibid.

5 China's gross domestic product reached US$ 1.4 trillion in 2003 (for comparison: Germany – US$1.8 trillion; USA – US$ 10.2 trillion). China, however, has shown no interest so far to join the exclusive G8(G9?) club.

6 *WirtschaftsWoche* ( *WiWo*), China edition Nr.1, 2003, p. 22.

7 During the WirtschaftsWoche-conference in Berlin in September 2004.

8 In 2003 BASF's turnover amounted to 33.4 billion Euro. China accounts for around 5 per cent of BASF's worldwide turnover.

9 Already since 2002. According to UNCTAD about one-third is accounted for by re-imports of Chinese balck money coming from Hongkong. See: www.globalpolicy.org. This practice is common in countries like the USA as well.

10 See: www.eiu.com.

11 This is what German Chancellor Schröder said in his keynote address on 7 December 2004, in Peking.

12 A.T. Kearney estimates that in the coming decade up to one-third of jobs will be moved to China.

13 See: Survey of Landesbank Rheinland-Pfalz, www.lrp.de.

14 Survey of Boston Consulting Group from October 2004. See: www.bcg.com, p. 24.

15 For comparison: The USA, comprising 4.5 per cent of the world population (292 Americans of 6.296 billion people) just below 30 per cent of global economic growth (US$ 11 trillion of 36.75 trillion), whereas China accounts for approximately 3.8 per cent of global growth (US$ 1.4 trillion of 36.75) with 20.2 per cent of global population (1.289 of 6.396 billion).

16 The globalisation debate did not get off the ground until this decade.

17 This, however, does not mean that one would be at the mercy of this phenomenon. It is the task of social science to 'make these blind, undesigned developments intellegible to the human

understanding; the task consists in providing orientation for the people in the midst of originally intransparent networks of integration which their own activities and needs have effectuated, as well as in enabling an increased control over these developments'. Elias (1986), p. 170.

18  For more than 20 years, China was growing at a rate of well above 8 per cent.
19  *Stern*, vol. 33/2004, p. 68.
20  *WiWo*, 20 May 2004, p. 40.
21  Data according to World Bank, July 2003.
22  McKinsey, China-edition, November 2004, p. 24.
23  Madisson, Angus: 'The World Economy. A Millenial Perspective', in OECD, 2001, p. 156.
24  Measured by the so-called Gini-Index the value is not even 10 per cent higher in China – 0.447 compared to 0.408 in the USA, but a value of 0.283 in Germany and in Japan even 0.249 (a value approximating one indicates a bad distribtution).
25  *WiWo*, China-edition, 2003, p. 2.
26  *Die Welt*, 7 April 2004, p. 12.
27  In an interview with the author in December 2003 in Canton.
28  *South China Morning Post (SCMP)*, 24 November 2003, p. 17.
29  Quote according to Klemens Ludwig, chairman of the Tibet Initiative. See: *Frankfurter Allgemeine Zeitung (FAZ)*, 8.December 2004, p. 37.
30  This includes Lardy, Studwell and Chang.
31  Only individual companies, such as Toyota, the world's most profitable carmaker, have made it – not the national economy as a whole. Germany may see a similar development.
32  On China's and Thailand's different roles during the Asian crisis, see Chapter 7.
33  When a US president threatens China with a trade embargo, lobbyists of Amercian companies which manufacture in China ask him whether he intends to damage the US economy. See: *WiWo*, China-edition 2003, p. 26.
34  www.eiu.com.
35  For detailed data concerning the comparison between India and China see: McKinsey, China-edition, November 2004, p. 32.
36  See: Copur and Schneider.
37  In an interview with the author on 19 March 2004, in in office in Bangkok.
38  Reuters, 22 April 2004.
39  Writes Reinhard Geissbauer, who co-authored the survey. In *Financial Times (FT)*, 24 August 2004.
40  In an interview with the author on 3 December 2004, in Canton.
41  There is a reason for this: Debts remain in the books, subsidies don't.
42  www.zeit.de
43  See: focup.msn.de
44  National savings depostits amount to US$ 2217 billion, 1260 billion of which are accounted for by private savings. See: HSBC archive.
45  *Süddeutsche Zeitung (SZ)*, 10 December 2004, p. 30.
46  www.eiu.com.
47  The author's research in Peking, Shanghai and Kunming.
48  Sieren et al.(2003).
49  Fell to 74.8 per cent. *FAZ*, 16 May 2003, p. 23.
50  See: Baseler Zeitung, 22 December 2003, p. 3.
51  In 2004 the USA for the first time in 50 years imported more agricultural products than it exported. See: *FAZ*, 25 September 2004, p. 11.
52  *FAZ*, 11 September 2004, p. 11. Since 1994 already foreign assets in the USA exceeded American assets abroad.
53  'The Asian central banks are big players which buy American federal bonds and do not seem to be interested in rates of return. It is highly unusual that financing a deficit depends on governmental players to this extent', says Harvard economist Kenneth Rogoff. *WiWo*, 15 January 2002. Of seven banks of issue with the highest assets, six are from Asia

(Japan, China, Taiwan, Hongkong, South Korea, Singapore). They hold assets worth just below US$ 900 billion. Only the ECB holds assets on a comparable scale – US$ 260 billion.

54  Andy Xie, Morgan Stanley Newsletter, 10 July 2004.

55  In 2004 exports into the USA exceeded those to China by 400 per cent. See: *Der Spiegel*, 3 November 2003, p. 99.

56  China alone accounts for one-fifth of the growth in global production.

57  *SZ*, 31 January 2004.

58  *FAZ*, 13 October 2004, p. 19.

59  www.unctad.org.

60  www.eiu.com.

61  Ibid.

62  *FAZ*, 24 November 2004, p. 24.

63  Chinese state media initially praised the book before it was blacklisted a few weeks later. In October Wu and Chen were awarded the 'Lettre Ulysses Award for the Art of Reportage' in Berlin.

64  Eight to ten thousand workers die every year in Chinese mines.

65  20 February 2004, See: www.bundestag.de.

66  Ibid.

67  www.eiu.com.

68  Ibid.

69  Ibid.

70  German direct investments: 1994: US$ 250 million. 2003: US$ 860 million. This is a growth of roughly 240 per cent.

71  www.iea.org.

72  Ibid.

73  www.world.newp.designerz.com.

74  Dow Jones, 15 November 2004.

75  Address by von Pierer during the German–Chinese WirtschaftsWoche Business Congress on 22 Septmeber 2004, in Berlin.

76  See: Brenner, Robert: 'Towards the Precipice', *London Review of Books*, 6 February 2004; www.lrb.co.uk.

77  *FAZ*, 6 September 2004, p. 12.

78  The German economy grew by merely 1.7 per cent. Even the Japanese economy, stagnating since more than a decade, grew twice as fast.

79  *WiWo*, 5 August 2004, p. 21.

80  *FAZ*, 8 October 2004, p. 13.

81  A survey by the Ifo-Institute for trade development. See: *WiWo*, 16 September 2004, p. 24.

82  According to Zhang Weiqing, minister for population and family planning in an interview with the author in July 2004.

83  Ibid., p. 79.

84  94 China ranks third with US$ 60 billion after the USA and Japan, ahead of Germany with its US$ 54 billion. See: *WiWo*, 13 November 2003, p. 8.

85  According to a survey in the World Competitiveness Yearbook of IMB Business School (International Institute for Management Development), one of the best business schools in the world. See: Cremer, Rolf: 'Beide Welten', *WiWo*, 25 November 2004, p. 80.

86  *WiWo*, 16 September 2004, p. 22.

87  Ibid., p. 21.

88  'We act on the assumption that the difference will remain on this high level over the next ten years, since absolute growth in Germany will be comparable to that in the low-wage countries', says a survey by the Boston Consulting Group from October 2004.

89  *WiWo*, 16 September 2004, p. 21.

90  www.janus-online.de. China will face problems with an aging population within the next 20 years as well due to the one-child policy. However, things look worse in Germany.

Until 2010, more than 53 million employable people will enter the market; in the United States it will be only 13 million.

91 *China Daily*, 24 October 2004.

92 See: Consumption survey by the *Far Eastern Economic Review (FEER)*, November 2003. www.feer.com.

93 From 1994 to 2003 the number grew by an average of 14 per cent annualy.

94 See: Walter, Franz: 'Zielloses Missvergnügen', *Internationale Politik*, May 2004, p. 11.

95 See: Buruma.

96 *FAZ*, 9 July 2004.

97 See: Beck.

98 *Der Spiegel*, 15 March 2004, p. 98.

99 www.eiu.com.

100 *FAZ*, 24 October 2003, p. 34.

101 Based on a poll by the Allensbach Institute. See: *FAZ*, 21 June 2004, p. 6.

102 'The observation of the leadership can, and typically will, use measures different from those used by the leadership itself; successes and failure, for instance, will be ascribed in a mode that sharply differs from that applied by those whose leadership and actions are being judged', Luhmann sums up this phenonenon. Luhmann (1994), p. 332.

103 Ibid., p. 346.

104 Ibid.

105 Ibid., p. 330.

106 Bin Wong.

107 Pomeranz, p. 38.

108 Ibid., p. 46.

109 Ibid., p. 40ff.

110 Fairbank (1989), p. 57.

111 Ibid., p. 264.

112 Pomeranz.

113 Pomeranz was awarded three academic prizes for his 'radical re-orientation' of the relative weight of the economic competitors Europe and China: The John K. Fairbank Prize, the Choice's Outstanding Academic Books in 2000, and the World History Assocations Book Prize in 2001. Simultaneously, critical objections were being raised, but those largely dealt with questions of historical detail. See: Wright, Tim: 'China Transformed. Historical Change and the Limits of European Experience', *Journal of Social History*, summer 2000.

114 This method has turned out to be effective in decoding the similarities and common points between East and West Germans. See: Engler.

115 This is the title of his most important work. Elias (1990).

116 Elias (1986), p. 187.

117 Elias (1992), p. 19. Elias initially talks about individuals. But his considerations can claim validity for larger units such as nations as well.

118 Ibid., p. 21. In view of the world wide web, which Elias could not know, his description of societies under the pressure of integration gain plausiblity in hindsight.

119 This only seems to be paradoxical, because – borrowing from Luhmann's terminology – different nations are facing an increasingly homogenized environment. Hence the feed-back in the overall system 'world' are increasing.

120 Elias (1992), p. 432.

121 Hensel, p. 4.

122 In this respect the notion coined by Elias can be extended.

123 See: Sunzi in his famous book on stratagems in war.

124 Geißler, Heiner: 'Wo bleibt euer Aufschrei?', 14 November 2004.

125 'All China Federation of Industry and Commerce'. September 2004.

126 *FAZ*, 20 January 2004, p. 10.

127 In 1913 it was 11 to 1, in 1950 35 to 1, in 1973 44 to 1 and in 1992 it was 72 to 1. Data according to statistics by the United Nation Development Program (UNDP). See: www.undp.org.

128  In: *Handelsblatt* (*HB*), 'The Twelve Disciples', 3 September 2004, p. 2.
129  Ibid.
130  Ibid.
131  Ibid.
132  Speech in Qinghua University in Peking on 11 October 2004.

# Chapter 2

1  Gentzler (Hg.), pp. 23–8.
2  In 1689 China had accepted for the last time a treaty with a country on an equal diplomatic level. Jesuit diplomats had played a part in negotiating this treaty with Russia. See: Roberts, p. 148.
3  The Shunzhi Emperor, born on 15 March 1638, died on 5 February 1661, was the second emperor of the Manchu dynasty.
4  Roberts, p. 144.
5  Ibid., p. 150.
6  Ibid., p. 157.
7  *FAZ*, 10 June 2003, See: Homann.
8  Ibid.
9  Ibid.
10  Elias (1992), p. 432.
11  Ibid., p. 176.
12  Yuan.
13  Fairbank (1989), p. 54.
14  Ibid., p. 57.
15  Pomeranz, p. 9f.
16  Ibid., p. 33.
17  Ibid., p. 68.
18  Fairbank (1989), p. 18.
19  Pomeranz, p. 68.
20  See: Haffner.
21  Hsi-Yang jen, See: Fairbank and Teng, p. 18.
22  Followinf Hannah Ahrend, who speaks of 'self-locked thinking'.
23  Fairbank (1989), p. 56. How proud can Germany be today of its position as Europe's largest economy if growth is limping since years while its neighbours are growing rapidly?
24  Ibid.
25  Spence (1995), p. 164ff.
26  Osterhammel (1989), p. 147.
27  Ibid., p. 146f.
28  Chang, Chih-Tung (1837–1909), from 'Exhortation to Study', 1898, quoted after Fairbank and Teng, p. 170.
29  Ibid., p. 187.
30  See: www.web.jjay.cuny.edu.
31  Fairbank and Teng, p. 25.
32  Hsü, Chi-yü, in 1848 one of the leading connoisseurs of the West. See: Ibid. p. 42f.
33  Fairbank and Teng, p. 36.
34  Polachek, p. 102.
35  Roberts, p. 168
36  Gregory, p. 89.
37  Osterhammel (1989), p. 147.
38  See: Levathes, p. 20.
39  Ibid.

40  Levathes, p. 21.
41  Ibid., p. 20.
42  Ibid., p. 179.
43  Ibid.
44  Ibid.
45  Ibid., p. 179.
46  Elias (1987), p. 19.
47  Ibid., p. 21.
48  Fairbank and Teng, p. 124.
49  Ibid., p. 142.
50  Ibid., p. 142.
51  Feng, Kuei-fen (1809–74), Ibid., p. 50.
52  Ibid., p. 52.
53  1873–1929.
54  Fairbank and Teng, p. 155.
55  1865–98.
56  Fairbank and Teng, p. 157.
57  Ibid., p. 154.
58  Gregory, p. 75.
59  Ibid., p. 74.

## Chapter 3

1  Elias (1992), p. 253.
 2  See: Denninger, Erhard and Gössner, Rolf: 'Wenn Recht zu Unrecht wird'. in Grass, Dahn and Stasser (eds), p. 505–22.
 3  Fukuyama, p. 7. Even the Berliner *Tageszeitung* (*TAZ*) counts this book among the most important publications of 2004.
 4  Fukuyama, p. 89.
 5  *Die Zeit*, 24 Februar 1999, p. 47.
 6  Karl Marx, *New York Daily Tribune*, 14 June 1853, in Marx.
 7  Spence (1995), p. 210.
 8  Ibid., p. 206.
 9  Lin Qing (1770–1813), www.asianlang.mq.edu.au.
10  See: Johnson, p. 126.
11  Shlomo (ed.), p. 49.
12  Fairbank and Teng, p. 8.
13  Ibid., p. 56f, p. 134.
14  Gregory, p. 106.
15  Roberts, p. 176.
16  Ibid., p. 179.
17  Ibid., p. 182.
18  Spence (1995), p. 221.
19  Elias (1986), p. 173. Luhmann assumes that this is not possible.
20  Ibid.
21  Ibid.
22  Ibid.
23  Spence (1995), p. 294.
24  Ibid., p. 224.
25  Roberts, p. 180.
26  Fredrick Townsend Ward from Massachusetts and Charles 'Chinese' Gordon. See: Spence (1995), p. 221.

27　Ibid., p. 239.
28　Roberts, p. 182.
29　Ibid., p. 184.
30　Roberts, p. 185.
31　He demanded this as early as 1842. See: Ibid., p. 184.
32　See: Spence (1995), p. 286.
33　See: Roberts, p. 201.
34　Already in 1895, Emperor Wilhelm II commissioned an allegorical painting by Herman Knackfuß of the European nations as a present for the Russian Czar. Germany was represented by a proud and martial archangel Michael equipped with shield and coat of arms, ready for battle.
35　Series of the German Federal Agency for Civic Education, vol. 274, p. 357.
36　Kaminski, p. 42.
37　Spence (1995), p. 290.
38　Ibid., p. 291.
39　Kaminski, p. 47.
40　Ibid.
41　Kaminski, p. 70.
42　Ibid., p. 71.
43　This includes the establishment of permanent foreign courts.
44　Roberts, p. 188.
45　Ibid.
46　Lu, p. 23.
47　Fairbank (1989), p. 67.
48　Kaminski, p. 106.
49　Ibid., p. 105.
50　Ibid., p. 107.
51　Roberts, p. 204.
52　Spence (1995), p. 307.
53　Jonathan Spence is overrating the country's stability when he states that 'apart from treaty ports and concessions the power of the state was unbroken'. See: Ibid., p. 318.
54　Ibid.
55　Ibid., p. 332.
56　Elias (1992), p. 441.
57　Gregory, p. 103.
58　Lu, p. 45.
59　Spence (1995), p. 321.

## Chapter 4

1　Spence (1995), p. 341.
2　Beiyang comprised today's Liaoning, Hebi and Shandong provinces.
3　Roberts, p. 224.
4　Ibid., p. 214.
5　The partners were England, France, Germany, Russia and Japan. See: Ibid., p. 214.
6　Ibid.
7　Frank Johnson Goodnow. Ibid., p. 216.
8　In July 1917.
9　Roberts, p. 220.
10　See: Rummel, p. 64.
11　Elias (1992), p. 418.
12　A professional army comprising a maximum of 100,000 troops.

13   Elias (1992), p. 250. Elias further writes: 'I remember in vivid detail how in 1932 the thread of violence increased in the form of public brawls'.

14   Ibid., p. 415.

15   Ibid., p. 286.

16   Elias (1990A), p. 57.

17   Elias (1992), p. 289. 'Finally the Weimar republic collapsed due to a structural weakness of its monopoly of violence and the purposeful exploitation of this weakness by bourgeois organisations in order to destroy the system of representative democracy'.

18   Ibid., p. 261.

19   Lu, p. 50.

20   Ibid., p. 51.

21   Roberts, p. 219.

22   Lu, p. 51.

23   See: McCord, p. 309–15.

24   Osterhammel (1997), p. 145.

25   Sun died in 1925.

26   Osterhammel (1997), p. 123.

27   *Hunan Daily*, 14 July 1919, p. 1.

28   Both sides had German support. The *Wunderwaffe* of the nationalists was colonel general Hans von Seeckt, chief of the Supreme Command of the German Reichswehr until 1926. The communists placed their hopes in the Moscow-educated Bavarian Otto Braun.

29   Osterhammel (1997), p. 123.

30   Ibid., p. 125.

31   So Sun Yat-sen, in: Spence (1995), p. 365.

32   Roberts, p. 234.

33   Ibid.

34   Ibid., p. 231.

35   Ibid., p. 232.

36   Ibid., p. 243.

37   Mao Zedong proclaimed the first 'Chinese Soviet Republic' in Ruijin, the capital of the area, in 1931.

38   The West gained insight into the CPCh only in the second half of the thirties. In 1938, the American journalist Edgar Snow had accompanied Mao during the last leg of the Long March. See his legendary book 'Red Star over China'.

# Chapter 5

1   Li, p. 73.

2   'Telling Asia's Story for Fifty Years'. *FEER*, 1996, p. 32.

3   See: Näth (1976), p. 7.

4   Li, p. 36.

5   Weber, volume 1, p. 311.

6   Mao Zedong: 'Über die demokratische Diktatur des Volkep. Zum 28. Jahrestag der Kommunistischen Partei Chinas', 30June 1949, in: www.marxistische-bibliothek.de.

7   Ibid.

8   Mao Zedong: Ausgewählte Werke, Peking, 1969, Bd. IV, p. 439f.

9   Ibid.

10   Mao Zedong: 'Über die demokratische Diktatur des Volkep. Zum 28. Jahrestag der Kommunistischen Partei Chinas', 30June 1949. www.marxisitische-bibliothek.de.

11   Ibid., p. 5.

12   Ibid.

13   'Telling Asia's Story for Fifty Years'. *FEER*, 1996, p. 38.

14   Ibid.

15 www.marxisitische-bibliothek.de.
16 Li, p. 138.
17 Ibid., p. 137.
18 Ibid., p. 90.
19 Ibid., p. 157.
20 Franz, p. 107.
21 Li, p. 106.
22 Ibid., p. 98.
23 Ibid., p. 145.
24 Spence (1995), p. 166.
25 Roberts, p. 260.
26 Ibid.
27 Ibid.
28 Li, p. 136.
29 Ibid., p. 137.
30 Ibid., p. 234.
31 Ibid.
32 Ibid., p. 238.
33 Ibid.
34 Ibid., p. 277.
35 Ibid., p. 278.
36 Schröder, p. 26.
37 Li, p. 226.
38 Four secret Sino-German talks were conducted in Bern in May, July, October and November 1964. See: Ruland, p. 360.
39 Ibid., p. 359.
40 Schröder, p. 34.
41 Li, p. 289.
42 Martin, p. 128.
43 Roberts, p. 259.
44 Ibid., p. 260.
45 Spence (1995), p. 612.
46 Ibid., p. 647.
47 *Der Spiegel*, vol. 5, 1967, p. 74.
48 Li, p. 219.
49 *Der Spiegel*, vol. 5, 1967, p. 74.
50 Ibid.
51 Li, p. 249.
52 Roberts, p. 267.
53 Ibid., p. 268.
54 Li, p. 263.
55 Becker.
56 Li, p. 300.
57 Ibid., p. 284.
58 Ibid., p. 324, on 2 July 1958, during a Politburo meeting.
59 Ibid.
60 Ibid., p. 417.
61 Li, p. 250.
62 Ibid.
63 German first edition 1967.
64 June 1996.
65 Li, p. 531.
66 Ibid., p. 493.
67 Ibid., p. 491.

68 *Der Spiegel*, vol.5, 1967, cover picture.
69 Li, p. 543.
70 An alternative version of this story includes the British Prime Minister.
71 On 11 October 1972. For the first time, Bonn and Peking had agreed to exchange embassadors. 'I can understand', remarked Gerhard Schröder, the former foreign minister and chairman of the foreign commission of the Bundestag, 'that a thriving country like the People's Republic of China attaches importance to establishing relations with an essential factor of global production and world trade'. Germany was then the fourth largest economy in the world. The 27-year-old Ma Canrong, today's ambassador, took part in the event. 'I witnessed the breakthrough as a small translator.' Ma had started to work in the Chinese foreign ministry one month before.
72 France had already established diplomatic relations with China in 1964.
73 Wang, p. 97.
74 See: Seitz, p. 221.

## Chapter 6

1 Franz, p. 174.
2 Ibid., p. 169.
3 Ibid.
4 Ibid., p. 255f.
5 Ibid., p. 174.
6 Ibid., p. 185.
7 On 30 January 1962, Mao had assumed responsibility for the failed policy.
8 Ibid.
9 Ibid., p. 204.
10 Ibid., p. 243.
11 Ibid., p. 239.
12 Spence (1995), p. 752.
13 Näth, p. 334.
14 The Chinese 'Gang of Four' comprised Jiang Qing, Zhang Chunqiao, Yao Wenyuan and Wang Hongwen.
15 Spence (1995), p. 254.
16 Ibid.
17 In 1981 the four members were brought to trial and accused of anti-party propaganda.
18 Franz, p. 271.
19 Ibid., p. 275.
20 Ibid.
21 Deng did not come too early: The economy was ramshackle. China by then had accumulated debts of US$ 1.8 billion.
22 Based on his statements in the standing committee of the Politburo on 25 Jaunary 1982.
23 Franz, p. 281.
24 *SZ*, 13 October 1978, p. 29.
25 *SZ*, 14 October 1978.
26 Franz, p. 281.
27 Näth, p. 345.
28 In a talk with the author in August 2004 in Peking.
29 Especially since the Chinese had already in the past been forced to cancel a deal over the purchase of a steel plant. The leaders during the Cultural Revolution had opined that China was capable of developing such a plant by itself. The displeased Germans had consequently sold the plant to Romania. See: Wang, p. 94.

30  Mann, p. 47.
31  Ibid., p. 46.
32  Jeep Maker plans Factory in Peking, *FT*, 2 May 1983, p. 1.
33  This happened since 1 October 1985.
34  *Time Magazine*, 2 June 1989, p. 40.
35  Ibid.
36  According to M. Posth in a talk with the author in December 2004.
37  He stayed in Shanghai until August 1988 (assumption of office in the board of directors of Volkswagen Inc.). He worked in VW's Hongkong-based board for Asia-Pacific from 1993 to 1997.
38  In a talk with the author on 6 December, 2004, in Peking. All further information is based on this talk.
39  Ibid.
40  Ibid.
41  According to Hartmut Heine, one of the participants in the talk with the author.
42  Fairbank (1989), p. 352.
43  *SZ*, 9 May 1989.
44  *Die Zeit*, 21 April 1989.
45  According to the *People's Daily*, mid-December 1984. This article had been so sensational that three days later it was rectified: Marx and Engels cannot solve all of today's problems.
46  Ibid.
47  Näth (1995), p. 347.
48  1985 in the Great Wall Sheraton. See Mann, p. 118. Governmental authorities demanded a monthly US$ 700 for a person who made 70 dollars. Installation of a telephone cost US$ 14,000. See Ibid.
49  23 September 1982.
50  September 1980, May 1983.
51  October 1983.
52  Mann, p. 117.
53  Ibid., p. 119.
54  Ibid., p. 137.
55  Seitz, p. 243.
56  *SZ*, 21 February 1997, p. 8.
57  Sieren (1990), p. 60.
58  Brahm, p. 7.
59  Ibid.
60  Wasserstrom, p. 304.
61  Zhang, p. 92.
62  *Die Zeit*, 7 April 1989.
63  Ibid., 31 March 1989.
64  Reuters, 14 April 1989.
65  *Frankfurter Rundschau (FR)*, 22 October 1988.
66  *Die Zeit*, 3 March 1989.
67  Ibid.
68  *SZ*, 8 March 1989.
69  Ibid., 25 March 1989.
70  Ibid.
71  *SZ*, 25 March 1989.
72  Ibid., 29 April/1 May 1989.
73  Näth, p. 354.
74  Ibid.
75  *SZ*, 22/23 April 1989.
76  Cremerius, Fischer and Schier, p. 77.

77  Ibid., p. 75.
78  Ibid., p. 76.
79  Ibid., p. 279. See: Li Peng's speech on 22 May during an extended meeting of the politburo.
80  Ibid.
81  *SZ*, 29/30 July 1989.
82  This is how the head of the university department summed up the results of the poll. See: *SZ*, 29 April/1 May 1989.
83  In a talk with the author in April 1999, see alao: *WiWo*, 15April 1999, p. 49.
84  *SZ*, 19 May 1989.
85  Ibid.
86  Cremerius, Fischer and Schier, p. 167.
87  Inflation had risen to more than 25 per cent in the first half of that year already. *SZ*, 29/30 July 1989.
88  *Die Zeit*, 6 January 2001.
89  *SZ*, 26 May 1989.
90  *SZ*, 20/21 May 1989.
91  A trranscript of the talk reached the demonstrators before 4 June but they did not recognise its significance.
92  *SZ*, 16 June 1989
93  The new head of state and party chief Jiang Zemin desribed the incidents soberly when he stated 'that a massacre has not occurred; the square has been cleared by military pressure. A carnage has not taken place. Conflicts occurred in the neighbouring streets, however, and about 400 people have been killed.' See: Sieren (1990), p. 61.
94  Ibid.
95  *SZ*, 19/20 May 1989.
96  *TAZ*, 16 June 1989.
97  *Libération*, 16 June 1989.
98  *TAZ*, 16 June 1989.
99  *Die Zeit*, 25 August 1989.
100  Cremerius, Fischer and Schier, p. 549.
101  Ibid.
102  *HB*, 24 October 1989.
103  Ibid.
104  7 June 1989.
105  *Die Zeit*, 6 October 1989.
106  On 15 December 1989, the official rate dropped from 3.7 to 4.72 RMB. Black market prices ranged from 9.4 to 9.8 RMB. A second devaluation in the following year brought the rate to 5.73 RMB. See: Brahm, p. 170.
107  Comment in a talk with the Japanese foreign minister Masayoshi. *Die Zeit*, 6 October 1989.
108  Ibid.
109  *HB*, 24 October 1989.
110  *SZ*, 14 November 1989.
111  Ibid., 27 September 1989. Otto Wolff von Amerongen was known in China since he had concluded a trade agreement between Germany and China in 1957. See: Wang, p. 78.
112  'Prime Minister Li explained that they had no experience whatsoever with mass rallies of this type', Weiss reports. After the talk he was convinced that what had happened could only be a 'fatal slip', and that 'a relapse into into the chaos of the Cultural Revolution [was] not to be expected', said Weiss in a talk with the author in August 2004.
113  The project was assisted by a 460 million Deutschmark credit. It was to be expected that the credit freeze would not last long.
114  *Die Zeit*, 6 October 1989.
115  *SZ*, 30 July 1989.

116 *HB*, 24 October 1989.

117 *WiWo*, 11 November 2004, p. 130.

118 The central committee document number 11 states that China's economic problems were a result of reforms which had been conducted too quick and too far, and which was now judged misconceived. Decision-making power in economic and monetary matters would have been decentralised too quickly, while the central government would have increasingly lost control. The plan to increase supply through consumption pressure would have failed. Both would have led to a chaotic situation and inflicted 'lethal wounds' to the Chinese economy. This analysis was competent and plausible. *SZ*, 5 December 1989.

119 Ibid., 23 November 1989.

120 Ibid., 5 December 1989.

121 *Die Zeit*, 2 January 1990.

122 *FAZ*, 9 December 1989.

123 In early November the former US President Nixon had already sounded out the situation.

124 In Taiwan, a state of emergency following rallies lasted for 14 years. It was lifted on 17 July 1987.

125 *FAZ*, 8 March 1990.

126 *FR*, 21 March 1991.

127 *SZ*, 29 January 1990.

128 Just below US$ 10 billion by the end of 1989.

129 Based on the estimates of German banks. See: *TAZ*, 23 March 1990.

130 *Time Magazine*, vol. 3, 1990, p. 74.

131 *TAZ*, 11 June 1990.

132 Ibid.

133 FAZ, 23 March 2002.

134 Ibid.

135 He assumed an even harder line when facing Western media. He had 'no regrets' concerning the incidents. 'If we had not succeeded in taking decisive measures, the entire capital of the People's Republic would have been plunged into chaos.' *Time Magazine*, May 1990.

136 The repression of the protest movement was a test of power, and it ended it China's favour – even though, or, as one may wonder, precisely because the CCP expelled 72,000 'liberal' or 'corrupt' party members and expelled another 256,000 between 1989 and 1990.

137 *FR*, 28 April 1990.

138 China, too, took great stock in this, because 50 per cent of the parts were already produced in China. This meant jobs and economic power.

139 *SZ*, 5 July 1990.

140 Ibid., 7 November 1990.

141 German weekly *Die Zeit* meanwhile commented on the Western dilemma: 'Ceausecu is dead, Honecker was admitted to a Soviet sick bay. Deng, however, is still receiving guests in the Great Hall of the People (…) In the long run nobody can ignore the giant of the Far East. The leadership in Peking can be confident that moral indignation has never lasted long in international politics; finally, interests override indignation.' *Die Zeit*, 1 June 1990.

142 *TAZ*, 2 June 1990.

143 Ibid., 11 June 1990.

144 Rheinischer Merkur, 4 January 1991.

145 Wang, p. 176. Wang, however, had been meeting board members of German banks.

146 *SZ*, 25 March 1991.

147 Ibid., 9 April 1991.

148 Seitz, p. 296.

149 Ibid.

150 Ibid.

151 Seitz, p. 302.
152 Ibid., p. 304.
153 Ibid.
154 Brahm, p. 13.


## Chapter 7

1 *WiWo*, 3 June 1999, p. 43.
2 www.sarswatch.org.
3 Sieren, Frank: 'Tal der Avantgarde' *WiWo*, 6 February 2002, p. 104.
4 Brahm, p. 14.
5 Ibid., p. 15.
6 Little by little the middle echelon got used to Zhu demanding more than he expected. His weapon blunted.
7 Brahm, p. 18.
8 Ibid., p. 43.
9 Ibid., p. 48.
10 Ibid., p. 61.
11 During a test-phase in 18 cities, 108 state-owned enterprises with altogether 77,000 employees declared bankruptcy; about one billion Yuan were saved. Ibid., p. 54.
12 Towards the end of his term, Zhu had to understand that he had underrated corruption even among his confidants. In 2002 the biggest Chinese financial scandal ever leaked out. Money to the tune of 800 million Euro had disappeared from the BoC. The former BoC president Wang Xuebing was found to be an accesory to the fraud, expelled from the party, and sentenced to a long prison term.
13 *WiWo*, 20 September 2001, p. 106.
14 Stephen Green, CEO of HSBC.
15 In 2003, the American investment firm Newbridge Capital acquired a 20 per cent share in the bank. During the Asian crisis, Newbridge had already saved a South Korean bank.
16 Data according to Professor Kellee Tsai of John Hopkins University.
17 Thailand's collapse was not entirely surprising. There had been signs of danger as early as spring 1997.
18 Brahm, p. 79: 17 January 1979 in the Great Hall of the People.
19 GDP Guangdong: US$ 153 billion (2003); GDP Thailand: US$ 143 billion (2003).
20 According to Dr Michael Thomas, head of Deutsche Bank Hongkong, China until 1991.
21 Brahm, p. 88.
22 By the end of the eighties the tropical island Hainan was decoupled from the centre and equipped with its own financial institutions.
23 Brahm, p. 88.
24 Jinrong Ribao, 14 October 1998, p. 3.
25 Reuters News, 25 November 1999.
26 Brahm, p. 71.
27 Wang Qishan, born in 1948, today mayor of Peking.
28 Xinhua News Agency, 27 September 1998.
29 *SCMP*, 18 December 1999.
30 Brahm, p. 95.
31 See: *Wall Street Journal Europe* (*WSJE*), 17 December 1999, and *SCMP*, 5 March 2003. During the first ten months the slump had diminished to just below 3 per cent.
32 Reuters, 25 November 1999: 'China's Guangdong Back in Business'.
33 Members of the US House of Representatives Banking and Financial Service Commitee, 30 January 1998: 'In the present crisis, the United States holds all the aces in order to

promote our principles, which should be the principles of world economy', it was stated during a meeting of the committee. 'We should use the opportunity of the crisis and insist that other nations will take measures accordingly.'

34 Brahm, p. 122.
35 'Many of these fears are rather psychological than legitimized by fact', says Fred Hu of Goldman Sachs. And Simon Orgus of Warburg Dillon Road in Hongkong even states: 'China is in a relatively good position'. See: *WiWo*, 8 September 1998.
36 During the first four months of 1998, the export growth had plunged from 8.6 to 1 per cent. Foreign investment abated sharply. In the first quarter, growth reached 7.2 per cent and remained well below the target of 8 per cent.
37 His father and grandfather had been professors at this elite institution.
38 Brahm, p. 100.
39 www.cnn.com.
40 Ibid.
41 See: 'Report Concerning the Current International Financial Situation and our Nations Reforms'. Brahm, p. 102.
42 *WiWo*, 27 June 1996, p. 25.
43 Debate in the Bundestag concerning the common initiative of CDU/CSU, SPD, The Greens, and FDP over the improvement of the human rights situation in Tibet. In April that year Kinkel had even pungently criticised the Chinese in a speech during the UN plenary meeting.
44 *Die Zeit*, 29 April 1999.
45 www.fmprc.gov.cn.
46 During this phase of the rallies, it increasingly seemed as though all demonstrators – mostly young high-school and university students – had been picked by the government and driven to to the rallies.
47 Brahm, p. 128.
48 In the first quarter of 1999 the savings rose by 19.2 per cent compared to the previous year. See: Ibid., pp. 136–44.
49 *WiWo*, China-Sonderheft 2003, p. 82.
50 Hai Yun: Xiamen Yuan Hua Da an, Beijing 2001, p. 6.
51 *People's Daily*, 30 October 2001.
52 Xinhua News Agency, 21 January 2000.
53 *WiWo*, 17 February 2000, p. 41.
54 Ibid.
55 Ibid.

## Chapter 8

1 'The naked concubine was wrapped in a red silk scarf embroidered with playing dragons and phoenixes, and carried into the emperor's chamber.' The China Auto Show is the most expensive and sumptuous in the world. Seagrave, p. 61.
2 Ibid., p. 4.
3 Ibid., p. 60.
4 Until 1997, foreign manufacturers had already sold about 50,000 vehicles including trucks and busses to China. See: Studwell, p. 19.
5 Ibid., p. 79. The investors, too, were convinced that the car industry was of central significance for China. When getting publically listed, the share was more than ten times oversubscribed.
6 *WiWo*, China edition 2004.
7 Brahm, p. 34.

8   This fact is not yet generally known.

9   *Der Spiegel*, 6 October 1999.

10  Xinhua News Agency, 6 November 2001.

11  Jinbei later was renamed Brilliance Automotive and today is BMWs production partner.

12  One of the reasons the negotiations kept dragging on was because GM was restructuring its operations until 1993.

13  Studwell, p. 129.

14  SAIC holds 25 per cent, 10 per cent is owned by the National Automotive Industrie Corporation, and 15 per cent by the Bank of China.

15  Studwell, p. 157.

16  Ibid., p. 166.

17  According to data from the production facility in Guangzhou from 16 July 2002: 1999 – 10008; 2000 – 32280; 2001 – 51048.

18  There are about 120 carmakers in China, including small and specialised companies.

19  *WiWo*, 23 September 2004, p. 52.

20  China Economic Information Network, 20 November 2003. GMs China business accounts for one third of the company's profits. Volkswagen denies this.

21  www.goldmansachp.com.

22  The committee was founded in 1993 during Helmut Kohl's first trip to China.

23  As reported by participants.

24  *Autonews*, 7 June 2000.

25  *Xiu Cai*, 7 February 2003, p. 6.

26  As reported by participants of the talk, which was later cancelled.

27  *Xiu Cai*, 7 February 2003, p. 6.

28  During a talk with the author in July 20002 in Peking.

29  In early 2004 40 per cent of all vehicles were credit financed; by the end of year it was merely 15 per cent.

30  Studwell, p. 131.

31  Xinhua News Agency, 19 June 1998.

32  Ibid.

33  *SZ*, 15 March 2001.

34  BBC Monitoring Service: Asia Pacific, 19 July 2000.

35  After a strategy meeting concering China on 16 and 17 July 2002. *Die Welt*, 19 July 2002.

36  In 2001 DaimlerChrysler acquired 37.2 per cent of Mitsubishi.

37  *WiWo*, 16 May 2002, p. 15.

38  The anger of the Mercedes owner was no doubt genuine; the press coverage, however, was a political trick and an old trick at that. In 1985 the government had tried to slow down a wave of Japanese imports by reporting about 'angry' buyers of Mitsubishi Trucks who wanted their money back: 'There are quality problems with all 31 trucks', *China Daily* said on 4 October 1985.

39  This had been the condition to prolong the Bank of China credit line. See: *Market Daily*, 5 June 2002, p. 5.

40  'Schrempp wird für DaimlerChrysler-Ergebnis immer zuversichtlicher' (DPA), 3 June 2002.

41  During a talk with the Author.

42  *Der Spiegel*, 8 September 2003.

43  *FT*, 15 October 2003.

44  Seagrave, p. 55.

45  *WiWo*, 9 December 2004, p. 50.

46  This figure refers to vehicles with 20 to 130 seats.

47  www.airshow.com.

48  www.english.people.com.cn.

49  Ibid.

50 This finally happened in early December 2003 in Peking.
51 According to von Pierer in Peking on 6 December 2003.
52 During a talk with the author on 14 April 2004 in Shanghai.
53 The angle for the ground wire tube was incorrect.
54 Bei den Quertraversen wurde beim Schleifen die Grundierung beschädigt.
55 www.heute.de.
56 *WiWo*, China edition 2003, p. 66.
57 The head of a think-tank said this during a talk with the author in May 2004.
58 Seagrave, p. 60.

# Chapter 9

1 The IMF during the eighties was affected by the republican administration under Ronald Reagan and the Thatcher era in Great Britain. The World Bank, on the other hand, saw an increase of its influence during Clinton's leadership in the nineties.
2 Stiglitz (2002), p. 26.
3 Ibid., p. 97.
4 Ibid., p. 93.
5 Krugman, p. 43.
6 Data according to the pre-crisis rates of US$1 = Baht 25. *The Nation*, 2 July 2004, p. B2.
7 Ibid., p. 101.
8 After his spectacular bankruptcy in 1994 Jürgen Schneider was sentenced to a perennial prison term.
9 Lafontaine, p. 183.
10 *The Nation*, 2 July 2004, p. 1B.
11 Ibid.
12 Kissinger, p. 198.
13 The foreign currency reserves had dwindled to US$ 3.9 billion by December 1997.
14 South Korean banks had supplied their customers with cheap money in order to boost consumption. In 2001 and 2002, public debts rose by approximately 12 per cent of the GDP. Brusseles grants only 3 per cent two member countries of the Euro zone. Overlall private debts reached just below two thirds of the annual gross national product. This was the highest dept rate in any OECD country relative to per capita income.
15 In a background paper for Managing Director Michel Camdessu. See: www.imf.org.
16 Ibid.
17 Ibid.
18 Ibid.
19 Ibid.
20 Dow Jones News, 27 August 2001.
21 Ibid.
22 Ibid., 15 June 1998.
23 www.morganstanley.com.
24 Dow Jones News, 15 June 1998.
25 *Financial News*, 15 June 1998. p. 1.
26 Ibid.
27 'If changing exchange rate exercise pressure on our foreign trade, I am sorry that we have to deal with the question of adjusting our exchange rate', Vice-minister for foreign trade Sun Zhenyu. Reuters, 17 June 1998, 06.27 CET.
28 The central bank concluded its transaction by 07.29 a.m. See: Reuters, 17 June 1998.
29 'China Welcomes US Intervention on Japanese Yen'. AFP, 18 June 1998.
30 Reuters, 12 April 2002.

31  www.imf.org.
32  Ibid.
33  Ibid.
34  Xinhua News Agency, 13 September 1997.
35  Ibid.
36  Ibid.
37  Ibid.
38  Ibid.
39  Ibid.
40  Lafontaine, p. 209.
41  Grefe, et al., p. 34.
42  www.imf.org.
43  Xinhua News Agency, 1 May 2002.
44  Ibid.
45  On 20 April 2002. The other speakers were far more reserved.
46  Xinhua News Agency, 1 May 2002.
47  15 and 16 May 2002 in Peking.
48  This, however, was not a Chinese invention. It was based on an agenda concering fiscal pol-
    icy that was developed in the eighties by John Williamson of the Institute for International
    Economics in Washington.
49  Lafontaine, p. 174.
50  Reuters, 20 November 1998.
51  Tiedtmayer. *Die Zeit*, vol. 48, 1998, p. 14.
52  Zhou, Xiaochuan: 3 October 2004. www.pbc.gov.cn.
53  www.imf.org.

## Chapter 10

1  During his first election campaign George W. Bush had already stated this. See: Harvard
   International Review: The Strategic Triangle, See: www.harvard.edu.
2  Goldstein, Avery: 'September 11, The Shanghai Summit and the Shift in U.P. China Policy'.
   www.fpri.org.
3  According to a co-worker.
4  www.wto.org.
5  A few weeks earlier, the Washingtion Post had still compared Peking's election as host city
   to the election of Hitler's Berlin in 1936. This assessment, however, was not generally shared
   in the Western media. *Washington Post*, Editorial, 21 May 2001: 'And while Hein Verbruggen,
   chairman of the Olympic Evaluation Committee, highlights that the IOC has "to keep up
   the unity of the olympic movement and hence must abstain from assuming a political
   position", the question remains what Mr. Verbruggen was really thinking. It is quite possible
   that the Olympic Committee followed the same line of thought when organising the
   games in 1936 in Nazi-Germany. This was a huge PR-success for Adolf Hitler and his
   friends, and it should not be repeated. If Mr. Verbruggen wants to freshen his memory he is
   recommended to rent a copy of Leni Riefenstahl's Olympia documentation, one of the
   most powerful propaganda prducts ever made.'
6  According to a non-public letter which is available to the author.
7  www.swissre.com.
8  According to a non-public paper which is available to the author.
9  According to a German producer of textile machines during a talk with the author.
10 According to a non-public paper which is available to the author.
11 www.eiu.com.
12 Xinhua News Agency, 12 May 2002.
13 *WiWo*, 2 July 1998, p. 9.

14 In 1997, 100,151 vehicles were imported from Hongkong to China. One year later the number had dropped to 60,136, and in 1999 to less than 20,000 vehicles. Since then the number is declining continuously. See: *WiWo*, 30 March 2002, p. 124.

15 According to a survey by Roland Berger.

16 It costs at least US$ 35,000 to license a model for the Chinese market.

17 Xinhua News Agency, 23 April 2002.

18 www.wallstreet-online.de.

19 In a worldwide ranking, the largest German bank, Deutsche Bank, ranks on 12th position; Commerzbank finds itself on rank 45.

20 APA-strategy paper from 21 November 2003. On top of that, there is no sufficient hedging available in China.

21 *FAZ*, 7 September 2004, p. 12.

22 Ibid.

23 *TAZ*, 23 August 2004.

24 *HB*, 3 September 2004, p. 2.

25 During that period the Dow Jones dropped by 16 and the S&P 500 by 25 per cent.

26 Within five days the Dow Jones plunged sharply three times. The decline during that week amounted to 7.7 per cent. The S&P 500, which covers a wider average of Wall Street stocks, declined by 7 per cent.

27 In Japan, stagnation had been dragging on through the nineties after the real-estate bubble burst in 1989 and 1900. It was to be expected that Japan would be shaken by a crisis triggered in the USA. Japanese banks and corporations had invested large sums in US federal bonds. And the USA were their most important export market. Japanese companies held US treasury bills worth US$ 350 billion, and company shares and bonds of still higher value.

28 Data according to Moodys Investors Service.

29 The Shanghai-Composite-Index in 2001 fell from its all-time high of more than 2200 to 1400 points. See: *China Daily*, 7 October 2004, p. 3.

30 According to the international real-estate company Cushman & Wakefield in October 2004.

31 *WiWo*, China edition 2003, p. 36.

32 Ibid.

33 Ibid.

34 Ibid.

35 Ibid.

36 China consumes 5.6 million barrel daily. Global consumption amounts to 79.1 million barrel. See: Energy Information Administration, 2003.

37 According to IEA estimates, China consumed 5.8 million barrels a day in 2004. The China National Petroleum Corporation (CNPC) acts on the assumption that in 2003 China consumed around 2003 tons of oil. The USA burned one billion tons annualy, Japan 3000 million. In 2003 China's consumption approximated Japan's (one ton is equal to about 7.3 barrels).

38 www.iea.org.

39 www.morganstanley.com.

40 Xinhua News Agency, 28 September 2001.

41 www.china-institut.org.

42 Professor Wu Lei of the Institute for International Relations, Yunan University, 16 January 2003.

43 www.china-institut.org.

44 *Die Zeit*, 2 December 1999.

45 China's head of state Hu Jintao had an ambitious agenda during his first trip abroad, which began on 25 May 2001. Until 5 June he visited Russia, Mongolia and Kazakhstan.

46 Reuters, Moscow, 5 December 2002.

47 *The Asian Wall Street Journal (AWSJ)*, 28 May 2003.

48 Ibid.

49 Peter Probert's partner and Asia chief at Jones Day. See: Ibid.
50 'Perhaps it will better serve the strategic interests of America if Washington openly acknowledges its interests', writes former chancellor Helmut Schmidt and highlights the 'maintenace of continuous oil-supplies'. Schmidt, p. 111.
51 According to two American oil-industry managers during a talk with the author in summer 2002 in Shanghai.
52 *The Economist*, 30 September 2004.
53 www.zdf.de, 30 July 2004.
54 Early October 2004.
55 *FAZ*, 13 October 2004, p. 19.
56 Ibid., p. 20.
57 *Die Netzeitung*, 'China kauft Stahlmarkt leer', 14 May 2004.
58 See: Equity Markets Weekly, HSH Nordbank, 24 September 2004.
59 *FAZ*, 28 October 2004, p. 11.
60 According to Commerzbank Securities in London.
61 Another angle is to let the USA finance its debts mainly in Asia. 'Savings rates are relatively high in Asia. That is why the American government can spend lavishly without significantly driving up interest rates. But the problem remains that the rest of the world will not finance America's deficite perpetually.' Professor Kenneth Rogoff of Harvard and former chief economist at the IMF. *FAZ*, 22 September 2004, p. 14.
62 Ibid.
63 The Chinese government bought 60 per cent of Aktjubinskmunai Oil in West Kazakhstan as early as 1997. Costs amounted to US$ 4.32 billion. An advance of US$ 4.32 billion was paid on signing the treaty. Just two months later China acquired 60 per cent of the Uzen oilfield. The overall costs amounted to US$ 1.3 billion, and once more China paid an advance, this time US$ 52 million. On top of that, Peking guaranteed an immediate investment of US$ 400 million. This bid was generally considered excessively high. See: www.dgap.org.
64 During a talk with the author on 27 November 2003. See also: *WiWo*, 4 December 2003, p. 34.
65 Ibid.
66 During a talk with the author in July 2004.
67 *WiWo*, 25 March 2004, p. 44.
68 Simultaneously, China is trying to decrease its dependence on international shipping companies. In 2004 China was the world's third largest ship-producer after Japan and South Korea.
69 James Brooke, www.accessasia.co.uk.
70 *The New York Times*, 28 December 2004.
71 Ibid.
72 *WiWo*, 11 November 2004, p. 36.
73 Prime Minister Wen, however, highlighted that China and the other Asian nations would grow in an environment of 'mutual respect instead of confrontation, mutual trust instead of suspicion, in cooperation, not competition, and in mutual benefit, not on the expense of the partner.' Xinhua News Agency, 30 November 2004.
74 www.parstimep.com/history/us_iran.html.
75 www.taz.de.
76 www.nti.org.
77 According to a lecture in Washington DC on 17 August 2004.
78 Interview with National Broadcasting Company (NBC), 10 September 2004.
79 Tagesschau, 14 November 2004.
80 www.world.newp.designerz.com.
81 Ibid.

82 Other Arab nations are welcoming China as well. In July 2004, Peking negotiated a skeleton agreement concerning economic and technological co-operation with Saudi Arabia, Kuwait and four furhter countries in the region.
83 Tagesschau, 14 November 2004.
84 Ibid.
85 *The New York Times*, 18 June 1998.
86 The intervention reached its peak during the operations in 1953.

# Chapter 11

1 Jones, p. 72f.
2 Ibid., p. 75.
3 Ibid., p. 39.
4 Ibid., p. 41.
5 *HB*, 3 September 2004, p. 2.
6 *WiWo*, 18 September 1997, p. 42.
7 The talk took place on 15 July 2004, in the Chinese foreign ministry. Both ministers expressed their views each in one go. To advance readability, the individual arguments have been arranged in dialogue form afterwards. I am indebted to Eva Corell of ARD in Peking for placing the transcript at my disposal.
8 A lecture during the German–Chinese congress organised by WirtschaftsWoche on September 22, 2004, in Berlin.
9 *Die Gazette*, vol. 33, February 2001. The foreign ministry denied this statement on the same day.
10 In 2004 Chan starred in the film-version of Jules Verne's 'Around the World in 80 Days'.
11 August 2002 in the proximity of Houston, Texas. Some of the billboards are in Chinese language.
12 The Chinese hurdle-racer levelled the 1993 world record of Great Britain's Colin Jackson.
13 5 June 2003, China–USA, Director: Zhang Yimou
14 *SCMP*, 15 March 2004, p. 1.
15 See: Rüdiger Suchsland. Artechock film: Hero (Ying xiong).
16 *FAZ*, 18 June 2003, p. N3.
17 Ekkehard Knörer. *Jump Cut* magazine: www.jump-cut.de.
18 *FAZ*, 9 July 2004.
19 Schmidt, Helmut: 'Wir verändern das Land gerade', *Die Zeit*, 4 March 2004.
20 Summer 2004 (in millions); world: 6396; Africa: 885; Latin America and Caribbean: 549; North America: 326; Europe: 728; Asia: 3875; Oceania: 33. See: www.wikipedia.org.
21 www.morganstanley.com

# BIBLIOGRAPHY

Albrecht, Peter-Alexis and Backes, Otto (Eds): Verdeckte Gewalt. Plädoyers für eine 'Innere Abrüstung'. Frankfurt a.M. 1990.

Beck, Ulrich: Die Erfindung des Politischen. Frankfurt a.M. 1993.

Becker, Jasper: Hungry Ghosts: China's Secret Famine. London 1996.

Bin Wong, Roy: China Transformed. Historical Change and the Limits of European Experience. Ithaca and London 1997.

Böckenförde, Ernst-Wolfgang: Staat, Nation, Europa. Frankfurt a.M. 1999.

Boos, Engelbert: Die neue Lokalisierungspolitik in der chinesischen Automobilindustrie. Unpublished script. Munich 2004.

Brahm, Laurence J.: Zhu Rongji and the Transformation of Modern China. Singapore 2002.

Buruma, Ian: Chinas Dissidenten. Munich 2003.

Cameron, Meribeth: The Reform Movement in China 1898–1912. New York 1963.

Chang, Gordon G.: The Coming Collapse of China. New York 2001.

Copur, Burak and Schneider, Anne-Kathrin: IWF & Weltbank. Die Dirigenten der Globalisierung. Berlin 2004.

Cremerius, Ruth, Fischer, Doris and Schier, Peter: Studentenprotest und Repression in China April–June 1989. Hamburg 1991.

Denninger, Erhard: Polizei in der freiheitlichen Demokratie. Frankfurt a.M.and Berlin 1968.

Elias, Norbert: Was ist Soziologie? Weinheim and Munich 1986.

Elias, Norbert: Engagement und Distanzierung. Frankfurt a.M. 1987.

Elias, Norbert: Über den Prozess der Zivilisation. Frankfurt a.M. 1990.

Elias, Norbert: Über sich selbst. Frankfurt a.M. 1990 (A).

Elias, Norbert: Die Gesellschaft der Individuen. Frankfurt a.M. 1991.

Elias, Norbert: Studien über die Deutschen. Frankfurt a.M. 1992.

Engler, Wolfgang: Die zivilisatorische Lücke. Frankfurt a.M. 1998.

Fairbank, John K. and Teng, Ssu-yü: China's Response to the West. Cambridge 1982.

Fairbank, John K.: Geschichte des modernen China 1800–1985. Munich 1989.

Farge, Arlette: Logik des Aufruhrs. Frankfurt a.M. 1989.

Franz, Uli: Deng Xiaoping: Chinas Erneuerer. Stuttgart 1987.

Fukuyama, Francis: Staaten bauen. Die neue Herausforderung internationaler Politik. Berlin 2004.

Geiss, Imanuel: Geschichte im Überblick. Daten und Zusammenhänge der Weltgeschichte. Reinbek 1995.

Geißler, Heiner: Was würde Jesus dazu sagen? Die politische Botschaft des Evangeliums. Berlin 2003.

Gentzler, J. Mason (Ed.): Changing China. Readings in the History of China from the Opium War to the Present. New York 1977.

Grass, Günter, Dahn, Daniela and Strasser, Johano (Eds): In einem reichen Land. Zeugnisse alltäglichen Leidens an der Gesellschaft. Göttingen 2002.

Grefe, Christiane, Greffrath, Mathias and Schumann, Harald: Attac. Was wollen die Globalisierungskritiker? Berlin 2002.

Gregory, John S.: The West and China 1500. Houndmills Basingstoke 2003.

Haffner, Sebastian: Von Bismarck zu Hitler. Ein Rückblick. Munich 1987.

Haiyun: Xiamen Yuan Da an. Beijing 2001.

Hensel, Jana: Die Zonenkinder. Reinbek 2002.

Holbig, Heike, Schüler, Margot and Liu, Kenkai: Volksrepublik China. Aktuelle politische und wirtschaftliche Entwicklung. Off print for Federal chancellor Gerhard Schröder. Hamburg 2004.

Homann, Karl: Überwindung von Politikblockaden. Tübingen 2002.

Huntington, Samuel P.: Der Kampf der Kulturen. Munich 1996.

Johnson, Chalmers: Revolutionary Change. London 1982.

Jones, David Martin: The Image of China in Western Social and Political Thought. Hampshire 2001.

Kaminski, Gerd: Wäre ich ein Chinese, so wäre ich ein Boxer. Wien 1988.

Keynes, John Maynard: The Problem of Longterm Unemployment. In: The Collected Writings of John Maynard Keynes. London 1980.

Kissinger, Henry: Die Herausforderung Amerikas. Weltpolitik im 21. Jahrhundert. Berlin 2003.

Kremb, Jürgen: Bis zum letzten Atemzug. Wei Jingsheng und das Schicksal einer chinesischen Familie. Munich 1997.

Krugman, Paul: Der Große Verkauf. Frankfurt a.M. 2004.

Lafontaine, Oskar: Die Wut wächst. Politik braucht Prinzipien. Berlin 2002.

Landes, S. David: Wohlstand und Armut der Nationen. Warum die einen reich und die anderen arm sind. Berlin 1999.

Lardy, Nicholas R.: China's Unfinished Economic Revolution. Washington 1998.

Leibnitz, Klaus: Sun Tsu über die Kriegskunst. Munich 1989.

Levathes, Louise: When China Ruled the Seas. New York 1996.

Li, Zhisui: Ich war Maos Leibarzt. Bergisch Gladbach 1994.

Lu, Aiguo: China and the Global Economy Since 1840. New York 2000.

Luhmann, Niklas: Die Wirtschaft der Gesellschaft. Frankfurt a.M. 1994.

Luhmann, Niklas: Soziologische Aufklärung. 6. Band. Opladen 1970–1995.

Madison, Angus: The World Economy. A Milliennial Perspective. OECD, 2001.

Mann, Jim: Beijing Jeep. A Case Study of Western Business in China. Colorado 1997.

Martin, Helmut (Ed.): Mao Zedong – Texte, Schriften, Dokumente, Reden und Gespräche, 1949–1976. Munich 1976.

Marx, Karl: Marx on China. New York 1975.

McCord, Edward: The Power of the Gun. The Emergence of Modern Chinese Warlordism. Berkley 1993.

Myers, James T.: Radical Resurgence and the Fall of Deng Xiaoping. Columbia 1989.

Näth, Marie-Luise: Chinas Weg in die Weltpolitik. Die nationalen und außenpolitischen Konzeptionen Sun Yat-sens, Chiang Kai-sheks und Mao Zedongs. Berlin 1976.

Näth, Marie-Luise: Die Volksrepublik China in Deutschland. Wahrnehmungen, Wissenschaftskonzeptionen und Wirklichkeiten. Frankfurt a.M. 1995.

Nölling, Wilhelm: Währungsunion und Weltwirtschaft. Stuttgart 1999.

Osterhammel, Jürgen: China und die Weltgesellschaft. Vom 18. Jahrhundert bis in unsere Zeit. Munich 1989.

Osterhammel, Jürgen: Shanghai 30.Mai 1925. Die Chinesische Revolution. Munich 1997.

Polachek, James M.: The Inner Opium War. Harvard 1992.

Pomeranz, Kenneth: The Great Divergance. China, Europe, and the Making of the Modern World Economy. Princeton 2000.

Rawski, Thomas: What's Happening to China's Statistics? Pittsburgh 2001.

Roberts, J.A.G.: A History of China. Houndmills Basingstoke 1999.

Ruland, Bernd: Deutsche Botschaft Peking. Das Jahrhundert deutsch–chinesischen Schicksals. Bayreuth 1973.

Rummel, Rudolph: China's Bloody Century. Genocide and Mass Murder Since 1900. New Brunswick 1991.

Schmidt, Helmut: Menschen und Mächte. Berlin 1987.

Schröder, Gerhard: Mission ohne Auftrag. Die Vorbereitung der diplomatischen Beziehungen zwischen Bonn und Peking. Bergisch-Gladbach 1988.

Seagrave, Sterling: Die Konkubine auf dem Drachenthron. Munich 1995.

Seitz, Konrad: China. Eine Weltmacht kehrt zurück. Berlin 2003.

Shlomo, Avineri (Ed.): Karl Marx on Colonialism and Modernization. New York 1969.

Sieren, Frank and Koehne, Ludwig (Eds): Günter Schabowski. Das Politbüro. Reinbek 1990.

Sieren, Frank, Boos, Engelbert and Boos, Christine: The China Management Handbook. London 2003.

Simmel, Johannis Mario: Es darf nicht immer Kaviar sein. Munich 2001.

Sinn, Hans Werner: Ist Deutschland noch zu retten? Berlin 2003.

Spence, Jonathan: Chinese Roundabout. New York 1992.

Spence, Jonathan: Chinas Weg in die Moderne. Munich 1995.

Spence, Jonathan: Mao. Munich 2003.

Stiglitz, Joseph: Die Schatten der Globalisierung. Berlin 2002.

Stolleis, Michael: Konstitution und Intervention. Studien zur Geschichte des öffentlichen Rechts im 19. Jahrhundert. Frankfurt a.M. 2001.

Streeck, Wolfgang (Ed.): Internationale Wirtschaft, nationale Demokratie. Herausforderungen für die Demokratietheorie. Frankfurt a.M. 1998.

Studwell, Joe: The China Dream. The Quest for the Last Great Untapped Market on Earth. London 2002.

Talbott, Strobe (Ed.): Chruschtschow erinnert sich. Reinbek 1971.

Trocki, Carl: Opium, Empire and the Political Economy. Routledge 1999.

Volckhart, Oliver: Wettbewerb und Wettbewerbsbeschränkungen im vormodernen Deutschland 1000–1800. Tübingen 2002.

Walravens, Hartmut: Neue Veröffentlichungen zur frühen Chinamission. Orientalische Literaturzeitschrift 88, 1993.

Wang, Shu: Maos Mann in Bonn. Frankfurt a.M. 2002.

Wasserstrom, Jeffrey N.: Student Protests in Twentieth-Century China. The View From Shanghai. Stanford 1991.

Weber, Max: Gesammelte Aufsätze zur Religionssoziologie. Tübingen 1988.

Weidenfeld, Werner (Ed.): Den Wandel gestalten. Strategien der Transformation, Gütersloh 2001.

Yuan, Yang: Tales of Emperor Qin Shihuang. Beijing 1999.

Zhang, Jie: Zwei Liebeserzählungen. Frankfurt a.M. 1990.

*What was the original date?

# COMPANIES INDEX

# PEOPLE INDEX

# WORD INDEX